Did you know that Benjamin Franklin started our nation's first public library? He also invented lightning rods, swim fins, and bifocal eyeglasses.

HARCOURT SOCIAL Studies

Our Communities

Series Authors

Dr. Michael J. Berson
Professor
Social Science Education
University of South Florida
Tampa, Florida

Dr. Tyrone C. Howard
Associate Professor
UCLA Graduate School of Education & Information Studies
University of California at Los Angeles
Los Angeles, California

Dr. Cinthia Salinas
Assistant Professor
Department of Curriculum and Instruction
College of Education
The University of Texas at Austin
Austin, Texas

Series Consultants

Dr. Marsha Alibrandi
Assistant Professor of Social Studies
Curriculum and Instruction Department
North Carolina State University
Chapel Hill, North Carolina

Dr. Patricia G. Avery
Professor
College of Education and Human Development
University of Minnesota
Minneapolis/St. Paul, Minnesota

Dr. Linda Bennett
Associate Professor
College of Education
University of Missouri–Columbia
Columbia, Missouri

Dr. Walter C. Fleming
Department Head and Professor
Native American Studies
Montana State University
Bozeman, Montana

Dr. S. G. Grant
Associate Professor
University at Buffalo
Buffalo, New York

C. C. Herbison
Lecturer
African and African-American Studies
University of Kansas
Lawrence, Kansas

Dr. Eric Johnson
Assistant Professor
Director, Urban Education Program
School of Education
Drake University
Des Moines, Iowa

Dr. Bruce E. Larson
Professor
Social Studies Education
Secondary Education
Woodring College of Education
Western Washington University
Bellingham, Washington

Dr. Merry M. Merryfield
Professor
Social Studies and Global Education
College of Education
The Ohio State University
Columbus, Ohio

Dr. Peter Rees
Associate Professor
Department of Geography
University of Delaware
Wilmington, Delaware

Dr. Phillip J. VanFossen
James F. Ackerman Professor of Social Studies
  Education
Associate Director, Purdue Center for
  Economic Education
Purdue University
West Lafayette, Indiana

Dr. Myra Zarnowski
Professor
Elementary and Early Childhood Education
Queens College
The City University of New York
Flushing, New York

Classroom Reviewers and Contributors

Connie Bingham
Teacher
Elm Tree Elementary
Bentonville, Arkansas

Lisa Johnson
Teacher
Whitely County School District
Corbin, Kentucky

Sheila McCoy
Teacher
Karns Elementary School
Knoxville, Tennessee

Charla Uhles
Teacher
Eastlake Elementary School
Oklahoma City, Oklahoma

Maps
researched and prepared by

Copyright © 2007 by Harcourt, Inc.

All rights reserved. No part of this publication may be reproduced or transmitted in any form or by any means, electronic or mechanical, including photocopy, recording, or any information storage and retrieval system, without permission in writing from the publisher.

Requests for permission to make copies of any part of the work should be addressed to School Permissions and Copyrights, Harcourt, Inc., 6277 Sea Harbor Drive, Orlando, Florida 32887-6777. Fax: 407-345-2418.

HARCOURT and the Harcourt Logo are trademarks of Harcourt, Inc., registered in the United States of America and/or other jurisdictions.

Printed in the United States of America

ISBN-13: 978-0-15-353081-4
ISBN-10: 0-15-353081-2

If you have received these materials as examination copies free of charge, Harcourt School Publishers retains title to the materials and they may not be resold. Resale of examination copies is strictly prohibited and is illegal.

Possession of this publication in print format does not entitle users to convert this publication, or any portion of it, into electronic format.

3 4 5 6 7 8 9 10 048 15 14 13 12 11 10 09 08 07

I1 **THE STORY WELL TOLD**
I4 **READING YOUR TEXTBOOK**
I8 **GEOGRAPHY REVIEW**

Unit 1: Communities Around Us

2 **UNIT 1 PREVIEW VOCABULARY**

4 **Reading Social Studies** (Focus Skill)
Compare and Contrast

6 **Start with a Story**
Be My Neighbor
by Maya Ajmera and John D. Ivanko

12 Chapter 1 Learning About Communities

Study Skills
Understand Vocabulary

14 **LESSON 1** What Is a Community?
20 **LESSON 2** Communities Are Different
26 **LESSON 3** Communities Near and Far
30 **Map and Globe Skills** Find Directions and Distances
32 **LESSON 4** Discover Your Community
38 Chapter 1 Review and Test Prep

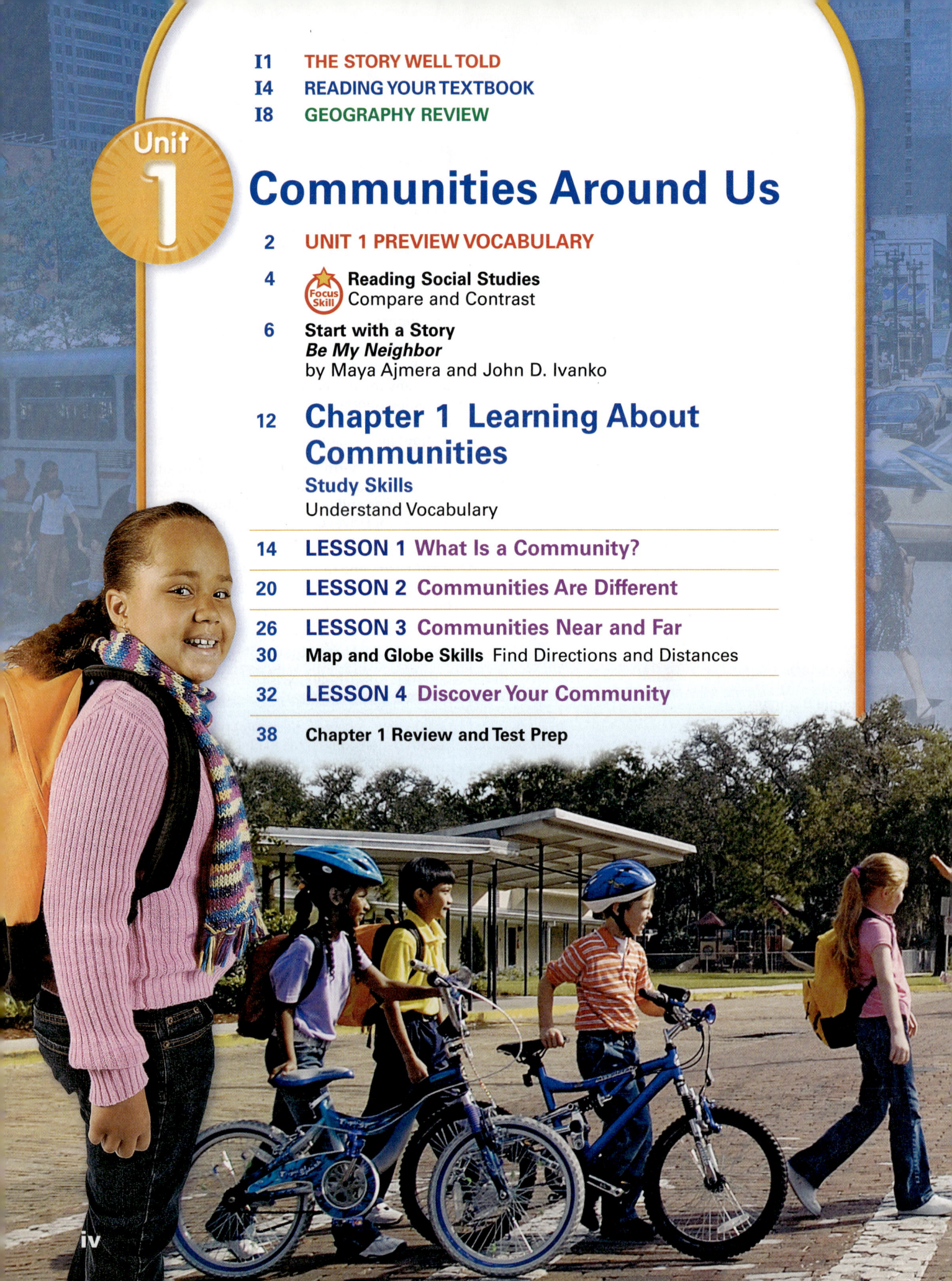

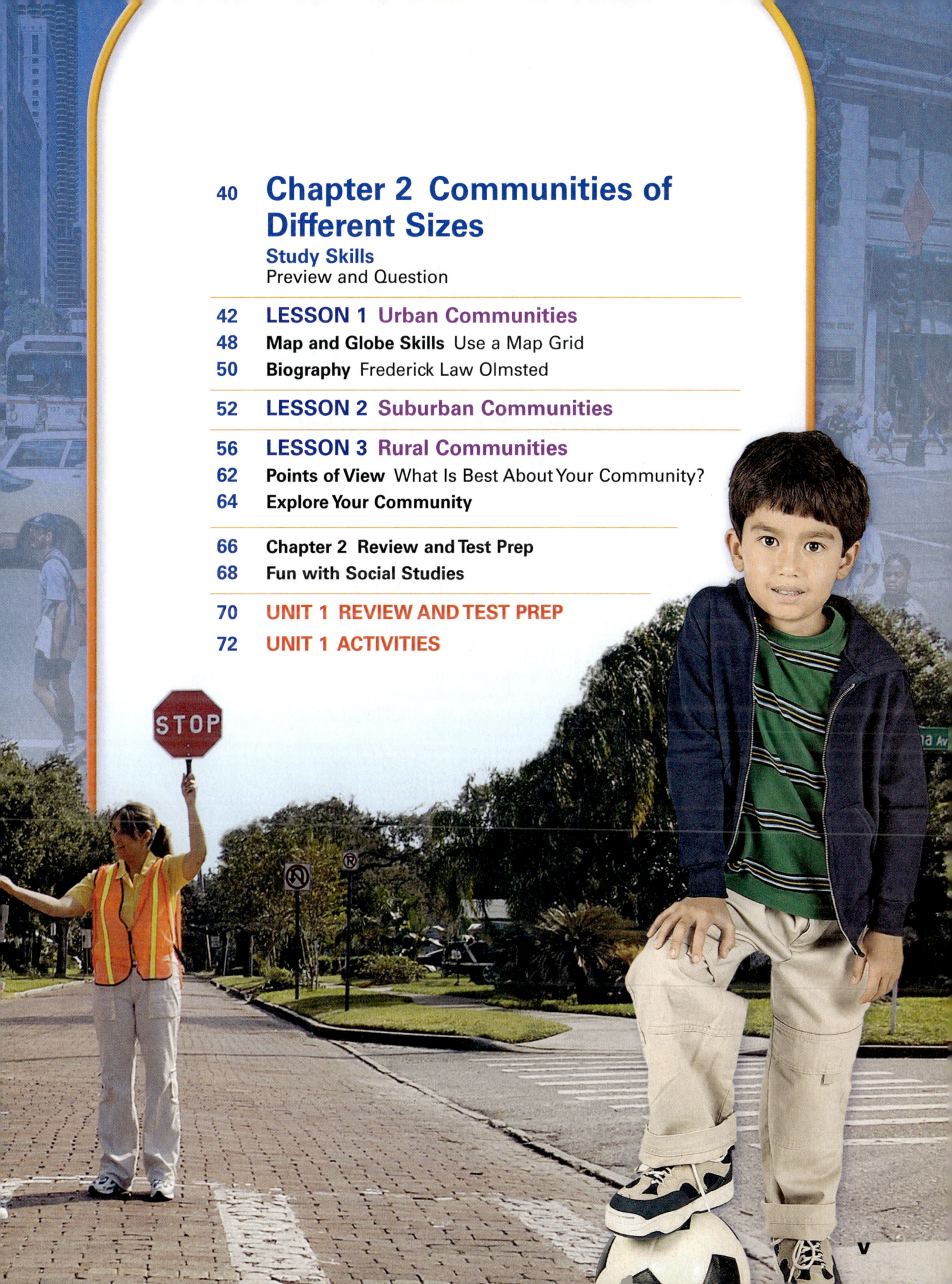

40	**Chapter 2 Communities of Different Sizes** **Study Skills** Preview and Question
42	**LESSON 1 Urban Communities**
48	**Map and Globe Skills** Use a Map Grid
50	**Biography** Frederick Law Olmsted
52	**LESSON 2 Suburban Communities**
56	**LESSON 3 Rural Communities**
62	**Points of View** What Is Best About Your Community?
64	**Explore Your Community**
66	**Chapter 2 Review and Test Prep**
68	**Fun with Social Studies**
70	**UNIT 1 REVIEW AND TEST PREP**
72	**UNIT 1 ACTIVITIES**

Unit 2
Communities and Geography

- **74** UNIT 2 PREVIEW VOCABULARY
- **76** **Reading Social Studies** Main Idea and Details
- **78** **Start with a Poem** "Walk Lightly" by J. Patrick Lewis illustrated by Alison Jay

- **80** **Chapter 3 Our Physical Geography** Study Skills Use Visuals
  - **82** LESSON 1 Our Location
  - **88** **Map and Globe Skills** Use Latitude and Longitude
  - **90** LESSON 2 Our Country's Geography
  - **98** **Map and Globe Skills** Use a Landform Map
  - **100** **Field Trip** Yellowstone National Park
  - **102** LESSON 3 Our Country's Regions
  - **106** LESSON 4 Natural Resources
  - **110** Chapter 3 Review and Test Prep

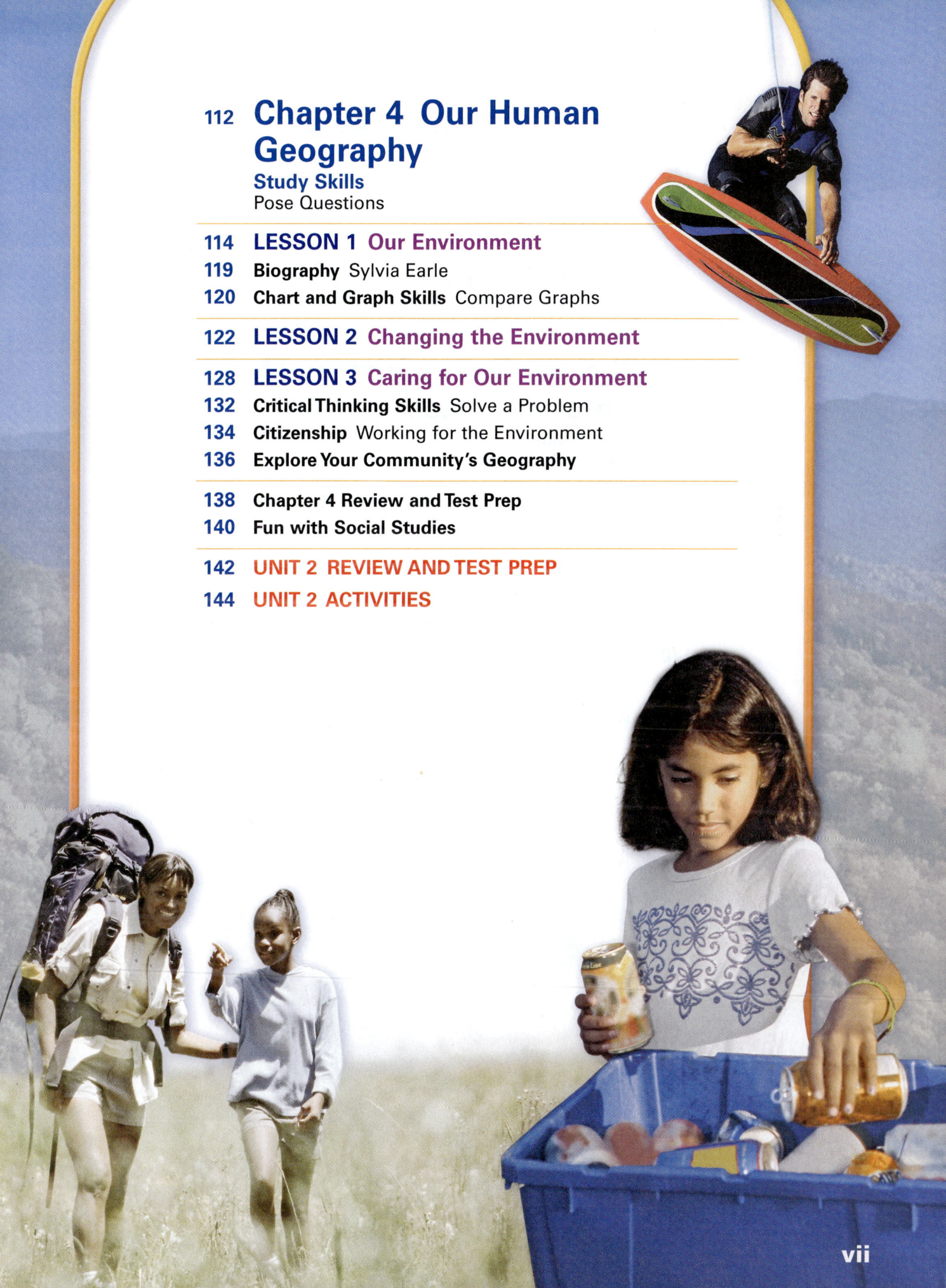

112 Chapter 4 Our Human Geography
Study Skills
Pose Questions

114 LESSON 1 Our Environment
119 **Biography** Sylvia Earle
120 **Chart and Graph Skills** Compare Graphs

122 LESSON 2 Changing the Environment

128 LESSON 3 Caring for Our Environment
132 **Critical Thinking Skills** Solve a Problem
134 **Citizenship** Working for the Environment
136 **Explore Your Community's Geography**

138 **Chapter 4 Review and Test Prep**
140 **Fun with Social Studies**

142 **UNIT 2 REVIEW AND TEST PREP**
144 **UNIT 2 ACTIVITIES**

Unit 3: Communities Over Time

146 UNIT 3 PREVIEW VOCABULARY

148 Reading Social Studies
Focus Skill Sequence

150 Start with a Story
A Place Called Freedom
by Scott Russell Sanders
illustrated by Thomas B. Allen

154 Chapter 5 Our History Through Time and Place
Study Skills
Make an Outline

156 LESSON 1 Communities Through Time
160 Chart and Graph Skills Read a Time Line

162 LESSON 2 People Bring Changes
168 Critical Thinking Skills Compare Primary and Secondary Sources

170 LESSON 3 Inventions in Communities
176 Chart and Graph Skills Read a Flowchart

178 LESSON 4 Communities Long Ago

186 Chapter 5 Review and Test Prep

188 Chapter 6 Our Country's History
Study Skills
Take Notes

190	**LESSON 1** The First Communities
194	**Points of View** How Did Change Affect Native Americans?
196	**LESSON 2** Building Communities
204	**LESSON 3** Fighting for Freedom
210	**Biography** Benjamin Franklin and Thomas Jefferson
212	**LESSON 4** Growth and Change
220	**Map and Globe Skills** Compare History Maps
222	**Primary Source** The Corps of Discovery
224	**Explore Your Community's History**
226	Chapter 6 Review and Test Prep
228	Fun with Social Studies
230	**UNIT 3 REVIEW AND TEST PREP**
232	**UNIT 3 ACTIVITIES**

Unit 4 Citizens and Government

- **234** UNIT 4 PREVIEW VOCABULARY
- **236** Reading Social Studies
  Summarize
- **238** Start with an Article
  "Becoming a Citizen—Just Like Me"
  as told to Diane Hoyt-Goldsmith
  by Shaddai Aguas Suarez
  photographs by Lawrence Migdale

- **242** Chapter 7 Citizenship
  Study Skills
  Use a K-W-L Chart
- **244** LESSON 1 Rights of Citizens
- **248** LESSON 2 Duties of Citizens
- **252** LESSON 3 Being a Good Citizen
- **258** Biography Cesar Chavez
- **260** Critical Thinking Skills Make a Thoughtful Decision
- **262** Chapter 7 Review and Test Prep

264 Chapter 8 Government
Study Skills
Skim and Scan

266	**LESSON 1 Structure of Government**
270	**Citizenship** Constitution Day
272	**LESSON 2 Local Governments**
278	**Map and Globe Skills** Read a Road Map
280	**LESSON 3 State and National Governments**
286	**Field Trip** The United States Capitol
288	**Citizenship Skills** Resolve Conflicts
290	**LESSON 4 Symbols of Our Nation**
296	**Chart and Graph Skills** Use a Line Graph
298	**Primary Sources** State Symbols
300	**LESSON 5 Governments of the World**
304	Explore Your Community's Government
306	Chapter 8 Review and Test Prep
308	Fun with Social Studies
310	**UNIT 4 REVIEW AND TEST PREP**
312	**UNIT 4 ACTIVITIES**

Unit 5

People in Communities

314 UNIT 5 PREVIEW VOCABULARY

316 Focus Skill **Reading Social Studies**
Cause and Effect

318 **Start with a Story**
Dreaming of America: An Ellis Island Story
by Eve Bunting
illustrated by Ben F. Stahl

322 **Chapter 9 Our American Culture**
Study Skills
Use an Anticipation Guide

324 **LESSON 1 Moving to New Places**
330 **Map and Globe Skills** Use a Population Map

332 **LESSON 2 Sharing Cultures**

338 **LESSON 3 Our American Heritage**
342 **Biography** Maya Lin

344 **Chapter 9 Review and Test Prep**

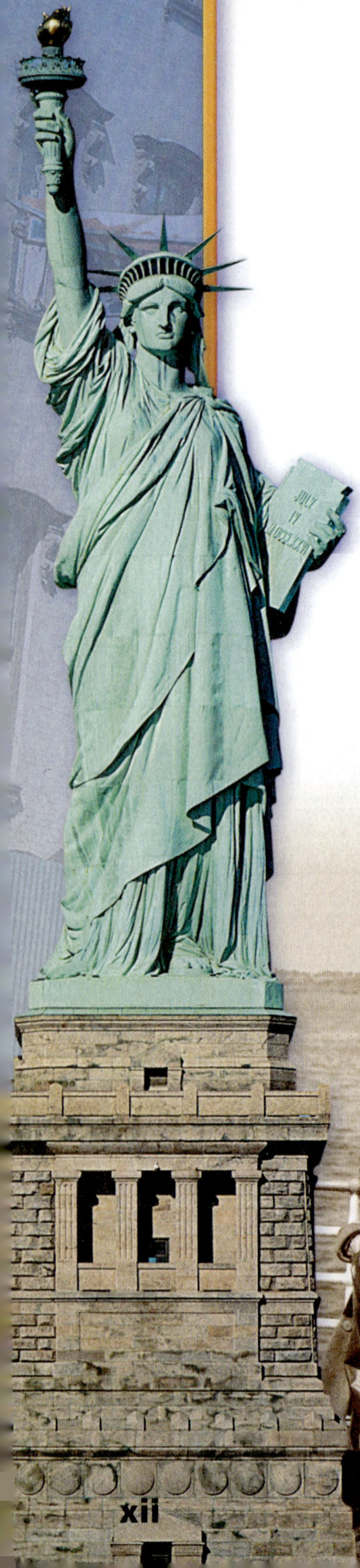

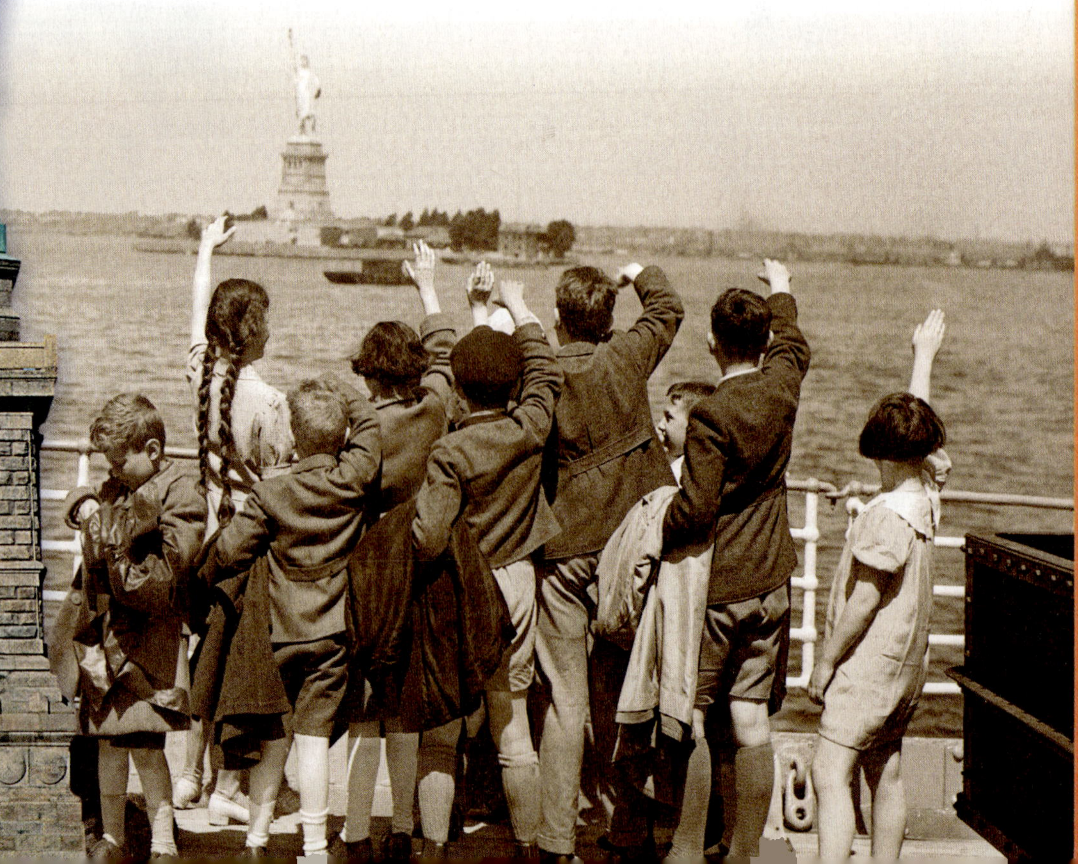

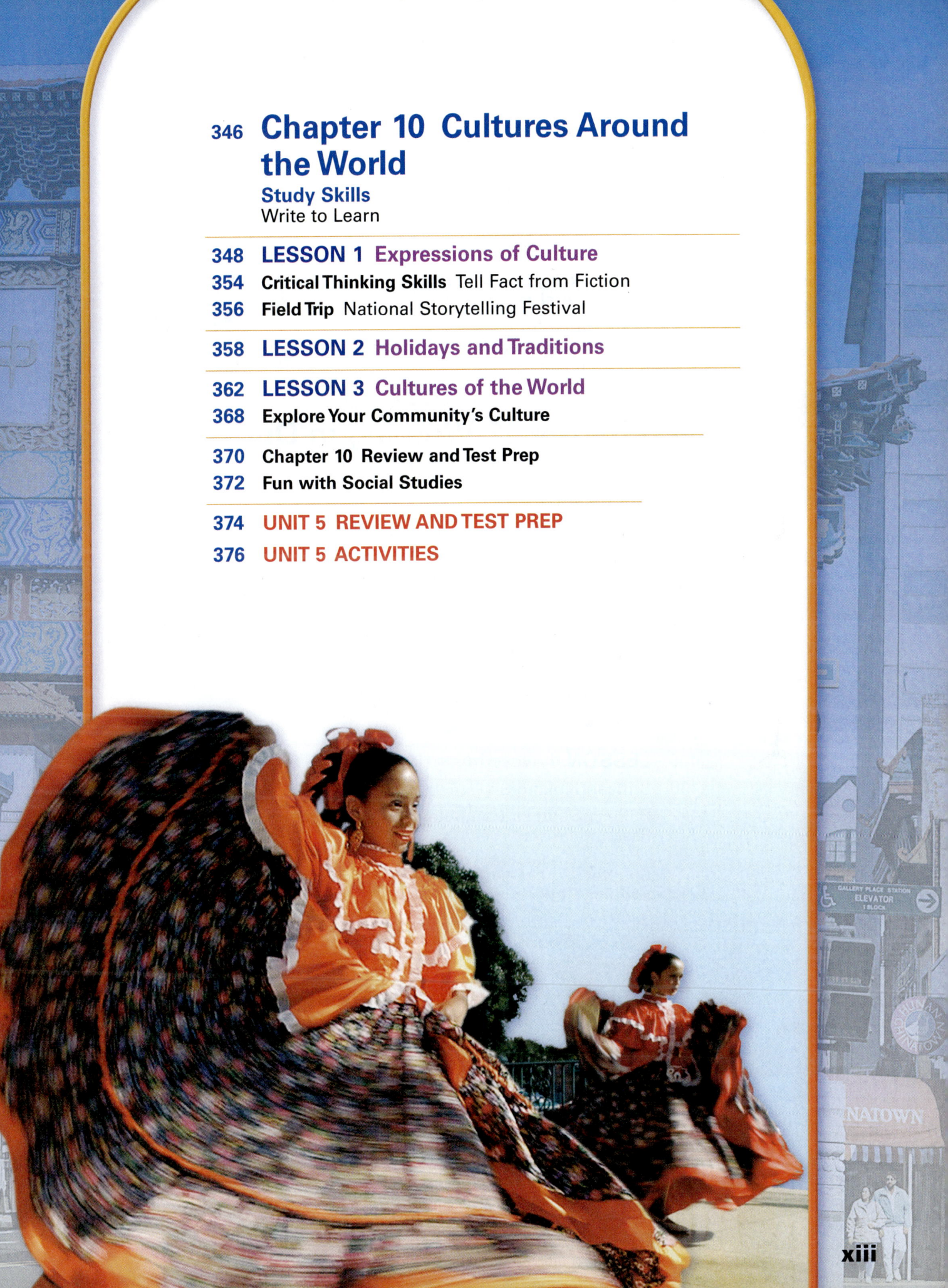

346 Chapter 10 Cultures Around the World
Study Skills
Write to Learn

348	**LESSON 1** Expressions of Culture
354	**Critical Thinking Skills** Tell Fact from Fiction
356	**Field Trip** National Storytelling Festival
358	**LESSON 2** Holidays and Traditions
362	**LESSON 3** Cultures of the World
368	Explore Your Community's Culture
370	Chapter 10 Review and Test Prep
372	Fun with Social Studies
374	**UNIT 5 REVIEW AND TEST PREP**
376	**UNIT 5 ACTIVITIES**

Unit 6
Working in Communities

378 **UNIT 6 PREVIEW VOCABULARY**

380 **Reading Social Studies** Focus Skill
Generalize

382 **Start with a Story**
Alex and the Amazing Lemonade Stand
by Liz and Jay Scott
illustrated by Pam Howard

386 **Chapter 11 Working in Our Community**
Study Skills
Connect Ideas

388 **LESSON 1** Workers and Consumers
393 **Biography** Madame C. J. Walker

394 **LESSON 2** How Business Works
398 **Map and Globe Skills** Read a Land Use and Products Map

400 **LESSON 3** Trading with the World
404 **Citizenship** Volunteering

406 **LESSON 4** New Inventions
410 **Critical Thinking Skills** Tell Fact from Opinion
412 **Primary Sources** Computers, Past and Present

414 Chapter 11 Review and Test Prep

416 Chapter 12 Saving and Spending Our Money
Study Skills
Organize Information

418 **LESSON 1 Forms of Money**

422 **LESSON 2 Free Market Economy**

426 **LESSON 3 Earn, Spend, and Save**
432 **Citizenship Skills** Make an Economic Choice
434 **Points of View** What Should You Do with Your Money?

436 **LESSON 4 World Businesses**
440 **Explore Your Community's Economy**

442 Chapter 12 Review and Test Prep
444 Fun with Social Studies

446 **UNIT 6 REVIEW AND TEST PREP**
448 **UNIT 6 ACTIVITIES**

FOR YOUR REFERENCE
R2 Atlas
R12 Research Handbook
R22 Biographical Dictionary
R27 Gazetteer
R33 Glossary
R40 Index

Features

Skills

CHART AND GRAPH SKILLS
- 120 Compare Graphs
- 160 Read a Time Line
- 176 Read a Flowchart
- 296 Use a Line Graph

CITIZENSHIP SKILLS
- 288 Resolve Conflicts
- 432 Make An Economic Choice

CRITICAL THINKING SKILLS
- 132 Solve a Problem
- 168 Compare Primary and Secondary Sources
- 260 Make a Thoughtful Decision
- 354 Tell Fact from Fiction
- 410 Tell Fact from Opinion

MAP AND GLOBE SKILLS
- 30 Find Directions and Distances
- 48 Use a Map Grid
- 88 Use Latitude and Longitude
- 98 Use a Landform Map
- 220 Compare History Maps
- 278 Read a Road Map
- 330 Use a Population Map
- 398 Read a Land Use and Products Map

READING SOCIAL STUDIES
- 4 Compare and Contrast
- 76 Main Idea and Details
- 148 Sequence
- 236 Summarize
- 316 Cause and Effect
- 380 Generalize

STUDY SKILLS
- 12 Understand Vocabulary
- 40 Preview and Question
- 80 Use Visuals
- 112 Pose Questions
- 154 Make an Outline
- 188 Take Notes
- 242 Use a K-W-L Chart
- 264 Skim and Scan
- 322 Use an Anticipation Guide
- 346 Write to Learn
- 386 Connect Ideas
- 416 Organize Information

Citizenship
- 134 Working for the Environment
- 270 Constitution Day
- 404 Volunteering

Points of View
- 62 What Is Best About Your Community?
- 194 How Did Change Affect Native Americans?
- 434 What Should You Do with Your Money?

Literature and Music
- 6 *Be My Neighbor* by Maya Ajmera and John D. Ivanko
- 78 "Walk Lightly" by J. Patrick Lewis illustrated by Alison Jay
- 150 *A Place Called Freedom* by Scott Russell Sanders illustrated by Thomas B. Allen
- 238 "Becoming a Citizen—Just Like Me" as told to Diane Hoyt-Goldsmith by Shaddai Aguas Suarez photographs by Lawrence Migdale
- 318 *Dreaming of America: An Ellis Island Story* by Eve Bunting illustrated by Ben F. Stahl
- 382 *Alex and the Amazing Lemonade Stand* by Liz and Jay Scott illustrated by Pam Howard

Primary Sources
- 206 The Declaration of Independence
- 222 The Corps of Discovery

298 State Symbols
412 Computers, Past and Present
420 Money Through Time

Documents
206 The Declaration of Independence
208 The Constitution of the United States
217 The Gettysburg Address
245 The Bill of Rights

Biography
50 Fredrick Law Olmsted
119 Sylvia Earle
210 Benjamin Franklin and Thomas Jefferson
258 Cesar Chavez
342 Maya Lin
393 Madame C. J. Walker

Children in History
60 Maya Angelou
130 The First Earth Day
215 Pioneer Schools
294 The Living American Flag
326 Edward Corsi
423 Kid Blink, A Famous Newsie

Field Trip
100 Yellowstone National Park
286 The United States Capitol

356 National Storytelling Festival

Fun with Social Studies
68 Unit 1
140 Unit 2
228 Unit 3
308 Unit 4
372 Unit 5
444 Unit 6

Charts, Graphs, and Diagram
4 Compare and Contrast
48 Grid System
54 Top Five Ways Suburban Workers Travel to New York City
76 Main Idea and Details
121 Pictograph of Tornado Season in Oklahoma
121 Bar Graph of Tornado Season in Oklahoma
148 Sequence
164 Some of the World's Tallest Buildings
176 The Assembly Line
236 Summarize
245 Basic Rights
261 Choices and Consequences
267 Levels of Government
268 Branches of the Federal Government
261 Flag Manners

297 Population of Bald Eagles, 1995–2000
316 Cause and Effect
327 Immigrants and Their Countries
353 Followers of Five Religions in the United States
380 Generalize
408 Online Buying and Selling
424 Supply and Demand Affects Prices

Maps
110 The World
111 Northern Hemisphere
111 Southern Hemisphere
112 The United States
28 Sister Cities
31 Missouri
49 Mount Vernon in Baltimore, Maryland
59 Communities in Arkansas
71 Stillwater, Oklahoma
83 Earth's Hemispheres
84 Salt Lake City
85 The World
86 North America
88 Latitude
88 Longitude
89 Ohio Latitude and Longitude
98 Landform Map of the United States
103 Regions of the United States
104 Lexington, Kentucky

xvii

143	Southeast States: Latitude and Longitude	
179	Ancient Mesopotamia	
180	Ancient Egypt	
181	Ancient China	
182	Ancient Greece	
183	Ancient Rome	
184	Ancient Mali	
191	Native American Groups	
205	The Thirteen Colonies	
213	Lewis and Clark's Journey	
216	Civil War States	
221	United States in 1803	
221	United States in 1903	
231	Frankfort, Kentucky, in 1800	
231	Frankfort, Kentucky, Today	
274	Counties of New Jersey	
279	Downtown Fayetteville, Arkansas	
281	States and Their Capitals	
301	Sharing Borders	
302	Bhutan	
311	Road Map of Norwood, Ohio	
325	Immigration to the United States	
331	Population Map of Illinois	
333	Washington, D.C.	
334	Cleveland, Ohio	
336	Chamblee, Georgia	
364	People of the World	
375	Population Map of Tennessee	
399	Land Use and Products of Minnesota	
402	Some Important Worldwide Exports	
437	Tokyo, Japan	
438	Manica, Mozambique	
447	New Jersey Land Use and Products	
R2	World: Political	
R4	World: Physical	
R6	Western Hemisphere: Political	
R7	Western Hemisphere: Physical	
R8	United States: Political	
R10	United States: Physical	

Time Lines

51	Frederick Law Olmsted Time Line
119	Sylvia Earle Time Line
160	Chicago's Early History
202	European Settlement
211	Benjamin Franklin and Thomas Jefferson Time Line
226	Visual Summary Time Line
258	Cesar Chavez Time Line
338	The Statue of Liberty Time Line
343	Maya Lin Time Line
393	Madame C. J. Walker Time Line

Illustrations

92	Bodies of Water
95	The Four Seasons
163	A Growing Community
192	Life on the Great Plains
282	The White House
396	A Yogurt Factory

Introduction

The Story Well Told

"The American city should be a collection of communities where every member has a right to belong."

—former President Lyndon B. Johnson

This year you will learn about different communities. You will read about what it was like to live in a different **time**. You will meet **people** from communities in other states and countries. You will visit many **places** to find out how people in different communities live.

Our Communities

The Story Is About Time, People, and Place

Every community has its own history. A **history** is the story of what has happened in a place. People who study the past are called historians. Historians study how the past and present are linked. They look for how things change over time. They look at how they stay the same.

To learn about communities long ago, historians study the objects used by people in the past. These objects are called **artifacts**.

Historians study people from the past to learn more about life long ago. They often read biographies of important people. A **biography** is the story of a person's life.

12 ■ Introduction

Historians also study the places where events happened. To better understand the place they are studying, historians study maps. A **map** shows a place's location. A map also tells historians about the land and the people who lived there.

Historians write the story of our past. They show us how time, people, and place are connected. You will learn to think like a historian as you study the history of your community.

Introduction • 13

Reading Your Textbook

GETTING STARTED

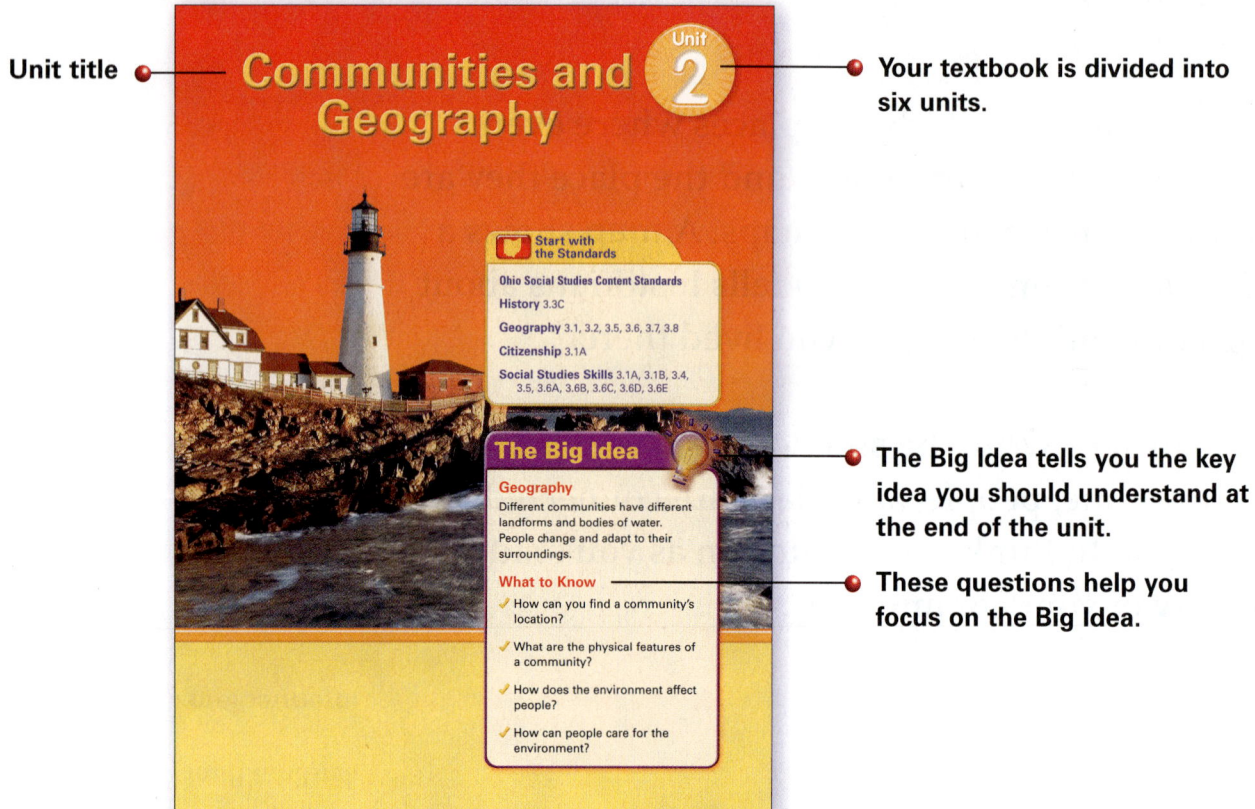

- Unit title
- Your textbook is divided into six units.
- The Big Idea tells you the key idea you should understand at the end of the unit.
- These questions help you focus on the Big Idea.

BEGINNING A UNIT

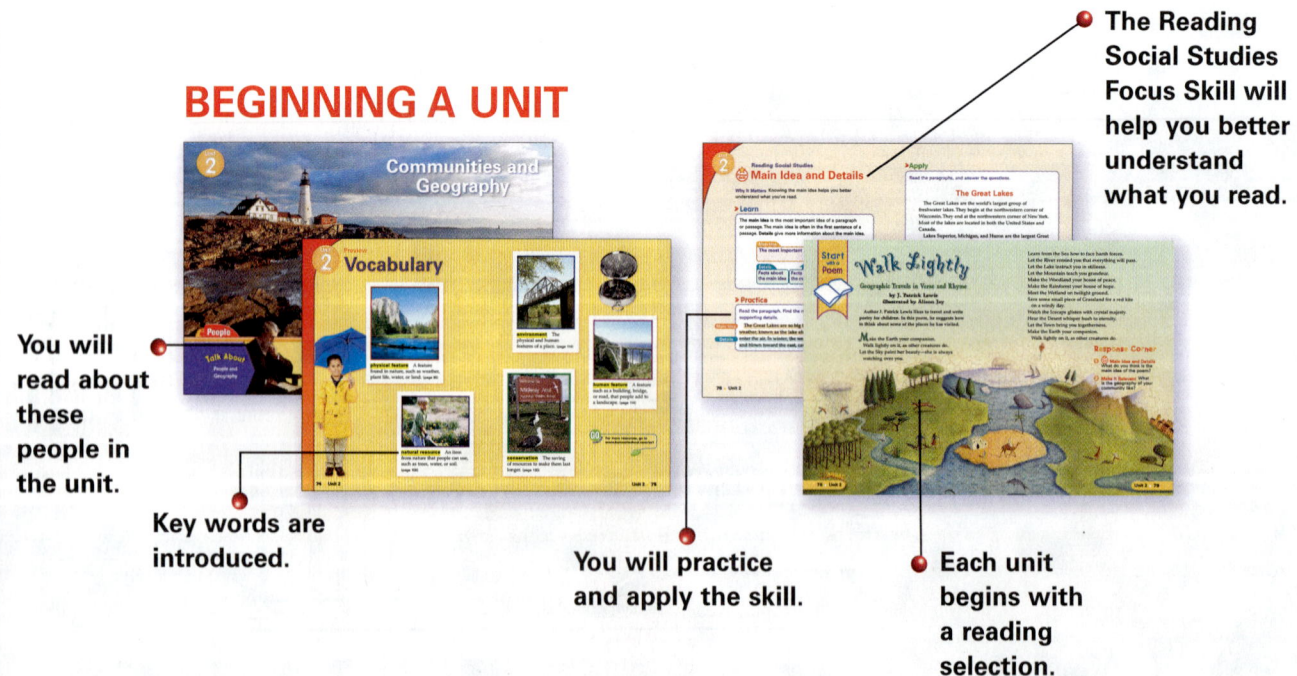

- You will read about these people in the unit.
- Key words are introduced.
- You will practice and apply the skill.
- The Reading Social Studies Focus Skill will help you better understand what you read.
- Each unit begins with a reading selection.

I4 ■ Introduction

BEGINNING A CHAPTER

Each unit is divided into chapters, and each chapter is divided into lessons.

The Study Skill provides a strategy you can use to remember or organize what you read.

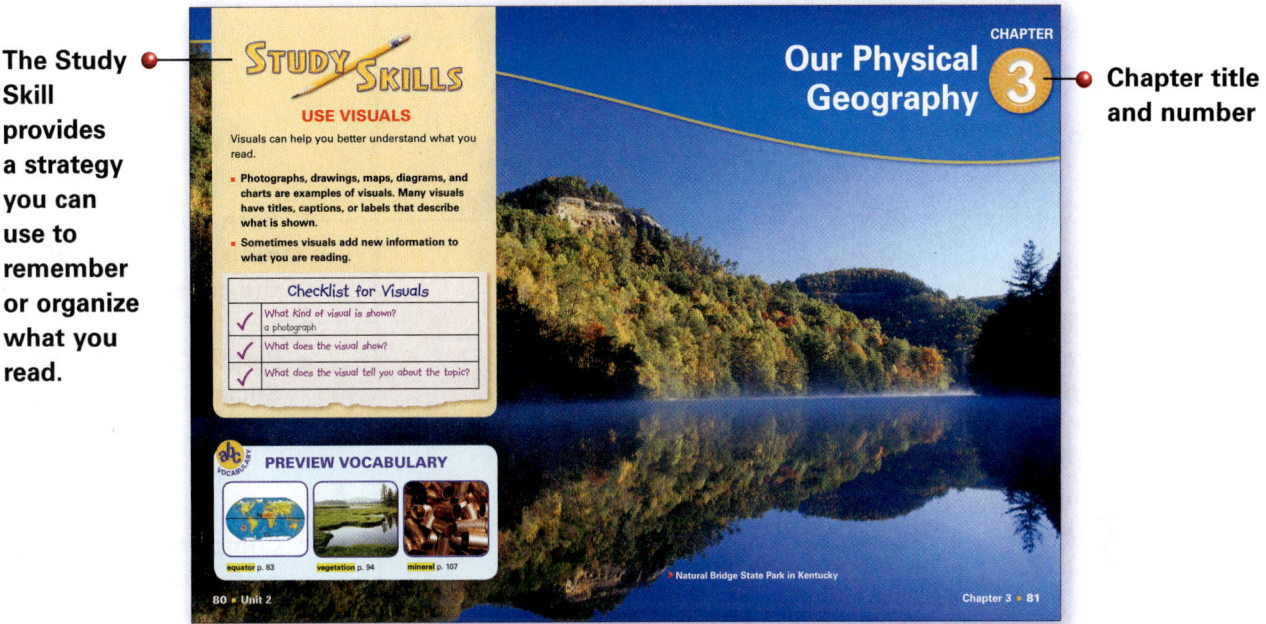

Chapter title and number

BEGINNING A LESSON

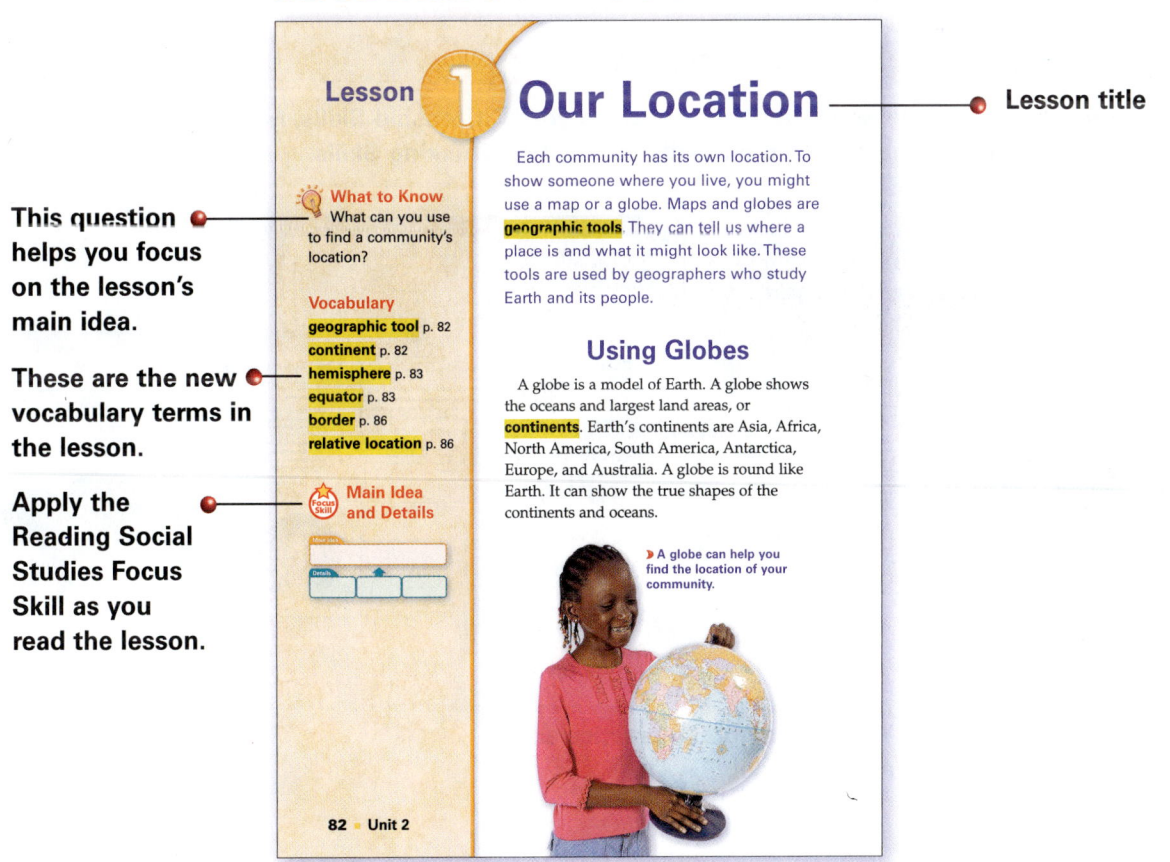

Lesson title

This question helps you focus on the lesson's main idea.

These are the new vocabulary terms in the lesson.

Apply the Reading Social Studies Focus Skill as you read the lesson.

Introduction ■ I5

CONCLUDING A LESSON

Each short section ends with a **Reading Check** question, which helps you check whether you understand what you have read.

Each lesson, like each chapter and unit, ends with a review. Questions and activities help you check your understanding of the lesson.

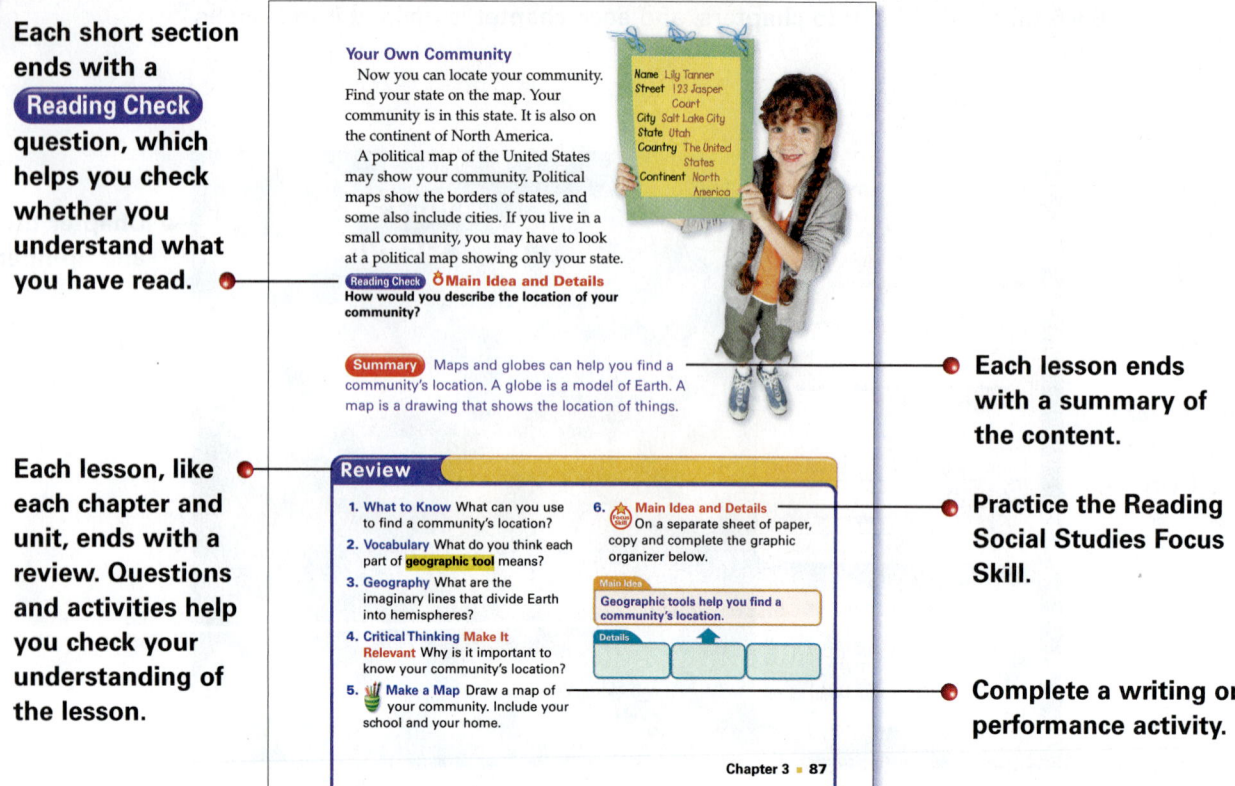

Each lesson ends with a summary of the content.

Practice the Reading Social Studies Focus Skill.

Complete a writing or performance activity.

LEARNING SOCIAL STUDIES SKILLS

Your textbook has lessons that help you build your Citizenship Skills, Map and Globe Skills, Chart and Graph Skills, and Critical Thinking Skills.

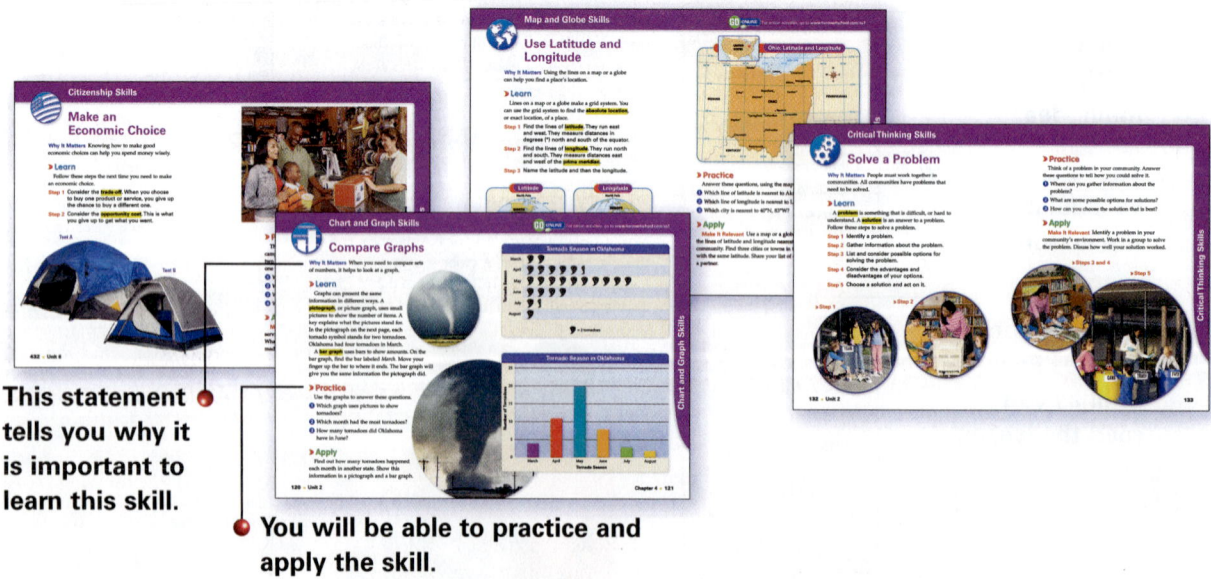

This statement tells you why it is important to learn this skill.

You will be able to practice and apply the skill.

I6 ■ Introduction

SPECIFIC FEATURES

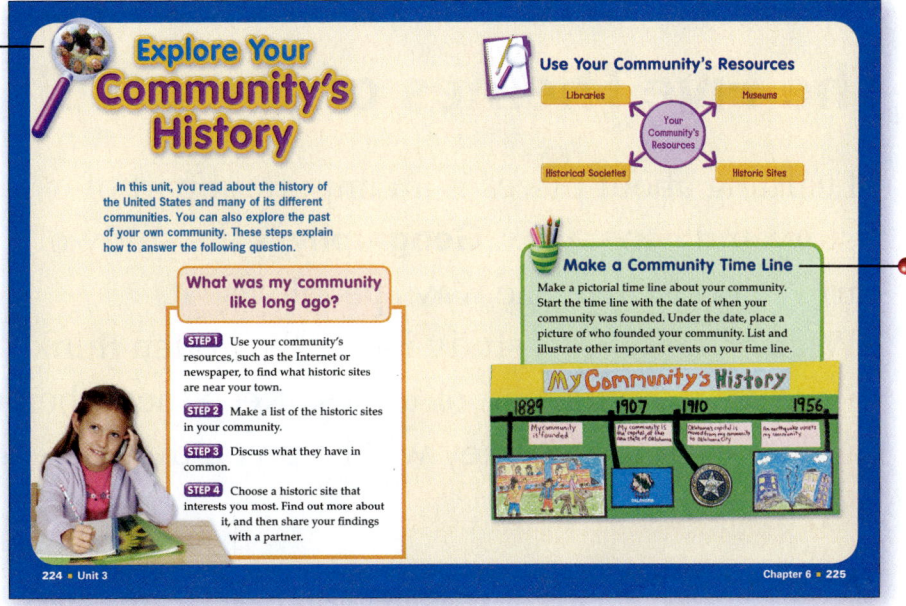

The Explore Your Community feature helps you research your local area.

You will do a project that helps you learn more about your community.

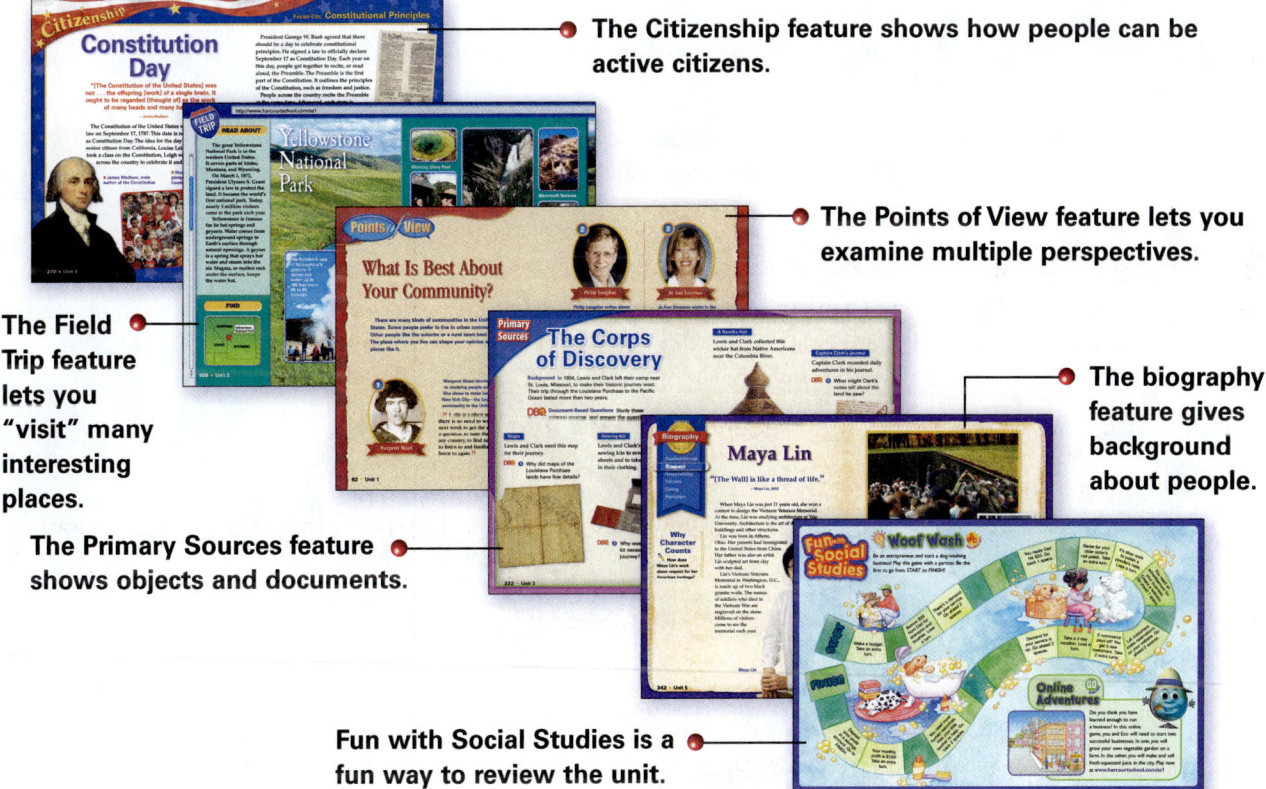

The Citizenship feature shows how people can be active citizens.

The Points of View feature lets you examine multiple perspectives.

The biography feature gives background about people.

The Field Trip feature lets you "visit" many interesting places.

The Primary Sources feature shows objects and documents.

Fun with Social Studies is a fun way to review the unit.

FOR YOUR REFERENCE

At the back of your textbook, you will find a section called For Your Reference. You can use it to look up words or to find out information about people, places, and other topics.

Introduction ■ I7

GEOGRAPHY REVIEW

The Five Themes of Geography

Learning about places is an important part of history and geography. **Geography** is the study of Earth's surface and the ways people use it.

When geographers study Earth, they often think about five main themes, or topics. Keep these themes in mind as you read. They will help you think like a geographer.

Location

Everything on Earth has its own **location** — the place where it can be found.

Place

Every place has physical and human characteristics, or features, that make it different from all other places. **Physical features** are formed by nature. **Human features** are created by people.

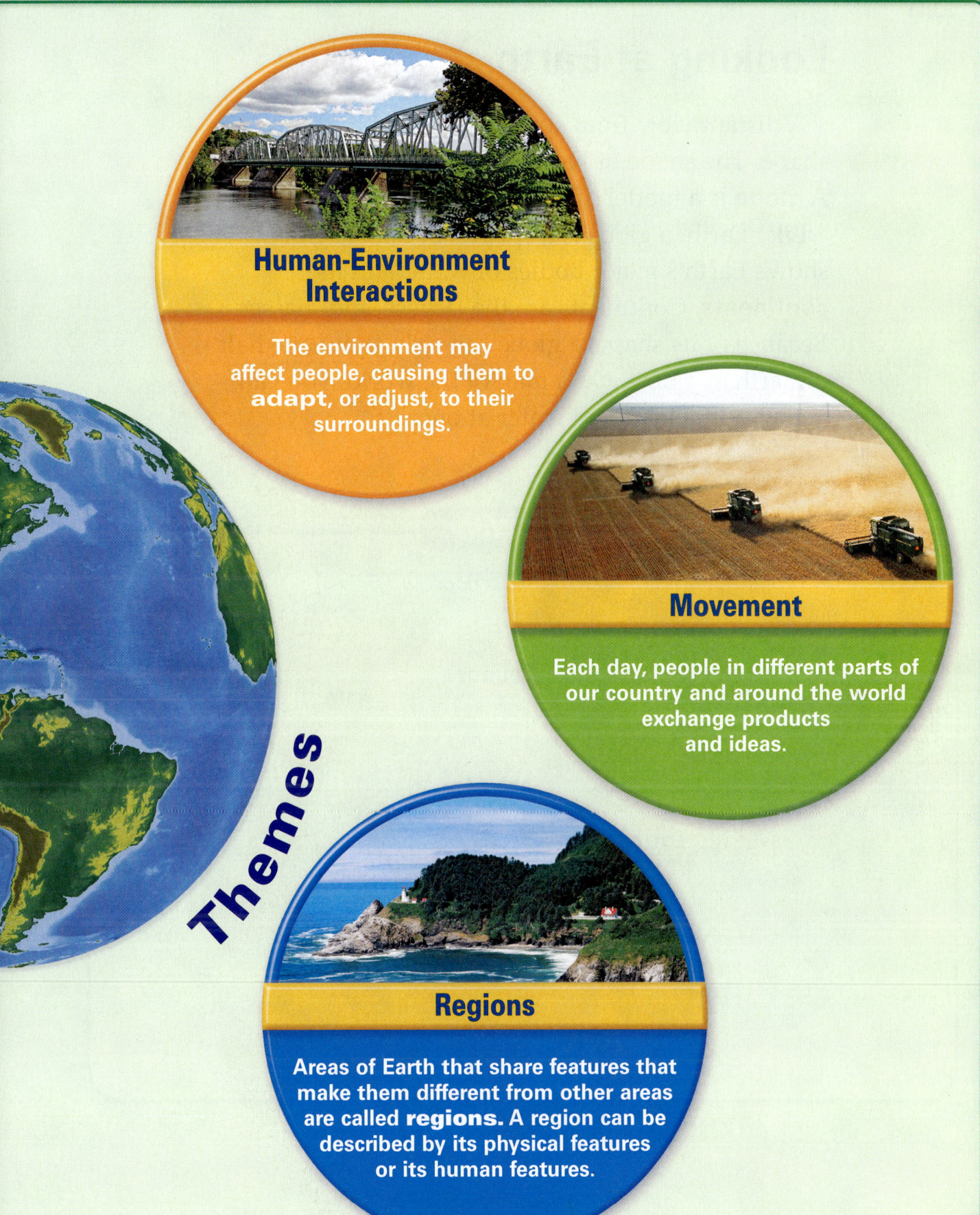

GEOGRAPHY REVIEW

Looking at Earth

A distant view from space shows Earth's round shape. The shape of Earth is shown best by a globe. A **globe** is a model of our planet.

Like Earth, a globe is a sphere, or ball. A globe shows Earth's major bodies of water and its **continents**. Continents are the largest land masses. Because of its shape, a globe can only show one half of Earth at a time. On a map of the world, you can see all of the land and water at once.

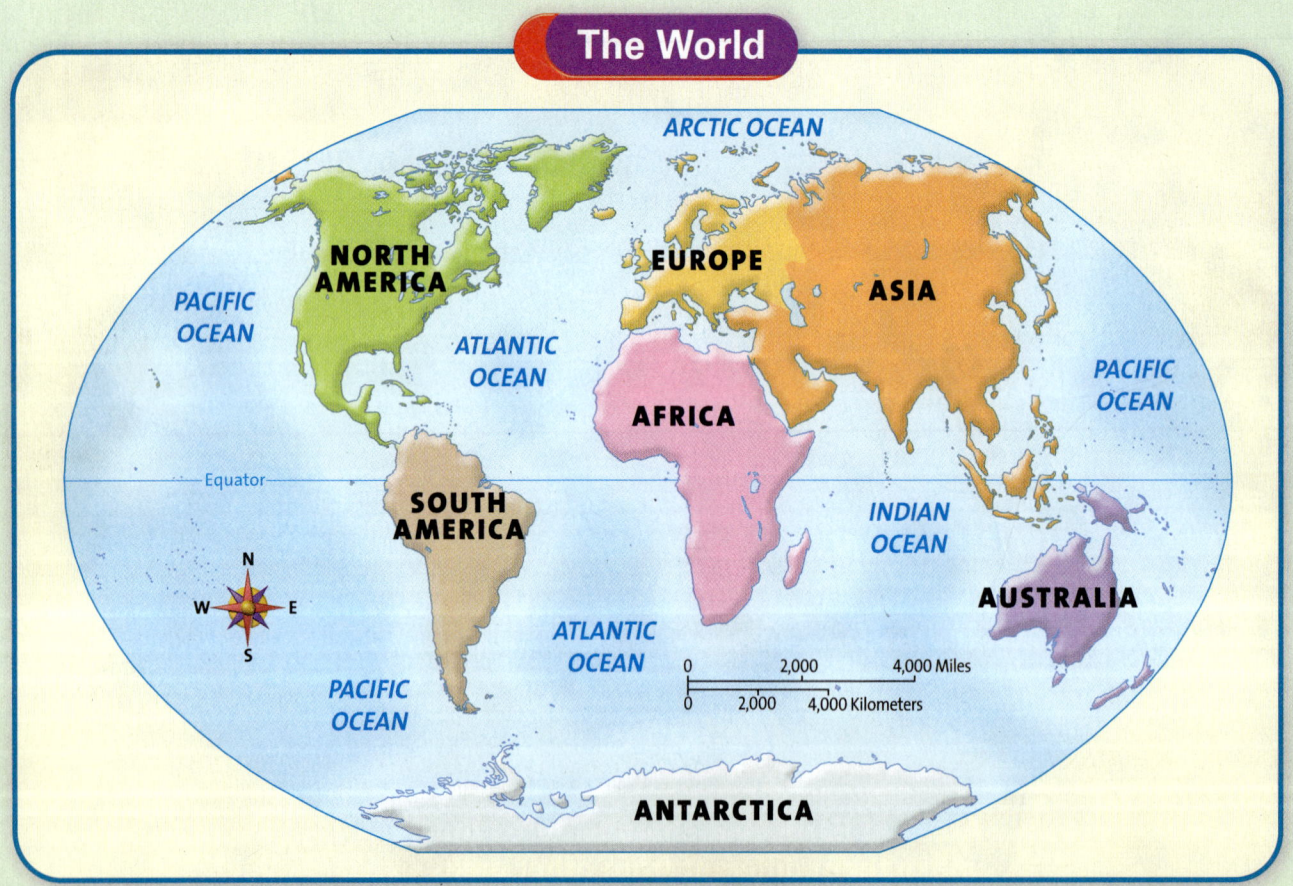

The World

Halfway between the North and South Pole is an imaginary line called the **equator**. It divides Earth into two equal halves, or **hemispheres**. The Northern Hemisphere is north of the equator. The Southern Hemisphere is south of it.

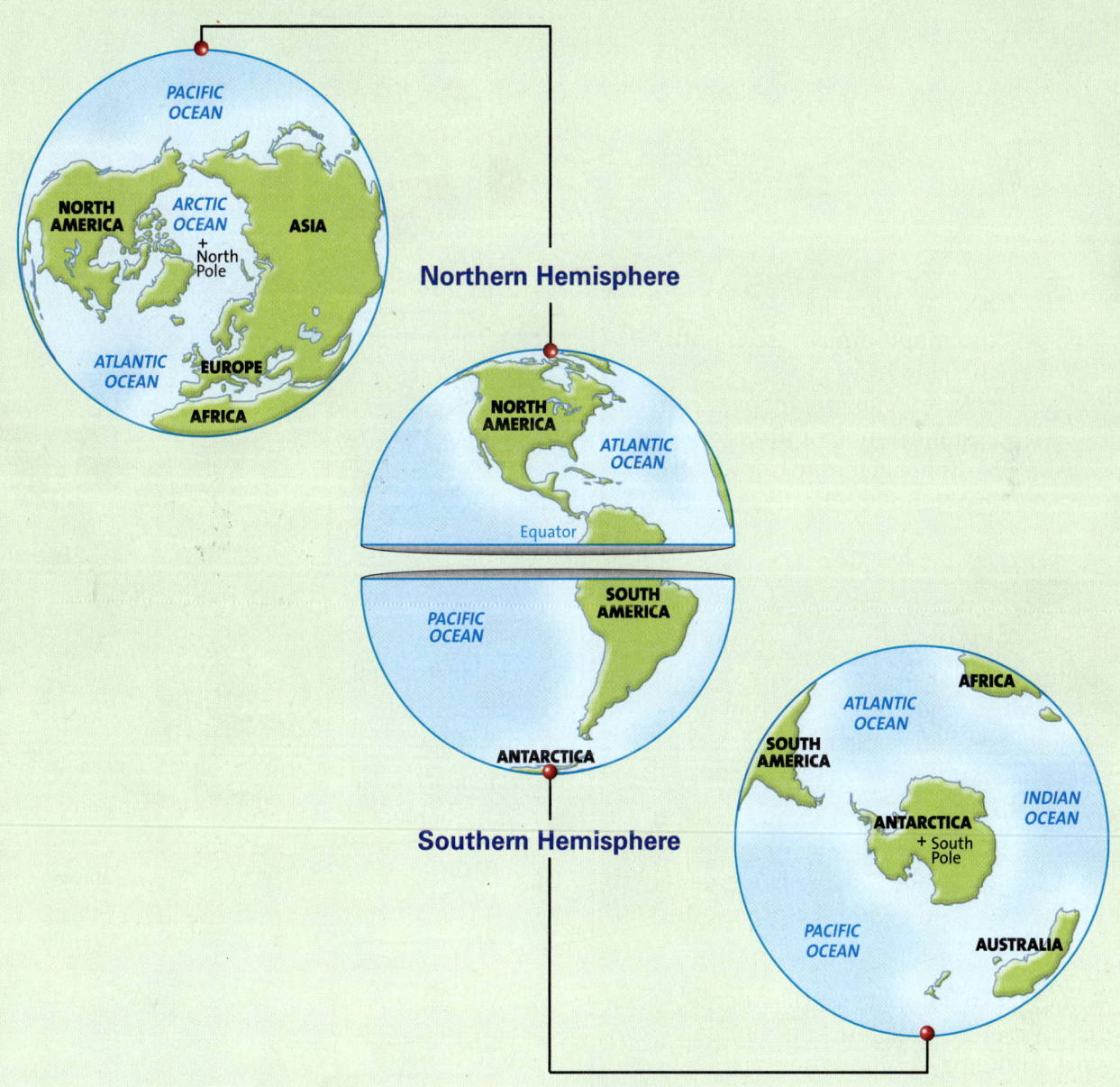

GEOGRAPHY REVIEW

Reading Maps

Maps can provide you with many kinds of information about Earth and the world around you. To help you read maps more easily, mapmakers add certain features to most maps they draw. These features usually include a title, a map key, a compass rose, a locator, and a map scale.

A **locator** is a small map or globe that shows where the place on the main map is located within a larger area.

A **map title** tells the subject of the map. It may also identify the kind of map.
- A political map shows cities, states, and countries.
- A physical map shows kinds of land and bodies of water.

A **map key**, or legend, explains the symbols used on a map. Symbols may be colors, patterns, lines, or other special marks.

An **inset map** is a smaller map within a larger one.

A **map scale** compares a distance on the map to a distance in the real world. It helps you find the real distance between places on a map.

I12 ■ Introduction

Mapmakers sometimes need to show places marked on a map in greater detail or places that are located beyond the area shown on the map. Find Alaska and Hawaii on the map on page R6. This map shows the location of these two states in relation to the rest of the country.

Now find Alaska and Hawaii on the map below. To show this much detail for these states and the rest of the country, the map would have to be much larger. Instead, Alaska and Hawaii are shown in separate inset maps, or a small map within a larger map.

- A **compass rose**, or direction marker, shows directions.
- The **cardinal directions** are north, south, east, and west.
- The **intermediate directions**, or directions between the cardinal directions, are northeast, northwest, southeast, and southwest.

Introduction ■ I13

GEOGRAPHY REVIEW

1. **desert** a large, dry area of land
2. **forest** a large area of trees
3. **gulf** a large body of ocean water that is partly surrounded by land
4. **hill** land that rises above the land around it
5. **island** a landform with water all around it
6. **lake** a body of water with land on all sides
7. **mountain** highest kind of land
8. **ocean** a body of salt water that covers a large area
9. **peninsula** a landform that is surrounded on only three sides by water
10. **plain** flat land
11. **river** a large stream of water that flows across the land
12. **valley** low land between hills or mountains

Communities Around Us

Frederick Law Olmsted 1822–1903
Designer of several city parks, such as Central Park in New York City

Maya Angelou 1928–Present
Missouri-born poet who wrote about growing up in the South as an African American girl

Unit 1 • 1

Preview
Vocabulary

community A group of people who live and work in the same place. (page 14)

citizen A person who lives in and belongs to a community. (page 14)

culture A way of life shared by members of a group. (page 15)

government A group of people who make rules and solve problems for a community. (page 19)

communication The sharing of information. (page 27)

GO ONLINE For more resources, go to www.harcourtschool.com/ss1

Unit 1 ■ 3

Unit 1

Reading Social Studies
 **Compare and Contrast**

Why It Matters Knowing how to compare and contrast will help you understand how things, people, and ideas are alike and different.

▶ Learn

> To **compare** things is to tell how they are alike, or similar. To **contrast** things is to tell how they are different.
>
>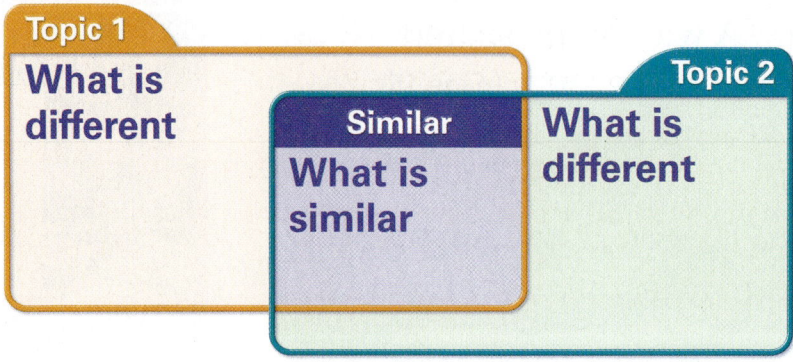
>
> - Words and phrases, such as *the same as, like, both,* and *similar,* are clues that two things are being compared.
> - Words and phrases, such as *different from, unlike, however,* and *but,* are clues that two things are being contrasted.

▶ Practice

> **Read the paragraph. Then compare and contrast the cities.**
>
> Lagos is in Nigeria, Africa. Washington, D.C., is in the United States, in North America. **Compare** Lagos and Washington, D.C., are both large, busy cities. **Contrast** However, they grew differently.

4 ▪ Unit 1

Apply

Read the paragraphs, and answer the questions.

Lagos and Washington, D.C.

Washington, D.C., is the capital of the United States. Lagos used to be the capital of Nigeria. These cities are very different in many ways. Yet they are alike in many ways, too.

Both cities are good places to buy and sell things because they are near water. Lagos is near the Gulf of Guinea. Washington, D.C., is mainly next to the Potomac River. Boats can carry people and things to and from cities that are near water.

The two cities grew in different ways. Lagos grew fast. It was not planned to become a large capital city. Washington, D.C., was planned to be the United States capital.

Today, Lagos and Washington, D.C., share large-city problems. Both need more homes and better ways for people to travel around the city.

Washington, D.C.

Lagos

 ## Compare and Contrast

1. How are Washington, D.C., and Lagos alike?
2. How are these cities different?
3. What problems do both cities have in common today?

Start with a Story

Be My Neighbor

by Maya Ajmera and John D. Ivanko

A community is a group of people who live in the same place. All communities are made up of different neighborhoods. Some neighborhoods are big, but some are small.

Neighborhoods are made up of different people. These people work to make their neighborhoods nice places to live. In this story, you will learn about the ways people live in neighborhoods around the world.

Israel

United States

Your neighborhood is a special place.

A neighborhood is where you live, learn, grow up, play, and work, surrounded by your family and friends. Each and every neighborhood is a special place. Yours might be in the mountains, along a coast, or somewhere in between. It might have important historical sites, such as a monument or the home of someone famous.

Canada

Mali

It may be part of a village, town, or big city.

Neighborhoods around the world can look very different. Some neighborhoods have lots and lots of people in them, while others have only a small population, such as those on a remote island, in the country, or high up in the hills. Some neighborhoods are made up of a few buildings in a town or village, while others stretch for miles and miles and are part of a big city.

Unit 1   7

Every neighborhood is made up of lots of different people . . .

Your neighborhood can be made up of people of all ages, interests, and backgrounds. Some members of your neighborhood may live like you and your family, and others may have different habits and customs that are celebrated in different kinds of festivals and community activities. The post office, town square, places of worship, and sports fields are places where people from your community come together.

Turkey

. . . and lots of different homes.

A house can be just for your family or it can be an apartment in a large building where many families live next to one another. Houses can be made from different materials, such as wood, brick, glass, or even mud, grass, or rocks. In places where the weather is cold, houses are made to keep you warm. In warm climates houses are built to keep you cool. No matter where you live, houses are for making you and your family comfortable, dry, and safe.

Mongolia

. . . and places to buy the things you need.

France

Many neighborhoods have markets, restaurants, shopping malls, or grocery stores to buy what you and your family need. Some places are large with lots of different things for sale, while other stores are small, selling only specific items like bread or cheese. You can even create your own place to sell something homemade to others in your community.

Mexico

In your neighborhood you share responsibilities . . .

People who live in the same neighborhood often work together to make it a better place. You might join your neighbors to clean up a river or work with a youth group to plant trees in a park. Neighbors look out for one another, perhaps helping someone find a lost dog or picking up fallen branches after a big storm. There are also people in your neighborhood whose job it is to take care of you: doctors, police officers, firefighters, and mail carriers, for example.

India

United States

Your neighborhood is where you feel at home.

Neighbors have in common the place where they live. You celebrate your neighborhood because you're a part of it and it's a part of you. Your neighborhood is a place where you learn about cooperation, respect, and friendship. It's the place you call home.

Papua New Guinea

United Kingdom

Response Corner

1 **Compare and Contrast** How are the neighborhoods that make up communities alike? How are they different?

2 **Make It Relevant** How is your neighborhood like other places in your community?

UNDERSTAND VOCABULARY

Using a dictionary can help you learn new words as you read.

- A dictionary shows the meanings of a word and describes where the word came from.
- You can use a chart to list the unknown words that you look up in a dictionary.

community (kə•myōō´nə•tē) *n* 1: a group of people who live and work in the same place.

Word	Definition
community	A group of people who live and work in the same place.

PREVIEW VOCABULARY

business p. 16

museum p. 17

law p. 18

Learning About Communities

CHAPTER 1

› A view of Main Street in Easton, Maryland

Lesson 1

What Is a Community?

 What to Know
What is a community?

Vocabulary
community p. 14
citizen p. 14
culture p. 15
business p. 16
museum p. 17
law p. 18
government p. 19

 Compare and Contrast

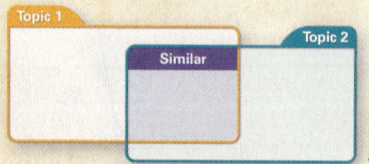

Like most people, you live in a community. A **community** is a group of people who live and work in the same place.

People live in communities all over the world. One reason they live in communities is that they like to be with others. In a community, people feel that they belong.

The people who live in and belong to a community are called **citizens**. Citizens are part of a community.

▶ Like many communities, New York City, New York, is made up of many groups of people.

14 ▪ Unit 1

Many People, One Community

The citizens of a community may belong to different groups. They may have different cultures. A **culture** is a way of life shared by members of a group. What people eat, how they speak and dress, and what they believe in are parts of their culture.

Sharing Cultures

Most communities have people from more than one culture. People often bring some of their culture to a community. They share their foods, clothing, music, and art. When a community has different cultures, people can enjoy other ways of life.

▶ Clothing is part of a person's culture. These girls in New Jersey dance at an Indian cultural event.

Reading Check ✲ **Compare and Contrast**
What is one way communities are alike?

Depending on One Another

People in a community depend on, or count on, one another. They depend on police and firefighters to keep them safe. People also depend on stores and other businesses. In a **business**, workers make or sell things or do work for others.

Businesses help people in communities meet their wants. A want is something that people would like to have, such as a television. Some wants are needs. Food, clothing, and a place to live are all needs.

Businesses provide jobs for people in a community. The money people earn from working can help them pay for their wants. In turn, businesses depend on the people in a community to buy what the businesses sell.

Reading Check **Generalize**
How do people in communities depend on one another?

> People depend on businesses for the things they want and need.

Coming Together

Most communities have places where people can come together. Schools are places where people come together to learn or hold meetings. People can also learn by using books and other materials at a library.

Communities have places where people can spend their free time. These may include parks, community centers, and playgrounds.

Some communities have interesting places to visit. Theaters may offer movies, plays, and concerts. A community might also have museums. People visit a **museum** to see objects from other places and times, such as clothing from the past. They can also see art there.

Reading Check **Main Idea and Details**
In what places in a community do people come together?

❱ Children study art at the Guggenheim Museum in New York City.

❱ The Guggenheim Museum

Chapter 1 ■ 17

Following Rules and Laws

Most of the time, people get along with one another. Sometimes they do not. Families often make rules to keep order and peace in their homes. At school, teachers have rules to help students learn and stay safe. Raising your hand before speaking is an example of a rule. Classroom rules tell students how to behave.

Communities also have rules. The rules that a community makes are called **laws**. People must follow the laws of their community. Laws keep order in a community. Laws help keep people safe. For example, traffic laws help people travel safely.

> **A crossing guard helps students obey the law.**

A Community Government

Most communities have a government to make laws and see that they are followed. A **government** is a group of people that makes laws for a community, a state, or a country. In many communities, citizens choose the members of government. Government members meet to talk about and solve problems.

Reading Check **Main Idea and Details**
What is one thing that members of the government do?

Summary Communities are places where people feel that they belong. People of different cultures live and work in communities. As citizens, they follow rules and laws.

▶ Citizens at a town meeting talk about community laws.

Review

1. **What to Know** What is a community?
2. **Vocabulary** Write a sentence that includes the word **government**.
3. **Culture** What are some ways of life that make up your culture?
4. **Critical Thinking** What might life be like in a community without businesses?
5. **Make a Word Web** Make a word web of a community. Include everything that can be found in a community.
6. **Compare and Contrast** On a separate sheet of paper, copy and complete the graphic organizer below.

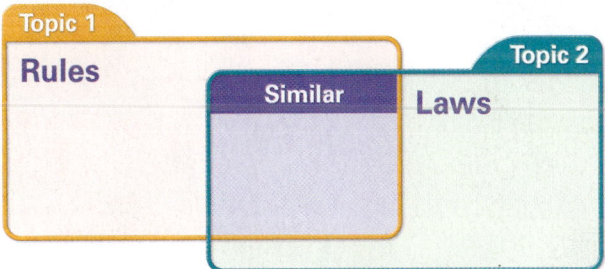

Chapter 1 ■ 19

Lesson 2 Communities Are Different

What to Know
How are communities different?

Vocabulary
climate p. 20
desert p. 21
landform p. 21
goods p. 24
service p. 24
bank p. 25

Focus Skill
Compare and Contrast

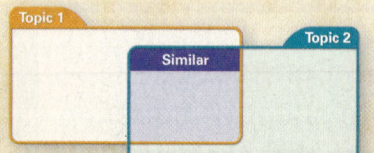

A community's land, bodies of water, and climate make it different. **Climate** is the weather that a place has over a long period of time. What has happened in a community's past also makes it different. So do its different types of businesses.

Different Geography

Every community is in a different place on Earth. That means the geography of every community is different. If you described your community's geography, you would probably begin with its climate, land, and water.

Seattle, Washington

Albuquerque, New Mexico

20 • Unit 1

Describing a Place

What kind of climate does your community have? Your community's climate might be hot or cold. It might change from season to season. You might live in a rainy place or in a desert. A **desert** is a place where the climate is dry.

What landforms are near your community? A **landform** is a kind of land. Your community might be on flat land, called a plain. Or you might live near mountains.

Are there any bodies of water near your community? A community might be located next to a river or a lake. People who live along the main coasts of the United States are near the Atlantic Ocean or the Pacific Ocean.

Reading Check **Compare and Contrast**
How can geography make communities different?

Burdett, Kansas

Chattanooga, Tennessee

Provincetown, Massachusetts

▶ This movie theater in Greenbelt is built in the Art Deco style of the 1930s.

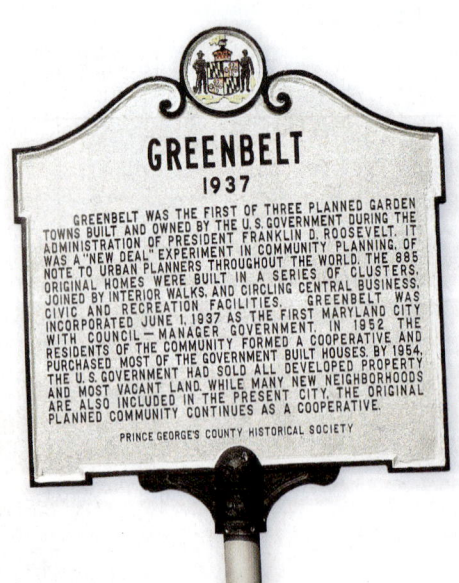

Different Pasts

Every community has its own history. Towns are started by different people and for different reasons. Some communities may be very old, while others are newer. Greenbelt, Maryland is a much newer town than Clarksville, Indiana.

Greenbelt, Maryland

By the time people began moving to Greenbelt in 1937, the whole town had already been built. The United States government planned this town. It was built for families who could not find a place to live in nearby Washington, D.C. The people of the new community made laws for the town. Greenbelt has grown and now includes new houses, new shops, and more people.

Clarksville, Indiana

Clarksville is named for George Rogers Clark. In the 1700s, Clark was a leader in the fight to make the United States a country. Clark and his soldiers camped in what is now Clarksville. It was a safe place for them to rest before moving on to fight their enemy.

In 1781, the United States government wanted to reward Clark and his soldiers. Leaders gave them the land that would become Clarksville. Today, more than 20,000 people live in this town.

Reading Check ⭐ **Compare and Contrast**
How are the towns of Greenbelt and Clarksville different?

▶ This cabin in Clarksville was built to look like one that George Rogers Clark built in about 1803.

Different Jobs

People do different kinds of jobs. Many choose to live in a community to be near their jobs. In some communities, people work in large businesses. In other places, they farm the land.

Jobs often depend on a community's location and geography. Many people who live near large bodies of water work on ships. Those who live near forests may cut down trees for wood.

Some workers make goods for others. **Goods** are things that can be bought or sold. Some goods, such as bicycles, are made. Other goods, such as vegetables, are grown.

Some workers provide services. A **service** is work that someone does for someone else. For example, doctors and nurses help people stay well.

▶ Tennis balls are goods.
A tennis lesson is a service.

Communities Built Around Jobs

Sometimes a community is known for goods that are made there. When people hear the name Hershey, Pennsylvania, they think of chocolate. The community was built around a famous candy company.

Other communities are known for services they provide. Many people in the United States depend on the banks in Charlotte, North Carolina. **Banks** are businesses that keep money safe.

Reading Check **Compare and Contrast**
How are goods and services different?

> Hershey, Pennsylvania, is known for the making of chocolate.

Summary Every community has things that make it different. Every community has its own geography, history, and places to work.

Review

1. **What to Know** How are communities different?
2. **Vocabulary** Use the term **climate** in a sentence to describe your own community's climate.
3. **Your Community** What landforms or bodies of water are found near your community?
4. **Critical Thinking Make It Relevant** Would you rather live in a new community or an older one? Why?
5. **Write a Description** Write a description of your community. Tell how it is different from other communities.
6. **Compare and Contrast** On a separate sheet of paper, copy and complete the graphic organizer below.

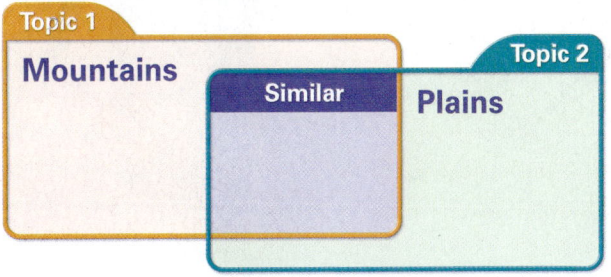

Chapter 1 ■ 25

Lesson 3 Communities Near and Far

What to Know
How are different communities connected?

Vocabulary
nation p. 26
communication p. 27
Internet p. 27

Focus Skill: Compare and Contrast

People live in communities all over the United States and the world. Whether they live nearby or far away, people still share with and learn from one another.

Communities Are Everywhere

The United States is a nation made up of many communities. A **nation**, or country, is an area of land with its own people and laws. There are many other nations around the world. All of these nations have their own communities.

26 • Unit 1

Community Connections

People often have family members or friends who live in different communities. Those communities may be in the United States or even in different nations. To see each other, people may have to travel thousands of miles by car, bus, train, or airplane.

Visiting people in another community is not the only way to stay in touch with them. **Communication** is the sharing of information. Using the telephone lets people speak to those who live far away.

People can also communicate with others by writing letters or by using the Internet to send e-mail. The **Internet** is a system that links computers around the world.

Reading Check ○ **Compare and Contrast**
How are speaking to someone on the telephone and writing an e-mail alike?

Fast Fact

Often, students on farms in Australia live many miles from the nearest school. They take part in classes by using radios and computers. This is called "the school of the air."

> Marrakech (ma•ruh•KESH) is a community in Morocco. How is Marrakech like your community? How is it different?

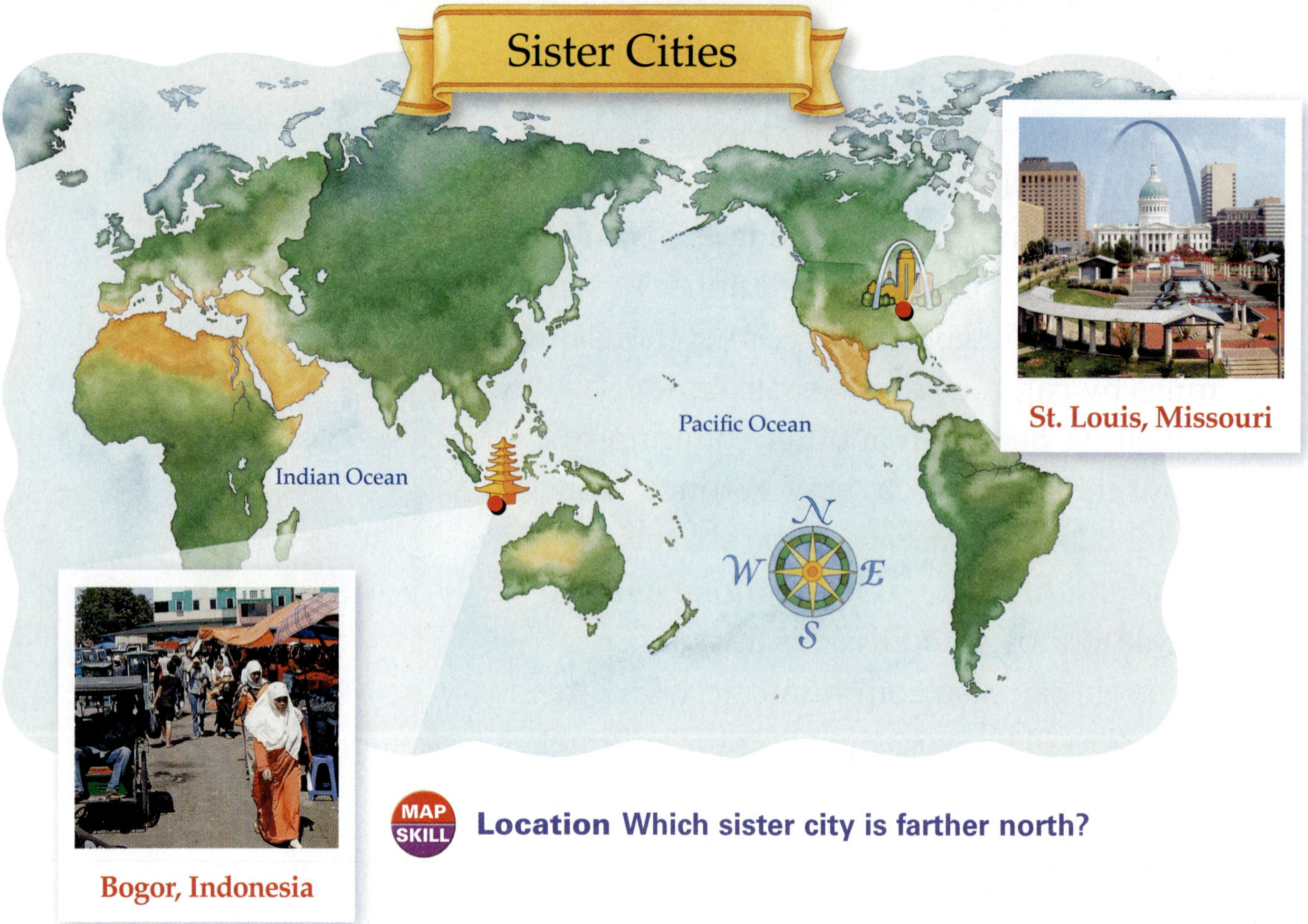

Sister Cities

St. Louis, Missouri

Bogor, Indonesia

MAP SKILL **Location** Which sister city is farther north?

▶ Leaders from Bogor and St. Louis meet.

Sister Cities

Communicating with citizens from other nations helps people learn about different ways of life. Some communities in different nations become partners to learn more about each other. These partner cities are called sister cities.

St. Louis, Missouri, in the United States, and Bogor (BOH•gawr), in Indonesia, are sister cities. Students, leaders, and business owners from each community visit their sister city.

They go to share ideas. When they return home, they share what they learned about their sister city. The citizens of St. Louis and Bogor also communicate through letters, telephone, and e-mail.

Helping Each Other

Members of sister cities also come together to help each other during times of need. In December 2004, a huge ocean wave called a tsunami (soo•NAH•mee) caused damage to Indonesia. The tsunami also damaged other communities on the Indian Ocean. Many people lost homes in the disaster. The people of St. Louis and Bogor gave money and supplies to help people in these communities.

Reading Check **Main Idea and Details**
How do sister cities share information?

Summary People in communities around the world communicate with and learn from one another. Sister cities, such as St. Louis and Bogor, show one way communities can be connected.

▶ Workers hand out needed supplies to people after the tsunami.

Review

1. **What to Know** How are different communities connected?
2. **Vocabulary** Explain how people can use the **Internet** for **communication**.
3. **Culture** Why do some communities become sister cities?
4. **Critical Thinking** Why is it important to communicate with people in other nations?
5. **Write an E-mail** Write an e-mail to someone in another country about your own community.
6. **Compare and Contrast** Copy and complete the graphic organizer below.

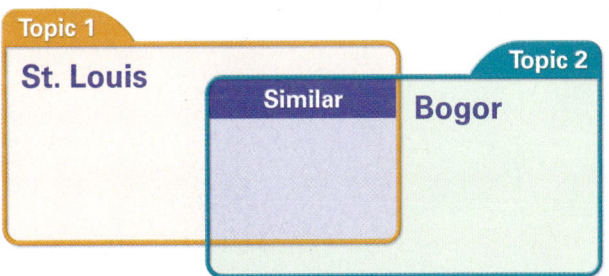

Map and Globe Skills

Find Directions and Distances

Why It Matters A map can show you a community's location. It can also show you directions and distances.

❯ Learn

A compass rose shows both cardinal and intermediate directions. The intermediate directions are in between the cardinal directions.

A map scale helps you find the real distances between places on a map. Follow these steps to use a map scale.

Step 1 Place a piece of paper next to the map scale.

Step 2 Mark the length of the scale on the paper.

Step 3 Use the scale as a ruler to find the distance.

❯ Practice

Use the compass rose and the map scale on the map on page 31 to answer these questions.

1. When a bus travels from Springfield to Jefferson City, in which direction is it going?
2. About how far is Joplin from Independence?

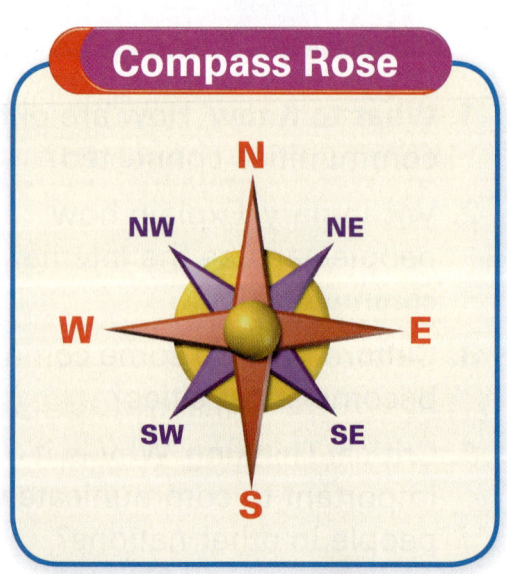

Compass Rose

❯ The intermediate directions are northeast, southeast, northwest, and southwest.

30 ■ Unit 1

 For online activities, go to www.harcourtschool.com/ss1

Missouri

▶ Apply

Make It Relevant Find your community on a map. Use the map scale and the compass rose to tell the distance and direction you would travel to get to a nearby community.

Chapter 1 ▪ 31

Lesson 4 Discover Your Community

What to Know
How can you learn about your community?

Vocabulary
reference work p. 33
ancestor p. 34
heritage p. 34
historic site p. 36
historical society p. 36

Compare and Contrast

Imagine that you are a detective. Detectives search for clues to discover the truth about events. They read books, talk to people, and visit places.

Detectives make notes about each discovery, both large and small. The clues they find are like puzzle pieces. When these pieces are put together, they form a complete picture of what happened.

> Students look at old community photographs.

32 • Unit 1

❯ Libraries have many resources you can use for community research.

Become a Detective

Like a detective, you can search for facts about your own community. You can learn what life was like in your community's past. You may learn about jobs and leaders. You might also discover facts about cultures in your community.

One way to find information about your community is to visit a library. A library has many **reference works**, or sources of facts. At a library, you can study maps to learn about your community's geography. You can also look at old and new photographs of your community. Ask a librarian to help you find what you need. Take notes when you find something useful.

Reading Check ○ **Compare and Contrast**
How is researching your community like being a detective?

Interview Other Citizens

Interviewing, or asking questions, is another good way to learn about your community. There are many people you can interview. You can ask business owners about jobs in your community. You can also talk to community members about different cultures found in your community.

Older family members are also good sources of information. They can tell you about your ancestors. An **ancestor** is someone in a person's family who lived long ago.

An older person can also tell you about your heritage. A **heritage** is the set of values and ways of life handed down from people who lived long ago.

▶ Students interview a person in their community of Nashville, Tennessee.

Plan the Interview
- Decide what the interview will be about.
- Write or call to ask for an interview.
- Tell the person who you are and why you would like to interview him or her.
- Set a time and a place to meet.

Before the Interview
- Find facts about your topic and the person.
- Make a list of questions to ask.

During the Interview
- If you want to use a digital video camera or tape recorder, ask the person first.
- Listen carefully, and do not interrupt.
- Take notes as you talk with the person. Write down some of his or her exact words.

After the Interview
- Before you leave, thank the person.
- Write the person a thank-you note.

Reading Check **Sequence**
What steps should you take before interviewing someone?

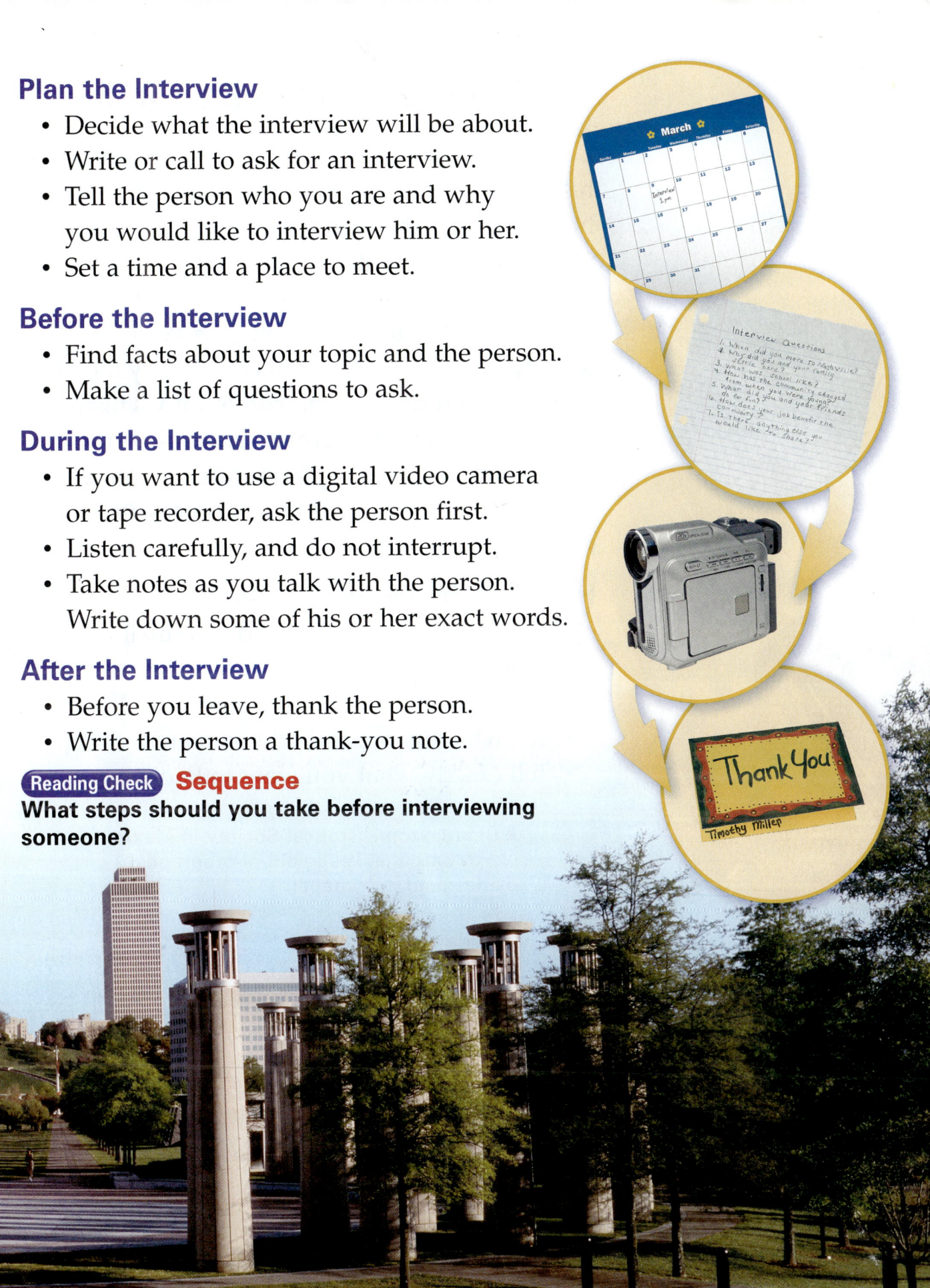

Write to or Visit Places

To get information about your community's history, you can write to or visit museums and historic sites. A **historic site** is a place where an important event took place.

Another source of information is your community's historical society. A **historical society** is an organization of community members who are interested in their community's history.

You can get more information about your community from other places, too. Businesses, parks, schools, and government offices are some of these places.

How to Write for Information

You can write a letter or send an e-mail to ask for information. Follow these steps.
- Write neatly, or use a computer.
- Tell who you are and why you are writing.
- Tell exactly what you want to know.

> **The Maxton Historical Society in Maxton, North Carolina, keeps old photographs, diaries, and newspapers.**

How to Ask Questions During a Visit

If you visit a museum, historical society, or historic site, be sure to do these things.
- Take along a list of questions to ask.
- Tell who you are and why you are visiting.
- Listen carefully, and take notes.
- Take any information that the place offers.
- Before you leave, thank the person you spoke with.

Reading Check **Compare and Contrast**
How are historical societies and historic sites different?

▶ A historian at the Maxton Historical Society studies his community.

Summary You can be a detective in your own community. To gather facts, you can visit a library, interview people, and write to or visit special places.

Review

1. **What to Know** How can you learn about your community?
2. **Vocabulary** What might you find at a **historic site**?
3. **Your Community** Whom can you interview to find out about your own community?
4. **Critical Thinking** How are museums and historical societies alike? How are they important to a community?
5. **Make a Web Page** Make a web page to show places where you can get information about your community.
6. **Compare and Contrast** On a separate sheet of paper, copy and complete the graphic organizer below.

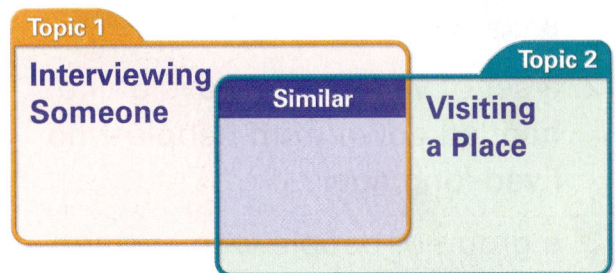

Chapter 1 ▪ 37

Chapter 1 Review

Visual Summary

Communities are places where people live and work.

Summarize the Chapter

Compare and Contrast Complete this graphic organizer to compare and contrast communities.

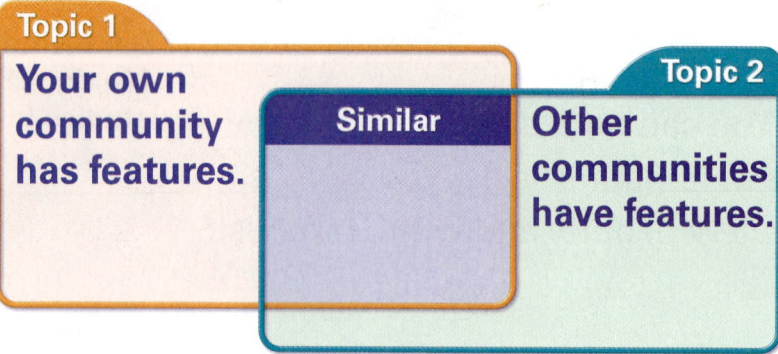

Vocabulary

Identify the term from the word bank that correctly matches each definition.

1. a group of people that makes laws for a community, a state, or a country

2. a set of values and ways of life handed down from people who lived long ago

3. a group of people who live and work in the same place

4. the weather a place has over a long period of time

5. an area of land with its own people and laws

Word Bank

community p. 14

government p. 19

climate p. 20

nation p. 26

heritage p. 34

38 ■ Unit 1

 Communities are similar and different in many ways.

 People can learn about their communities.

Facts and Main Ideas

Answer these questions.

6. What do people from different cultures share with others in their community?

7. What could you talk about to describe a community's geography?

8. How can people communicate with others who live far away?

Write the letter of the best choice.

9. Which of the following is a landform?
   A mountain
   B climate
   C region
   D weather

10. Which of the following is a place where an important event happened?
    A library
    B museum
    C historic site
    D historical society

Critical Thinking

11. **Make It Relevant** If your community chose a sister city, what might you learn from that city?

12. **Make It Relevant** What would your community be like without its businesses?

Skills

Find Directions and Distances
Use the map on page 31 to answer the question.

13. In what direction would you travel to go from Maryville to Hannibal? How far is it between the two cities?

writing

- **Write an Article** Write an article telling how libraries can help you learn about the past.

- **Write a Poem** Make a list of words about your community. Use the words to write a poem.

Chapter 1 ■ 39

STUDY SKILLS

PREVIEW AND QUESTION

Previewing a lesson helps you identify main ideas. Asking questions about these ideas can help you find important information.

- Reading the lesson titles and section titles gives clues about the main topic. Think of any questions you have about the topic.
- Read to find the answers to your questions.
- Finally, review what you have read.

Communities of Different Sizes

Preview	Questions	Read	Review
Lesson 1 A city is an urban community.	What is it like to live in an urban community?	✓	✓
Lesson 2			

PREVIEW VOCABULARY

urban p. 43

suburban p. 52

rural p. 56

Communities of Different Sizes

CHAPTER 2

▶ Navy Pier and Chicago's skyline

Lesson 1

Urban Communities

What to Know
What is an urban community?

Vocabulary
region p. 42
population p. 42
urban p. 43
harbor p. 45
transportation p. 46

Compare and Contrast

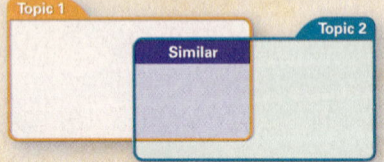

Communities are different. They have different people, jobs, and histories. They also may be located in different regions. A **region** is an area with at least one feature that makes it different from other areas.

The features of a community might include its landforms or climate. Another feature that makes a region different from others is its population. The **population** of a place is the number of people living there.

▶ The skyline of Chicago, Illinois

42 ■ Unit 1

Communities Large and Small

How would you describe the population of your own community? It may be large, small, or in between. Your community may have a lot of people or just a few.

Urban Regions

Most people in the United States live in or near **urban**, or city, regions. A city is the largest kind of community.

A city has busy streets, many people, and tall buildings. Cities need more schools and businesses than smaller communities do. In a city, crowded buses and trains carry people from place to place.

Reading Check **Compare and Contrast**
How is an urban community different from other communities?

> State Street in Chicago

Baltimore, an Urban Community

Kelsey lives in a row house building in Baltimore, Maryland. On her way to school, Kelsey sees people opening businesses for the day. Other people are catching buses to their jobs.

A Picture of Kelsey's City

The city of Baltimore is located on the Patapsco (puh•TAP•skoh) River. More than half a million people live in the city. Long ago, Baltimore began as a place where goods were loaded and unloaded onto ships. Over time, it grew into the city it is today.

Kelsey's area of Baltimore has people of many cultures. Living in Baltimore allows Kelsey to learn about these cultures.

> Kelsey leaves her Baltimore home to go to elementary school.

Living in Baltimore

Kelsey's parents moved to Baltimore to work there. Her mother rides the subway, or underground train, to her job at a local hospital. Baltimore also has a lightrail system. A lightrail is like a train. It rides on a rail and carries people. Kelsey's father works in a skyscraper, a very tall building. The building is in downtown Baltimore, the city's main business district. A business district is where many businesses are located.

On the weekends, Kelsey and her family visit many places in Baltimore. At the Inner Harbor, they go to museums and watch boats on the river. A **harbor** is a protected place with deep water that allows ships to come close to shore.

▶ The Inner Harbor is located near downtown Baltimore, along the waterfront.

Reading Check **Main Idea and Details**
What makes Baltimore an urban area?

Chapter 2 ■ 45

Other Urban Communities

Baltimore is at the center of one of many urban regions in the United States. Some other cities are even larger than Baltimore. New York City, New York, is the nation's largest city. It is located near a harbor on the Atlantic Ocean.

Cities are often located near harbors and rivers because this location makes transportation easier. **Transportation** is the movement of people and goods.

People in New York City have many ways to get around. They ride the bus or the subway to get from place to place. Many people choose to walk or ride bikes.

Chicago, Illinois, the nation's third-largest city, sits in the middle of the country near Lake Michigan. Like Baltimore and New York City, Chicago has many businesses and people. People in Chicago ride elevated trains that circle the city.

❯ New Yorkers use MetroCards to ride the subway.

❯ The subway in New York City is mostly underground. In some places, however, the tracks are above ground.

Cities with Different Cultures

Los Angeles, the nation's second-largest city, is near the Pacific coast in southern California. As in other cities, many of its citizens came from different parts of the United States or from other countries. They moved to Los Angeles to work at jobs, go to school, and make new lives. In Los Angeles, you can find neighborhoods in which people of many different cultures live together.

Reading Check ö Compare and Contrast
How is New York City different from Chicago?

Summary A city is the largest kind of community. Urban regions are filled with people, buildings, jobs, and different forms of transportation.

❯ Many people celebrate Hispanic culture in Los Angeles.

Review

1. **What to Know** What is an urban community?
2. **Vocabulary** Write a sentence about **population**, using the term **urban**.
3. **Geography** Why are many cities located near bodies of water?
4. **Critical Thinking Make It Relevant** Do you think your community is in an urban area? Why or why not?
5. **Create a Postcard** Create a picture postcard of an urban community. Write about what makes this community special.
6. **Compare and Contrast** On a separate sheet of paper, copy and complete the graphic organizer below.

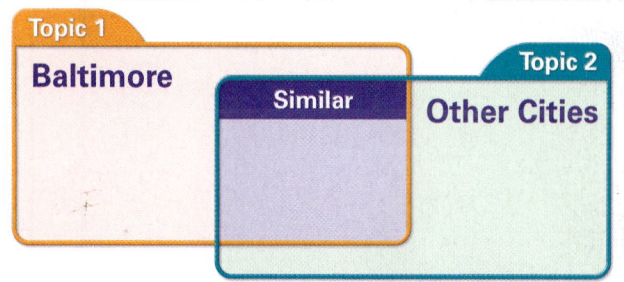

Chapter 2 ■ 47

Map and Globe Skills

Use a Map Grid

Why It Matters Sometimes you need to find the exact location of a park, a school, or a road.

▶ Learn

To find the exact location of a place, you can use a map that has a grid system. A **grid system** is a set of lines the same distance apart that cross one another to form boxes. The grid on this page shows rows and columns of boxes. The rows are labeled with letters, and the columns are labeled with numbers. Follow these steps to use a map grid.

Step 1 Put a finger on the red box. Slide your finger to the left, to the letter D.

Step 2 Now put a finger on the red box again. Slide your finger to the top, to the number 3. The exact location of the red box is D-3, or row D, column 3.

▶ Grid system

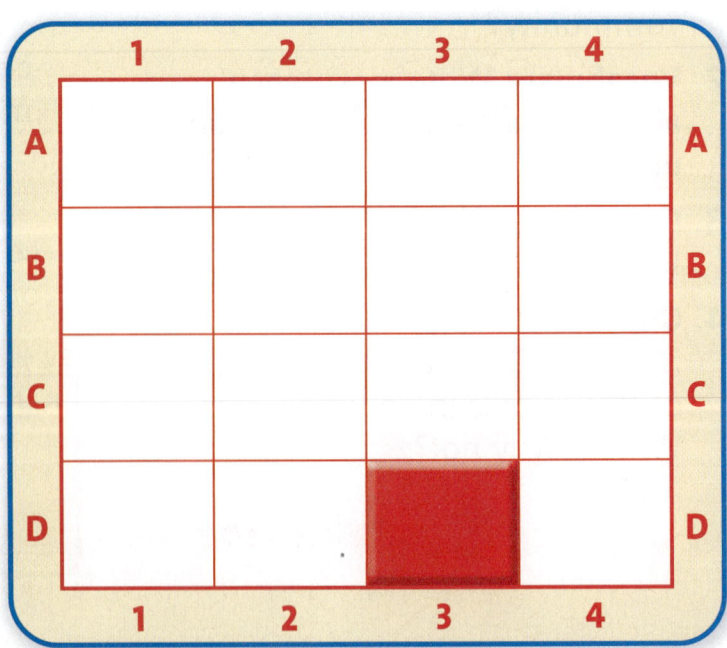

48 ▪ Unit 1

 For online activities, go to www.harcourtschool.com/ss1

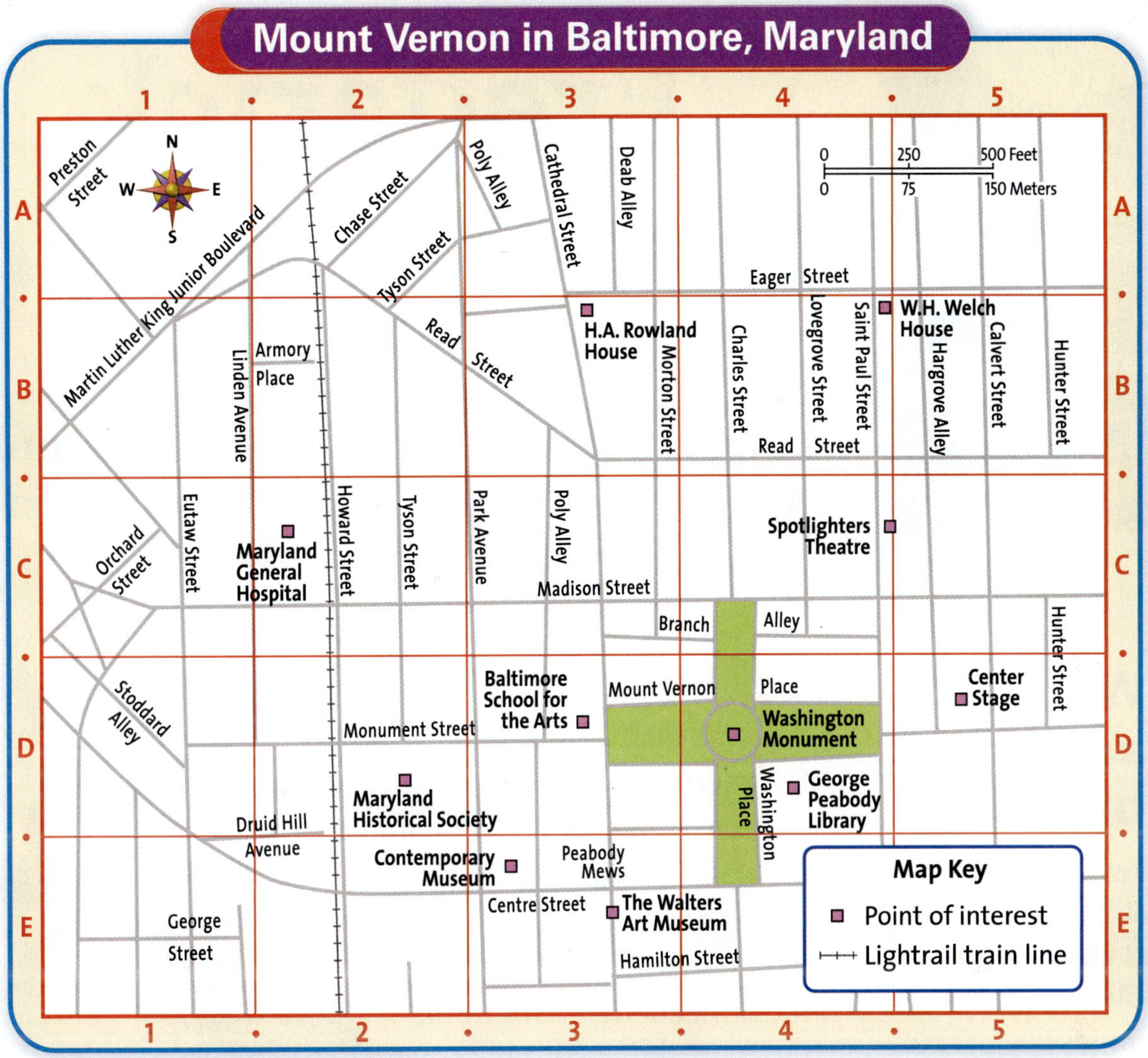

Mount Vernon in Baltimore, Maryland

Map and Globe Skills

▶ Practice

Use this map and its grid system to answer the questions. Give exact locations by using a letter and a number.

1. Where is the Contemporary Museum?
2. What point of interest do you see in the box at D-5?
3. Where is the Maryland General Hospital?

▶ Apply

Make It Relevant Draw a map of your school, house, or community. Add a grid, and label places on your map. Then share your map with classmates.

Chapter 2 ■ 49

Biography

- Trustworthiness
- Respect
- Responsibility
- Fairness
- **Caring**
- Patriotism

Frederick Law Olmsted

"An artist, he paints with lakes and wooded slopes; . . . with mountain sides and ocean views."

— Architect Daniel Burnham on Frederick Law Olmsted

Why Character Counts

✏️ **How did Frederick Law Olmsted show caring for people in urban communities?**

Frederick Law Olmsted designed many of our country's famous urban parks. He wanted people in urban communities to enjoy nature.

Olmsted grew up on a farm in Connecticut. Early in his life, he began reading books about natural landscapes.

As a young man, Olmsted spent time traveling throughout Europe. During his travels, he studied parks and landscapes.

Frederick Law Olmsted

Central Park in New York City

Olmsted worked as the supervisor for planning Central Park in New York City. In 1858, the city held a contest to choose a new park design. Olmsted worked with Calvert Vaux, another parks designer, on a plan. Their design won the contest.

Olmsted then spent nearly 40 years planning and creating parks in communities across the United States. One of his last projects was the Emerald Necklace, a 7-mile system of parks around Boston, Massachusetts.

Frederick Law Olmsted is remembered for his landscaping. Landscaping is the use of natural materials, such as plants and rocks, to create outdoor spaces. His landscape designs have improved many urban areas.

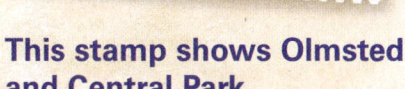

This stamp shows Olmsted and Central Park.

 For more resources, go to www.harcourtschool.com/ss1

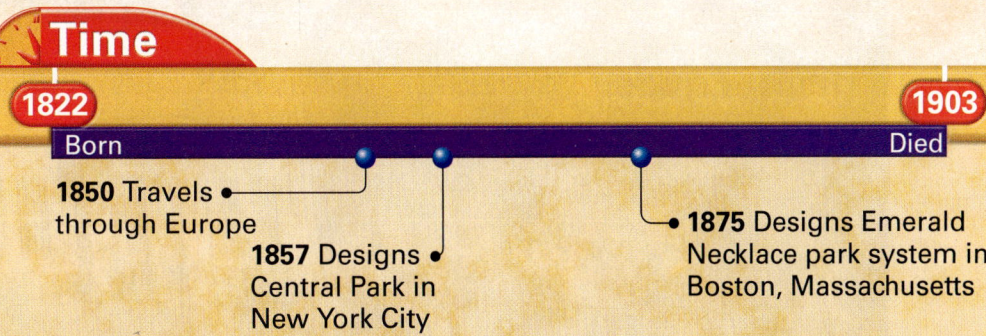

Time

- **1822** Born
- **1850** Travels through Europe
- **1857** Designs Central Park in New York City
- **1875** Designs Emerald Necklace park system in Boston, Massachusetts
- **1903** Died

Chapter 2 ■ 51

Lesson 2

Suburban Communities

What to Know
What is a suburban community?

Vocabulary
suburb p. 52
suburban p. 52

Compare and Contrast

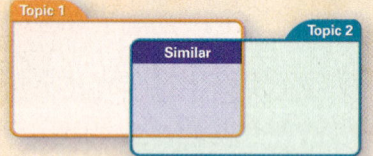

Many large cities have smaller communities around them. A smaller city or town built near a large city is called a **suburb** (suh•berb).

Maplewood, a Suburban Community

Maplewood, New Jersey, is a suburb of New York City. It is one of hundreds of suburbs around New York City. This suburban region includes communities in New York, New Jersey, Pennsylvania, and Connecticut. A **suburban** region is made up of all the suburbs around a large city.

Living in Maplewood

Years ago, John's parents lived in a New York City apartment. After John was born, they decided to move to Maplewood, just 18 miles away. Now, they live in a house with a large yard on a tree-lined street. They have more space for their growing family.

Like many suburbs, Maplewood has its own government and its own businesses. John and his family shop at the local supermarket, at small stores in downtown Maplewood, and at shopping centers at the edge of town. They also enjoy the town's parks and movie theater.

John attends one of the elementary schools in Maplewood. Every school day, his parents drive him to school. Then they ride the train into New York City, where they work.

Reading Check **Compare and Contrast**
How is life in a suburb different from life in a city?

❯ People in this suburban community enjoy spending time with their neighbors.

❯ John likes to play soccer in his front yard in Maplewood, New Jersey.

Top Five Ways Suburban Workers Travel to New York City
1. By subway
2. By train
3. By car
4. By bus
5. By ferry

Table How do most workers travel to New York City?

▶ Many people drive to and from the suburbs and New York City.

Urban Connections

Long ago, communities were often built near railroad stations. As people moved from large cities to these communities, the communities grew into suburbs. As more and more people began driving cars, more suburbs were built near roads and highways. Today, people in suburbs travel on trains, subways, and highways to nearby cities.

Maplewood is its own town, but it is closely connected to New York City. Like John's parents, many people in Maplewood work in New York City.

Suburban citizens also travel to urban areas to visit interesting places. Many suburbs have their own theaters and museums, but nearby cities offer people more choices. John and his family visit New York City to see his favorite sports teams compete.

Suburbs Grow

Today, more and more people are living in suburban regions. Businesses are moving to the suburbs. This allows them to be closer to people's homes. It also costs less to run a business in the suburbs.

Museums and other cultural sites are also being built in the suburbs. In many suburbs, people attend music concerts and other events. Though still connected to cities, these suburbs are their own communities.

Reading Check **Main Idea and Details**
How are suburban and urban areas connected?

❯ Most suburban communities have parks.

Summary Suburban communities are smaller communities near urban areas. They are connected to cities through transportation and jobs.

Review

1. **What to Know** What is a suburban community?
2. **Vocabulary** Write a description of a **suburban** area.
3. **History** Where did many suburban areas start?
4. **Critical Thinking** Why do you think people live in suburbs?
5. **Make a Flyer** Make a flyer about a suburban community. Describe what it is like to live there.
6. **Compare and Contrast** On a separate sheet of paper, copy and complete the graphic organizer below.

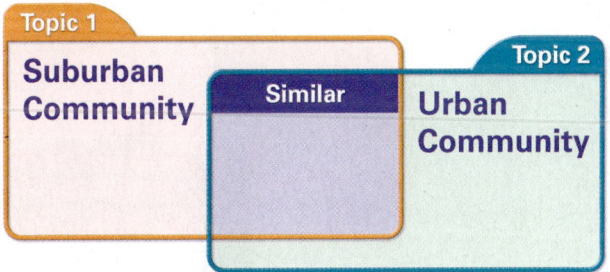

Chapter 2 ■ 55

Lesson 3 Rural Communities

What to Know
What is a rural community?

Vocabulary
rural p. 56
agriculture p. 60
economy p. 60

Compare and Contrast

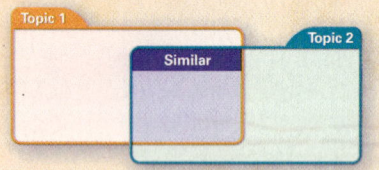

Many people live in urban and suburban communities in the United States. Other people live in small towns far away from these areas.

Searcy, a Rural Community

A rural region is in the countryside, away from cities and large towns. Small towns, farms, fields, and woods make up rural regions. Searcy (SER•see) is a rural community in Arkansas.

> Corn and other crops are grown near Searcy, Arkansas.

Small Town Life

Mallory lives in a small house in Searcy. Her father works at a store in the town. Her mother works at the community's newspaper. The newspaper provides important local information to the citizens of Searcy.

Mallory attends one of the elementary schools in Searcy. She enjoys playing soccer with her friends at a nearby soccer field. She also spends time at the community center, where people play basketball, tennis, and other sports.

In the fall, Mallory visits the county fair. She enjoys looking at the many animals that are brought to the fair from the surrounding countryside. She also enjoys the rides and games at the carnival.

Reading Check **Compare and Contrast**
How is Searcy different from a large city?

❯ The White County Fair in Searcy

❯ Mallory lives in Searcy, a rural community.

Urban and Suburban Connections

Rural, urban, and suburban communities may all be different, but they are important to each other. Colleges in each kind of area provide education for students from the other areas. Many rural areas grow and produce food for other communities.

People in rural areas sometimes travel long distances to visit cities. Some cities have more choices in stores and more choices of doctors to visit.

Sherwood and Little Rock, Arkansas

Little Rock, Arkansas, is the large city nearest to Searcy. It is located 50 miles from the town. Little Rock is an urban community and the center of the state's government. A few miles south is Sherwood, a suburb of Little Rock. Many people in Sherwood work in Little Rock. People in Searcy sometimes drive to Little Rock to visit hospitals or shop at stores.

Reading Check **Summarize**
How are all types of communities connected?

❯ This farmer grows cotton in Arkansas.

Communities in Arkansas

Rural Community  — Searcy

Suburban Community — Sherwood

Urban Community — Little Rock

MAP SKILL **Location** Searcy, Sherwood, and Little Rock are communities of different sizes. Along which river is Little Rock located?

Chapter 2 • 59

Other Rural Communities

Many people in Searcy work in agriculture. **Agriculture** is the raising of farm animals and the growing of crops for sale. Not all rural communities have farms and ranches.

A College Town

Stillwater is a town in Oklahoma. The economy of Stillwater is based on the university there. An **economy** is the way a community or country makes and uses goods and services.

Many people who live in Stillwater work or take classes at Oklahoma State University. The university is important to Stillwater. When the school grows, so does the town. Students who go to the university live in Stillwater's apartments and houses. Students also eat at restaurants in Stillwater. The town's businesses hire students.

› In Stillwater, many people attend and work at Oklahoma State University.

Children in History

Maya Angelou

Writer Maya Angelou (AN•juh•loh) lived in a rural community in Arkansas in the 1930s. Angelou helped at a store her grandmother owned.

She later wrote her memories in a book about her life. She wrote, "Customers could find food staples [common foods], a good variety of colored thread . . . corn for chickens, coal oil for lamps, light bulbs for the wealthy, shoestrings, hair dressing, balloons, and flower seeds."

Make It Relevant What businesses in your community sell these goods?

60 ■ Unit 1

Outdoor Activities and Historic Towns

Rural areas offer outdoor activities, such as fishing, skiing, and hiking. Some towns have historic sites. Michigan's Mackinac (MA•kuh•naw) Island offers both. Visitors fish and go boating on Lake Michigan. They explore history at Fort Mackinac. This site has the oldest buildings in Michigan.

Reading Check **Compare and Contrast**
How can rural communities be different from each other?

Summary Rural areas are far from cities. Urban, suburban, and rural communities all depend on each other.

Fast Fact

In the 1920s, Mackinac Island no longer allowed automobiles on the island. Horses and bikes are now the main kinds of transportation.

Review

1. **What to Know** What is a rural community?
2. **Vocabulary** Use the terms **agriculture** and **rural** in a sentence.
3. **Your Community** How is your own community connected to rural, suburban, or urban areas?
4. **Critical Thinking** Why are rural communities important?
5. **Write a Diary Entry** Write a diary entry about the type of community you live in. What makes your community different from other communities?
6. **Compare and Contrast** On a separate sheet of paper, copy and complete the graphic organizer below.

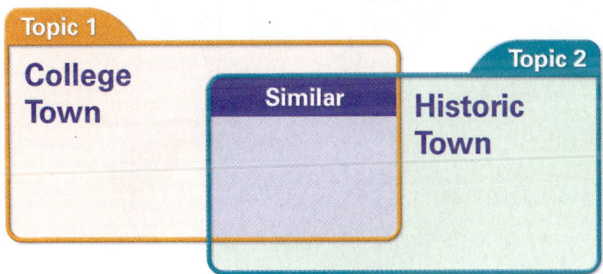

Chapter 2 ■ 61

Points of View

What Is Best About Your Community?

There are many kinds of communities in the United States. Some people prefer to live in urban communities. Other people like the suburbs or a rural town best. The place where you live can shape your opinion about places like it.

Margaret Mead

Margaret Mead devoted her life to studying people and places. She chose to make her home in New York City—the largest urban community in the United States.

"A city is a place where there is no need to wait for next week to get the answer to a question, to taste the food of any country, to find new voices to listen to and familiar ones to listen to again."

2

Philip Langdon

Philip Langdon writes about communities and design. In one book, he describes what he likes about East Aurora, an older suburban community in New York.

66 Stores, churches, restaurants, offices, and civic buildings were strung along a pleasant, maple-shaded Main Street.... Nearly everything the inhabitants [community members] needed ... was close to home. 99

3

Jo Ann Emerson

Jo Ann Emerson works in the government. Each year, she tours southern Missouri to learn about rural communities.

66 Many Americans who live in urban or suburban areas may not realize just how important our rural communities are to them and to America. Our farming and ranching neighbors feed the country. 99

It's Your Turn

Compare Points of View Review each point of view, and answer the questions.

1. Who would most likely want to live in a rural area?

2. What words in Margaret Mead's quote tell about the different cultures in a city?

3. What does Philip Langdon like about East Aurora?

Make It Relevant Why might people have different points of view about the size of a community?

Chapter 2 • 63

Explore Your Community

In this unit, you learned about the different features of a community. There are resources in your community to help you learn about those features.

Your Community's Resources

Family and Neighbors

Libraries

Museums

Find Out About Your Community

- What are some different features in your community?
- Where can people come together in your community?
- Do you live in a rural, a suburban, or an urban community?
- What is your community's population?

Create a Community Collage

Make a collage of your community. Gather pictures from magazines or newspapers that show its different features. Include pictures of climate, landforms, businesses, transportation, and places where people come together.

Chapter 2 ■ 65

Fun with Social Studies
Postcard Mania

	1	2	3	4	5
A	a	b	c	d	e
B	f	g	h	i	j
C	k	l	m	n	o
D	p	q	r	s	t
E	u	v	w	x	y

Use the grid to find the missing words in the postcards. Then decide what kind of region each person has moved to—urban, rural, or suburban.

Hi All!

We're here!

There are [E-3, C-5, C-5, A-4, D-4] near our house. I can't wait for the [B-1, A-1, B-4, D-3]! There will be a lot of [A-1, C-4, B-4, C-3, A-1, C-2, D-4].

Your buddy,

Josh

Dear Grace,

We're here!

Our house has a huge [E-5, A-1, D-3, A-4], so now I can have a [A-4, C-5, B-2]. Dad drops me off at [D-4, A-3, B-3, C-5, C-5, C-2].

Bye for now,

Stacie

Dear Grandpa Joe,

We're here!

There are so many [D-1, A-5, C-5, D-1, C-2, A-5]. Mom likes all the [D-3, A-5, D-4, D-5, A-1, E-1, D-3, A-1, C-4, D-5, D-4] and [D-4, D-5, C-5, D-3, A-5, D-4]. This place is fun!

Love,

Terry

Take One Out

VOCABULARY

Each book in the historical society's library has a mixed-up word in its title. Fix it. Then find the book that doesn't belong in the library.

A Guide to the renInett

A Hard Life: A Journey of Our torscesAn

swaL in Our Community

Life in Our ruRla Community

Online Adventures

GO ONLINE

Join Eco to play a game in this online community. A scavenger hunt is taking place in town today. You'll need to explore the police station, the grocery store, the town hall, and other buildings. If you can find all the items in time, you win! Play now at www.harcourtschool.com/ss1

Unit 1 • 69

Unit 1 Review and Test Prep

The Big Idea

Communities Communities are alike and different and are found all over the world.

Chattanooga, Tennessee

Reading Comprehension and Vocabulary

Communities Around Us

People live in communities all over the world. Citizens in these communities follow laws, depend on one another, and have their own cultures. They stay connected to others through communication.

Communities are different in many ways. They have different landforms, climates, histories, and jobs. Communities are also different sizes, depending on their populations. Urban, suburban, and rural communities depend on each other.

Read the summary above. Then answer the questions that follow.

1. Which of the following is a citizen?
   A a school
   B a place to find resources
   C a person living in a community
   D a business

2. Which of the following is a form of communication?
   A the Internet
   B a train
   C farming
   D a library

3. What makes each community different?
   A landforms
   B climate
   C history
   D all of the above

4. How would you describe the population of an urban community?
   A few people
   B few cultures
   C many people
   D few businesses

Facts and Main Ideas

Answer these questions.

5. How do communities around the world communicate?

6. What resources can you use to learn about a community?

7. What are some different kinds of communities?

Write the letter of the best choice.

8. Which of the following jobs would likely be found in a community near water?
   A tree farmer
   B fisher
   C dairy farmer
   D mountain-climbing guide

9. Which of the following is not a good?
   A a television
   B a fruit
   C a doctor's visit
   D a computer

10. Which of the following groups depend on each other?
    A businesses and workers
    B citizens in the same community
    C urban and rural communities
    D all of the above

 Critical Thinking

11. What do you think a community would be like if its people did not share their culture with others?

12. **Make It Relevant** What is one feature in your community that makes it different from another community?

 **Skills**

Find Directions and Distances

Use the map below to answer the following questions.

13. Which is closer to Stillwater—Enid or Durant? Find the distances.

14. Name a town northwest of Stillwater.

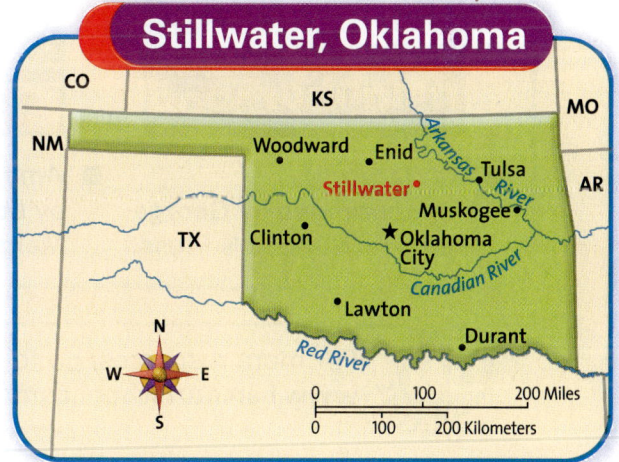

Unit 1 ■ 71

Unit 1 Activities

Show What You Know

 ### Unit Writing Activity

Write an Article Write an article about two communities.

- Research two communities.
- Compare and contrast facts about the communities.
- Explain how people live, work, and play in each community.

 ### Unit Project

Community Catalog Create a catalog of the resources in your community.

- List the resources, and tell where they can be found.
- Explain what each resource can tell about your community.

Read More

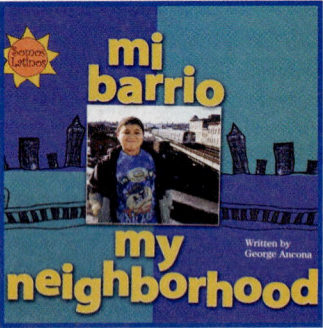

- *Mi Barrio/My Neighborhood* by George Ancona. Children's Press.

- *America Is . . .* by Louise Borden. Margaret K. McElderry.

- *If the World Were a Village* by David J. Smith. Kids Can Press.

GO ONLINE For more resources, go to www.harcourtschool.com/ss1

Unit 2

Communities and Geography

Start with the Standards

OHIO SOCIAL STUDIES CONTENT STANDARDS

History 3.3C

Geography 3.1, 3.2, 3.5, 3.6, 3.7, 3.8

Citizenship 3.1A

Social Studies Skills 3.1A, 3.1B, 3.4, 3.5, 3.6A, 3.6B, 3.6C, 3.6D, 3.6E

The Big Idea

Geography
Different communities have different landforms and bodies of water. People change and adapt to their surroundings.

What to Know
- How can you find a community's location?
- What are the physical features of a community?
- How does the environment affect people?
- How can people care for the environment?

Where Is Ohio?

OHIO CONNECTION

Did You Know?
The lowest temperature ever recorded in Ohio was −39 °F, on February 10, 1899.

Earth is divided by imaginary lines that help you find where places are located. Five major lines of latitude circle earth. The equator is the line that is halfway between the North Pole and the South Pole. The Arctic Circle marks the area around the North Pole. The Antarctic Circle marks the area around the South Pole.

The Tropic of Cancer and the Tropic of Capricorn are the northernmost and southernmost latitudes where the sun can be seen directly overhead. The area between these two lines is called the tropics. The climate in the tropics is hot and humid all year. Many areas in this climate zone get a large amount of rain. Rain forests are located in the tropics.

OH 73A • Ohio Connection

Ohio is located between the North Pole and the Tropic of Cancer. Ohio's climate is temperate. The state has warm, humid summers and cold winters. Snow falls in the winter. The northeastern part of the state has places where people can ski.

▶ Lake Erie's East Harbor Beach

▶ Skiing in Ohio

Ohio TEST PREP

1 What kind of climate do the tropics have?
  A. hot and humid all year
  B. warm, humid summers and cold winters
  C. cold and rainy all year

2 What kind of climate does Ohio have?
  A. tropical
  B. temperate
  C. cold

3 How do lines of latitude help us describe places?

Ohio Connection ▪ OH 73B

Unit 2

People

Talk About
People and Geography

John Muir
1838–1914
Naturalist and writer who helped protect our national parks

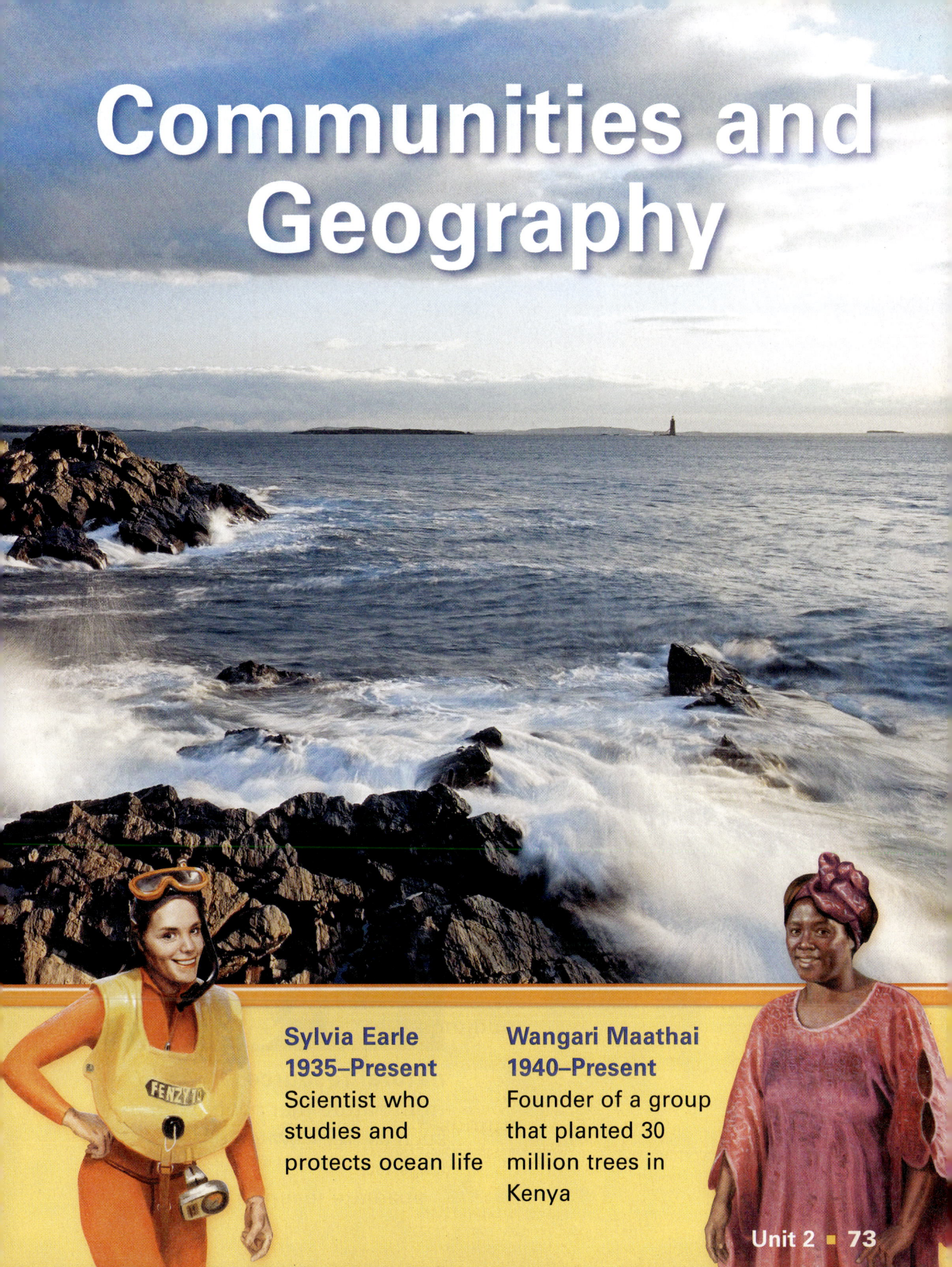

Communities and Geography

Sylvia Earle
1935–Present
Scientist who studies and protects ocean life

Wangari Maathai
1940–Present
Founder of a group that planted 30 million trees in Kenya

Unit 2 Preview
Vocabulary

physical feature A feature found in nature, such as weather, plant life, water, or land. (page 90)

natural resource An item from nature that people can use, such as trees, water, or soil. (page 106)

environment The physical and human features of a place. (page 114)

human feature A feature such as a building, bridge, or road, that people add to a landscape. (page 114)

conservation The saving of resources to make them last longer. (page 130)

For more resources, go to www.harcourtschool.com/ss1

Unit 2 75

Start with a Poem

Walk Lightly

Geographic Travels in Verse and Rhyme

by J. Patrick Lewis
illustrated by Alison Jay

Author J. Patrick Lewis likes to travel and write poetry for children. In this poem, he suggests how to think about some of the places he has visited.

Make the Earth your companion.
Walk lightly on it, as other creatures do.
Let the Sky paint her beauty—she is always watching over you.

Learn from the Sea how to face harsh forces.
Let the River remind you that everything will pass.
Let the Lake instruct you in stillness.
Let the Mountain teach you grandeur.
Make the Woodland your house of peace.
Make the Rainforest your house of hope.
Meet the Wetland on twilight ground.
Save some small piece of Grassland for a red kite
   on a windy day.
Watch the Icecaps glisten with crystal majesty.
Hear the Desert whisper hush to eternity.
Let the Town bring you togetherness.
Make the Earth your companion.
   Walk lightly on it, as other creatures do.

Response Corner

1 Main Idea and Details What do you think is the main idea of the poem?

2 Make It Relevant What is the geography of your community like?

Study Skills

USE VISUALS

Visuals can help you better understand what you read.

- **Photographs, drawings, maps, diagrams, and charts are examples of visuals. Many visuals have titles, captions, or labels that describe what is shown.**
- **Sometimes visuals add new information to what you are reading.**

Checklist for Visuals

✓	What kind of visual is shown? a photograph
✓	What does the visual show?
✓	What does the visual tell you about the topic?

PREVIEW VOCABULARY

equator p. 83

vegetation p. 94

mineral p. 107

Our Physical Geography

CHAPTER 3

> Natural Bridge State Park in Kentucky

Lesson 1 Our Location

Each community has its own location. To show someone where you live, you might use a map or a globe. Maps and globes are **geographic tools**. They can tell us where a place is and what it might look like. These tools are used by geographers who study Earth and its people.

What to Know
What can you use to find a community's location?

Vocabulary
geographic tool p. 82
continent p. 82
hemisphere p. 83
equator p. 83
border p. 86
relative location p. 86

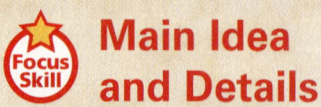

Main Idea and Details

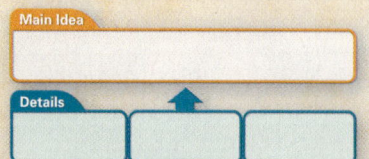

Using Globes

A globe is a model of Earth. A globe shows the oceans and largest land areas, or **continents**. Earth's continents are Asia, Africa, North America, South America, Antarctica, Europe, and Australia. A globe is round like Earth. It can show the true shapes of the continents and oceans.

> A globe can help you find the location of your community.

82 ▪ Unit 2

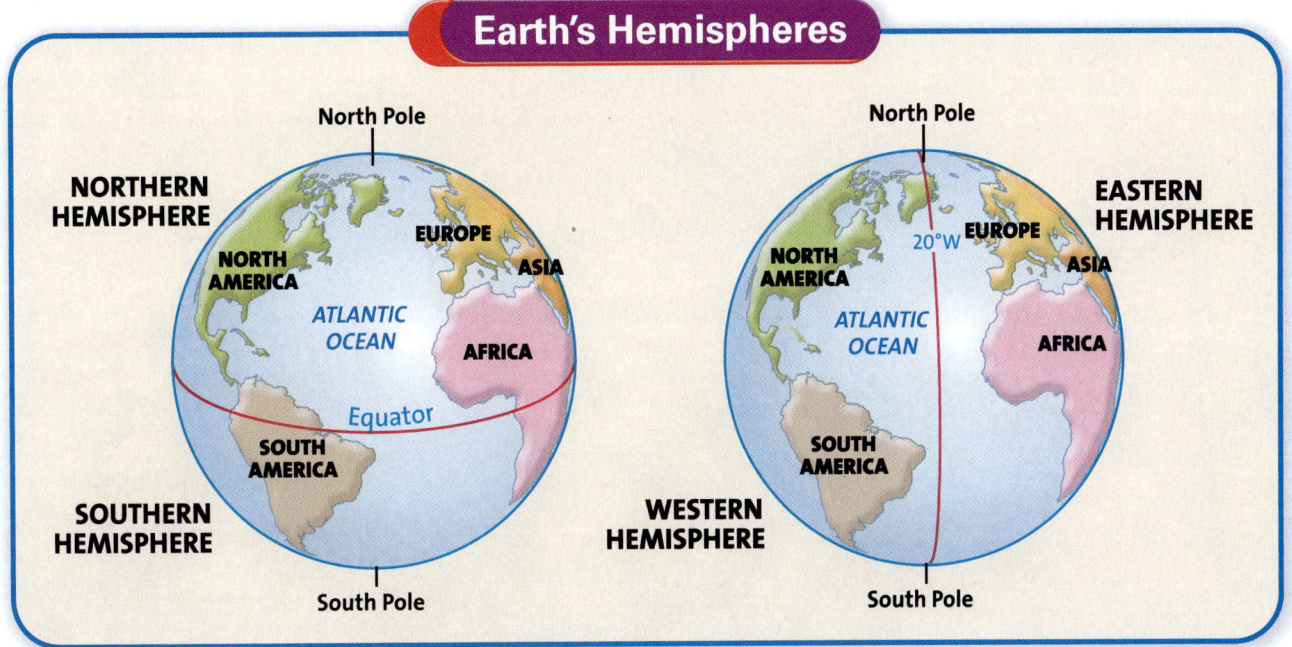

 Location In which two hemispheres is Asia located?

Hemispheres

On a globe, Earth can be divided into halves. A half of Earth is called a **hemisphere** (HEH•muh•sfeer). One way to divide Earth in half is to use the equator. The **equator** is an imaginary line that is halfway between the North Pole and the South Pole. It divides Earth into a Northern Hemisphere and a Southern Hemisphere.

Another imaginary line runs from the North Pole to the South Pole. It is often used to divide Earth into a Western Hemisphere and an Eastern Hemisphere.

Every place on Earth is in two hemispheres. North America, for example, is in the Northern Hemisphere and also in the Western Hemisphere.

Reading Check **Main Idea and Details**
In which two hemispheres is North America located?

Location The aerial photo and the map above show the same location—Salt Lake City, Utah. Which features do you see in both?

Using Maps

While a globe is round, a map is flat. A map is a drawing that shows the location of places.

An Aerial View

Looking at a map of a community is like seeing it from an airplane. A map shows an aerial (AIR•ee•uhl) view of the location of a place. An aerial view is the view from above. Aerial photographs, or photographs taken from above, also show what a community looks like from the air.

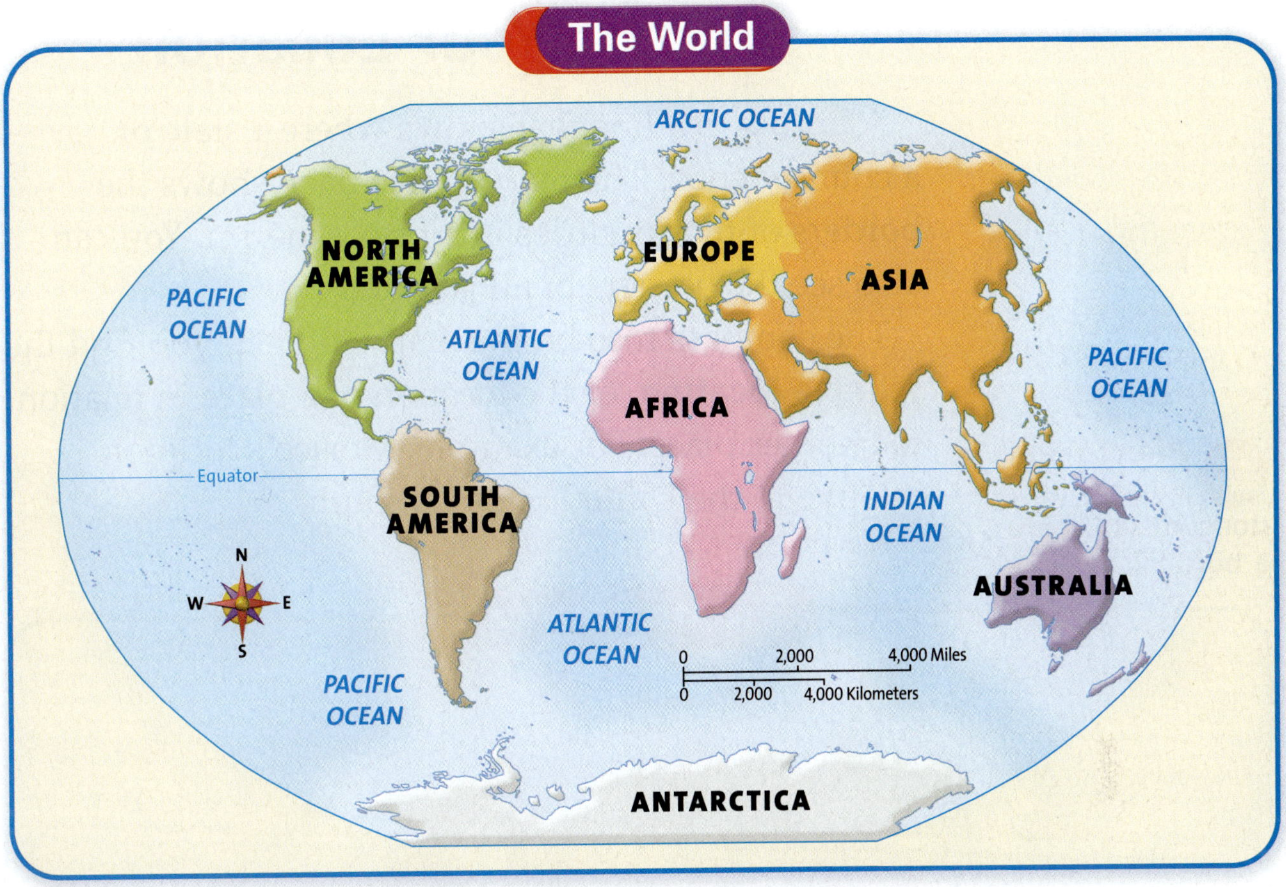

The World

MAP SKILL Location What are the four oceans on this map?

Maps

Unlike photographs, maps use colors, drawings, and symbols to show places on Earth. Because a map is flat, it is easy for people to carry. Maps can also give more information about a place.

A map can show the whole Earth or just a small part of it. Unlike a globe, however, a map cannot show the true shapes of oceans and continents.

Reading Check Compare and Contrast
How are maps and aerial photographs alike?

Finding Your Location

A **border** is a line that shows where a state or a country ends. The map on this page shows the borders of the countries in North America. You can also see the borders of all 50 states.

The compass rose on the map will help you find the **relative location**, or the location of a place in relation to another place. For example, Mexico's location relative to the United States is south.

MAP SKILL **Place** With what country does Alaska share a border?

Your Own Community

Now you can locate your community. Find your state on the map. Your community is in this state. It is also on the continent of North America.

A political map of the United States may show your community. Political maps show the borders of states, and some also include cities. If you live in a small community, you may have to look at a political map showing only your state.

Reading Check ⭐ **Main Idea and Details**
How would you describe the location of your community?

Summary Maps and globes can help you find a community's location. A globe is a model of Earth. A map is a drawing that shows the location of things.

Review

1. **What to Know** What can you use to find a community's location?
2. **Vocabulary** What do you think each part of **geographic tool** means?
3. **Geography** What are the imaginary lines that divide Earth into hemispheres?
4. **Critical Thinking Make It Relevant** Why is it important to know your community's location?
5. **Make a Map** Draw a map of your community. Include your school and your home.
6. **Main Idea and Details** On a separate sheet of paper, copy and complete the graphic organizer below.

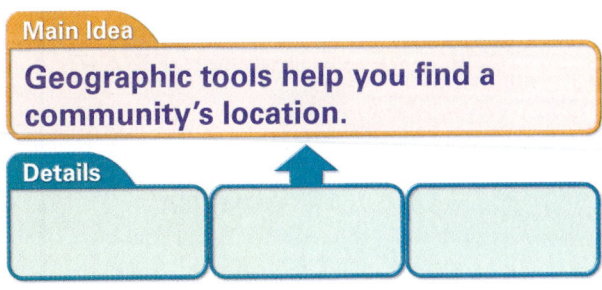

Chapter 3 • 87

Map and Globe Skills

Use Latitude and Longitude

Why It Matters Using the lines on a map or a globe can help you find a place's location.

▶ Learn

Lines on a map or a globe make a grid system. You can use the grid system to find the **absolute location**, or exact location, of a place.

Step 1 Find the lines of **latitude**. They run east and west. They measure distances in degrees (°) north and south of the equator.

Step 2 Find the lines of **longitude**. They run north and south. They measure distances east and west of the **prime meridian**.

Step 3 Name the latitude and then the longitude.

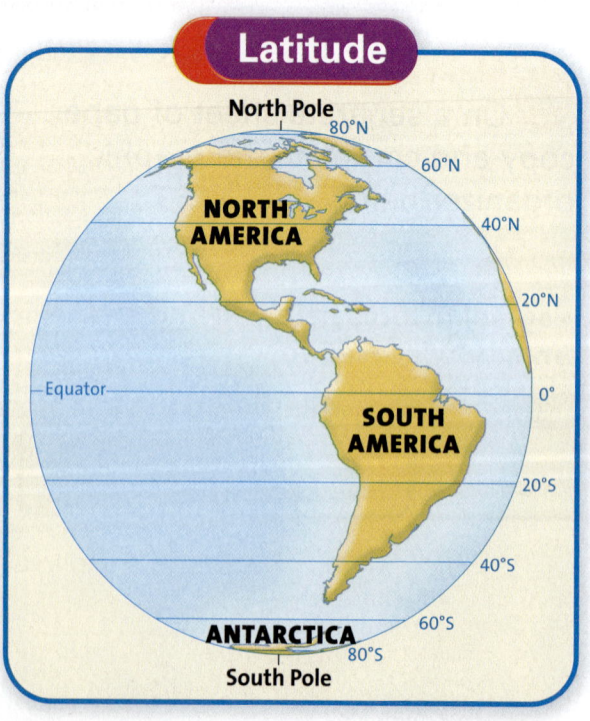

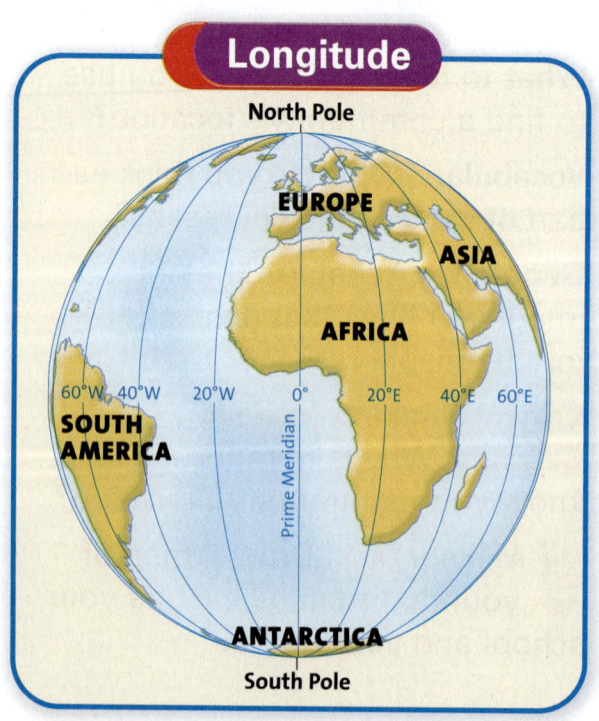

88 ■ Unit 2

GO ONLINE For online activities, go to www.harcourtschool.com/ss1

Ohio: Latitude and Longitude

Practice

Answer these questions, using the map.

1. Which line of latitude is nearest to Akron?
2. Which line of longitude is nearest to Lima?
3. Which city is nearest to 40°N, 83°W?

Apply

Make It Relevant Use a map or a globe to find the lines of latitude and longitude nearest your community. Find three cities or towns in the world with the same latitude. Share your list of cities with a partner.

Map and Globe Skills

Chapter 3 ▪ 89

Lesson 2
Our Country's Geography

What to Know
What are the physical features of a community?

Vocabulary
physical feature p. 90
mountain range p. 91
valley p. 91
plateau p. 91
vegetation p. 94
growing season p. 94
erosion p. 96
ecosystem p. 97

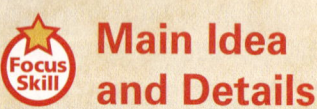
Main Idea and Details

All places on Earth have features that make them special. Some of these are physical features. **Physical features** include land, water, climate, and plant life.

Land Features

You can describe a place by listing its physical features. Many communities have both land and water features.

> The Appalachian Mountains are a mountain range in the eastern United States.

90 ■ Unit 2

Different Landforms

The United States is a large country with many kinds of landforms. A large area of plains, called the Great Plains, stretches across the middle of our country. Often plains lie along a coast. The Coastal Plain stretches along the Atlantic Ocean and along the Gulf of Mexico.

Like other landforms, mountains can be different shapes and sizes. There are many mountain ranges in the United States. A **mountain range** is a chain of mountains. The Appalachian (a•puh•LAY•chuhn) Mountains in the eastern United States are low and rounded. The Rocky Mountains in the west are tall and sharply pointed.

Other landforms include valleys and plateaus. A **valley** is a low area of land that lies between hills or mountains. A **plateau** (pla•TOH) is a landform with steep sides that rise to a flat top.

❯ Hiking lets people enjoy the natural landscape.

Reading Check ⭐ **Main Idea and Details**
What are some examples of land features?

Chapter 3 ■ 91

Water Everywhere

Bodies of water are another kind of physical feature. The largest bodies of water are the oceans, which cover more than half of Earth. All ocean water is salty.

On the continents are many smaller bodies of water, such as lakes, ponds, rivers, and streams. Most of these contain fresh water, or water that is not salty. Fresh water, after it is treated, is the kind of water we drink and use in our homes.

▶ A waterfall in Tennessee

Bodies of Water

Illustration Which kinds of bodies of water are near your community?

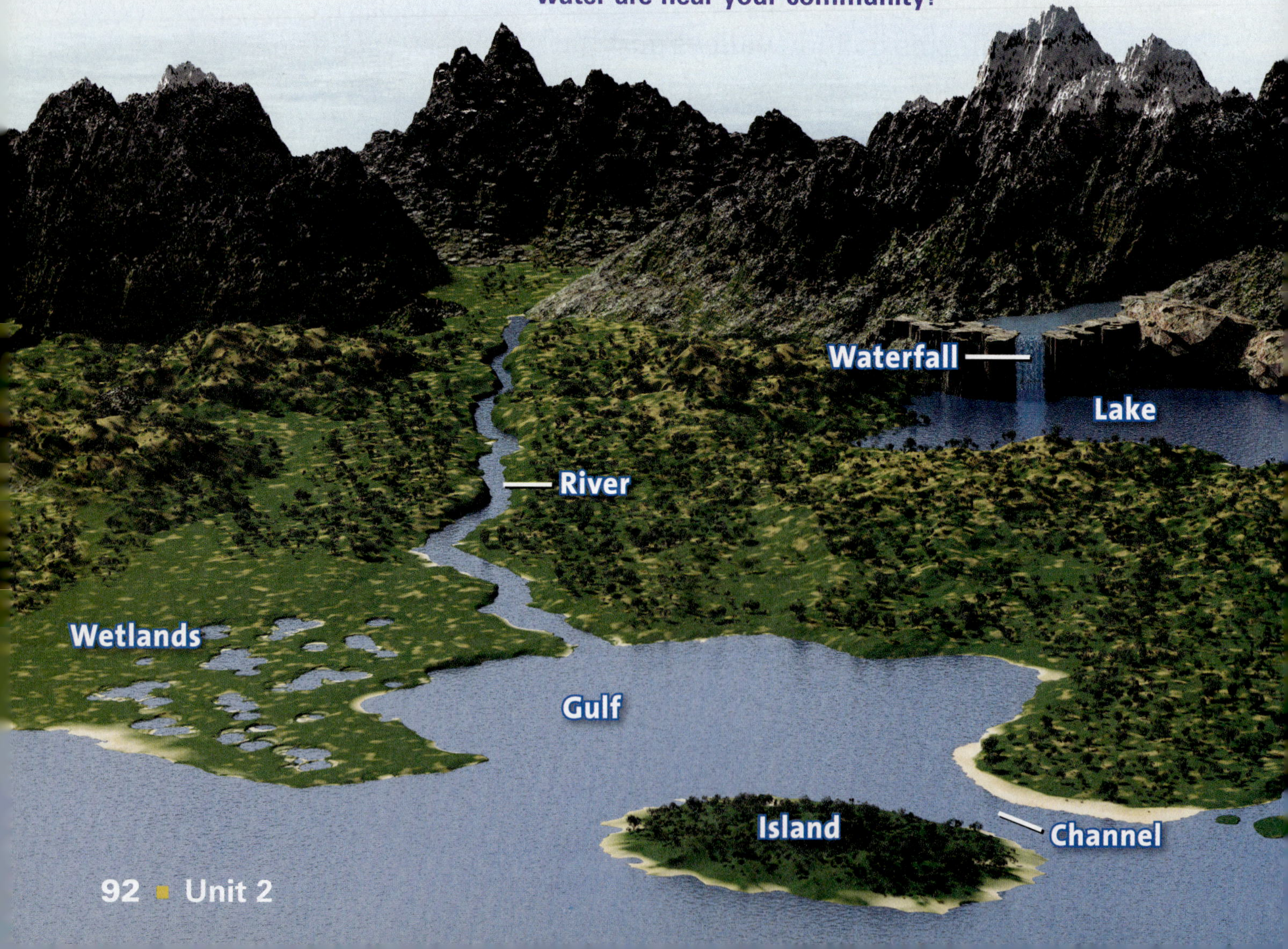

- Waterfall
- Lake
- River
- Wetlands
- Gulf
- Island
- Channel

Lakes and Rivers

The United States has many bodies of fresh water. The Great Lakes are a chain of giant lakes located in the northeastern United States, along the border with Canada. Together, they form the largest group of freshwater lakes in the world.

The Mississippi River flows from Minnesota to the Gulf of Mexico. Many other rivers, such as the Ohio River, flow in to the Mississippi River.

Many communities are built near bodies of water. You might describe your community as being near an ocean, a lake, or a river. Some communities are located on an island—land that has water on all sides.

> The Mississippi River begins in Minnesota.

Reading Check **Main Idea and Details**
What are some examples of bodies of water?

Stream

Lake

Delta

Bay

Ocean

Chapter 3 ■ 93

Climate and Weather

Climate and weather are also physical features. Climate is a place's usual weather over the year. It includes how hot and cold the temperatures are and how much rain or snow falls.

Earth and the Sun

A community's climate is affected by its location on Earth. Sunlight hits Earth at different angles in different places. It is most direct near the equator. Places there are often hotter and wetter than places farther away from the equator.

❯ Wet Climate

Climate and Plant Life

The **vegetation**, or plant life, in a place is another physical feature. Vegetation is affected by the climate. Cactuses grow well in hot, dry places. Palm trees grow well in hot, wet places.

Climate also affects the **growing season**, or the time when plants can grow. Places with short, warm winters have longer growing seasons.

Reading Check ★ Main Idea and Details
How does climate affect a place?

❯ Cold Climate

❯ Dry Climate

The Four Seasons

Illustration When is North America warmest?

Summer

Fall

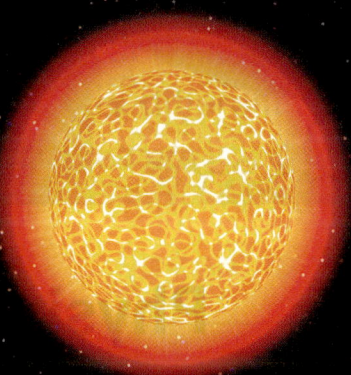

Winter

Spring

FIELD TRIP

http://www.harcourtschool.com/ss1

Yellowstone National Park

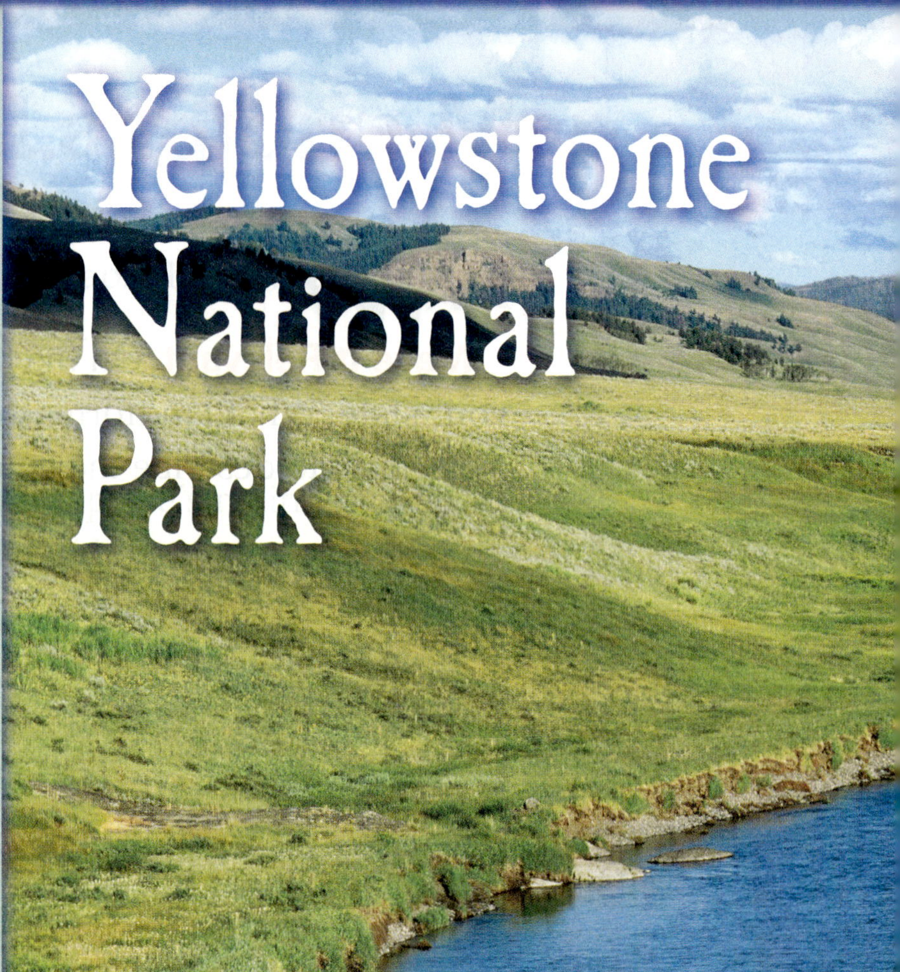

READ ABOUT

The great Yellowstone National Park is in the western United States. It covers parts of Idaho, Montana, and Wyoming.

On March 1, 1872, President Ulysses S. Grant signed a law to protect the land. It became the world's first national park. Today, nearly 3 million visitors come to the park each year.

Yellowstone is famous for its hot springs and geysers. Water comes from underground springs to Earth's surface through natural openings. A geyser is a spring that sprays hot water and steam into the air. Magma, or molten rock under the surface, keeps the water hot.

FIND

Old Faithful is one of Yellowstone's geysers. It sprays hot water up to 184 feet every 65 to 90 minutes.

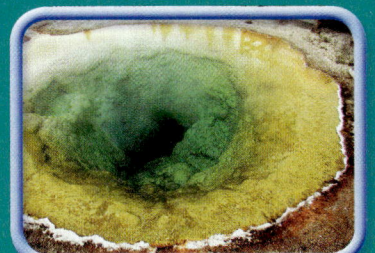
Morning Glory Pool

A park ranger

The Lower Falls of the Yellowstone River

Mammoth Terraces

A bald eagle

A VIRTUAL TOUR

GO ONLINE For more resources, go to www.harcourtschool.com/ss1

Chapter 3 ■ 101

Lesson 3 Our Country's Regions

What to Know
What are our country's regions?

Vocabulary
preserve p. 104

Main Idea and Details

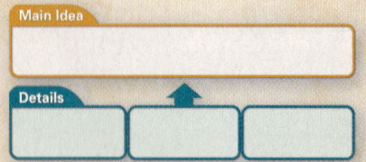

Geographers sometimes divide countries and states into regions. A region is an area with at least one feature that makes it different from other areas. The parts of a region may share many features, such as location, landforms, culture, or economy.

The Regions

The United States is often divided into five large regions. These regions are the Northeast, the Southeast, the Midwest, the Southwest, and the West. The states in each region share a relative location in the country.

Reading Check **Main Idea and Details**
What are the five regions of the United States?

West

Southwest

Regions of the United States

Map Key
- Northeast
- Southeast
- Midwest
- Southwest
- West

MAP SKILL **Regions** In which region is your state located?

Midwest

Southeast

Northeast

Chapter 3 • 103

Other Regions

Geographers can study a region based on any of its features. The features of a region include its culture and economics.

One Community, Many Regions

A community can be part of more than one kind of region. Lexington, Kentucky, is part of the Southeast region of the United States. Lexington is also closely connected with Appalachia, the region in and around the Appalachian Mountains.

In the past, the people of Appalachia were separated from the rest of the United States by the Appalachian Mountains. They developed their own culture, which includes music and storytelling. Today, the people of Lexington work to **preserve**, or save, Appalachian culture.

This business district is in Lexington's urban region.

Lexington, Kentucky

Diagram In which region of the United States is Lexington?

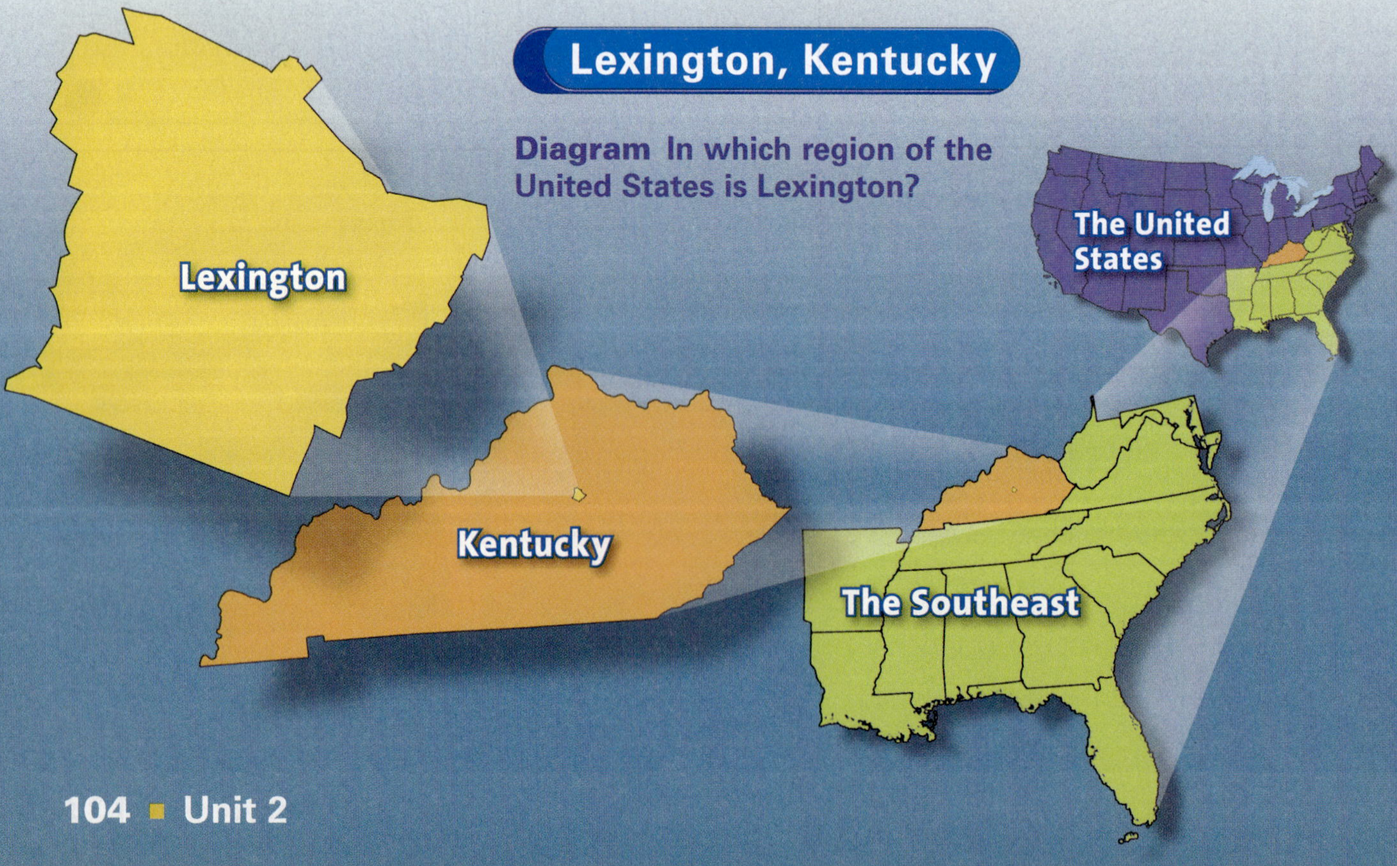

Lexington

Kentucky

The Southeast

The United States

104 ■ Unit 2

Lexington is also part of an economic region that depends on horses. The region has grasses that are good food for horses. Today, many businesses in Lexington are connected with raising horses.

Reading Check ⏱ **Main Idea and Details**
With what cultural region is Lexington closely connected?

Summary Regions in the United States include the Northeast, Southeast, Midwest, Southwest, and West. A community can be part of more than one kind of region.

Lexington's Appalachian Heritage Festival

Lexington is known as The Horse Capital of the World.

Review

1. **What to Know** What are our country's regions?
2. **Vocabulary** Use the term **preserve** in a paragraph about the Appalachian culture.
3. **Your Community** What regions is your community a part of?
4. **Critical Thinking Make It Relevant** What are some physical features of your region of the country?
5. ✏️ **Write a Travel Brochure** Write about the different types of features of your region. Include things visitors can see and do.
6. **Main Idea and Details** On a separate sheet of paper, copy and complete the graphic organizer below.

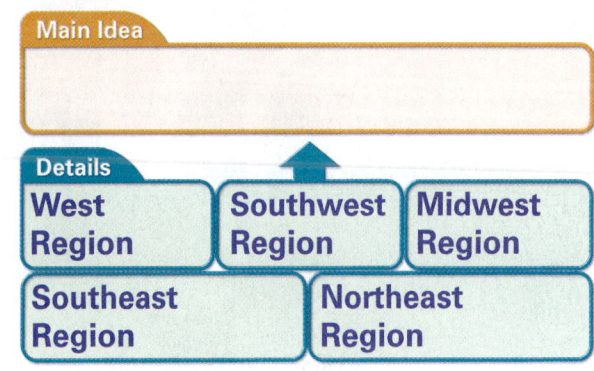

Chapter 3 ■ 105

Lesson 4 Natural Resources

What to Know
What are natural resources?

Vocabulary
natural resource p. 106
mineral p. 107
renewable p. 108
nonrenewable p. 108
fuel p. 108

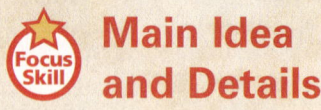
Main Idea and Details

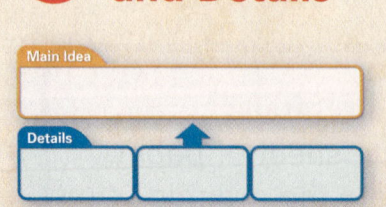

The naturalist John Muir wrote, "So extraordinary [amazing] is Nature with her choicest [best] treasures." The treasures Muir wrote about can still be found today. They are Earth's natural resources. A **natural resource** is something from nature that people can use, such as trees, water, and soil. Many of Earth's "choicest treasures" are found here in the United States.

Our Resources

Forests cover a lot of land in the United States. Trees, a natural resource, are used to build houses, to make furniture and paper, and to burn for heat.

Another natural resource is the land itself. The soil of many states in the United States is rich. Rich soil allows people to grow many crops. For example, cotton is grown to make clothing. Cows, chickens, and other animals are also raised on farmland.

Water is another natural resource. People use water for drinking, watering crops, and fishing.

Other natural resources are found underground. These are called **minerals**. Gold, iron, copper, and salt are some of Earth's many minerals.

Reading Check **Main Idea and Details**
How is land a natural resource?

❯ On farms, land is used for growing crops, such as corn, and for raising animals, such as cows.

Chapter 3 ▪ 107

Types of Resources

There are different types of natural resources. Some can be replaced quickly, but others cannot.

Renewable and Nonrenewable Resources

A **renewable** resource is one that can be made again by nature or people. Trees and other plants are renewable resources. When trees are cut down, new trees can be planted. Wild animals, such as fish, are also renewable. People just have to let the fish populations stay steady by not fishing too much.

A **nonrenewable** resource cannot be made again quickly by nature or people. Minerals are nonrenewable. It might take thousands of years for Earth to replace a mineral that has been used. Many fuels, such as coal and oil, are also nonrenewable. A **fuel** is a natural resource that is burned to make heat or energy.

▶ Third graders plant trees, an important renewable resource.

▶ Pine trees are grown on a tree farm.

Living and Nonliving Resources

Natural resources can also be living or nonliving. Plants, trees, and wild animals are all examples of living resources. Nonliving resources include water, metals, soil, and minerals.

Reading Check **Main Idea and Details**
What are some nonrenewable resources?

Summary Natural resources are materials from nature that people use. Renewable resources can be replaced, but nonrenewable resources cannot.

Oil is a nonliving resource found deep underground. Wells are drilled to get to the oil.

Review

1. **What to Know** What are natural resources?
2. **Vocabulary** Write a sentence that includes the terms **fuel** and **nonrenewable**.
3. **Economics** Why might a resource that is nonrenewable, such as gold, cost a lot of money?
4. **Critical Thinking** What might happen if a nonrenewable resource, such as oil, were used up?
5. **Draw a Picture** Draw a picture that shows some natural resources in your community.
6. **Main Idea and Details** On a separate sheet of paper, copy and complete the graphic organizer below.

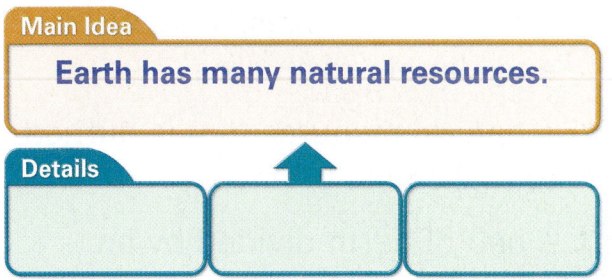

Chapter 3 ■ 109

Chapter 3 Review

Visual Summary

Our country's geography has many physical features.

Summarize the Chapter

Main Idea and Details Complete the graphic organizer to show that you understand the important main idea and details about our country's geography.

Main Idea
Our country's geography has many special features.

Details
- Our country has different physical features.
-
- Our country has many regions.

Vocabulary

Identify the term from the word bank that correctly matches each definition.

1. the plants, animals, land, water, and climate of an area
2. a natural resource that is burned to make heat or energy
3. a half of Earth divided by an imaginary line
4. to save
5. one of Earth's largest land areas
6. a natural resource found underground.

Word Bank

continent p. 82
hemisphere p. 83
ecosystem p. 97
preserve p. 104
mineral p. 107
fuel p. 108

110 ■ Unit 2

 A community can be part of more than one region.

 Communities have many natural resources.

 Facts and Main Ideas

Answer these questions.

7. What are some causes of erosion?
8. What three regions is Lexington, Kentucky, part of?
9. Where are minerals found?

Write the letter of the best choice.

10. How are maps and globes similar?
    A They show the true shapes of oceans and continents.
    B They are flat.
    C They show locations.
    D They are round.

11. Which natural resource do people use to make paper?
    A trees
    B animals
    C land
    D minerals

 Critical Thinking

12. **Make It Relevant** How might your community be different if it had a different climate?
13. **Make It Relevant** How might physical processes affect you?

Skills

Use Latitude and Longitude
Use the map on page 89 to answer the question.

14. Near which lines of latitude and longitude is Zanesville, Ohio?

Use a Landform Map
Use the map on pages 98 and 99 to answer the question.

15. What landforms are found in southeastern Oklahoma?

Write a Postcard Describe a physical feature in a postcard to a friend.

Write a Paragraph Write a paragraph about why people use maps.

Chapter 3 ■ 111

STUDY SKILLS

POSE QUESTIONS

Asking questions as you read can help you understand what you are learning.

- Ask questions about events and ideas as you read.
- Look for the answers to your questions as you read.

Our Human Geography

Questions	Answers
How can people use land?	They may use land to farm.
How can we protect the environment?	

PREVIEW VOCABULARY

canal p. 123

irrigation p. 124

recycle p. 130

Our Human Geography

CHAPTER 4

▸ Glen Canyon Dam in Arizona

Landforms of the United States

140 • Unit 2

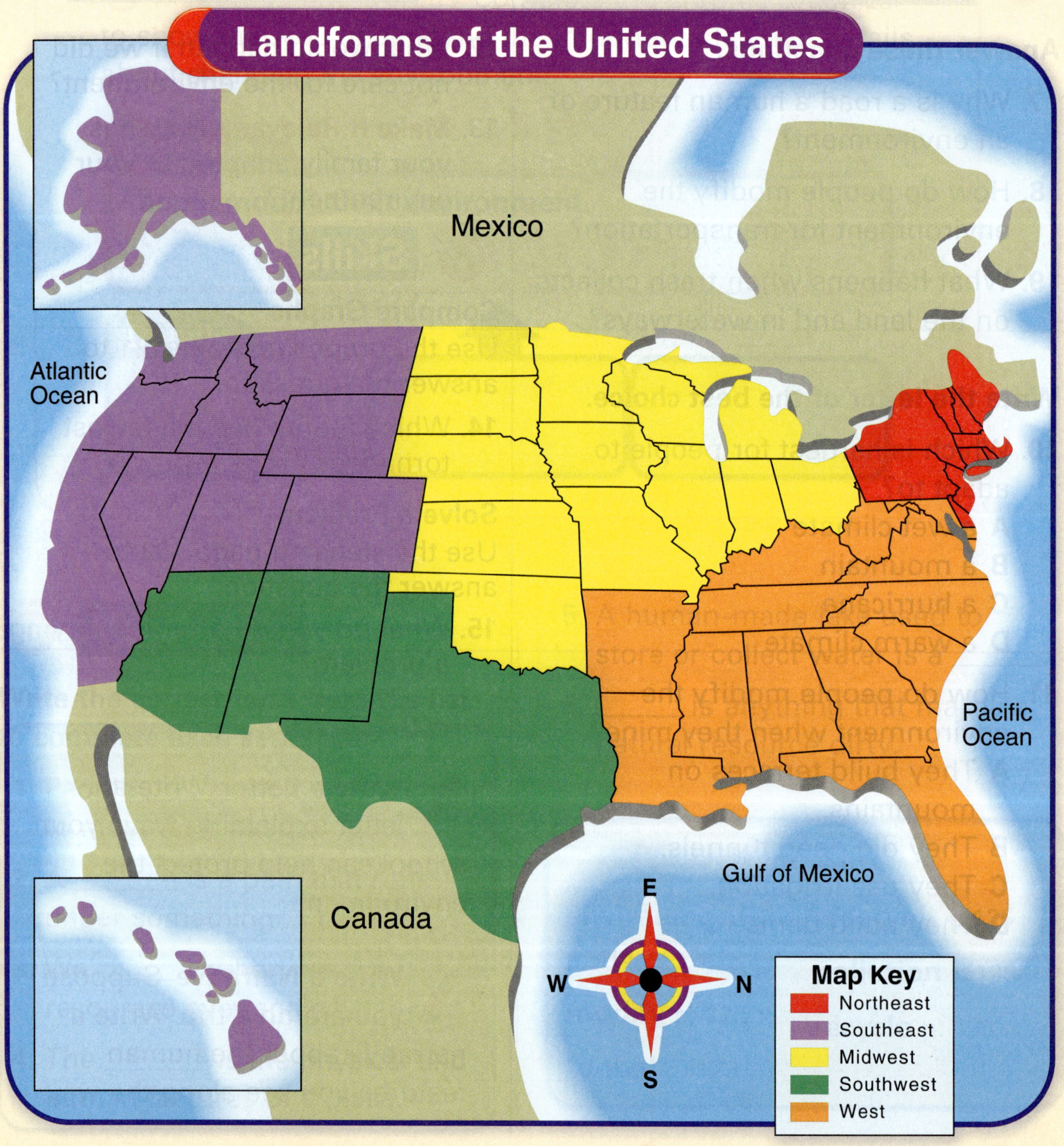

Figure It Out

Vocabulary

Use the rebus to figure out each two-word term.

geographic +  = ?

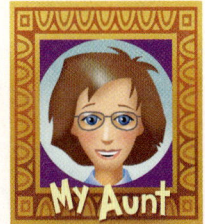 + location = ?

growing +  = ?

 + range = ?

Online Adventures

GO ONLINE

Get ready to race! Join Eco on the online landform road race to see how far you can travel. In this game, you'll explore mountains, plains, rivers, and oceans. There is a special surprise waiting for you at the end. Play now at www.harcourtschool.com/ss1

Unit 2 Review and Test Prep

💡 The Big Idea

Geography Different communities have different landforms and bodies of water. People change and adapt to their surroundings.

Reading Comprehension and Vocabulary

Communities and Geography

Earth is covered by many physical features. People can find the locations of these features by using geographic tools, such as maps and globes. People use natural resources, such as trees, water, soil, and minerals. People must adapt to their environment. They modify their environment to meet their needs. They build human features such as terraces, mines, and dams. People in all communities should conserve and protect natural resources.

Read the summary above. Then answer the questions that follow.

1. What are physical features?
   A aerial photographs
   B maps and globes
   C land, water, climate, plants
   D mines

2. How can people find the locations of physical features?
   A by protecting natural resources
   B by building dams
   C by using geographic tools
   D by modifying their environment

3. What does natural resources mean in the passage above?
   A human features
   B pollution
   C the time when plants grow
   D something from nature people can use

4. Why do people build human features?
   A to change the climate
   B to prevent pollution
   C to look at maps and globes
   D to meet their needs

142 ■ Unit 2

Facts and Main Ideas

Answer these questions.

5. What are the imaginary lines that divide Earth into four hemispheres?

6. What are some renewable resources?

7. What are some causes of pollution?

Write the letter of the best choice.

8. Which of the following has the hottest climate?
   - **A** a city in the Western Hemisphere
   - **B** a community with a short growing season
   - **C** a place near the equator
   - **D** a town in the mountains

9. Which human feature can help produce electricity?
   - **A** tunnel
   - **B** dam
   - **C** canal
   - **D** mine

10. How does recycling help the environment?
    - **A** It cleans smog from the air.
    - **B** It adds less trash to landfills.
    - **C** It uses less gas.
    - **D** It cleans polluted water.

 Critical Thinking

11. **Make It Relevant** How do you use relative location to locate places that are near your community? Give examples.

12. **Make It Relevant** How can your community prepare for a natural disaster?

 **Skills**

Use Latitude and Longitude

Use the map below to answer the following questions.

13. Which line of longitude is closest to the western tip of North Carolina?

14. Which line of latitude runs through southeastern North Carolina?

Southeast States: Latitude and Longitude

Unit 2 ■ 143

Unit 2 Activities

Show What You Know

 Unit Writing Activity

Write a Story Write a story about a community that worked to protect its environment.
- Talk about the community's environment or resources.
- Tell why and how the community saved its natural treasures.

 Unit Project

Community Nature Center Exhibit Create a nature exhibit that tells about your community.
- Describe the climate, land, water, vegetation, and natural resources.
- Show information on posters.

Read More

- *Mapping Penny's World* by Loreen Leedy. Owlet.

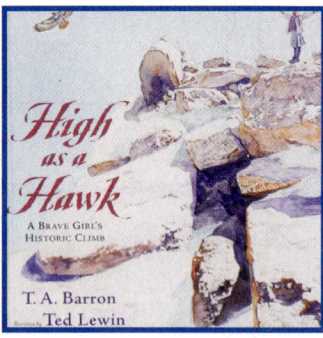
- *High as a Hawk* by T. A. Barron. Philomel.

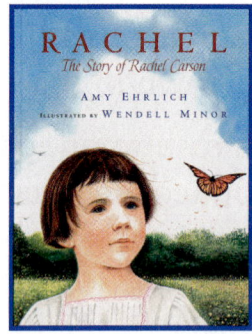
- *Rachel: The Story of Rachel Carson* by Amy Ehrlich. Silver Whistle.

GO ONLINE For more resources, go to www.harcourtschool.com/ss1

144 ▪ Unit 2

Unit 3

Communities Over Time

Start with the Standards

OHIO SOCIAL STUDIES CONTENT STANDARDS

History 3.1, 3.2, 3.3B, 3.3E, 3.3F, 3.3G, 3.3H, 3.3I

People in Societies 3.1B, 3.1C, 3.3

Geography 3.1, 3.8

Social Studies Skills 3.1A, 3.1B, 3.1C, 3.1F, 3.1G, 3.3, 3.4

The Big Idea

History
Every community has a unique history. Some features of a community change, while others stay the same, over time.

What to Know
- How do communities change and stay the same?
- How have people changed communities?
- Who formed the first communities in North America?
- How did the United States grow and change?

Ohio Schools Long Ago

Did You Know?

Woodward High School in Cincinnati, Ohio, is one of the oldest public high schools in the United States. It opened in 1831.

The first schools in Ohio were built by pioneer families. They were made from logs and had dirt floors. These schools had one room, which was heated by a stone or mud fireplace. Ohio's earliest schools had few books.

After about 1850, one-room schools in Ohio were made from wood or brick. They were heated by iron stoves. Each morning, students raised the flag and sang a patriotic song. Then came time for the lessons. Students in all eight grades learned in the same room. The teacher called the students in each grade to the front to say their lessons. Students learned reading, writing, arithmetic, and history.

▷ Students at one-room schools used slates (left) to write their lessons.

▶ Students and teachers gather outside a one-room school.

▶ A school desk

During recess, students played outside. Some of the games they played, such as tag and Red Rover, are still played today. Another game students played was called Ante, Ante, Over the Shanty. During the winter, children went sledding and played in the snow. Students also helped the teacher with chores in the schoolhouse. They helped build the fire and carried water.

Ohio

1 What were most early Ohio schools made from?
  A. logs
  B. mud
  C. brick

2 How did students help the teacher at the schoolhouse?
  A. They played outside during recess.
  B. They sang songs.
  C. They did chores.

3 How were schools in Ohio long ago different from schools today? How were they the same?

Unit 3

People

Talk About

People and History

Sacagawea
1786?–1812
Guide to Meriwether Lewis and William Clark on their journey west

Communities Over Time

**Abraham Lincoln
1809–1865**
President of the United States during the Civil War

**Dr. Martin Luther King, Jr.
1929–1968**
National leader who led peaceful marches for equal rights

Unit 3 Preview
Vocabulary

invention An object that has been made for the first time. (page 162)

technology The inventions that people use. (page 170)

explorer A person who goes to find out about a place. (page 196)

settlement A new community. (page 197)

colony A place that is ruled by another country. (page 204)

For more resources, go to www.harcourtschool.com/ss1

Unit 3 • 147

Unit 3

Reading Social Studies

Focus Skill: Sequence

Why It Matters Identifying the order in which events happen helps you understand what you read.

> ## Learn

Sequence is the order in which events happen.

- Words, such as *first, next, then, last, after,* and *finally,* are sequence clues.
- Sometimes events are not listed in the order in which they happened.

> ## Practice

Read the paragraph. Look for sequence clues.

Sequence

At first, Memphis was a small city. When Memphis was built, it had only 50 people and was just four blocks wide. Then its harbor on the Mississippi River made it important. Ships brought and took away people and goods, causing the city to grow. Today, Memphis has more than 650,000 people.

148 ■ Unit 3

Apply

Read the paragraphs, and answer the questions.

The Story of Memphis, Tennessee

The city of Memphis, in southwestern Tennessee, has a long history. It was not always a city. In 1541, Hernando de Soto (er•NAHN•doh day SOH•toh), from Spain, explored the area. Next, Europeans came to live there. Before then, however, Native Americans, the Chickasaw, lived in the area.

In 1818, the United States government forced the Chickasaw to give up their land. Memphis was founded there in 1819. It was named after Memphis, Egypt, because both cities sit by large rivers.

Later, during the 1900s, Memphis became a center for blues music. Blues was a new style of music that began in the region. Musicians, such as Muddy Waters and B. B. King, played at clubs on Beale Street. They helped create the style of music known as Memphis blues.

Today, Memphis is Tennessee's largest city. People visit from all over the world to hear Memphis blues.

 Sequence

1. What word clue tells you Europeans arrived after the Chickasaw?
2. What happened before Memphis was founded in 1819?
3. Which paragraph tells about Memphis today?

Start with a Story

A Place Called FREEDOM

by Scott Russell Sanders

illustrated by Thomas B. Allen

In this story, James Starman, his parents, and his sister, Lettie, were once enslaved. In this story, they leave their home in Tennessee and move to Indiana. They help start the community of Freedom. The Starman family want a place to begin a new life after they become free.

At last one morning, just after sunrise, we came to the Ohio River. A fisherman with a face as wrinkled as an old boot carried us over the water in his boat. On the far shore we set our feet on the free soil of Indiana. White flowers covered the hills that day like feathers on a goose.

By and by we met a Quaker family who took us into their house, gave us seed, and loaned us a mule and a plow, all because they believed that slavery was a sin. We helped on their farm, working shoulder to shoulder, and we planted our own crops.

That first year Papa raised enough corn and wheat for us to buy some land beside the Wabash River, where the dirt was as black as my skin. Papa could grow anything, he could handle horses, and he could build a barn or a bed.

Before winter, Papa and Mama built us a sturdy cabin. Every night we sat by the fire and Papa told stories that made the shadows dance. Every morning Mama held school for Lettie and me. Mama knew how to read and write from helping with lessons for the master's children. She could sew clothes that fit you like the wind, and her cooking made your tongue glad.

While the ground was still frozen, Papa rode south through the cold nights, down to the plantation in Tennessee. We fretted until he showed up again at our door, leading two of my aunts, two uncles, and five cousins. They stayed with us until they could buy land near ours and build their own cabins.

Again and again Papa went back to Tennessee, and each time he came home with more of the folks we loved.

Hearing about our settlement, black people arrived from all over the South, some of them freed like us, some of them runaways. There were carpenters and blacksmiths, basket weavers and barrel makers.

Soon we had a church, then a store, then a stable, then a mill to grind our grain. For the first time in our lives, we had money, just enough to get by, and we watched every penny.

After a few years, the railroad decided to run tracks through our village, because so many people had gathered here. If our place was going to be on the map, it needed a name. At a meeting, folks said we should call it Starman, in honor of Mama and Papa. But Mama and Papa said, "No, let's name it Freedom."

And that's how we came to live in a place called Freedom.

Response Corner

1. **Sequence** What happened after the Quakers took the family into their home?

2. **Make It Relevant** This story is about how a community started. Do you know how your community started?

STUDY SKILLS

MAKE AN OUTLINE

An outline organizes topics, main ideas, and details.

- Topics are shown by Roman numerals.
- Main ideas about each topic are shown by capital letters.
- Details about each main idea are shown by numbers.

Our History Through Time and Place

I. Communities Through Time
   A. Communities change in some ways over time.
      1. Many old buildings are replaced with new ones.
      2.
   B. Communities stay the same in some ways.
      1. The kind of work some people do can stay the same.
      2.

PREVIEW VOCABULARY

equality p. 166

primary source p. 168

civilization p. 178

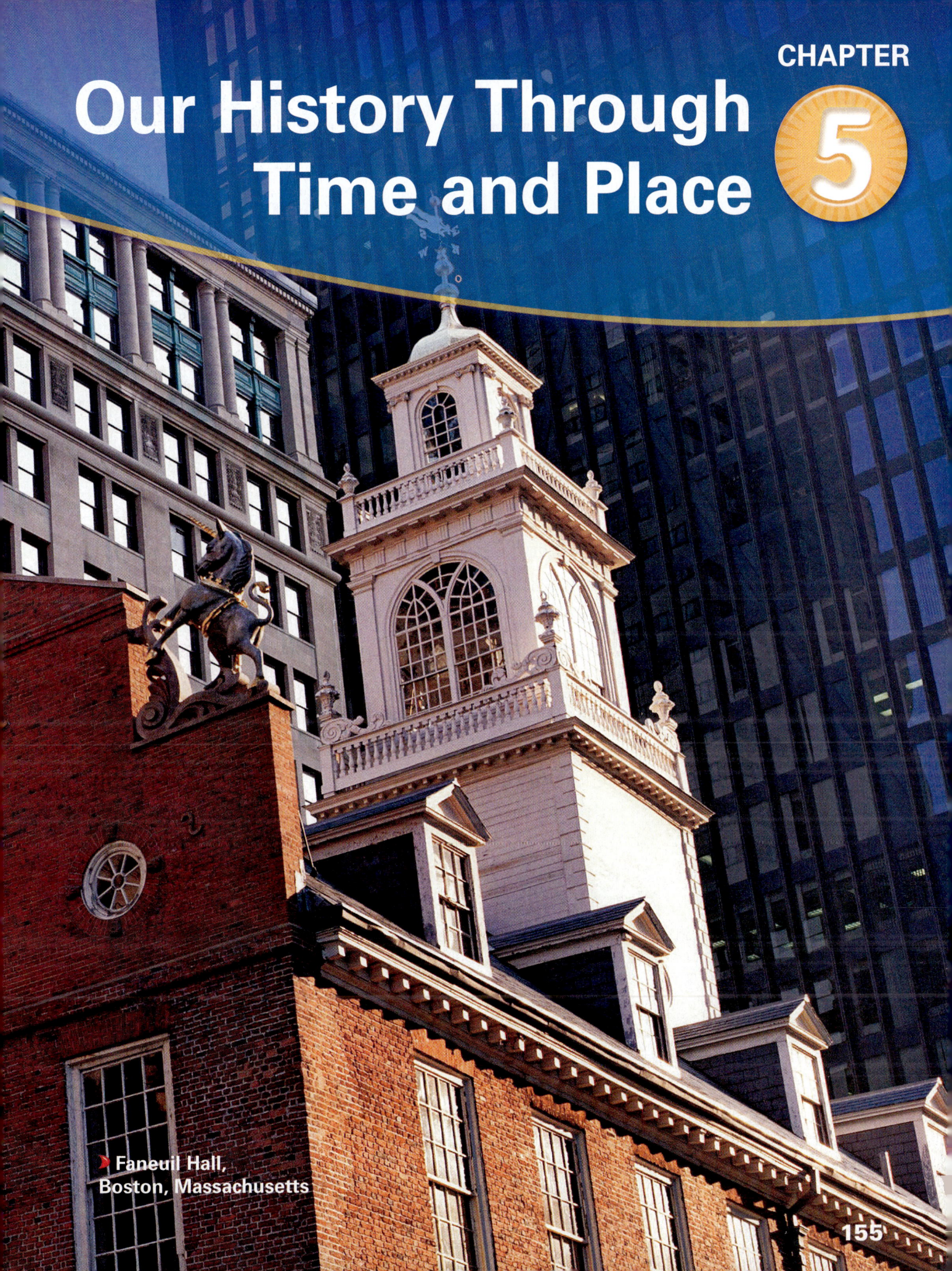

Our History Through Time and Place

CHAPTER 5

› Faneuil Hall, Boston, Massachusetts

Lesson 1 Communities Through Time

What to Know
How do communities both change and stay the same?

Vocabulary
decade p. 156
century p. 156
continuity p. 157

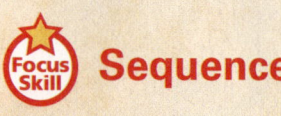

Sequence

Events that happened long ago often affect communities today, or in the present. What happens today will affect communities in the future, or in the time still to come.

Changes Over Time

All communities change in some ways and stay the same in other ways. Change may take place in a day, a week, a month, a year, a decade, or a century. A **decade** is 10 years. A **century** is 100 years.

You can use old and new photographs to see change. The photos on these pages show Chicago, Illinois. What changes can you see in this community?

▶ The skyline of Chicago today

Continuity in a Community

You can also use the same photographs to see continuity (kahn•tuhn•OO•uh•tee) in Chicago. **Continuity** is continuing without changing.

In communities everywhere, some things stay the same. Many old buildings in Chicago are still used today. They just have new things in them, such as computers. Some kinds of work in the community can stay the same, but the work may be done in new ways.

Reading Check ⭐ **Sequence**
Which is longer—a decade or a century?

> Built in 1869, the Chicago Water Tower still stands today. The tower shows continuity, while the area around it has changed.

Long Ago

Today

Chapter 5 ■ 157

▶ This painting shows the Great Chicago Fire.

▶ This photograph shows Chicago's streets after the Great Chicago Fire.

Fast Changes

Changes in communities usually happen slowly. A community may grow larger as more people move there. New roads may be built, and old roads may be made wider. People may start new businesses. They may tear down old buildings.

The Great Chicago Fire

Some changes happen very fast. In October 1871, a fire started in a barn in Chicago. Some people believe that a cow kicked over a lighted lantern.

At that time, most of Chicago's buildings were made of wood. The buildings burned easily. When the fire was finally put out more than a day later, thousands of homes and businesses had burned down. Chicago was rebuilt after that terrible fire. It is now one of the country's largest cities.

Jerome, Arizona

Some changes can cause a community to grow fast and then nearly disappear. In the 1870s, Jerome, Arizona, grew from a few tents into a town of almost 15,000. People came to mine the copper that had been found there. By 1953, the mines had closed. Soon, only 50 people lived there.

Today, people visit Jerome to see what it was like to live in a mining town. Because of the visitors, more people now work in Jerome than when the mines closed.

Reading Check ⭐ **Sequence**
What happened after the mines closed in Jerome?

Summary Communities both change and stay the same. Sometimes, changes are fast and unplanned.

Long Ago

Today

▶ Jerome, Arizona

Review

1. **What to Know** How do communities both change and stay the same?
2. **Vocabulary** Write the meaning of the term **continuity**.
3. **History** How has Chicago, Illinois, changed and stayed the same?
4. **Critical Thinking Make It Relevant** What are some ways in which your community has changed over time?
5. ✏️ **Make a Brochure** Make an illustrated brochure that shows both change and continuity in your community.
6. ⭐ **Sequence** On a separate sheet of paper, copy and complete the graphic organizer below.

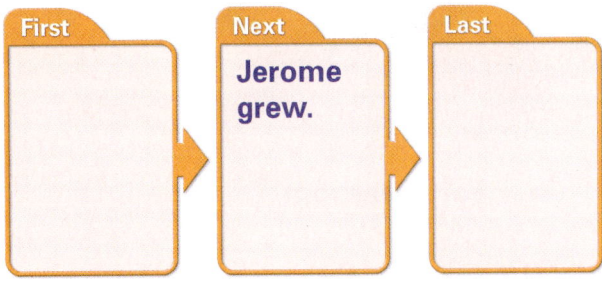

Chapter 5 ▪ 159

Chart and Graph Skills

Read a Time Line

Why It Matters Knowing the order of events helps you understand history. Knowing how time is measured is also helpful.

▶ Learn

A **time line** is a diagram that shows when and in what order events took place. You read a time line from left to right. The events on the left happened first. The events on the right happened later.

Time lines are divided into equal time periods. A time period can be any length. It can be a year, a decade, a century, or a millennium (muh•LEH•nee•uhm). A **millennium** is 1,000 years.

Chicago's Early History

1801 | 1811 | 1821 | 1831 | 1841 | 1851

1803 The United States adds its first fort to the area

1818 Illinois becomes a state

1837 Chicago becomes an official city

1848 Galena and Chicago Union Railroad is built

Fort Dearborn

Galena and Chicago Union Station

160 ■ Unit 3

The time line below shows events in Chicago's history. They happened during the nineteenth century. This includes the years from 1801 to 1901.

> Practice

Use the time line to answer these questions.

1. When did Chicago become an official city?
2. Was the Water Tower built before or after the Great Chicago Fire?
3. How many years passed between the coming of the railroad and the World's Columbian Exposition?

> Apply

Make It Relevant Make a time line showing the events of a year in your life. You may wish to add pictures to your time line.

1869 — The Water Tower is built

1871 — The Great Chicago Fire burns much of the city

1893 — The World's Columbian Exposition is held

The Water Tower

The Great Chicago Fire

Poster about World's Columbian Exposition

Lesson 2 People Bring Changes

What to Know
How have people changed their communities?

Vocabulary
invention p. 162
engineer p. 164
right p. 165
vote p. 165
suffrage p. 165
slogan p. 165
equality p. 166
civil rights p. 167

 **Sequence**

People change communities with their actions and inventions. **Inventions** are things that are made for the first time. New ideas also help communities grow and change.

Building Outward

Communities grow as people move to them. New streets and roads are built. New businesses open, and new buildings go up near the edges of communities. Often, a town's borders move outward to include the new areas.

Businesses

Passengers

162 ▪ Unit 3

Improving Transportation

As towns grow, people build roads to connect their communities. Early roads were rough. Most people traveled on horseback or by horse and wagon. Travel was slow.

People wanted better and faster ways to travel. They built canals to connect rivers. Later, they built railroads. In Britain, George Stephenson developed a train engine that could run on a track. Many people call Stephenson "the Father of the Railways."

Railroads brought change to communities. Businesses used railroads to move goods to markets. New businesses opened, and older communities located along tracks grew. New communities also grew along the tracks. All of these communities were now connected because it was easy to travel between them by train.

❯ George Stephenson developed a widely used train engine.

Reading Check ⭕ **Sequence**
Which were built first—railroads or canals?

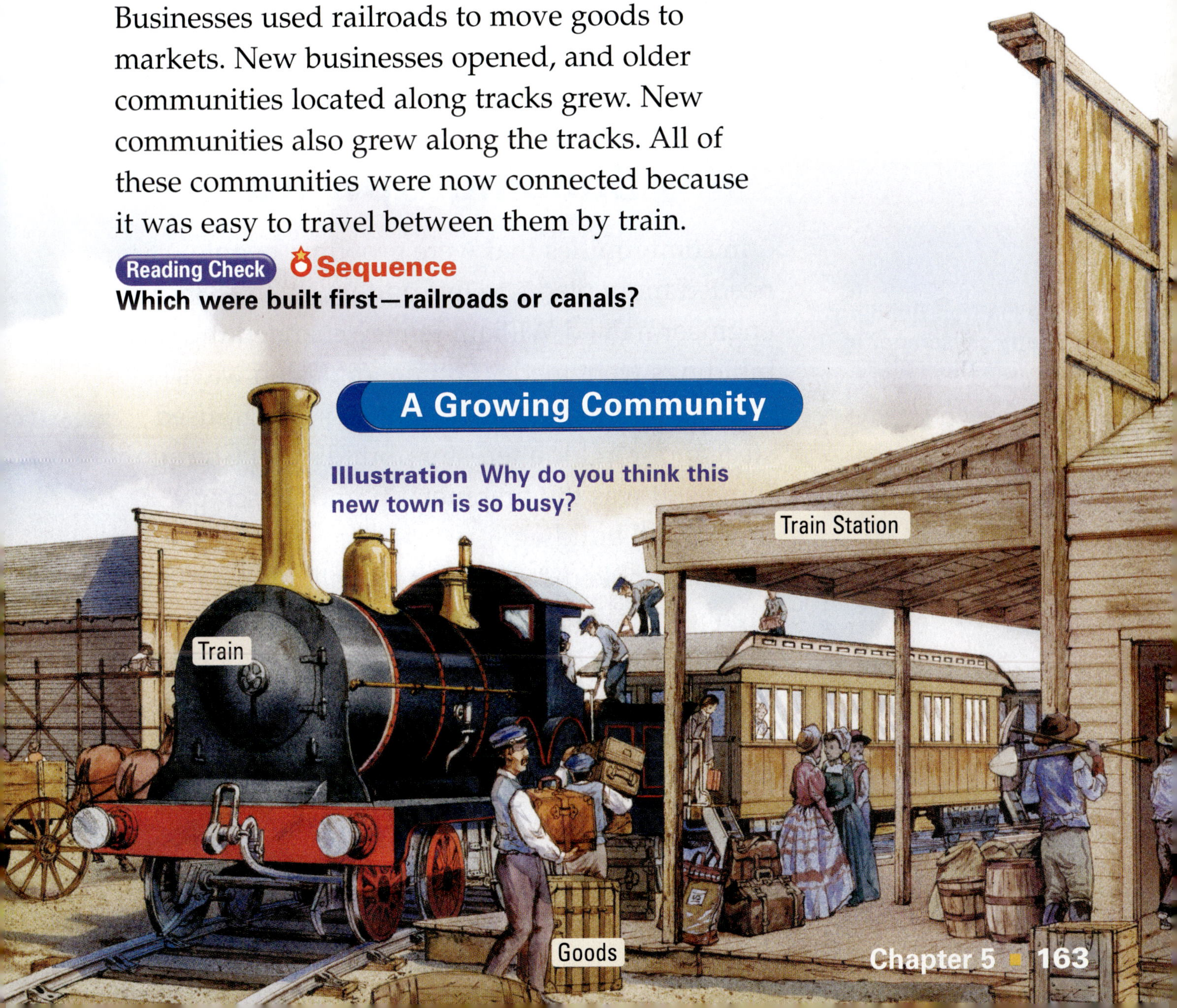

A Growing Community

Illustration Why do you think this new town is so busy?

Train Station

Train

Goods

Some of the World's Tallest Buildings

Height (in feet): 0, 150, 300, 450, 600, 750, 900, 1,050, 1,200, 1,350, 1,500

Transamerican Building (San Francisco, California, United States)
Eiffel Tower (Paris, France)
Empire State Building (New York City, New York, United States)
Sears Tower (Chicago, Illinois, United States)
Petronas Towers (Kuala Lumpur, Malaysia)

Graph Which is taller—the Sears Tower or the Eiffel Tower?

▶ The Flatiron Building, an early skyscraper in New York City

Building Upward

In communities that were growing, people needed more places to live and work. In 1885, an engineer named William Jenney changed the way buildings were made. **Engineers** design ways to build and make things. Jenney's design used steel and iron for a ten-story building in Chicago, Illinois. It was the first metal-frame skyscraper, or very tall building.

Most people did not want to walk up the many flights of stairs tall buildings needed. In the late 1800s, Elisha Otis designed the first elevator that could safely carry people. Elevators made it possible for people to build taller skyscrapers.

Reading Check **Cause and Effect**
How did elevators help people build taller buildings?

Working for Suffrage

People also use ideas to change communities. Many have worked to make sure that everyone has the same **rights**, or freedoms.

United States citizens have the right to vote. To **vote** is to make a choice that gets counted. In the early 1900s, women could not vote. Susan B. Anthony believed this should change. In the mid-1800s, she and Elizabeth Cady Stanton set up groups of people to work for woman's suffrage. **Suffrage** is the right to vote.

People printed **slogans**, or short sayings, on buttons and signs to tell their message. They held meetings and talked to people about the importance of giving suffrage to women. Finally, in 1920, women won the right to vote.

Reading Check Main Idea and Details
When did women win the right to vote?

› Susan B. Anthony (below left) and others worked for woman's suffrage.

▶ Gandhi was a leader for equality in India.

Working for Equality

In the 1900s, many worked for equality, or equal treatment, for all people. Both Mohandas Gandhi (moh•HAHN•dahs GAHN•dee) and Dr. Martin Luther King, Jr., believed that everyone should have the same rights.

Mohandas Gandhi

Gandhi wanted people in India to have freedom. At the time, India was ruled by Britain. Britain's leaders made the laws for India. Many people were not treated fairly or equally.

Instead of fighting, Gandhi used peaceful actions to work for equality. He did not want people to hurt others. He led marches and refused to follow laws that he felt were wrong.

In 1947, India became its own country. Gandhi had helped the people of India become free.

Dr. Martin Luther King, Jr.

Dr. Martin Luther King, Jr., believed that laws should treat all people equally. The rights to be treated equally are called **civil rights**. In Dr. King's lifetime, laws in the United States separated people. For example, African Americans could not go to the same schools as white people.

Dr. King led peaceful marches and spoke against unfair laws. In the 1960s, laws were passed to support equality.

Reading Check **Compare and Contrast**
What did Gandhi and Dr. King both do?

▶ Dr. Martin Luther King, Jr., agreed with Gandhi about using peaceful actions to work for equality.

Summary People cause change all over the world. They help communities grow. They also work for equality.

Review

1. **What to Know** How have people changed their communities?
2. **Vocabulary** Use the term **slogan** in a sentence about **suffrage**.
3. **Your Community** How has a person or group changed your community?
4. **Critical Thinking** How did Gandhi help change the way people around the world work for change?
5. **Write a Paragraph** Write a paragraph about a person in this lesson who has brought change to many communities.
6. **Sequence** On a separate sheet of paper, copy and complete the graphic organizer below.

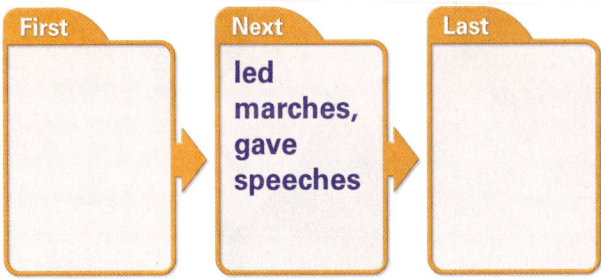

Chapter 5 ■ 167

Critical Thinking Skills

Compare Primary and Secondary Sources

Why It Matters People use both primary sources and secondary sources to learn about history.

▶ Learn

A **primary source** is a record made by people who saw or took part in an event. A letter, diary entry, photo, or film can be a primary source.

A **secondary source** is a record of an event that was made by a person who was not there. An encyclopedia article is an example of a secondary source.

The record below is part of the "I Have a Dream" speech made by Dr. Martin Luther King, Jr. The photo below shows him making this speech.

Primary sources about Dr. King include
1. a photograph of him
2. a speech
3. a Nobel Peace Prize, which he won in 1964.

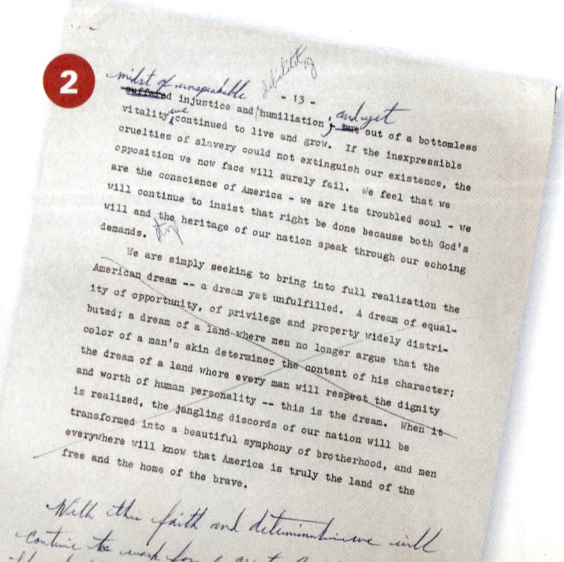

> ## Practice

Use the primary and secondary sources on these pages to answer these questions.

1. Which images show primary sources?
2. Which images show secondary sources?
3. How is a primary source different from a secondary source?

> ## Apply

Make It Relevant Find one primary source and one secondary source about an event or a person in your community. Share these sources with your class.

Secondary sources about Dr. King include
4. websites and
5. reference books.

169

Lesson 3 Inventions in Communities

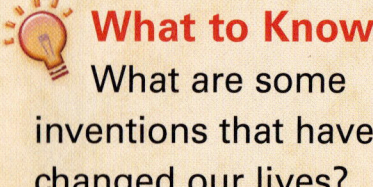
What to Know
What are some inventions that have changed our lives?

Vocabulary
technology p. 170

Sequence

New inventions add to **technology**, or all of the tools people can use every day. Changes in technology change the ways people live and work.

Changes in Communication

Long ago, people did not have many ways to communicate with others who were far away. Most messages were sent by mail, but a letter could take days or weeks to arrive. In the 1800s, new inventions made it faster and easier to communicate.

▶ The Pony Express made mail delivery faster. This painting by Frederic Remington is called *Coming and Going of the Pony Express*.

❯ Samuel Morse invented the telegraph.

❯ Alexander Graham Bell's telephone was one of the first of many designs.

Samuel Morse and the Telegraph

Samuel Morse was a painter, but he had many ideas for inventions. In 1840, Morse invented the telegraph. This machine used a code of dots and dashes to send messages over wires. Before long, telegraph wires were strung across the country. People could now get news quickly from far away.

Alexander Graham Bell and the Telephone

Alexander Graham Bell also changed the way people communicated. Bell had improved the telegraph. In 1876, he built a telephone. The next year, he started the first telephone company. For the first time, people could speak to and hear others who were far away.

Reading Check ❂ **Sequence**
Which was invented first—the telegraph or the telephone?

Chapter 5 ■ 171

Changes in Transportation

Canals and then railroads had made travel faster and easier. However, the invention of the automobile in the late 1800s made it possible for people to travel on their own.

Henry Ford and the Automobile

At first, cars cost a lot of money. In 1908, Henry Ford made a car that more people could buy. It was called the Model T. Because all Model Ts were the same, they could be made faster and at a lower cost.

As more people bought them, cars became the main form of transportation. People could now live outside of cities and drive to work. The automobile also led to the building of highways all across the country.

> Henry Ford with his Model T

The Wright Brothers and the Airplane

Airplanes also changed transportation. In 1903, Orville Wright made a 12-second flight in an airplane. He and his brother, Wilbur, had built the plane. They had been building and improving airplanes for several years.

Later, airplane companies used the Wright brothers' ideas to build larger airplanes. Today, airplanes carry both people and goods around the world.

Reading Check **Sequence**
What happened after the Wright brothers made an airplane that could fly?

❯ Orville Wright and the Model A Flyer

❯ The Model T was the first car in the United States that many people could afford to buy.

Chapter 5 ■ 173

▶ Inventions such as the vacuum cleaner and the television changed daily life.

Changes in the Home

Homes are filled with inventions. Toasters, vacuum cleaners, and lightbulbs are all inventions that make life easier. These inventions have changed the way people live.

Thomas Edison, Lewis Latimer, and the Lightbulb

Many inventors worked together to bring electricity to homes. In the 1880s, Thomas Edison and Lewis Latimer invented the first practical electric lightbulbs. Before the lightbulb, people used candles, oil lamps, and gas lamps for light.

The lightbulb let people light their homes without the danger of causing a fire. Because of the lightbulb, they could do more evening activities.

▶ Edison (top) and Latimer (bottom) invented the first practical lightbulb.

174 ■ Unit 3

Other Home Inventions

Many inventors worked on inventions that led to the radio in the late 1800s and the television in the early 1900s. These inventions now bring people news from all over the world.

Other inventions have changed people's homes. Many items in kitchens today were once the ideas of inventors. These include stoves, ovens, dishwashers, and refrigerators.

Reading Check **Main Idea and Details**
When was the first practical electric lightbulb invented?

Summary Inventions have changed the way people live. Many people have worked to invent the things we use every day.

▶ **Josephine Cochran (top) invented the first practical dishwasher. Guillermo Gonzalez Camarena (bottom) invented the color television and the remote control.**

Review

1. **What to Know** What are some inventions that have changed our lives?
2. **Vocabulary** Write about how you use **technology** in your life.
3. **History** Which inventions changed the way people communicate?
4. **Critical Thinking Make It Relevant** What would your life be like if the lightbulb had not been invented?
5. **Make a Chart** Make a chart of inventors and inventions.
6. **Sequence** On a separate sheet of paper, copy and complete the graphic organizer below.

Chapter 5 ■ 175

Chart and Graph Skills

Read a Flowchart

Why It Matters People often need to know how to do something or how something works. A chart that shows the steps in order can help them understand.

❯ Learn

A **flowchart** shows how to do something or how something works. It shows the steps in order.

The flowchart below uses words, pictures, and arrows to show the steps to building a car. Cars are put together on assembly lines. On an **assembly line**, each worker adds one kind of part to a product as it passes on a moving belt.

Assembly Line

The car frame is placed on the assembly line.

The top and sides of the car are added to the frame.

176 ▪ Unit 3

Practice

Follow the arrows on the flowchart to answer the questions.

1. What is the next step after the car frame is placed on an assembly line?
2. What happens after the top and sides are added to the frame?
3. When are the engine parts put into the car?

Apply

Make It Relevant Make a list of the things you do every morning to get ready for school. Use your list to make a flowchart that shows the sequence in which you do these things. Draw pictures, label them, and add arrows to show how to read the steps of your chart.

Wheels are attached to the car.

Engine parts are put into the car.

Chapter 5 ■ 177

Lesson 4 Communities Long Ago

What to Know
What ideas from ancient communities are used today?

Vocabulary
ancient p. 178
civilization p. 178
modern p. 178
democracy p. 182
republic p. 183
empire p. 184
trade p. 184
port p. 185

Sequence

Since **ancient** times, or times very long ago, people have lived in communities. In even the earliest groups, people often shared a government and a culture.

Some of those communities grew to become great civilizations. A **civilization** is a large group of people living in a well-organized way. Ideas from some of those ancient civilizations are still used in modern times. **Modern** is how we describe the time we live in today.

▶ Ruins of ancient Mesopotamia still stand in what is now Iraq.

178 • Unit 3

◗ This piece of clay shows Sumerian writing.

◗ This Mesopotamian artwork called *Standard of Ur* shows a wheeled cart.

Ancient Mesopotamia

One of the world's earliest civilizations was in southwestern Asia. It was in a place called Mesopotamia (meh•suh•puh•TAY•mee•uh). It had some of the world's earliest cities. People built them in a part of Mesopotamia called Sumer (SOO•mer).

The Sumerians developed many new ideas and inventions. They built carts with wheels. Wheels made it easier for people to move things from place to place.

Writing was another important idea developed by the Sumerians. Before people learned to write, they had to keep track of things by remembering them. Writing gave the Sumerians a way to record important information and their history.

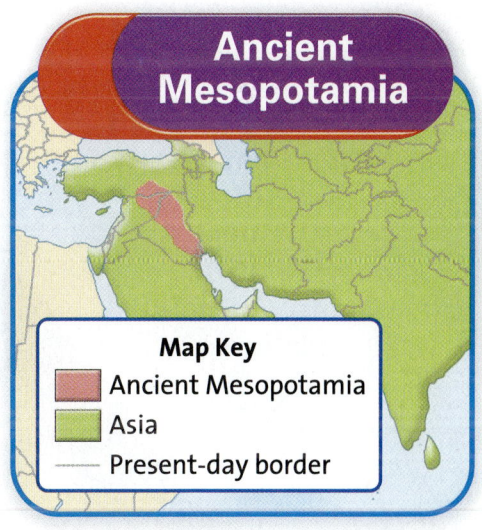

Ancient Mesopotamia

Map Key
- Ancient Mesopotamia
- Asia
- Present-day border

Reading Check ◉ **Sequence**
Was writing developed during or after the time of the Sumerians?

Ancient Egypt

The ancient civilization of Egypt, in Africa, is known for its pyramids. An Egyptian pyramid is a tomb, or burial place, for a dead king or queen.

The Great Pyramid is the largest of the pyramids that are still standing today. It is more than 450 feet high. It was built about 4,500 years ago for an Egyptian pharaoh (FAIR•oh), or king, named Khufu (KOO•foo).

The pyramids were made by stacking huge stone blocks in layers. Some of the blocks in the Great Pyramid weigh 5,000 pounds. The ancient Egyptians did not have wheels and pulleys for moving things. They put the giant blocks in place by pushing them up ramps on rollers made of logs.

Reading Check **Summarize**
How was the Great Pyramid of Egypt built?

❯ Hatshepsut (hat•SHEP•soot) was one of Egypt's leaders.

❯ The Great Pyramid took 20 years to build. As many as 10,000 people worked on it at all times.

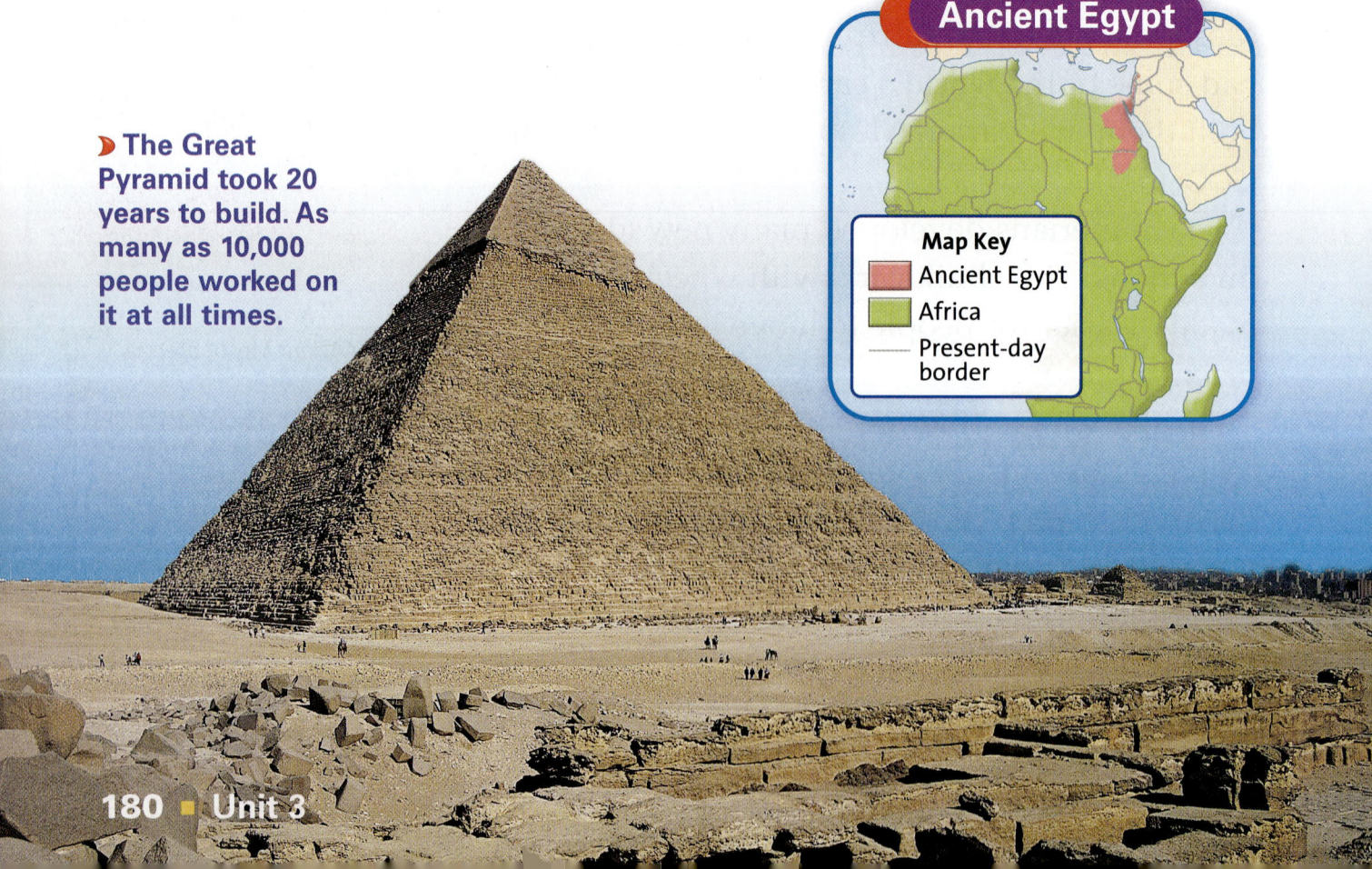

Ancient Egypt

Map Key
Ancient Egypt
Africa
Present-day border

Chinese Paper Making

Illustration The ancient Chinese made paper by
① cutting reeds and soaking them to make pulp,
② mashing the pulp,
③ heating the pulp,
④ pounding the pulp,
⑤ stretching the paper, and
⑥ drying the paper.

What happened to the pulp after it was heated?

Ancient China

Every Fourth of July, fireworks light up the night sky all across the United States. But fireworks are not an American invention. They were invented thousands of years ago in China.

The ancient Chinese also invented paper and printing. First, they wrote on paper with brushes and ink. Later, they invented a way to print copies of pages. They carved the writing for a page on a wooden block. Then they put ink on the block and pressed it against paper to make a print. This let them make many copies of a page much faster than they could write them by hand.

Ancient China

Map Key
- Ancient China
- Asia
- Present-day border

Reading Check **Summarize**
What inventions from ancient China are still used?

Chapter 5 ▪ 181

Greek Alphabet

Greek Letter	English Sound
Α	a
Β	b
Γ	g
Δ	d
Ε	e

Table In what ways is the Greek alphabet like the alphabet we use today?

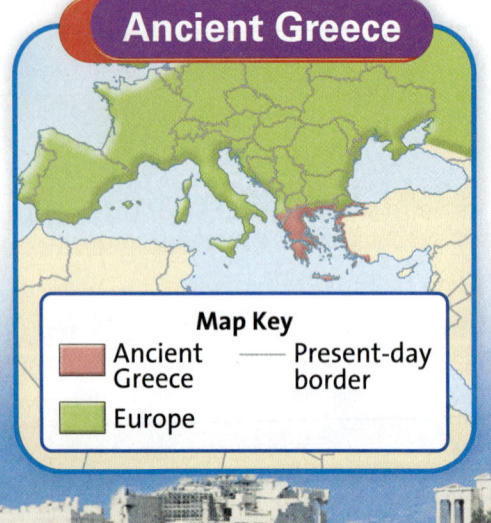

Map Key
- Ancient Greece
- Europe
- Present-day border

Ancient Greece

The Greek civilization began in what is now the country of Greece, in Europe. Athens was one of its most important communities.

The government of Athens was the world's first democracy. In a **democracy**, citizens make the decisions. All free men over the age of 18 could take part in the government of Athens.

In ancient Greece, the male citizens met in a large group, or assembly. Each man had the right to speak. They talked about ideas for new laws and voted on them.

The people of Athens loved the arts and learning. Ancient Greece is still known for its sculptors, potters, painters, builders, and writers.

Reading Check **Main Idea and Details**
What kind of government did Athens have?

❯ The Acropolis (uh•KRAH•puh•luhs) was a religious center in ancient Athens.

▶ The Forum was a public square in the center of Rome. Romans met there to talk about government and business.

Ancient Rome

The Roman civilization began with a number of tiny villages. These were scattered over seven hills above the Tiber (TY•ber) River, in what is today the country of Italy. As the villages grew, they combined to form the city of Rome.

The people of ancient Rome had the world's first republic. In a **republic**, citizens vote to choose government leaders. These leaders make decisions for all the people.

To make the city strong, Rome's leaders built good roads and public buildings. Rome became one of the world's richest cities up to that time.

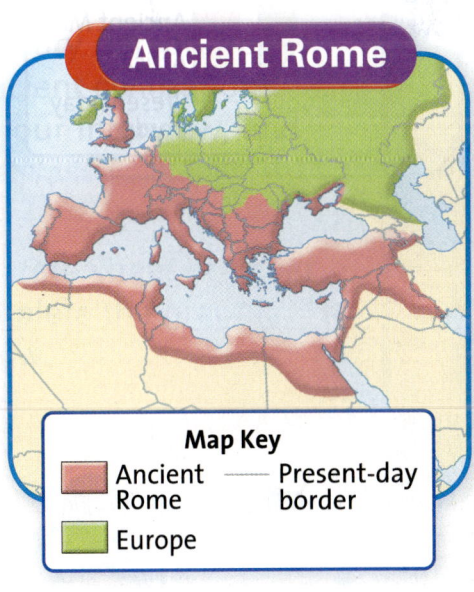

Ancient Rome

Map Key
- Ancient Rome
- Europe
- Present-day border

Reading Check **Main Idea and Details**
What form of government did Rome have?

Chapter 5 ■ 183

STUDY SKILLS

TAKE NOTES

Taking notes can help you remember important ideas in what you read.

- Write important facts and ideas in your own words.
- Organize your notes so that they are easy to understand.

Our Country's History

Main Ideas	Facts
Lesson 1: • Our First Communities • How the People Lived • _____	• Native Americans formed the first communities in North America. • Native Americans belonged to different tribes. • _____

PREVIEW VOCABULARY

shelter p. 191

patriotism p. 208

pioneer p. 214

CHAPTER 6
Our Country's History

▶ Musicians in Colonial Williamsburg, Virginia

Lesson 2

Building Communities

What to Know
Why did Europeans build communities in North America?

Vocabulary
explorer p. 196
religion p. 197
claim p. 197
settlement p. 197
settler p. 199
conflict p. 200
slavery p. 201

Sequence

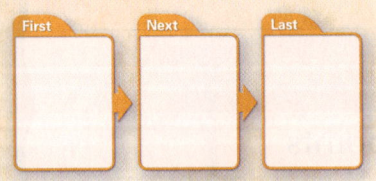

In 1492, an Italian explorer named Christopher Columbus sailed from Spain. An **explorer** is a person who goes to find out about a place. Columbus thought that if he sailed west across the Atlantic Ocean, he would reach the part of Asia that Europeans called the Indies.

Instead, he reached an island off the coast of North America. At that time, people in Europe did not know about the Americas, or the continents of North America and South America.

▶ Christopher Columbus came to the Americas with three sailing ships.

196 ■ Unit 3

▶ This fort at St. Augustine, completed in 1695, is one of the few remaining Spanish buildings in Florida.

▶ In 1513, Spanish explorer Juan Ponce de León (HWAHN POHN•say day lay•OHN) first claimed the land that is now Florida for Spain.

Exploring North America

Soon, other European explorers came to the Americas. Some hoped to find treasure and to spread their **religion**, or belief system. Others came to claim land. To **claim** something is to say it belongs to you.

Spanish Explorers

In 1565, the king of Spain sent Pedro Menéndez de Avilés (may•NAYN•days day ah•vee•LAYS) to what is now Florida. He built a fort named St. Augustine there. St. Augustine is the oldest lasting settlement in the United States. A **settlement** is a new community.

Spain claimed much of South America and the southern part of North America. Mexico and most countries to its south share a Spanish heritage.

Reading Check ✪ **Sequence**
Was St. Augustine built before or after the United States was a country?

> Native Americans and settlers leaving after trading fur near what is now Missouri.

A French Settlement

French explorers also came to North America. They claimed much of what is today Canada. The French also claimed the middle part of what is now the United States.

In 1763, Pierre Laclède (lah•KLED) traveled up the Mississippi River. He was looking for a good place for a fur-trading post. Laclède chose a spot near a cliff along the river. He knew he could use the river to move furs.

In 1764, he began a settlement there that later became St. Louis. It was named for King Louis XV of France. Laclède said, "This settlement will become one of the finest cities in America."

> Pierre Laclède founded St. Louis, in what is now Missouri.

Building St. Louis

The settlers first built shelters in which to live and work. A **settler** is one of the first people to live in a new community. These buildings included a large house for trading furs, cabins for workers to sleep in, and sheds for storing things. The settlers later built a church and a fort.

Many people traveling west passed through St. Louis. Some stayed and settled there. By 1765, St. Louis had more than 300 settlers. In the 1800s, the city became one of the largest river ports in the nation. Today, St. Louis is a large city.

❯ St. Louis today

Reading Check ◎ **Sequence**
What did the settlers add to St. Louis after building shelters?

❯ St. Louis was a busy river port in 1874.

Chapter 6 ■ 199

An English Settlement

In 1607, three ships sailed from England to North America. They landed in what is now the state of Virginia. Some of the 105 passengers hoped to find riches and a way to the Pacific Ocean. Others wanted to spread their religion. They named their settlement after their king, James I. Jamestown was the first lasting English settlement in North America.

Conflict and Change

An early leader of Jamestown, John Smith, traded with Native Americans to get food for the settlers. Over time, the settlers came into **conflict**, or disagreement, with Native Americans. They fought over food and land.

> Today, Jamestown is a National Historic Site.

In 1612, John Rolfe began growing tobacco in Jamestown. To grow tobacco and other crops, the settlers needed more workers. Beginning in the 1600s, people were brought from Africa and forced into slavery. **Slavery** is a system under which people have no choices.

The Africans had been taken from their homes and families. Then traders had brought them to North America, where they worked as enslaved people. An enslaved person is owned by another person and forced to work without pay.

Reading Check **Main Idea and Details**
Why did the English settlers come to North America?

▶ Pocahontas was the daughter of Chief Powhatan. He was the leader of the Powhatan, the Native Americans who lived near Jamestown.

Another English Settlement

The Wampanoag (wahm•puh•NOH•ag) were the first people to live where Plymouth, Massachusetts, is today. They fished the nearby Atlantic Ocean and grew corn and other crops.

Pilgrims Come to Plymouth

In 1620, a ship called the *Mayflower* carried more people from England to North America. They wanted to live where they could be free to follow their religion. Because they traveled for religious reasons, they became known as Pilgrims.

The Pilgrims looked for a good place to build a settlement. They found a harbor with deep water where ships could come close to shore. John Smith had named the place Plymouth.

> Native Americans taught the Pilgrims how to grow corn.

Time Line Which of these settlements was built first?

European Settlements

- **1565** Pedro Menéndez de Avilés builds a fort named St. Augustine
- **1607** Jamestown is settled for King James I of England
- **1620** People from England start the community of Plymouth
- **1764** Pierre Laclède founds St. Louis for France

The Mayflower Compact

The Pilgrims wrote a compact, or agreement, that set up a government for their community. In the Mayflower Compact, the Pilgrims agreed to make fair laws for the new community. They also promised to obey these laws. The Pilgrims would govern themselves.

Reading Check ⚪ **Sequence**
Who were the first people to live in what is now Plymouth, Massachusetts?

Summary Explorers from Europe claimed many areas of North America. Settlers from different countries built new communities in what is now the United States.

> In the fall of 1621, the Pilgrims celebrated their first harvest with the Wampanoag. Many people think of this as the first Thanksgiving.

Review

1. **What to Know** Why did Europeans build communities in North America?
2. **Vocabulary** What is the difference between an **explorer** and a **settler**?
3. **Your Community** Find out who started your community.
4. **Critical Thinking** Why do you think there was conflict between the settlers and Native Americans?
5. **Make a Chart** Make a chart showing early settlements. Include their locations, the dates when they were started, and who built them.
6. **Sequence** On a separate sheet of paper, copy and complete the graphic organizer below.

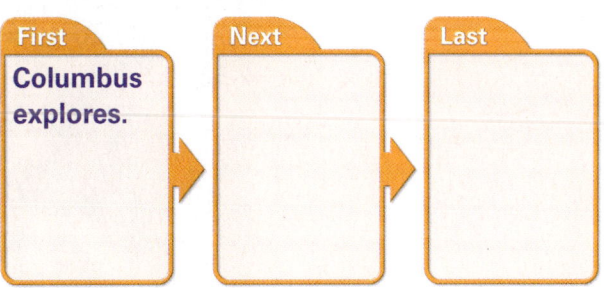

Chapter 6 ■ 203

Lesson 3 Fighting for Freedom

What to Know
Who fought for our freedom?

Vocabulary
freedom p. 204
colony p. 204
tax p. 205
revolution p. 205
independence p. 206
constitution p. 208
patriotism p. 208
President p. 209

Sequence

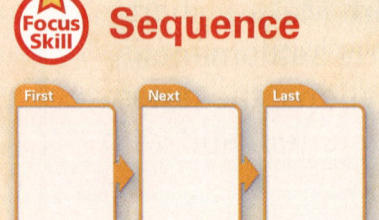

In the United States, we have many freedoms. **Freedom** is the right to make your own choices. It is one of the ideas on which our country was founded.

Freedom from England

Long ago, most of the settlements along the eastern coast of North America were colonies of England, or Britain. A **colony** is a settlement ruled by a country that is far away. By the 1700s, there were 13 colonies. These colonies were the beginning of the United States.

Fast Fact

The Boston Tea Party was an action taken in 1773 by colonists who were angry about taxes on tea. The colonists dumped 342 crates of tea into Boston Harbor.

The colonists were people living in the colonies. For a long time they did not mind being ruled by Britain. Then Britain's lawmakers began passing new laws. The colonists felt the laws were unfair. The colonists were also angry that they had no part in making the laws.

Many of the laws included new taxes on goods from Britain, such as sugar and tea. A **tax** is money that people pay to the government.

In 1773, some colonists dumped tea into Boston Harbor. This is known as the Boston Tea Party. The colonists said they would rather throw away tea than pay taxes on it.

Fighting broke out between colonists and soldiers who had been sent from Britain. This fighting was the beginning of the American Revolution, or Revolutionary War. In a **revolution**, people fight for a change in government.

Reading Check Sequence
What happened after Britain made the colonists pay new taxes?

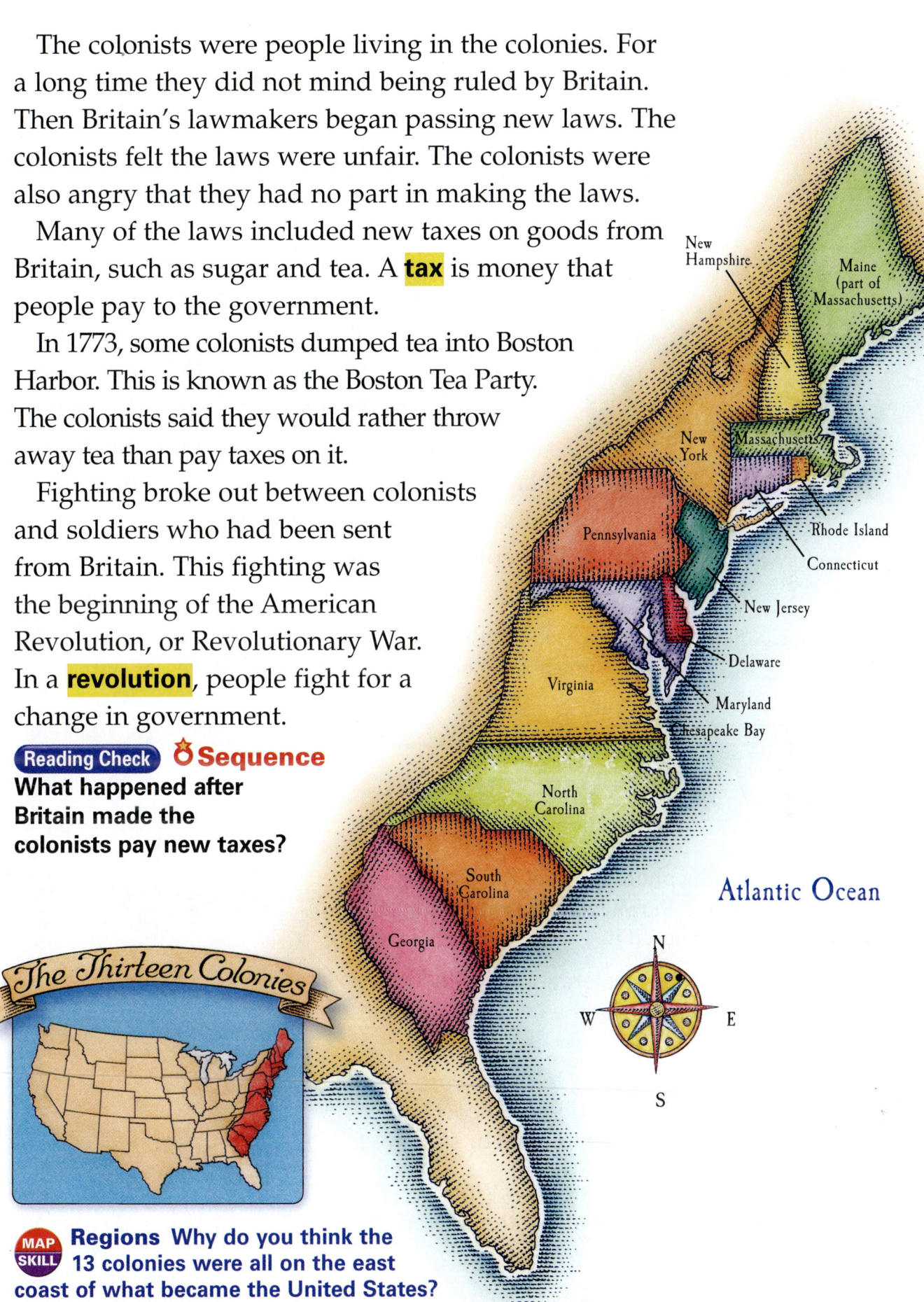

The Thirteen Colonies

MAP SKILL Regions Why do you think the 13 colonies were all on the east coast of what became the United States?

Chapter 6 ■ 205

A Declaration Is Made

In 1776, John Adams, Benjamin Franklin, Thomas Jefferson, and other leaders of the colonies met in Philadelphia, Pennsylvania. They wrote a statement listing reasons the colonists wanted independence. **Independence** is freedom from another country's control.

The statement is called the Declaration of Independence. It says that all people have the right to "Life, Liberty, and the pursuit of Happiness." *Liberty* means "freedom."

On July 4, 1776, the leaders voted to accept the Declaration of Independence. The declaration said that the colonies no longer belonged to Britain. They were now states in a new country, the United States of America.

▶ The Declaration of Independence was worked on by Benjamin Franklin, John Adams, and Thomas Jefferson.

 **Primary Sources**

The Declaration of Independence

Background This photograph of the Declaration of Independence shows what Thomas Jefferson wrote and who signed it.

The first part of the Declaration is called the Preamble. This says why the colonists wanted independence.

One of the colony leaders, John Hancock, wrote his name large. The term *John Hancock* came to mean a person's written name, or signature.

DBQ Document-Based Question What does this photograph tell you about the Declaration of Independence?

206 ▪ Unit 3

▶ This engraving shows George Washington and his army in Morristown, New Jersey.

The War Begins

The Revolutionary War began in 1775, a year before the Declaration of Independence was written. George Washington was chosen to lead the American troops against Britain.

Washington's army was made up of colonists who wanted to help. They were not well trained and sometimes had to get supplies from the towns for which they were fighting. The British soldiers, though, were better trained. Their supplies were sent to them on ships from Britain.

The American soldiers fought many battles. They won some, but they lost others. In 1783, the Americans finally won the war and their independence from Britain. The United States is still an independent country today.

▶ American soldiers wore clothes like these in the Revolutionary War.

Reading Check ⭐ **Sequence**
Was the Declaration of Independence written before or after the start of the Revolutionary War?

New Laws Are Made

After the war, people in the United States could make their own laws. They formed a government for the new nation. However, the new government turned out to be weak. By 1787, the country's leaders decided they needed a new constitution. A **constitution** is a set of laws that tells how a government will work.

The leaders wanted to form a government that was strong enough to get things done but would not take away freedoms. They met in Philadelphia to write the Constitution of the United States. In 1789, the Constitution was approved.

The Constitution helped found the republic of the United States. The leaders were proud of the country they had started. A feeling of pride in one's country is called **patriotism**.

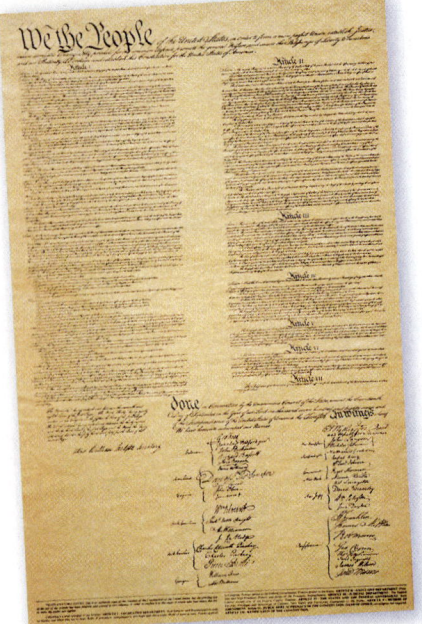

▸ The Constitution of the United States

▸ This painting shows the signing of the Constitution of the United States.

Our First President

The new Constitution said that the people would choose a **President**, or leader for the country. On April 30, 1789, Americans chose General George Washington to become their first President. He is often called "the father of our country."

Reading Check ⭐ **Sequence**
What happened after the Constitution was approved?

▶ George Washington arriving in New York City to be sworn in as President

Summary The American colonists fought for freedom from Britain in the Revolutionary War. After the war, their leaders wrote the Constitution of the United States of America.

▶ The quarter coin features George Washington.

Review

1. **What to Know** Who fought for our freedom?
2. **Vocabulary** How are **freedom** and **independence** related?
3. **Civics and Government** What document did the leaders of the United States write to form a new government?
4. **Critical Thinking Make It Relevant** How might your life be different if the colonists had not won their independence?
5. **Make a Time Line** Make a time line of important events in the colonists' fight for freedom.
6. **Sequence** On a separate sheet of paper, copy and complete the graphic organizer below.

Chapter 6 ■ 209

Biography

- Trustworthiness
- Respect
- Responsibility
- Fairness
- Caring
- **Patriotism**

Franklin and Jefferson

> "We hold these truths to be self-evident, that all men are created equal, that they are endowed by their Creator with certain unalienable Rights, that among these are Life, Liberty, and the pursuit of Happiness."
>
> — The Declaration of Independence

Why Character Counts

✏️ How did Franklin and Jefferson show patriotism in their lives?

It was June 1776. The leaders of the 13 colonies had only one thing on their minds—writing a Declaration of Independence. They chose some of the finest minds in the colonies to help. They asked Thomas Jefferson to do the writing, with the help of Benjamin Franklin and John Adams.

Jefferson and Franklin had very different backgrounds. Jefferson was a rich landowner from Virginia. He had a college education. Franklin was from a working-class family. He went to school for only two years and had a job by the age of ten.

Benjamin Franklin

Thomas Jefferson

This painting is called *Congress Voting the Declaration of Independence*.

Yet Jefferson and Franklin were alike in many ways. They both were great writers and thinkers. Each loved science and new ideas. They both loved the land of their birth. They believed it could and should be a free and united country. They worked toward a dream of a country that was governed by its people.

On July 4, 1776, the leaders of the 13 colonies approved the Declaration that Jefferson and Franklin had worked so hard to write. With the help of these two patriots, the United States of America began.

The first page of Thomas Jefferson's rough draft of the Declaration of Independence

 For more resources, go to www.harcourtschool.com/ss1

Time

1700			1830
1775 Jefferson and Franklin represent their states in the Continental Congress	**1776** Jefferson, Franklin, and John Adams draft the Declaration of Independence	**1787** Franklin signs the Constitution of the United States	**1801** Jefferson becomes third President of the United States

Chapter 6 ▪ 211

Lesson 4

Growth and Change

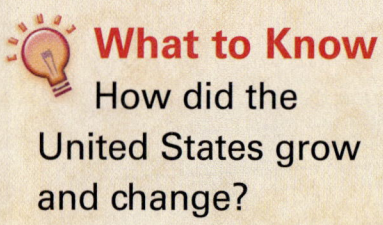
What to Know
How did the United States grow and change?

Vocabulary
pioneer p. 214
civil war p. 216
territory p. 217
amendment p. 217
immigrant p. 218

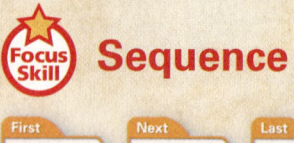
Sequence

After the Revolutionary War, Americans began to move farther west. They moved across the Appalachian Mountains toward the Mississippi River. Many people believed that one day the United States would stretch from ocean to ocean.

The Louisiana Purchase

In 1803, President Thomas Jefferson bought a huge area of land called Louisiana from the French. The Louisiana Purchase made the United States more than twice as large as it had been. Now the nation stretched from the east coast to the Rocky Mountains.

> Meriwether Lewis and William Clark (center) explored the West with Sacagawea (right) and York (left).

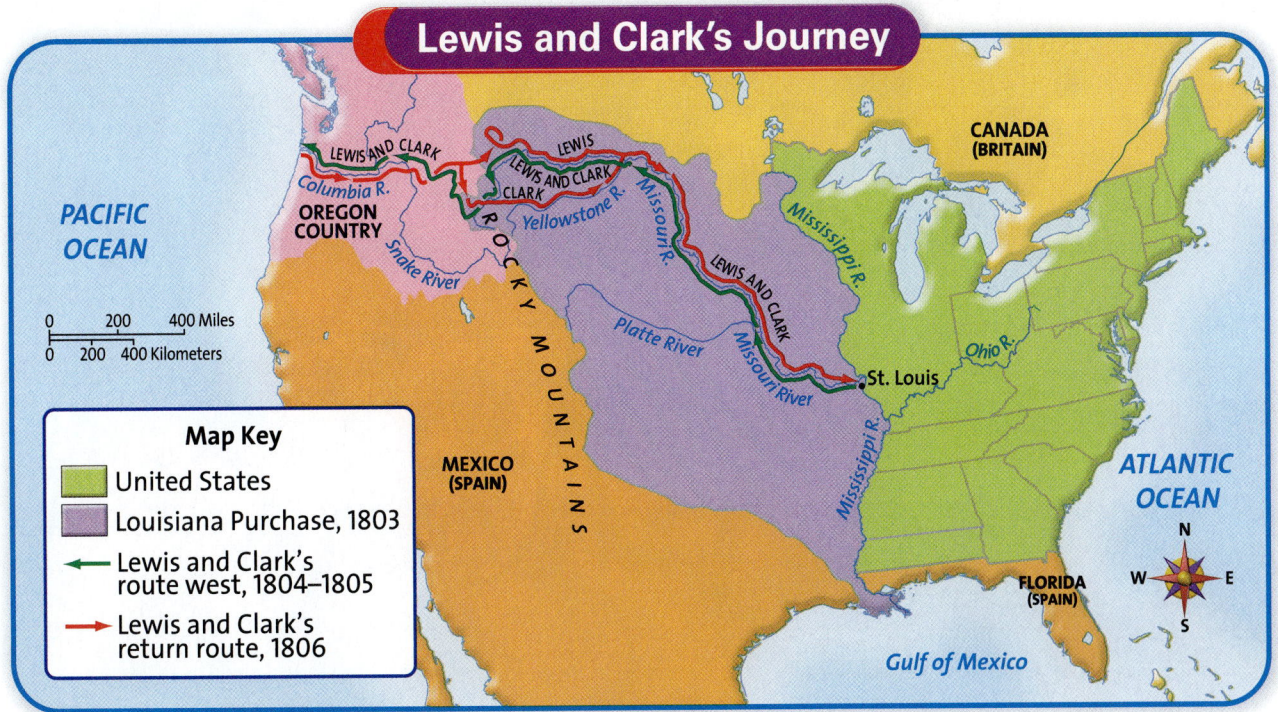

Map Skill **Movement** In which direction did Lewis and Clark travel at the beginning of their trip?

The Corps of Discovery

President Jefferson asked Meriwether Lewis and William Clark to explore the Louisiana Purchase. He also wanted them to find a way to the Pacific Ocean.

Lewis and Clark traveled with nearly 40 other people, including soldiers and guides. They called themselves the Corps of Discovery. One of the Corps was York, an enslaved African American. York was skilled at hunting and fishing.

A Native American woman of the Shoshone (shuh•SHOH•nee) became a guide for Lewis and Clark. Sacagawea (sa•kuh•juh•WEE•uh) helped them find paths through the mountains.

Reading Check **Sequence**
Was the Corps of Discovery formed before or after the Louisiana Purchase?

› The compass that William Clark used

Chapter 6 ■ 213

▶ Often children could not ride in the wagon because it was full of goods.

▶ Pioneers used churns to make their own butter.

Moving West

On their travels, Lewis and Clark wrote about and drew pictures of plants, animals, and Native Americans. They also drew maps to show rivers and mountain paths. This information helped open the western lands to new settlement. Many people wanted to see this land after they heard or read about it.

The Pioneers

In the 1800s, many Americans moved west. They traveled in long lines of covered wagons. These **pioneers**, or people who settle lands, included men, women, and children.

Pioneers had many reasons for moving. Some wanted land for farming. Others wanted to find new jobs in the West.

Life in the West

The trip west was very hard. Pioneers faced sickness, accidents, and bad weather along the way. Conflict with Native Americans made some areas unsafe.

Life was not any easier for the pioneers as they settled. First, they had to find water. Many settled near waterways. Others dug wells to reach water under the ground.

Next, they needed shelter. On the plains, some people made homes in the sides of mounds of mud and grass. In forests, people cut trees and used the logs to build cabins. They also planted gardens to grow food.

Reading Check ⭐ **Sequence**
What did pioneers have to find first as they settled?

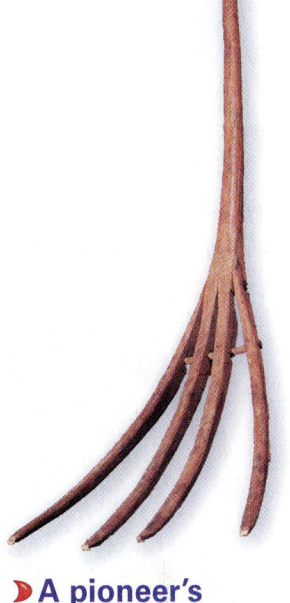

▶ A pioneer's pitchfork

Children in History

Pioneer Schools

Children of pioneer families went to school every day of the week except Sunday. In the 1800s, children stayed home during the summer to help their parents plant and gather crops. The schoolhouses had only one room. There were very few books in early classrooms, and often students had to memorize their lessons. The teacher taught all eight grades in the same room. The subjects were math, reading, spelling, and geography. After lunch, students could play outside. They had an entire prairie for their playground!

Make It Relevant How is your school similar to a pioneer school?

The Civil War

In 1861, the American Civil War began between the Northern states and the Southern states. In a **civil war**, people of one country fight each other.

People on both sides of the war had different views on many things, including slavery. Many people in the North thought that slavery was wrong. They wanted a law saying that no one in the country could own enslaved people. Many people in the South disagreed. Their way of life was based on enslaved people working for free on their plantations, or large farms.

▶ Harriet Tubman helped enslaved people escape to freedom.

▶ Frederick Douglass wrote and spoke out against slavery.

MAP SKILL **Regions** Northern states were called Union states. Border states were part of the Union but still had slavery. Where were the border states located?

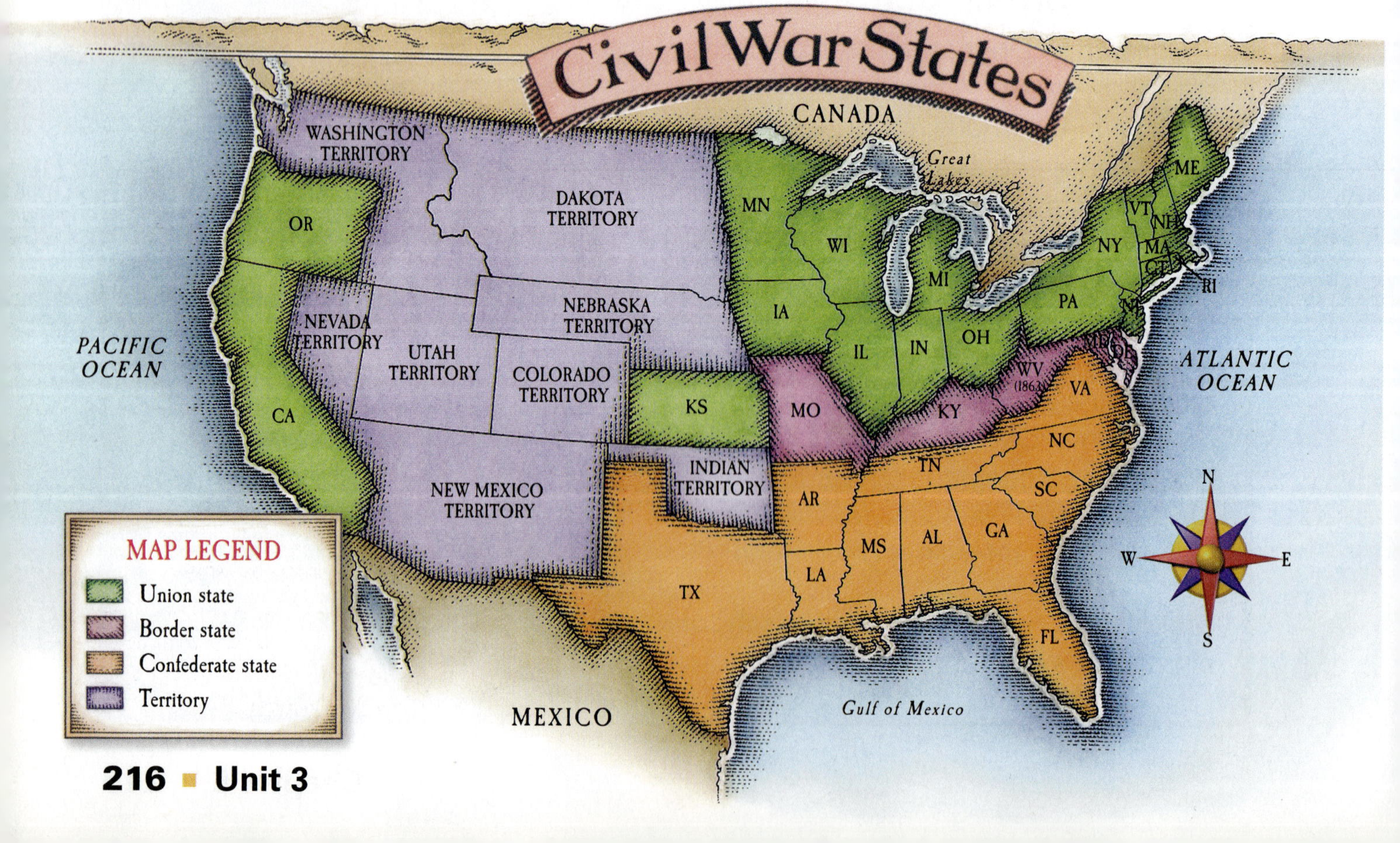

Civil War States

MAP LEGEND
- Union state
- Border state
- Confederate state
- Territory

216 ■ Unit 3

▶ Abraham Lincoln (center) meets with Northern troops during the Civil War.

Abraham Lincoln

The Southern states started their own country, the Confederate States of America. Abraham Lincoln, President of the United States, felt strongly that the country should stay together.

Lincoln also felt that slavery should not be allowed in new territories. A **territory** is land that belongs to a government but is not a state or a colony. In 1863, Lincoln signed the Emancipation Proclamation. This called for many enslaved people in the Confederate states to be free.

The Civil War ended in 1865. The Thirteenth Amendment to the Constitution was soon passed. An **amendment** is a change to something that is already written. This amendment made slavery against the law.

▶ Lincoln gave the Gettysburg Address speech to honor soldiers who had died in a famous battle.

Reading Check **Cause and Effect**
What was an effect of the Civil War?

Chapter 6 ■ 217

Growing into Today's World

After the Civil War ended, the United States continued to grow and change. Communities were affected by changes in transportation, technology, and population.

From Ocean to Ocean

By 1869, railroads starting on the east coast had connected with those from the west coast. All across the country, new routes for travel were built. This opened up more areas to settle.

Ships carried more immigrants to the United States. **Immigrants** come to live in a country from somewhere else in the world. Today, immigrants still move to the United States.

By 1959, Hawaii and Alaska had become states. In less than 200 years, the United States had grown from a small nation of 13 states to a large nation of 50 states.

▶ An airplane flies above San Diego, California.

Space Exploration

In the 1960s, the people of the United States began exploring another new area—space. Astronauts Neil Armstrong and Edwin Aldrin walked on the moon in 1969. Today, nations work together to explore space.

Reading Check **Summarize**
What changes happened after the Civil War?

Summary The settling of the West and the Civil War changed the United States. Changes are still taking place today.

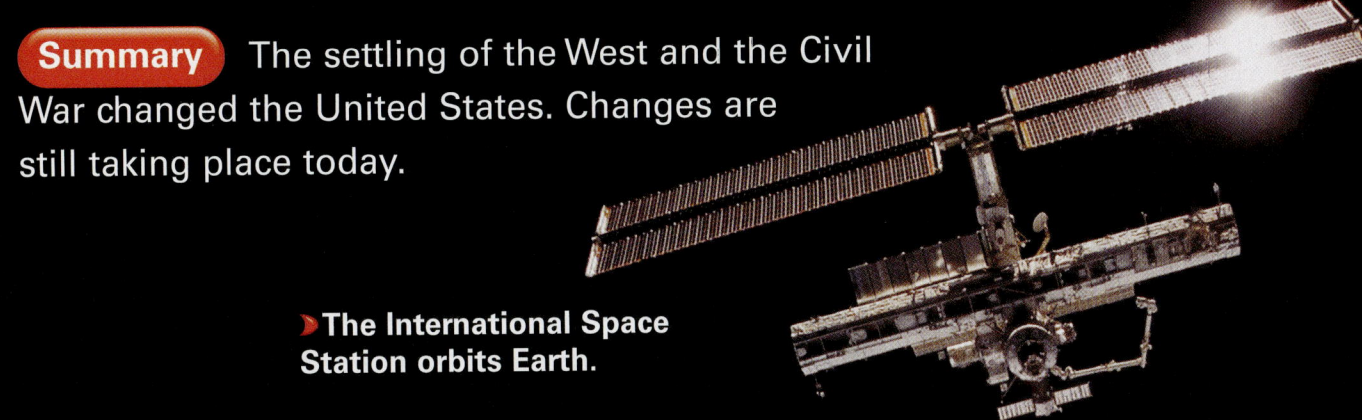

▶ The International Space Station orbits Earth.

Review

1. **What to Know** How did the United States grow and change?
2. **Vocabulary** Use the term **civil war** in a sentence.
3. **Culture** How was pioneer life different from the life of people who did not move west?
4. **Critical Thinking** How might the United States be different if the Lousiana Purchase had not happened?
5. **Write a Journal Entry** Imagine you are a pioneer. Write a journal entry telling about your journey west.
6. **Sequence** On a separate sheet of paper, copy and complete the graphic organizer below.

Chapter 6 ■ 219

Map and Globe Skills

Compare History Maps

Why It Matters Comparing maps that show the same area at different times helps you see how the area has changed. It also helps you see what has stayed the same.

Learn

A **history map** shows what a place looked like at an earlier time. The maps on page 221 show the United States at two different times. The first shows the United States just before the Louisiana Purchase, in 1803. The other shows the United States in 1903.

Practice

Look at the map keys to see what each color, line, and label shows. Then use the maps to answer these questions.

1. What river marked the western border of the United States before the Louisiana Purchase?
2. How many more states did the United States have in 1903 than it had in 1803?

Apply

Make It Relevant Compare an old map and a new map of your community. What has changed? What has stayed the same?

▶ This telescope was owned by Meriwether Lewis.

 For online activities, go to www.harcourtschool.com/ss1

Primary Sources

The Corps of Discovery

Background In 1804, Lewis and Clark left their camp near St. Louis, Missouri, to make their historic journey west. Their trip through the Louisiana Purchase to the Pacific Ocean lasted more than two years.

DBQ Document-Based Questions Study these primary sources, and answer the questions.

Map

Lewis and Clark drew this map during their journey.

DBQ 1 Why do some areas of the map have few details?

Sewing Kit

Lewis and Clark's team used sewing kits to sew tents and sheets and to take care of rips in their clothing.

sewing needle

DBQ 2 Why would a sewing kit be necessary on the journey?

A Nootka Hat

Lewis and Clark collected this wicker hat from Native Americans near the Columbia River.

Captain Clark's Journal

Captain Clark recorded daily adventures in his journal.

DBQ ⑤ What might Clark's notes tell about the land he saw?

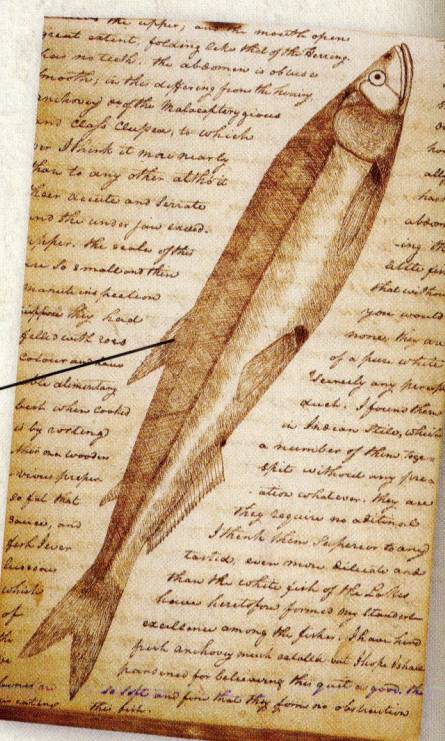

Clark illustrated his journal with drawings.

DBQ ③ Why would the explorers want to take back Native American crafts?

Peace Medal

Lewis and Clark gave peace medals and other gifts to the Native Americans.

DBQ ④ Why does the peace medal show a picture of Thomas Jefferson?

Thomas Jefferson

WRITE ABOUT IT

What do these primary sources tell you about the journey?

GO ONLINE For more resources, go to www.harcourtschool.com/ss1

Explore Your Community's History

In this unit, you read about the history of the United States and many of its different communities. You can also explore the past of your own community. These steps explain how to answer the following question.

What was my community like long ago?

STEP 1 Use your community's resources, such as the Internet or newspaper, to find what historic sites are near your town.

STEP 2 Make a list of the historic sites in your community.

STEP 3 Discuss what they have in common.

STEP 4 Choose a historic site that interests you most. Find out more about it, and then share your findings with a partner.

Use Your Community's Resources

- Libraries
- Museums
- Historical Societies
- Historic Sites

Your Community's Resources

Make a Community Time Line

Make a pictorial time line about your community. Start the time line with the date of when your community was founded. Under the date, place a picture of who founded your community. List and illustrate other important events on your time line.

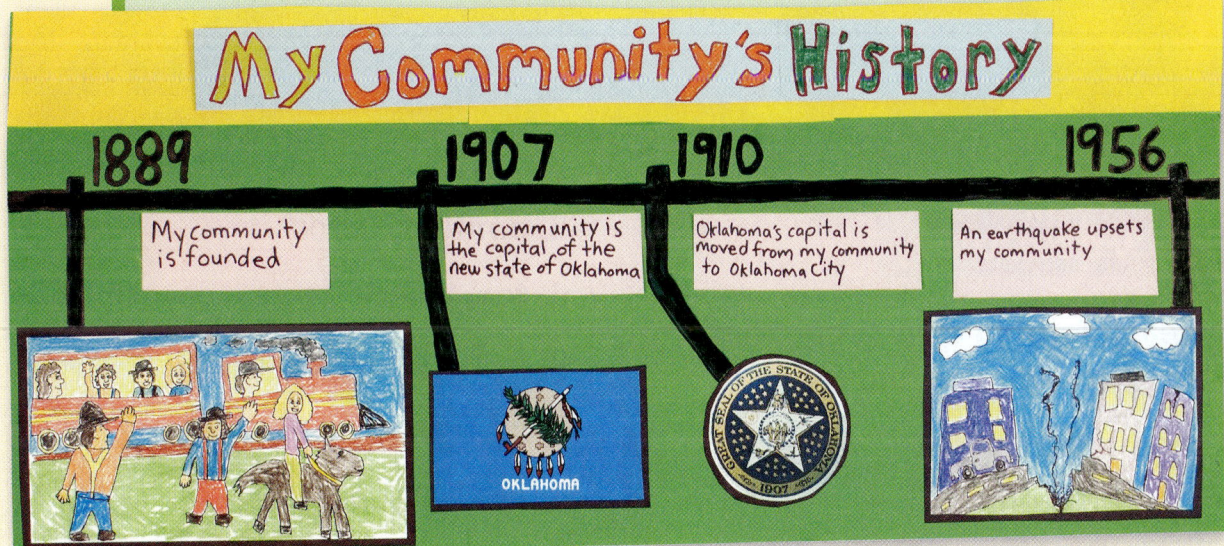

Chapter 6 Review

Visual Summary

Time

1400

1492 Christopher Columbus reaches North America

1600

1620 Pilgrims found Plymouth in Massachusetts

Summarize the Chapter

Sequence Complete the graphic organizer to show you understand the sequence of events in the chapter.

First
Native Americans formed North America's first communities.

Next

Last
The Louisiana Purchase more than doubled the size of the United States.

Vocabulary

Use each term in a sentence that tells the meaning of the term.

1. **oral history**, p. 190
2. **shelter**, p. 191
3. **explorer**, p. 196
4. **settlement**, p. 197
5. **conflict**, p. 200
6. **tax**, p. 205
7. **independence**, p. 206
8. **civil war**, p. 216
9. **territory**, p. 217
10. **immigrant**, p. 218

226 ■ Unit 3

1800

1776 The Declaration of Independence is approved

1861 Civil War begins

1969 Astronauts Neil Armstrong and Edwin Aldrin walk on moon

 **Present**

Facts and Main Ideas

Answer these questions.

11. What happened during the Boston Tea Party?

12. Why did pioneers move west in the 1800s?

13. What was the Emancipation Proclamation?

Write the letter of the best choice.

14. Who were the very first people to live in North America?
    A the Spanish
    B the French
    C the Pilgrims
    D the Native Americans

15. What is the oldest lasting European settlement in what is now the United States?
    A Jamestown, Virginia
    B St. Louis, Missouri
    C St. Augustine, Florida
    D Plymouth, Massachusetts

Critical Thinking

16. Why do you think St. Louis, Missouri, grew between 1763 and the 1800s?

17. **Make It Relevant** What do you think our country would be like without the Constitution?

Skills

Compare Historical Maps
Use the map on page 221 to answer the question.

18. In 1803, which country claimed the land that later became the Arizona Territory?

writing

Write a Speech Imagine that you live in one of Britain's 13 colonies. Write a speech persuading other colonists to join you in the fight for freedom.

Write a Log Entry Imagine that you are Lewis or Clark. Write a log entry about a day in your travels.

Chapter 6 ■ 227

Fill It In

 **VOCABULARY**

What's the word? Add the missing letters.

Clue	Word
10 decades	_ e _ t _ r y
what every citizen has	_ _ g h t s
very old	_ n c i e n _
likes to build things	e n _ i n e _ r
makes life easier	_ e c _ n o l o _ y
the government of ancient Greece	_ e _ o c r _ c y

Which Came First?

Which object in each pair was invented first?

 or

 or

 or

People Tic-Tac-Toe

Play Explorers and Inventors Tic-Tac-Toe. Find three people in a row who were either explorers or inventors.

 Wright Brothers	 William Clark	 Sacagawea
 Meriwether Lewis	 Neil Armstrong	 Elisha Otis
 Alexander Graham Bell	 Juan Ponce de León	 Henry Ford

Online Adventures GO ONLINE

Eco is on a field trip to the time museum, but something is wrong. The different times and places have become all mixed up! If you and Eco can't solve the mystery in this online game, the past might never be the same again. Play now at www.harcourtschool.com/ss1

Unit 3 Review and Test Prep

The Big Idea

History Every community has a unique history. Some features of a community change, while others stay the same, over time.

Reading Comprehension and Vocabulary

Communities Over Time

All communities have different histories. People change communities by sharing ideas and inventions. Inventions have changed the way people live. Communities are also changed by ideas such as democracy and civil rights.

Our nation's first communities were formed by Native Americans. Then, European explorers and settlers built new communities in North America. Later, colonists in Britain's 13 colonies fought for their freedom. Today, communities in the United States continue to grow.

Read the summary above. Then answer the questions that follow.

1. Which of the following has not changed communities?
   A inventions
   B automobilies
   C continuity
   D ideas

2. What are civil rights?
   A ancient ideas
   B equal treatment under the law
   C inventions
   D community events

3. What is an explorer?
   A a person who goes to find out about a place
   B a pioneer
   C a person who fights for independence
   D an inventor

4. What did the colonists fight for in the Revolutionary War?
   A new inventions
   B continuity
   C new ideas
   D freedom

Facts and Main Ideas

Answer these questions.

5. What inventions for the home have changed the way people live?

6. How did the Native Americans get food?

7. Who was President of the United States during the Civil War?

Write the letter of the best choice.

8. How did George Stephenson change communities?
   A He worked for civil rights.
   B He voted for women's suffrage.
   C He wrote slogans.
   D He developed a train engine.

9. How did John Smith help the settlers in Jamestown?
   A He disagreed with Native Americans.
   B He brought enslaved people to Jamestown.
   C He traded with Native Americans to get food.
   D He agreed with John Rolfe.

10. Which of the following describes an American soldier in the Revolutionary War?
    A well trained
    B received supplies from Britain
    C not well trained
    D did not want to help

 Critical Thinking

11. What might have happened if Sacagawea had not helped Lewis and Clark?

12. **Make It Relevant** How might your community change?

 Skills

Compare Historical Maps

Use the maps below to answer the following question.

13. What do these maps show about how Frankfort has changed?

Unit 3 • 231

Unit 3 Activities

Show What You Know

 ### Unit Writing Activity

Write a Journal Entry Imagine visiting your community in 100 years. Write a journal entry to describe your experience.
- Explain what has changed.
- Tell which features of your community have stayed the same and why.

 ### Unit Project

Community History Scrapbook Make a scrapbook of your community's history.
- Research your community.
- Write short reports about events in your town's past.
- Add the reports and visuals to a scrapbook.

Read More

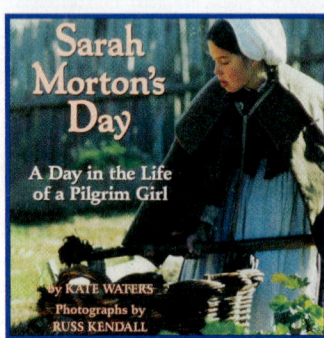
- *Sarah Morton's Day: A Day in the Life of a Pilgrim Girl* by Kate Waters. Scholastic Paperbacks.

- *My Brother Martin* by Christine King Farris. Simon & Schuster Children's Publishing.

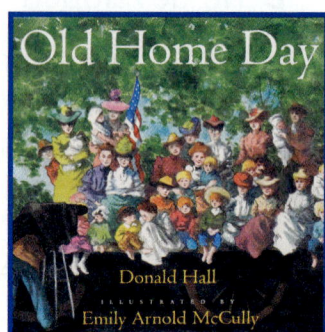
- *Old Home Day* by Donald Hall. Browndeer Press.

GO ONLINE For more resources, go to www.harcourtschool.com/ss1

Citizens and Government

Unit 4

Start with the Standards

OHIO SOCIAL STUDIES CONTENT STANDARDS

History 3.3E, 3.3I

Geography 3.1

Government 3.1A, 3.1B, 3.1C, 3.1D, 3.1E, 3.2, 3.3, 3.4, 3.5, 3.6

Citizenship 3.1A, 3.1B, 3.1C, 3.1D, 3.1E, 3.2A, 3.2B, 3.2C, 3.2D, 3.2E, 3.2G, 3.3A, 3.3B, 3.3C, 3.3D, 3.3E

Social Studies Skills 3.1A, 3.1F, 3.1G, 3.6B, 3.6C, 3.6D, 3.6E

The Big Idea

Government
Communities depend on citizens to participate in their government.

What to Know
- ✓ What are our rights?
- ✓ What are our responsibilities?
- ✓ What are the three branches and levels of our government?
- ✓ How do other world communities govern their people?

Local Government in Ohio

Did You Know?

Ohio has 255 cities and 694 villages.

Every community in Ohio has a government. Counties, townships, cities, and villages each have their own governments. Each level of government has its own responsibilities.

Ohio is divided into 88 counties. Most counties are governed by three county commissioners. They meet in the county seat, the city where the main offices of the county government are located. The commissioners make laws and collect taxes. County governments also provide services, such as hospitals, libraries, and courthouses.

OH 233A ■ Ohio Connection

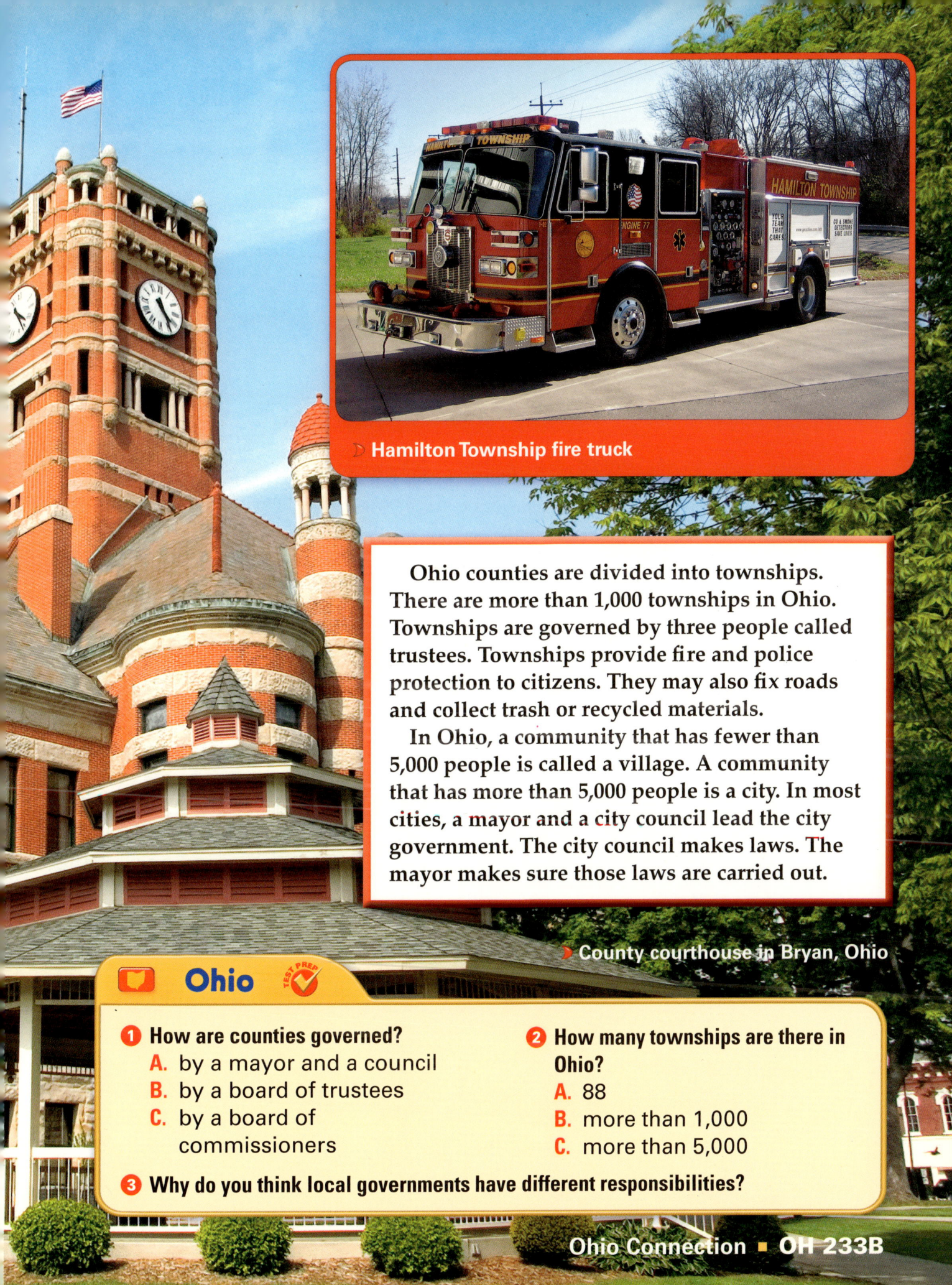

▶ Hamilton Township fire truck

Ohio counties are divided into townships. There are more than 1,000 townships in Ohio. Townships are governed by three people called trustees. Townships provide fire and police protection to citizens. They may also fix roads and collect trash or recycled materials.

In Ohio, a community that has fewer than 5,000 people is called a village. A community that has more than 5,000 people is a city. In most cities, a mayor and a city council lead the city government. The city council makes laws. The mayor makes sure those laws are carried out.

▶ County courthouse in Bryan, Ohio

Ohio TEST PREP

1 How are counties governed?
  A. by a mayor and a council
  B. by a board of trustees
  C. by a board of commissioners

2 How many townships are there in Ohio?
  A. 88
  B. more than 1,000
  C. more than 5,000

3 Why do you think local governments have different responsibilities?

Ohio Connection ■ OH 233B

Unit 4

People

Talk About
People and Government

**Francis Scott Key
1779–1843**
American lawyer who wrote "The Star-Spangled Banner"

Unit 4 Preview
Vocabulary

election A time set aside for voting. (page 246)

volunteer A person who chooses to work without getting paid. (page 251)

government service Work that is done by the government for everyone in a city or town, state, or country. (page 267)

patriotic symbol Something that stands for the ideas in which people believe. (page 290)

monument Something built to honor a person or event. (page 292)

For more resources, go to www.harcourtschool.com/ss1

Start with an Article

Becoming a Citizen—Just Like Me

As told to Diane Hoyt-Goldsmith
by Shaddai Aguas Suarez
photographs by Lawrence Migdale

Shaddai was born in the United States. That makes her a citizen of this country. This is the story of how Shaddai's father earns his citizenship.

Usually it's the grown-ups who do things first. Even though I'm just a kid, I became a citizen of the United States long before my parents did. My parents were born in Jalisco, Mexico. They both immigrated to the United States when they were just teenagers.

My dad was a student and wanted to become a lawyer. At that time, however, there was no opportunity for him in Mexico. He couldn't afford to pay for college or buy books. My father decided to move to the United States, where he could follow his dreams.

❯ Shaddai and her brother help their mother prepare dinner.

▶ Shaddai's father still likes to fish, just as he did as a boy in Mexico. He likes to take Shaddai with him.

▶ Shaddai's father has his own gardening business. He helps people plant flowers and take care of their lawns.

My mother is the eldest of eleven children. Her mother was struggling to raise the family on her own. So my mother came to the United States to find a good job. That way she could send money back to her family in Mexico.

My father tells me that it was very hard to leave his family and move to a new country. He went to Santa Barbara, California, where he found work. On the job, my father learned how to grow and care for roses. Even though he often felt sad and homesick, my father worked very hard.

My father could speak only Spanish when he came to the United States. He knew he had to learn English in order to succeed. Each night after work, my father went to an ESL class. ESL means "English as a second language." For eight months he studied. Finally he learned enough to begin speaking English.

My parents met in Santa Barbara and soon they were married. My brother came along first, and I was born a few years later. It wasn't until I started going to school that my father decided to become a citizen.

For him, becoming a citizen was hard work. My father had to study the history of the United States. He had to learn about the Constitution and the Bill of Rights. He also had to learn to say the Pledge of Allegiance. After he had learned it, he was so proud.

Soon it was time for my father to take the Citizenship Test. No one was surprised when my father passed.

Then came a special ceremony. On that happy day, in the company of more than a thousand other immigrants, my father was sworn in as a citizen of the United States. Everyone received a special Citizenship certificate.

❯ A friend helped Shaddai's father study for the Citizenship Test.

❯ After studying for many months, Shaddai's father was ready to take the Citizenship Test.

▶ Shaddai's father likes to play soccer on the weekends—and the whole family likes to watch.

Each year on September 17, my family celebrates Citizenship Day. My father knows that on this date in 1787, the Constitution was signed.

He reminds us that we have reasons to be thankful. My father says, "This country has given us everything we have—our home, our jobs, and the chance to build a good life. This country is a place where anyone has the chance to succeed—no matter what his or her race or religion or background might be."

Response Corner

1. **Summarize** How did Shaddai's father become a citizen of the United States?

2. **Make It Relevant** Describe some ways people at your school help new students from other countries. How have you helped your new friends?

Unit 4 ■ 241

Study Skills

USE A K-W-L CHART

A K-W-L chart helps you identify what you know and what you want to learn.

- Use the *K* column to list what you know about a topic.
- Use the *W* column to list what you want to know.
- Use the *L* column to list what you learned after reading.

Citizenship

What I Know	What I Want to Know	What I Learned
Communities have rules and laws.	How do laws help citizens? Why is it important to follow laws?	

PREVIEW VOCABULARY

responsibility p. 248

jury p. 248

hero p. 257

Citizenship

CHAPTER 7

Students hold a 15-star American flag and learn about the history of Fort McHenry, Maryland.

Lesson 1

Rights of Citizens

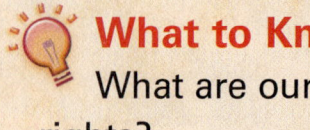
What to Know
What are our rights?

Vocabulary
elect p. 246
election p. 246
ballot p. 246
majority rule p. 247
minority rights p. 247

Summarize
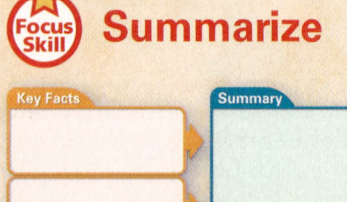

Every citizen of the United States has certain rights, or freedoms. Some of these rights are named in the first ten amendments to the Constitution. Together, these amendments are called the Bill of Rights. The Bill of Rights was added to the Constitution to keep people's rights safe.

The Bill of Rights

The Bill of Rights lists the basic rights that belong to all citizens of the United States. These rights cannot be taken away by the government. Respecting the rights of others is an important part of being a good citizen.

▶ The Constitution is on display in Washington, D.C.

Some Basic Rights

Freedom of speech is one of our basic rights. It allows citizens to speak in public about their ideas and beliefs. This right protects people who say good or bad things about their government.

Another right is the freedom to gather peacefully in a group. This is called freedom of assembly. People who share the same opinion can assemble, or get together.

Citizens can share their opinions in the media. Media include newspapers, radio, television, and film. Freedom of the press allows people to write, read, and watch what they want.

All citizens are free to practice any religion, too. This is called freedom of religion.

> The Bill of Rights

Reading Check **Summarize**
What are some basic rights of all Americans?

Diagram Which right allows you to read whatever you want?

Freedom of Speech

Freedom of Religion

Freedom of Assembly

Freedom of the Press

Some Basic Rights

Chapter 7 ■ 245

Citizens Make Choices

Citizens also have the right to vote for their leaders. Voting allows them to help make choices in their government. To vote, people must be at least 18 years old. They must also meet any other requirements their state may have.

By voting, citizens help **elect**, or choose, their government's leaders. Many go to special voting places on the day of an election. An **election** is a time set aside for voting. Voters mark their choice on a paper ballot or on a ballot shown on a voting machine. A **ballot** lists all the possible choices in an election.

Each citizen's vote in an election is kept secret. Only the results are announced. This way, people can vote without worrying about what other people may think of their choices.

> Voters must register, or sign up, to vote.

> At a voting booth, people can make their choice without anyone seeing it.

Majority Rule and Minority Rights

When more than half of the voters vote in the same way, they are the majority. In **majority rule**, these people rule, or get what they want.

The voters who did not vote for the winner are the minority. However, the Constitution protects the rights of the people in the minority. This idea is called **minority rights**. It helps keep people from being mistreated.

Reading Check ⭕ **Summarize**
How do citizens choose their government leaders?

▶ Voters do not put their names on their ballots.

Summary Citizens of the United States have rights. Some of these rights are listed in the Bill of Rights. Citizens use their right to vote to choose their government's leaders.

Review

1. **What to Know** What are our rights?
2. **Vocabulary** Use the term **ballot** in a sentence about an **election**.
3. **Civics and Government** When might people use their freedom of assembly?
4. **Critical Thinking Make It Relevant** How can people use their freedom of speech? What does freedom of speech mean to you?
5. **Write a Speech** Write a speech that tells about the rights of United States citizens.
6. **Summarize** On a separate sheet of paper, copy and complete the graphic organizer below.

Chapter 7 ■ 247

Lesson 2

Duties of Citizens

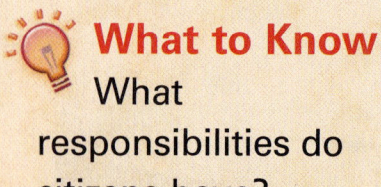

What to Know
What responsibilities do citizens have?

Vocabulary
responsibility p. 248
jury p. 248
consequence p. 249
common good p. 250
volunteer p. 251

Summarize

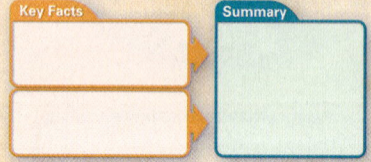

For every right, there is a responsibility. A **responsibility** is a duty, or something a person must do because it is necessary or important. Voting, for example, is both a right and a responsibility.

Our Responsibilities

Citizens of the United States have many responsibilities. They have a responsibility to obey laws and to settle differences peacefully. They also have to pay taxes and to serve on a jury. A **jury** is a group of people who meet to decide whether a person has broken a law.

> Voters have a responsibility to learn about the people trying to be elected.

248 • Unit 4

▶ A jury has a responsibility to make careful decisions.

People who break laws face consequences. A **consequence** (KAHN•suh•kwens) is something that happens because of what a person does.

If someone breaks a traffic law, one of the consequences may be an accident. A person who breaks any law may have to pay a fine or go to jail.

Knowing Limits

Citizens need to know the limits to their rights. For example, we have the right to gather in groups, but we must do so peacefully. We have the right to share our opinions, but we should also respect other people's opinions.

Reading Check ⭕ Summarize
What are some responsibilities citizens have?

▶ One consequence of breaking a traffic law is paying a fine.

Chapter 7 ■ 249

Serving Your Community

Some responsibilities, such as paying taxes and serving on a jury, are the law. Other responsibilities are not required by law but are still important. One responsibility of being a citizen is to work for the **common good**—the good of everyone in a community.

Wheaton, Illinois

People in communities help one another every day. Helping others is one way to work for the common good.

The community of Wheaton, Illinois, helped one of its citizens. Joel Gomez was hurt while fighting in the war in Iraq. He could no longer move his body and had to use a wheelchair.

> **Volunteers help build a house for Joel Gomez in Wheaton, Illinois.**

A group of volunteers worked together to build Joel Gomez a new house. **Volunteers** are people who choose to work without getting paid. Gomez's new house had technology that would help him live a better life.

Volunteers from more than 50 groups in Wheaton helped in other ways. School groups and firefighters held events to raise money for Gomez. One citizen even bought him a special van.

Reading Check **Summarize**
How can citizens work for the common good?

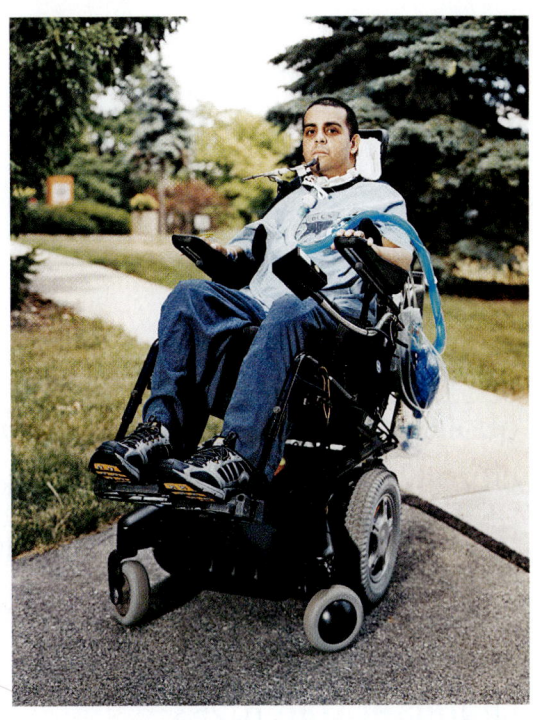

▶ Joel Gomez

Summary Citizens have many responsibilities. These include paying taxes, obeying laws, and helping others.

Review

1. **What to Know** What responsibilities do citizens have?
2. **Vocabulary** Use the terms **responsibility** and **jury** in a sentence.
3. **Civics and Government** What responsibilities do voters have?
4. **Critical Thinking Make It Relevant** What responsibilities do you have in your community?
5. **Write a Report** Write a short report that tells how to be a responsible citizen.
6. **Summarize** On a separate sheet of paper, copy and complete the graphic organizer below.

Chapter 7 ■ 251

Lesson 3

Being a Good Citizen

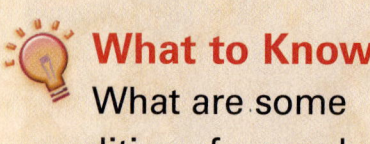

What to Know
What are some qualities of a good citizen?

Vocabulary
cooperate p. 252
character trait p. 253
justice p. 253
boycott p. 255
hero p. 257

Summarize

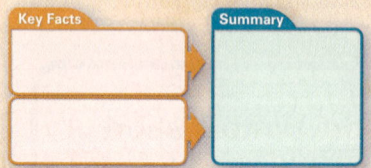

What does it take to be a good citizen? Good citizens take action. They **cooperate** (koh•AH•puh•rayt), or work together, for the good of the community. They try to make the community a better place for everyone.

What Is a Good Citizen?

Good citizens follow the laws of the nation, the state, and the community. They speak out against laws that they think are unfair. They pay taxes and take part in the government by voting. Good citizens also show respect for themselves and for the people around them.

▶ Cooperating with classmates is one way to be a good citizen.

252 ▪ Unit 4

> Students in Kentucky made these posters to support Kentucky's Adopt-A-Highway program.

Being Good Citizens

Students are being good citizens when they show respect for their classmates and teachers. They follow rules, do their best work, and take part in class activities.

Good citizens often show helpful character traits. A **character trait** is a quality that a person has, such as responsibility, trustworthiness, respect, fairness, patriotism, and caring. Helpful character traits usually make good citizenship traits, too.

Some citizens become leaders and bring big changes to people's lives. Others work with their neighbors to solve problems. They show a belief in **justice**, or fairness, for everyone.

Reading Check ⭐ **Summarize**
How would you describe a good citizen?

▶ Jimmy Carter and Rosalynn, his wife, help build homes for Habitat for Humanity.

▶ Jimmy Carter received the Nobel Peace Prize in 2002.

Jimmy Carter

Jimmy Carter was once President of the United States. Now he works for peace in countries around the world. He helps nations that disagree solve their problems peacefully. In 2002, Carter was awarded the Nobel Peace Prize for his work.

Carter also volunteers for Habitat for Humanity. This is a group that builds homes for people who cannot pay for them. Volunteers like Jimmy Carter give their time and effort for free. They feel a responsibility to help other people.

Reading Check ⓢ **Summarize**
How is Jimmy Carter a good citizen?

Rosa Parks

Rosa Parks wanted to change laws that were unfair to African Americans. In some places in the 1950s, African Americans had to sit in the back of public buses. They could sit in the middle only if the seats were not needed for white people.

In 1955, Parks was sitting in a middle seat of a bus in Montgomery, Alabama. When the bus filled up, Parks refused to give up her seat. The driver called the police, and she was arrested.

Parks and other African Americans in Montgomery had been planning a bus boycott. During a **boycott**, people refuse to buy or use something. After Parks was arrested, many people refused to ride the bus. Their boycott caused the bus company to lose money. After almost a year, the law was changed.

Reading Check **Summarize**
How did Rosa Parks help her community?

▶ Rosa Parks worked for justice.

▶ The bus on which Rosa Parks refused to give up her seat is now in a museum.

> Dolores Huerta worked with Cesar Chavez to form the National Farm Workers Association.

Dolores Huerta

As a teacher, Dolores Huerta saw her students come to school hungry and poorly dressed. She decided to help them by helping their parents. The parents were mostly farmworkers from Mexico and other countries. The families traveled all over the United States to find work picking fruits and vegetables.

Because many of the farmworkers were not United States citizens, they did not have many rights. Huerta started classes to teach the workers how to become citizens and how to vote. Later, she helped them earn more money so they could buy the food and clothing they needed.

Reading Check ⚛ **Summarize**
How did Dolores Huerta help farmworkers?

Everyday Heroes

Many people in a community show that they care by being everyday heroes. A **hero** is a person who does something important and sets an example for others. Some everyday heroes in your community may be parents, firefighters, police officers, teachers, and volunteers.

Reading Check ⭕ **Summarize**
What is an everyday hero?

Summary Good citizens are responsible, caring, and fair. They work to help people in their community. They may be community leaders or act as everyday heroes.

Fast Fact

Ryan Hreljac learned at the age of six that some people did not have clean water. That year, Ryan raised $70 to build a well in Africa. He kept working and has now raised more than 1 million dollars. Ryan is shown here with his adopted brother, Jimmy.

Review

1. **What to Know** What are some qualities of a good citizen?
2. **Vocabulary** Write a short description of a **character trait**.
3. **Your Community** Who are some of the everyday heroes in your community?
4. **Critical Thinking Make It Relevant** What are some ways you can be a good citizen?
5. **Make a Poster** Make a poster about justice and respect.
6. **Summarize** On a separate sheet of paper, copy and complete the graphic organizer below.

Key Facts → Summary: A good citizen takes action to help the community.

Chapter 7 ■ 257

Biography

Trustworthiness
Respect
Responsibility
Fairness
Caring
Patriotism

Cesar Chavez

Why Character Counts

✏️ How did Cesar Chavez work for fairness for migrant field workers?

"My motivation comes from my personal life—from watching what my mother and father went through when I was growing up."

— Cesar Chavez, 1984

When Cesar Chavez was born in 1927, his family was facing hard times. The family members were migrant, or traveling, workers. They worked mostly with other Mexican Americans, picking grapes, beans, carrots, and lettuce.

Field work is seasonal. Workers are needed only at different times and places. Like other migrant workers, the Chavez family was always traveling around California and Arizona for work.

Cesar Chavez

Cesar Chavez talks to farm workers in Salinas, California.

Buttons and patches like these were worn by Cesar Chavez supporters.

As an adult, Chavez never forgot his family's hardships. In 1958, he became the national director of the Community Service Organization. This group worked to gain civil rights for Hispanic Americans. In 1962, Chavez helped form the National Farm Workers Association. This group worked for higher pay and a better work environment for migrant farmers.

Chavez did not believe in violence. He organized peaceful actions to help the workers. He held public hunger strikes in which he did not eat for many days. These hunger strikes brought attention to the lives of the workers.

Cesar Chavez died in 1993. More than 50,000 people came to his funeral. In 1994, former President Bill Clinton honored him with the Medal of Freedom.

 For more resources, go to www.harcourtschool.com/ss1

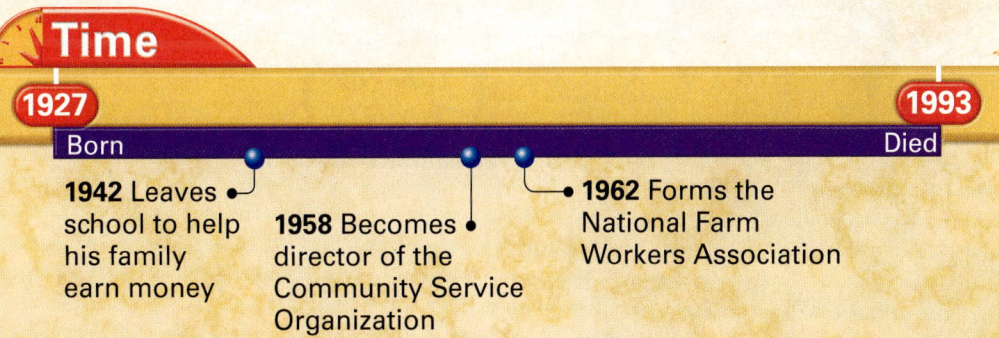

Time

- **1927** Born
- **1942** Leaves school to help his family earn money
- **1958** Becomes director of the Community Service Organization
- **1962** Forms the National Farm Workers Association
- **1993** Died

Chapter 7 ■ 259

Critical Thinking Skills

Make a Thoughtful Decision

Why It Matters Thinking about consequences can help you make the best choice.

❯ Learn

A choice is also called a **decision**. Follow these steps to make a thoughtful decision.

Step 1 List the choices.

Step 2 Gather all the information you need.

Step 3 Think about the consequences of each choice.

Step 4 Decide which choice will have the best consequences.

Step 5 Make a choice, and act on it.

▶ Practice

Miguel makes a chart to help him decide what to do with his free time. He wants to volunteer at an animal shelter, but he also wants to play with his friends. He uses the steps in this lesson to make a thoughtful decision.

1. What are Miguel's choices?
2. What information does he need?
3. What consequences will each choice have?
4. Which choice do you think Miguel should make?

▶ Apply

Make It Relevant Think about a decision you have made recently. Make a chart like Miguel's to show the choices and consequences you faced.

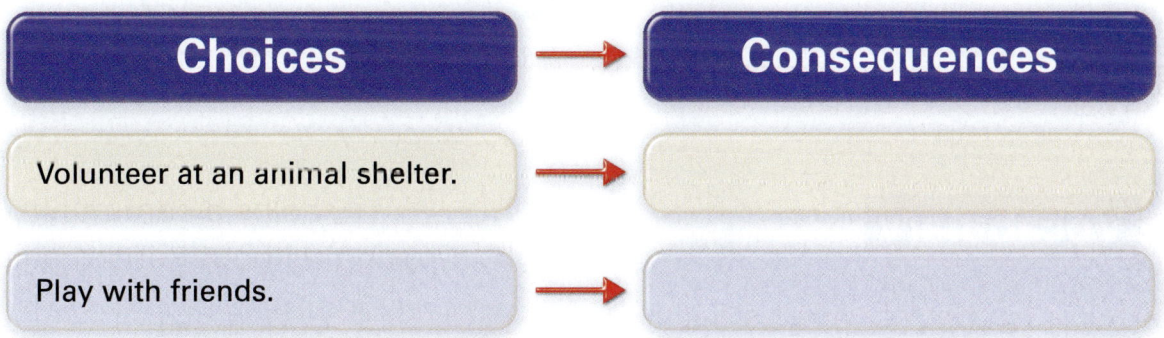

Chapter 7 Review

Visual Summary

Citizens of the United States have rights.

Summarize the Chapter

Summarize Complete the graphic organizer to show what you have learned about being a citizen.

Key Facts

Citizens have rights, including freedom of religion and the right to vote.

Responsibilities include voting and obeying laws.

Summary

Vocabulary

Write the term that completes each sentence.

1. People vote for a leader in a(n) _____.

    election, p. 246   **ballot**, p. 246

2. There are _____ when someone breaks a law.

    responsibilities, p. 248

    consequences, p. 249

3. A _____ helps a community by working without getting paid.

    common good, p. 250

    volunteer, p. 251

4. Respect is a _____.

    character trait, p. 253

    hero, p. 257

262 ■ Unit 4

 Citizens of the United States have responsibilities.

 Good citizens work to improve their community.

 ## Facts and Main Ideas

Answer these questions.

5. What does freedom of speech allow citizens to do?
6. How is voting a responsibility?
7. How can students be good citizens?

Write the letter of the best choice.

8. Which responsibility is required by law?
   A working for the common good
   B voting in elections
   C paying taxes
   D volunteering

9. How did Dolores Huerta work for the common good?
   A She solved conflicts in other nations.
   B She helped farmworkers become citizens.
   C She boycotted buses.
   D She served as United States President.

 ## Critical Thinking

10. **Make It Relevant** How can you show a belief in justice in your daily life?
11. Why is it important to know the limits to your rights?

 ## Skills

Make a Thoughtful Decision
Use the steps on page 260 to answer the question.

12. What do you do after you decide which choice will have the best consequences?

writing

Write an Article Write an article comparing your responsibilities at home, at school, and in your community.

Write a Brochure Create a brochure informing people about their freedoms of the press, assembly, speech, and religion.

Study Skills

SKIM AND SCAN

Skimming and scanning are two ways to learn from what you read.

- **To skim, read lesson and section titles to identify main ideas. Look at the pictures, and read the captions.**
- **To scan, look for key words or facts.**

Skim	Scan
Lesson: Workings of Government	**Key Words and Facts** • There are three levels of government—local, state, and national. • _____ • _____
Main Idea: Voters elect leaders to all three levels of government.	
Titles/Headings: • The Levels of Government • _____	

PREVIEW VOCABULARY

council p. 273

mayor p. 273

court p. 275

CHAPTER 8

Government

> The State capitol building in Oklahoma City, Oklahoma

Lesson 1

Structure of Government

What to Know
What are the three levels and three branches of our government?

Vocabulary
authority p. 266
government service p. 267
legislative p. 268
executive p. 268
judicial p. 268

Summarize

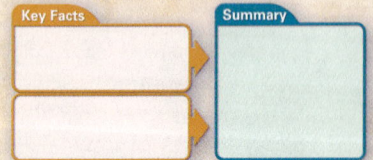

The Constitution is the plan of government for the United States. That plan is based on the idea that government gets its **authority**, or power, from the people. By voting, people give government leaders the authority to make decisions and take action for them.

In the United States, voters elect leaders to run three levels of government—local, state, and national. The three levels handle different kinds of problems for areas that are different sizes.

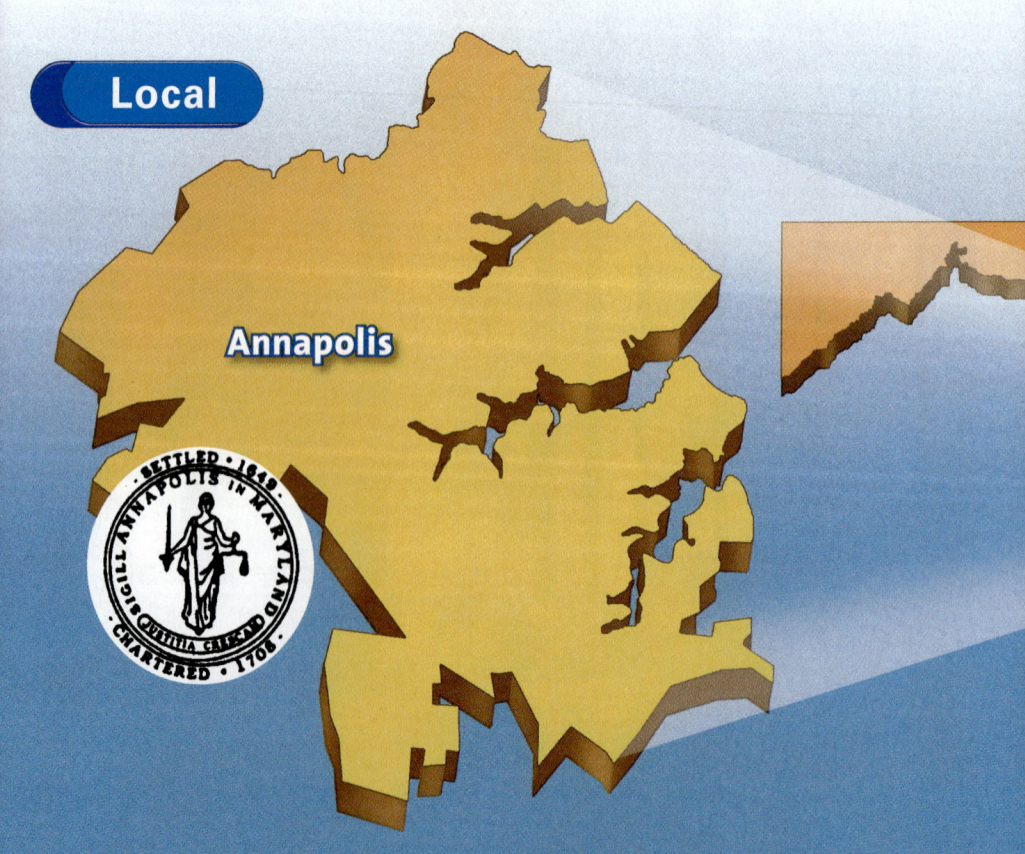

Local

Annapolis

266 • Unit 4

The Levels of Government

A local government governs just one community, such as a city or town. Each of the 50 states is run by a state government. The national government is also called the federal government. It makes laws for the whole nation. Each level of government must obey the Constitution.

Purposes of Government

All three levels of government make laws to keep people safe and to protect their rights and property. However, all three levels of government have their own responsibilities, or jobs to do. Each one provides different government services. A **government service** is work that the government does for the people in its area. People pay for these services with their taxes.

Reading Check ⚬**Summarize**
What are the three levels of government?

Levels of Government

Diagram This diagram shows the levels of government. Which level governs the city of Annapolis?

Chapter 8 ■ 267

Branches of the National Government

Legislative Branch	Executive Branch	Judicial Branch
Makes the laws	Carries out the laws	Makes sure laws are fair
U.S. Capitol Building	White House	Supreme Court Building

Chart Which branch of the United States government makes laws?

The Branches of Government

The Constitution divides the national government into three branches, or parts. The three branches are the legislative, executive, and judicial branches. These branches are separate but connected, like the branches of a tree.

Each branch of government has a different job to do. The **legislative** branch makes laws. The **executive** branch sees that the laws are obeyed. The **judicial** branch judges whether the laws are fair and based on the Constitution. The judicial branch also settles conflicts between citizens and businesses.

› The President of the United States, George W. Bush, is the leader of the executive branch.

State governments and most local governments also have three branches. The branches of the state and local levels also make laws, make sure that laws are obeyed, and judge whether laws are fair.

Reading Check **Summarize**
What are the three branches of the United States government?

> Members of Kentucky's state government talk about laws.

Summary The three levels of government are local, state, and national. Each level provides services for people in its area. Each level of government also has three branches. Each branch of government does different jobs.

Review

1. **What to Know** What are the three levels and three branches of our government?
2. **Vocabulary** What do you think each word of the vocabulary term **government service** means?
3. **Civics and Government** What document is the plan for our government?
4. **Critical Thinking** What might happen if people did not pay taxes?
5. **Make a Chart** Make a chart that shows the main job of each branch of the national government.
6. **Summarize** On a separate sheet of paper, copy and complete the graphic organizer below.

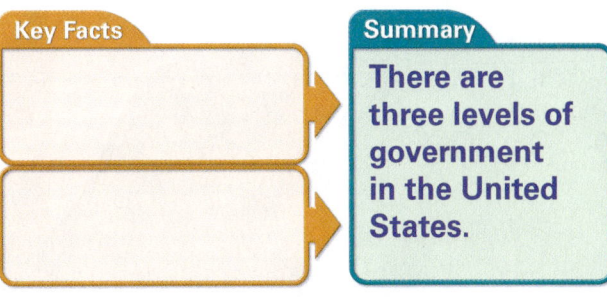

Chapter 8 ■ 269

Citizenship

Constitution Day

"[The Constitution of the United States] was not . . . the offspring [work] of a single brain. It ought to be regarded [thought of] as the work of many heads and many hands."

—James Madison

The Constitution of the United States was signed into law on September 17, 1787. This date is now celebrated as Constitution Day. The idea for the day began with a senior citizen from California, Louise Leigh. After she took a class on the Constitution, Leigh wanted people across the country to celebrate it and learn about it.

▶ James Madison, main author of the Constitution

▶ Students recite the pledge of Allegiance on Constitution Day.

Focus On: Constitutional Principles

President George W. Bush agreed that there should be a day to celebrate constitutional principles. He signed a law to officially declare September 17 as Constitution Day. Each year on this day, people get together to recite, or read aloud, the Preamble. The Preamble is the first part of the Constitution. It outlines the principles of the Constitution, such as freedom and justice.

People across the country recite the Preamble at the same time. Afterward, each state is expected to ring bells. The bells can be heard across the country.

Make It Relevant How will you celebrate Constitution Day this year?

▶ The United States Constitution

▶ A Constitution Day concert

Lesson 2 Local Governments

What to Know
What are local governments?

Vocabulary
county p. 272
council p. 273
mayor p. 273
county seat p. 274
court p. 275
recreation p. 276
public works p. 277

Summarize

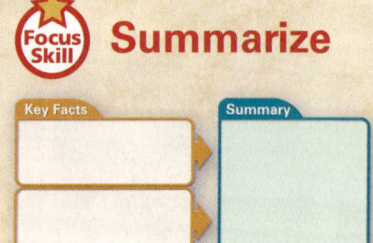

Local governments serve communities, such as cities and towns, as well as counties. A **county** is a part of a state. A county often has several towns or cities within its borders.

City and Town Government

Each city and town in a county has its own local government. In some community governments, all citizens decide things at a town meeting. In others, elected leaders meet to make decisions.

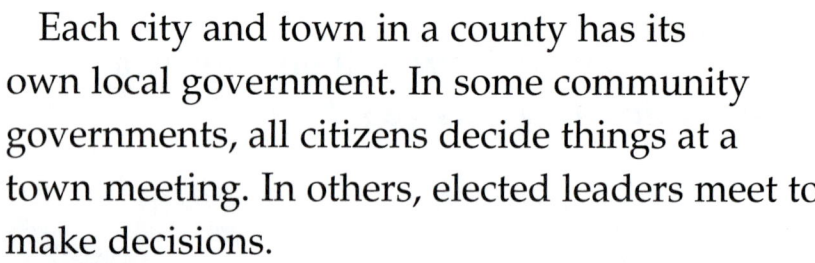

> City Hall in Columbus, Ohio, is where members of that city's government meet.

▶ A city council meeting in Columbus, Ohio

Different Local Governments

There are two main types of city government. Both include a **council**, or a group of people who meet to make laws. This is the legislative branch of local government.

In a mayor-council government, voters in a city elect the mayor and the council members. A **mayor** is the leader of a community government. He or she leads the executive branch and makes sure city laws are carried out. The council makes laws and collects taxes.

In a council-manager government, voters also elect council members. Then the council chooses one of its members to be the mayor. It also hires a city manager to help run the city. The city manager hires people to run the fire, police, and other departments.

▶ The mayor of Columbus, Michael Coleman

Reading Check ⭐ **Summarize**
What are the two main types of city government?

273

Counties of New Jersey

Map Key
- ● County seat
- ★ State capital
- — County border
- — State border

Location What is the county seat of Ocean County in New Jersey?

County Government

Most states are divided into counties. For example, New Jersey has 21 counties. Each county has its own local government.

The County Board

In New Jersey, a group of people is elected by citizens of the county to form a county board. The board members discuss problems in the county and make laws to solve them. These laws affect only the people and area of the county.

The board members meet in the county seat. A **county seat** is the city or town in which the main offices of the county government are located.

› County board members meet in Warren County, New Jersey.

274 ■ Unit 4

County Courts

County governments often have their own courts. A **court** is a place for deciding whether a person has broken a law. County courts are the judicial branch of county government.

Judges are chosen to lead courts. Judges are usually lawyers. Within certain guidelines, a judge may decide what the consequences for breaking a law will be.

Large cities also have their own courts. These courts make decisions about traffic, parking, and other matters important to the community. But most laws are judged in county courts.

Reading Check ⓢ **Summarize**
What are the parts of a county government?

▸ **The county courthouse in Essex County, New Jersey**

▶ Many communities have parks and centers where people can meet and have fun.

Community Services

A community government provides services for the people in its town or city. The fire department puts out fires and rescues people who are sick or hurt. The police department makes sure traffic laws and other laws are followed.

Education is also a government service. Some communities have groups of citizens who serve on school boards. These citizens make decisions about the community's schools.

Local governments also provide places, such as parks, pools, and sports fields, for recreation (reh•kree•AY•shuhn). **Recreation** is any activity that is done just for fun.

▶ Firefighters protect communities.

The Public Works Department

The **public works** department provides services to meet the daily needs of citizens. It repairs streets, collects trash, and makes sure that the community has clean water. It also takes care of wastewater. Pipes carry the wastewater to water treatment plants. There, it is cleaned before it is returned to rivers and lakes.

Reading Check ◊ **Summarize**
What kinds of services does a local government provide?

Summary Local governments include towns, cities, and counties. A city government runs a city or town. A county government runs a county.

▸ **This water treatment center in Christmas, Florida, is also a wetlands park.**

Review

1. **What to Know** What are local governments?
2. **Vocabulary** Write a sentence that explains what a **council** is.
3. **Your Community** Do you live in a county? Which city is the county seat for your county?
4. **Critical Thinking** What are some ways citizens in a community can take part in local government?
5. **Make a Diagram** Create a Venn diagram that compares a mayor-council government and a council-manager government.
6. **Summarize** On a separate sheet of paper, copy and complete the graphic organizer below.

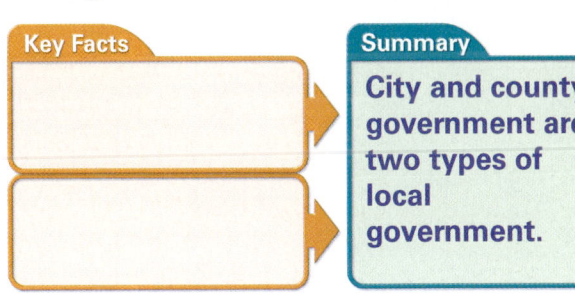

Chapter 8 ▪ 277

Map and Globe Skills

Read a Road Map

Why It Matters A road map can help you locate places and find your way around a community.

▶ Learn

A **road map** shows you the roads and other local features of a community. Follow these steps to read a road map.

Step 1 Find the roads. Roads are shown as solid lines. Thicker lines are used for main roads.

Step 2 Look for points of interest or other local features, such as parks, schools, or railroad tracks. These features will have labels.

Step 3 Trace a road route with your finger. Follow the solid lines from where you are to where you want to go.

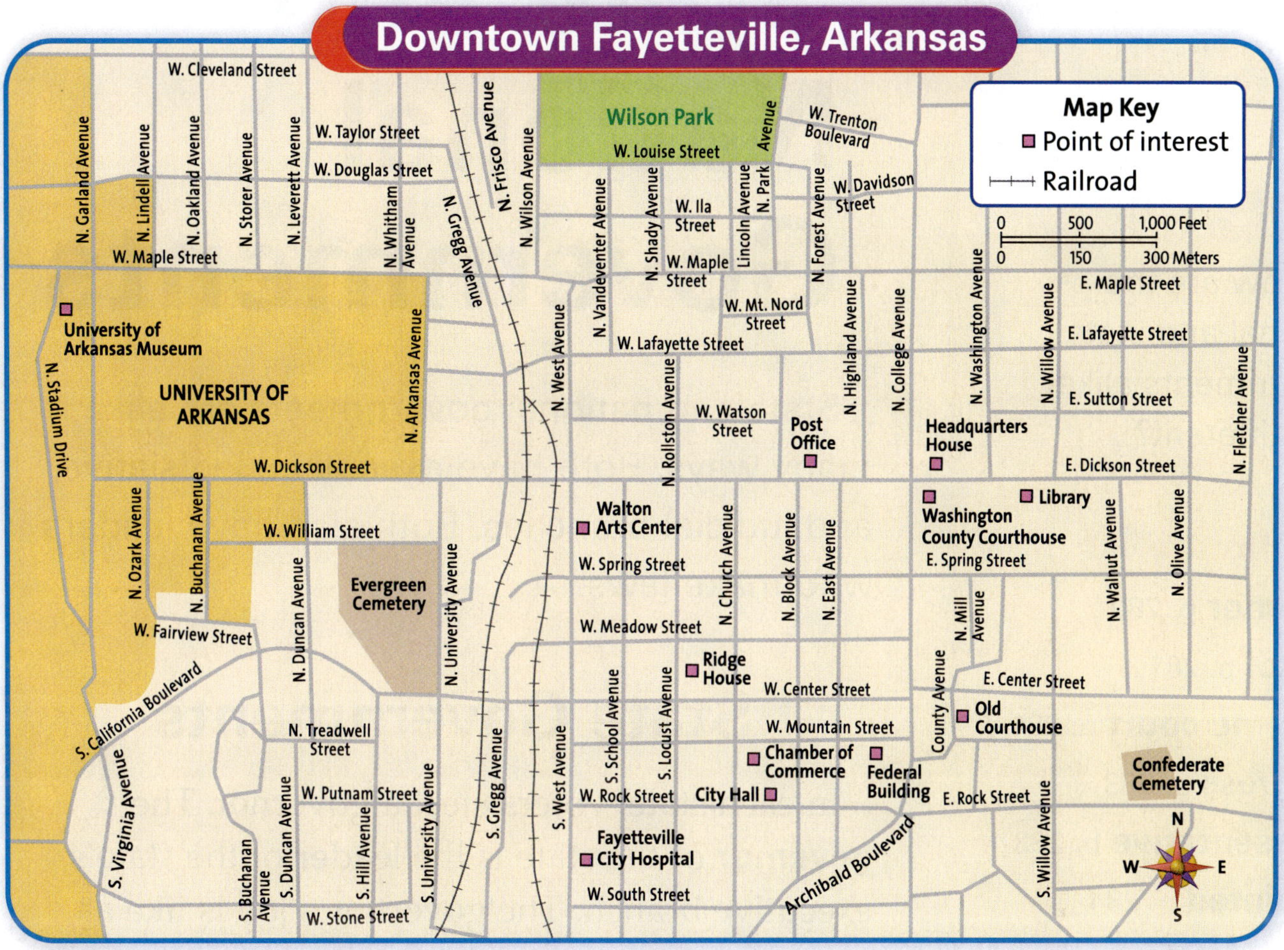

For online activities, go to www.harcourtschool.com/ss1

Downtown Fayetteville, Arkansas

Practice

Use the road map of downtown Fayetteville, Arkansas, to answer these questions.

1. What are some local features shown on this map?
2. Which road would you take to reach Wilson Park—Lincoln Avenue or Maple Street?

Apply

Make It Relevant Find a road map of your community. Trace the route from your home to your school. List the roads you take to get there.

Chapter 8 ■ 279

Lesson 3
State and National Governments

What to Know
How are the national and state governments alike and different?

Vocabulary
governor p. 280
capitol p. 281
supreme court p. 281
Congress p. 283
representative p. 283
appointed p. 284

Summarize

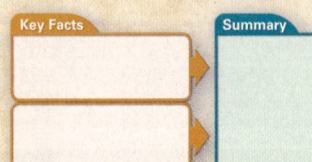

State and national governments are alike in many ways. Both have executive, legislative, and judicial branches. Both also have leaders who make laws.

State Governments

In each state, voters elect a governor. The **governor** of the state is the leader of the state's executive branch. The governor's job is like a mayor's job in many ways. A governor suggests laws for the state and sees that the laws are carried out.

❯ Jennifer Granholm is the governor of Michigan.

280 ▪ Unit 4

States and Their Capitals

 Location What is the capital of your state?

State Lawmakers

Each state has its own constitution. The legislative branch makes state laws that all the counties and communities in the state must obey. The lawmakers meet in a building called the **capitol** in the state's capital city.

State Judges

A state's **supreme court** is the most important court in that state. The courts and judges make up the state's judicial branch.

Reading Check ⚡ **Summarize**
What are the three branches of a state government?

❯ The state capitol in Lansing, Michigan

Chapter 8 ■ 281

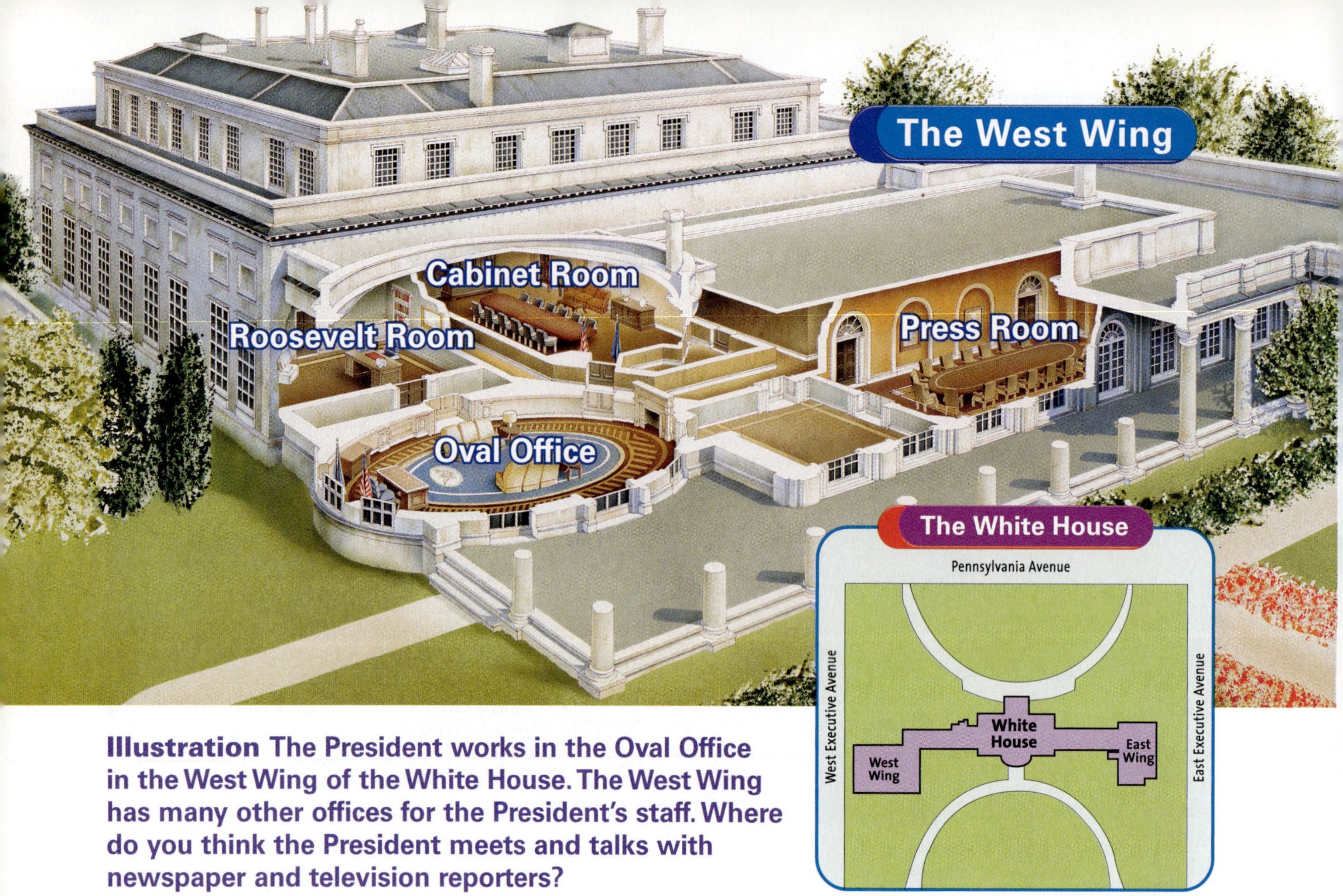

Illustration The President works in the Oval Office in the West Wing of the White House. The West Wing has many other offices for the President's staff. Where do you think the President meets and talks with newspaper and television reporters?

The National Government

The government of the United States is our national, or federal, government. It is located in our nation's capital, Washington, D.C.

The President

The President is elected by all the country's voters. The President is the leader of the executive branch of the federal government. The President leads our military. The President also enforces laws and suggests new ones.

The President lives and works in the White House in Washington, D.C. This famous building has rooms for the President's family to live in. It also has offices in the West Wing, along the west side of the building.

❯ **President George W. Bush often works with members of the legislative branch and the leaders of other nations.**

Congress

Congress is the legislative branch of the national government. Congress has two parts, the House of Representatives and the Senate. A **representative** is a person chosen by a group of people to act or speak for them. The number of representatives a state has in the House of Representatives depends on its population. Each state has two members in the Senate.

Members of Congress are elected by voters in their states. They discuss national problems and vote on how to solve them. They write new laws and decide how tax money should be spent. Senators and representatives must agree on a law to pass it. Then it goes to the President for approval. Laws passed by the national government must be followed in all 50 states.

Reading Check **Main Idea and Details**
What are the parts of Congress?

▶ United States senators from North Carolina, Elizabeth Dole and Richard Burr

▶ Members of the Senate and the House of Representatives sometimes meet for special events.

Chapter 8 ■ 283

▶ This photograph shows the United States Supreme Court justices in 2006. STANDING: Stephen G. Breyer, Clarence Thomas, Ruth Bader Ginsburg, and Samuel Anthony Alito, Jr. SEATED: Anthony M. Kennedy, John Paul Stephens, Chief Justice John Roberts, Antonin Scalia, and David Hackett Souter.

The Supreme Court

▶ The Supreme Court uses the Great Seal of the United States as its seal.

The federal courts make up the judicial branch of the national government. The Supreme Court is the most important court in the United States. Nine judges, called justices, serve on the Supreme Court. They decide whether a law agrees with the Constitution.

Supreme Court justices are not elected. They are **appointed**, or chosen, by the President. The Senate can approve or reject the President's choice. Once appointed, a justice serves for his or her lifetime or until the justice chooses to retire.

Reading Check ⭐ **Summarize**
What is the Supreme Court, and what does it do?

State and National Services

The state and national governments also provide important services. One national service is to keep the country safe. Other national services make life easier for people. For example, people can send mail by using the United States Postal Service. State services include building highways and caring for state parks.

The national and state governments also provide goods. Some books are published by the national government.

Reading Check ⭕ **Summarize**
What are some state and national services?

▶ National parks are protected as a service of the national government.

Summary Both the state and national governments have three branches. Each level has different types of leaders and services.

Review

1. **What to Know** How are the national and state governments alike and different?

2. **Vocabulary** What clue can you use to remember the meaning of **representative**?

3. **Civics and Government** What are the three branches of both the state and national governments?

4. **Critical Thinking Make It Relevant** Who is the governor of your state? Where does he or she live?

5. ✏️ **Write a Letter** Write a letter to a representative in your state. Share your ideas about an important state issue.

6. ⭐ **Summarize** On a separate sheet of paper, copy and complete the graphic organizer below.

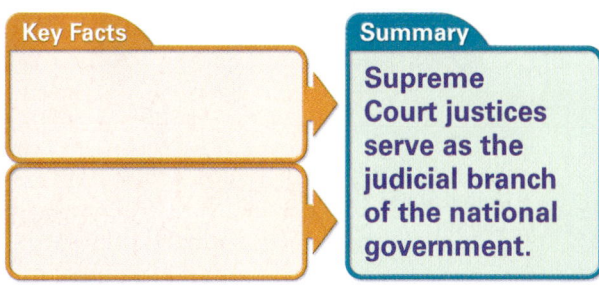

Chapter 8 ■ 285

FIELD TRIP

http://www.harcourtschool.com/ss1

The United States Capitol

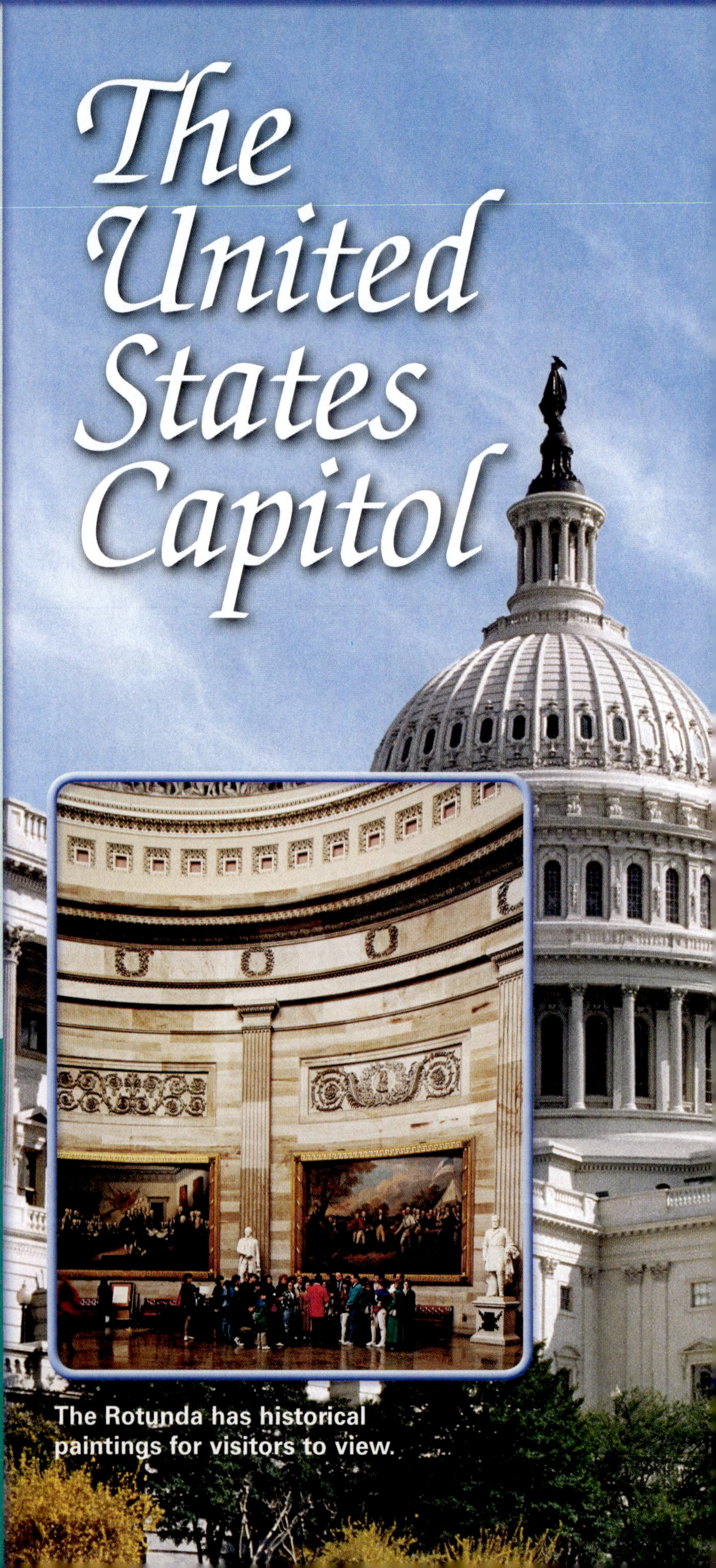

READ ABOUT

The United States Capitol building in Washington, D.C., is where Congress meets to make laws. It was first built in 1793, when George Washington was President. Since then, the building has burned down, been rebuilt, and been expanded. Today, the building has 540 rooms, 658 windows, and 850 doorways.

One famous room is the beautiful Rotunda. This 96-foot circular room is directly under the iron dome. It connects the House and Senate wings, or sections, of the Capitol. The Senate meets in the North wing. The House of Representatives meets in the South wing.

FIND

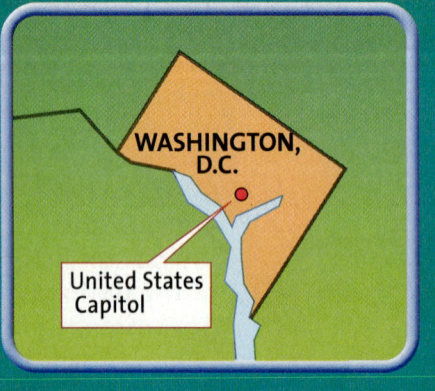

The Rotunda has historical paintings for visitors to view.

Statuary Hall

The *Freedom* Statue on top of the Capitol dome

The iron dome of the Rotunda

The Senate meeting hall

Members of the House of Representatives meet.

A VIRTUAL TOUR

GO ONLINE For more resources, go to www.harcourtschool.com/ss1

Chapter 8 ■ 287

Citizenship Skills

Resolve Conflicts

Why It Matters People can have different ideas about things. This can lead to a conflict. Knowing how to resolve, or settle, a conflict is important.

▶ Learn

Follow these steps when you need to resolve a conflict with someone.

Step 1 *Walk Away* Wait until both people can talk calmly about the conflict.

Step 2 *Smile About It* It is easier to resolve a conflict if both people are friendly about it.

Step 3 *Compromise* Two people **compromise** (KAHM•pruh•myz) when each person gives up some of what he or she wants.

Step 4 *Ask for Help* A **mediator** (MEE•dee•ay•ter) is a person who helps other people settle a conflict.

Conflict

Resolution

> Practice

With a partner, roleplay solving a conflict. Tell what happens as you try each of the steps.

1. What happens when one person smiles?
2. What happens when one person is willing to compromise?
3. What happens when one person asks a mediator for help?

> Apply

Make It Relevant Think about a conflict you have seen at school. How was the conflict resolved? Write a paragraph that compares the way the people resolved their conflict with the steps in this lesson.

Lesson 4 Symbols of Our Nation

What to Know

What are some of the symbols of our country?

Vocabulary

patriotic symbol p. 290
monument p. 292
memorial p. 292
anthem p. 294

Summarize

People everywhere feel patriotism for their country. One way they show this feeling is through their patriotic symbols. A **patriotic symbol**, such as a flag, stands for the ideas in which people believe.

Our Nation's Symbols

The United States flag is a symbol of our country's history and beliefs. There are 13 stripes and 50 stars on the flag. The stripes stand for the original 13 colonies. Each star represents one of the 50 states.

> A Boy Scout troop carries the United States flag during a parade. The United States flag is a symbol of our country's unity.

290 ■ Unit 4

Flag Manners

Saluting the Flag

- Stand and look at the flag. Place your right hand over your heart.
- If you have a hat on, remove it and hold it with the hand that is over your heart.

Displaying the Flag

- Fly the flag of the United States above any other flag on the same pole. Raise the United States flag first, and lower it last.
- Flying the flag at half-mast is a sign of mourning, or sorrow for a death. Raise the flag to the top of the pole, and then lower it halfway. At night, raise it to the top before lowering it.

The Bald Eagle

The American bald eagle is the national bird of the United States. It lives only in North America. President John F. Kennedy said, "The fierce beauty and proud independence of this great bird aptly [very well] symbolizes the strength and freedom of America."

> The bald eagle is a symbol of the strength and freedom of the United States.

The Liberty Bell

The Liberty Bell, in the city of Philadelphia, Pennsylvania, is another patriotic symbol. It was rung after the first public reading of the Declaration of Independence. People often think of the Liberty Bell when they hear the words *Let freedom ring*.

Reading Check **Summarize**
What do our flag's stars and stripes represent?

> The Liberty Bell is a symbol of freedom.

▶ The National Mall in Washington, D.C., has many monuments.

A City of Monuments

Many patriotic symbols are located in Washington, D.C. Some are monuments. A **monument** is built to honor a person or an event in history. It can be a sculpture, a fountain, a building, or any lasting marker. The Washington Monument is a huge stone column in honor of our country's first President.

Some monuments are built as memorials. A **memorial** helps keep the memory of a person or an event alive. The Lincoln Memorial helps people remember President Abraham Lincoln.

▶ The Korean War Veterans Memorial

▶ The Franklin Delano Roosevelt Memorial

War Memorials

Some memorials remember people who died in wars. The Vietnam Veterans Memorial and the Korean War Memorial honor citizens who fought in Vietnam and Korea.

The National World War II Memorial honors soldiers who fought in World War II in the 1940s. It was built in 2004. It is located between the Washington Monument and the Lincoln Memorial.

Reading Check ⓞ **Summarize**
What is the purpose of monuments and memorials?

▶ The National World War II Memorial

Chapter 8 ■ 293

Words of Patriotism

People often use words to express patriotism. Francis Scott Key wrote about his feelings in a poem called "The Star-Spangled Banner." His poem later became the national **anthem**, or song of patriotism.

The Story Behind the Song

Key wrote his poem during the War of 1812. He had watched from a ship as the British attacked a fort in Baltimore, Maryland. The battle went on into the night. When the fighting stopped, it was too dark for Key to tell which side had won.

The next morning, Key could see the American flag flying above the fort. He knew then that the United States had won the battle.

❯ Francis Scott Key

Children in History

The Living American Flag

Each year in May, schoolchildren in Baltimore, Maryland, gather for Flag Day. Wearing red, white, and blue, they create a large "living flag." This tradition began in 1914 to celebrate the 100th anniversary of the battle that defended Baltimore.

The children also wanted people to remember the writing of "The Star-Spangled Banner." To make the first "human flag," 6,500 Baltimore schoolchildren wore colored coats and waved matching handkerchiefs. They made the flag look as if it were waving in the wind!

Make It Relevant How do you take part in patriotic events?

294 ■ Unit 4

The Pledge of Allegiance

The Pledge of Allegiance is a promise that people make to be loyal, or true, to the United States. They stand at attention as they say the words. They place their right hand over their hearts to show respect.

Reading Check · Summarize
Why do people say the Pledge of Allegiance?

Summary People show their patriotism through symbols. Monuments and memorials are symbols that honor and remember a person or an event. Patriotic words tell the way people feel about their country.

> Students say the Pledge of Allegiance in their Maryland school.

Review

1. **What to Know** What are some of the symbols of our country?
2. **Vocabulary** How is "The Star-Spangled Banner" an **anthem**?
3. **History** Why is the Liberty Bell a symbol of freedom?
4. **Critical Thinking Make It Relevant** Are there any monuments in your community? How does a monument honor a person or an event?
5. **Draw a Symbol** Draw a picture of a patriotic symbol. Write a sentence to tell what the symbol means.
6. **Summarize** On a separate sheet of paper, copy and complete the graphic organizer below.

Chapter 8 ■ 295

Chart and Graph Skills

Use a Line Graph

Why It Matters Sometimes people need to see how things change over time. Graphs can help them.

❯ Learn

A <mark>line graph</mark> uses a line to show changes over time. Look at the graph on page 297. It shows how the number of pairs of bald eagles has grown. The number of bald eagles was once so few that the government made a plan to protect them. You can follow these steps to read the graph.

Step 1 Read the title to learn what the graph shows.

Step 2 Read the labels along the bottom and side of the graph. They tell what the numbers represent.

Step 3 Use the dots on the graph and the numbers along the bottom and side to find the number shown.

Step 4 Follow the line on the graph to see how the number changes over time.

❯ A pair of bald eagles is two eagles that nest together.

 For online activities, go to www.harcourtschool.com/ss1

> ## Practice

Use the line graph to answer these questions.

1. What information is shown along the bottom? Along the side?
2. Between which years did the biggest change in bald eagle population take place?

> ## Apply

Make It Relevant Make a line graph that shows how your town's population has changed over time.

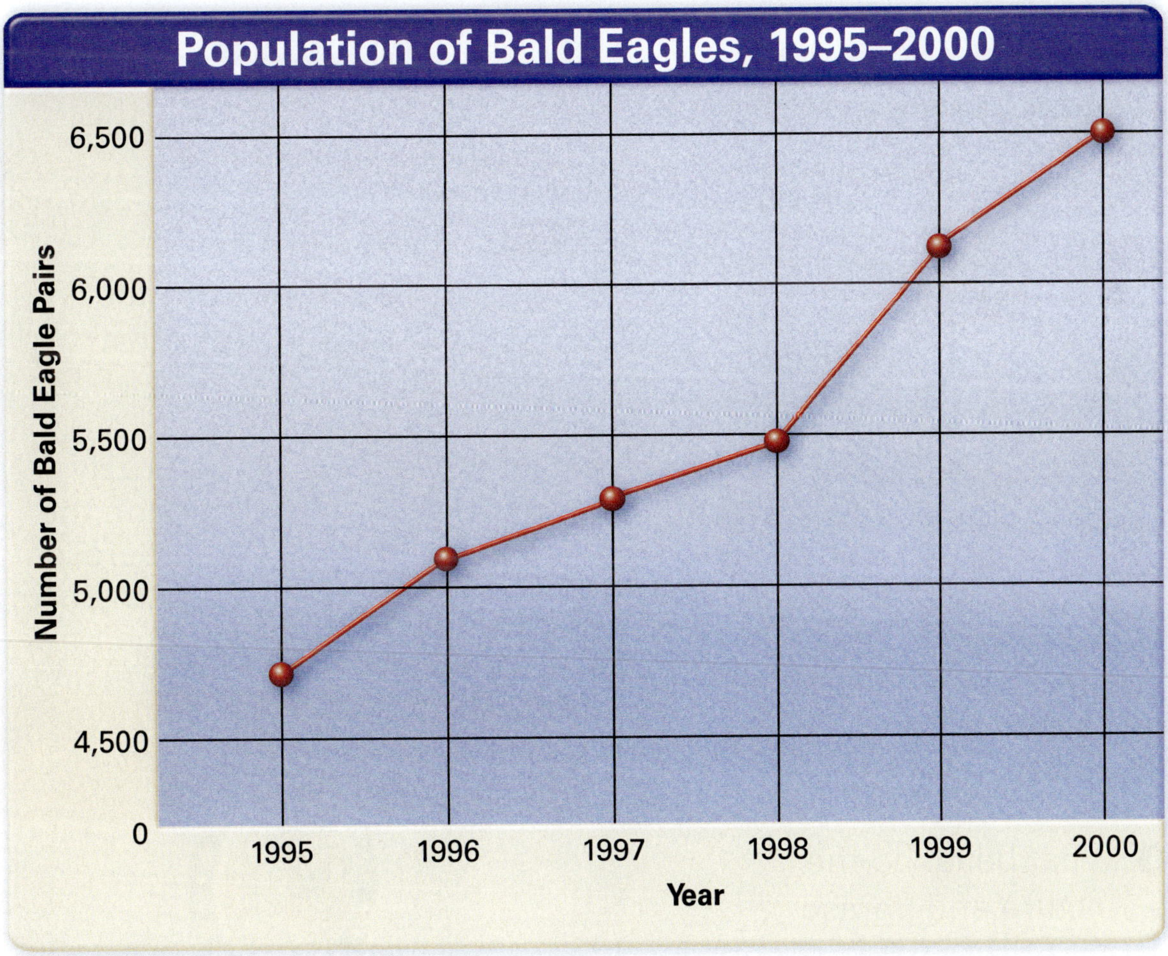

Population of Bald Eagles, 1995–2000

Chart and Graph Skills

Chapter 8 ▪ 297

Primary Sources

State Symbols

Background States have symbols that can tell about life in the states or values important to their citizens. A state flag can express feelings of state pride. A state seal on government buildings or papers is a sign of authority.

DBQ **Document-Based Questions** Study these primary sources, and answer the questions.

Kentucky State Flag

This flag shows a pioneer and a government worker.

"United we stand, divided we fall" is Kentucky's state motto.

DBQ ❶ What belief do the picture and phrase show?

Missouri State Flag

The Missouri flag shows the Missouri state seal.

DBQ ❷ What values are represented on the Missouri state seal?

The grizzly bears on the seal represent strength and courage.

Missouri state seal

Ohio State Seal

The Ohio state seal shows a bundle of wheat and a bundle of arrows.

DBQ ❸ Why might the seal show wheat?

New Jersey State Seal

The New Jersey state seal shows two women.

DBQ ❹ What values are most important to the state of New Jersey?

Liberty holds the liberty cap on her staff.

Plenty holds a container filled with food.

"Liberty and prosperity" is the state's motto.

Oklahoma State Flag

The Oklahoma state flag was adopted in 1925. The shield is decorated with symbols of peace.

DBQ ❺ What does Oklahoma's flag tell you about who might have lived in the state?

WRITE ABOUT IT

Write a paragraph about your state's flag and seal.

GO ONLINE For more resources, go to www.harcoutschool.com/ss1

Chapter 8 ■ 299

Lesson 5

Governments of the World

What to Know
How do other countries govern their people?

Vocabulary
Parliament p. 301
prime minister p. 301
constitutional monarchy p. 302

Summarize

Countries around the world have different governments. Some countries, like the United States, have democracies. Others have governments in which leaders are not chosen by the citizens.

Neighboring Governments

The government of Mexico is somewhat like the government of the United States. Both governments have executive, legislative, and judicial branches. In both countries, the president is the leader of the executive branch.

▶ Government leaders from different countries often meet.

300 ▪ Unit 4

▶ Government members from the United States and Mexico meet to discuss business.

Canada's government is also like that of the United States in certain ways. Canada's legislative branch is **Parliament**. Parliament works with another group called the Cabinet of Ministers. This group is led by the **prime minister**, who heads the executive branch.

Working Together

As neighbors, the United States, Mexico, and Canada have close relationships. Their governments often work together. The three countries also do business together. Mexico, for example, sends most of its goods to the United States.

Reading Check ⓢ **Summarize**
How are the governments of Mexico and Canada like that of the United States?

Sharing Borders

MAP SKILL **Location** Which country shares the northern border of the United States?

Chapter 8 ■ 301

Fast Fact

King Jigme Singye Wangchuck became the king of Bhutan when he was 17 years old.

Bhutan's Government

The government of Bhutan (boo•TAHN) is different from the government of the United States. Bhutan is a country in Asia. Instead of a president, Bhutan has a monarch, or king. King Jigme Singye Wangchuck (JEE•mee SING•ee WANG•choo) is the king of Bhutan. Like other kings, he was born into a royal family. His father and his grandfather were also kings.

A Constitutional Monarchy

Bhutan's government is changing. It is turning into a constitutional monarchy. A **constitutional monarchy** has both a monarch and a government elected by the people. King Wangchuck gave up some of his power to help Bhutan make this change.

▶ The Himalayas in Bhutan

Bhutan's legislative branch is the National Assembly. Some of its members are elected. Others are chosen by the king and by religious groups. Wangchuck has given the National Assembly most of his powers.

The executive branch is the Council of Ministers. Its members are chosen by the king but must be approved by the National Assembly.

Reading Check ○ **Summarize**
How is Bhutan's government different from the United States government?

▶ Members of Bhutan's government

Summary Countries around the world have different forms of government. The United States, Mexico, Canada, and Bhutan govern their people in different ways.

Review

1. **What to Know** How do other countries govern their people?
2. **Vocabulary** Write a description of a **constitutional monarchy**.
3. **Civics and Government** How does a person usually become a monarch?
4. **Critical Thinking** How are a president and a monarch alike? How are they different?
5. ✏️ **Write a Paragraph** Write a paragraph to compare the governments you learned about in this lesson.
6. **Summarize**
   Focus Skill On a separate sheet of paper, copy and complete the graphic organizer below.

Key Facts	Summary
	National governments can be similar to or different from our own.

Chapter 8 ■ 303

Explore Your Community's Government

In this unit, you read about the different levels and branches of government. You can learn about your own community's government by using the resources below.

Your Community's Resources

Newspapers

Government Offices

Community Websites

Find Out About Your Community

- What type of local government does your community have?
- Who are some leaders in your community?
- Where and when do your community's leaders meet?
- What government services are offered in your community?

Make a Community Website

Make a website for the citizens of your community. Include important information about your community's government, such as your leaders' names, local government offices, and meeting times. Explain what government services your community offers its citizens.

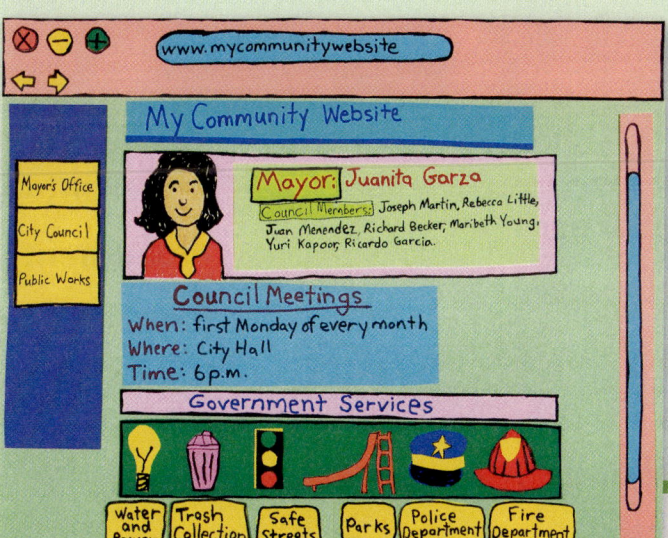

Chapter 8 Review

Visual Summary

The United States has three levels of government.

Summarize the Chapter

Summarize Complete the graphic organizer to show what you have learned about your nation's government.

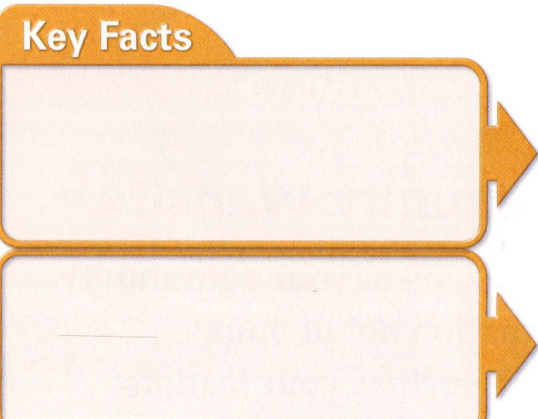

Key Facts

Summary
There are three levels of government in the United States. Each level has three branches.

Vocabulary

Write a definition for each term.

1. **government service**, p. 267
2. **judicial**, p. 268
3. **county**, p. 272
4. **public works**, p. 277
5. **governor**, p. 280
6. **Congress**, p. 283
7. **representative**, p. 283
8. **monument**, p. 292
9. **anthem**, p. 294
10. **prime minister**, p. 301

 Executive, legislative, and judicial are three branches of government.

 Citizens show patriotism for their country through symbols.

Facts and Main Ideas

Answer these questions.

11. Who gives the authority to leaders of our country?

12. What are the three branches of national and state government?

13. What does the Vietnam Veterans Memorial honor?

Write the letter of the best choice.

14. Which best explains a mayor-council government?
    A Voters elect the mayor and council members.
    B Voters hire a judge.
    C The council hires a city manager.
    D The council chooses a mayor.

15. Which of the following governments is a constitutional monarchy?
    A Canada
    B United States
    C Mexico
    D Bhutan

Critical Thinking

16. Why do we need government?

17. **Make It Relevant** What government services does your community provide?

Skills

Read a Road Map
Use the road map on page 279 to answer the question.

18. Which street runs along the southern end of Wilson Park?

Resolve Conflicts
Use the steps on page 288 to answer the question.

19. What happens when one person walks away during a conflict?

writing

✏️ **Write a Paragraph** Write a paragraph about the United States President.

✏️ **Write a Song** Imagine that you saw an important event in history. Write a patriotic song about the event.

Chapter 8 ■ 307

Picture Clues

This crossword puzzle is complete, but which picture clues match the puzzle words? One is done for you.

```
              6.
               M
    1. P A T R I O T I C S Y M B O L
               N            7.
               U             R
      2. V O L U N T E E R
               M             E
               E             C
         8.    N             R
          M                  E
    3. B A L L O T      4. H E R O
          Y                  A
          O                  T
          R    5. A N T H E M
                             O
                             N
```

Across
1.   2.   3.   4.   5.

Down
6.   7.   8.

308 • Unit 4

Good Citizens

These four good citizens made a difference. What are their names?

I won the Nobel Peace Prize in 2002. Now I help build houses for people in need.

I did not give up my seat on the bus and went to jail. That helped change unfair laws.

I wrote a poem that was set to music. Now many people sing my words.

I have helped farmworkers and their families.

Online Adventures

GO ONLINE

In this online game, you'll visit City Hall on Election Day. Somebody is trying to stop citizens from voting. To save the election, you'll have to meet all the challenges and catch the person who is responsible. Can you figure out what is happening in time to save the election? Play now at www.harcourtschool.com/ss1

Unit 4 Review and Test Prep

The Big Idea

Government Communities depend on citizens to participate in their government.

Reading Comprehension and Vocabulary

Citizens and Government

As citizens of the United States, we have rights. We also have responsibilities. For example, we have the responsibility to obey laws. To be good citizens, we must cooperate for the good of the community.

Our government has three levels—local, state, and national. Each level provides different government services and has different types of leaders. For example, a mayor leads a community government.

The national, state, and most local governments have three branches that do different jobs. These three branches are the executive, legislative, and judicial branches.

Read the summary above. Then answer the questions that follow.

1. What is one responsibility of citizens?
   A following a religion
   B sharing beliefs
   C obeying laws
   D working

2. What do all three levels of government provide?
   A government services
   B a good community
   C rights
   D responsibilities

3. What does a mayor do?
   A leads state government
   B leads community government
   C leads county government
   D leads national government

4. How many branches do the national, state, and most local governments each have?
   A 2
   B 4
   C 5
   D 3

310 ■ Unit 4

Facts and Main Ideas

Answer these questions.

5. What right is also a responsibility?

6. What are two kinds of local government?

7. What are the two parts of Congress?

Write the letter of the best choice.

8. What did Jimmy Carter do to be a good citizen?
   A refused to give up a bus seat
   B helped nations solve conflicts peacefully
   C started classes for poor farmworkers
   D helped plan a bus boycott

9. What is the Pledge of Allegiance?
   A our national anthem
   B a promise to be loyal to the United States
   C a war memorial
   D the Constitution

10. How did Bhutan's king become the monarch?
    A He was born into the royal family.
    B He was elected.
    C He was appointed.
    D He was hired by the National Assembly.

 Critical Thinking

11. **Make It Relevant** How does the United States Constitution affect you?

12. Why does a state need a government?

 **Skills**

Read a Road Map

Use the map below to answer the following questions.

13. What are some features on the map?

14. Which road would you take to get to Waterworks Park—Forest Avenue or Montgomery Road?

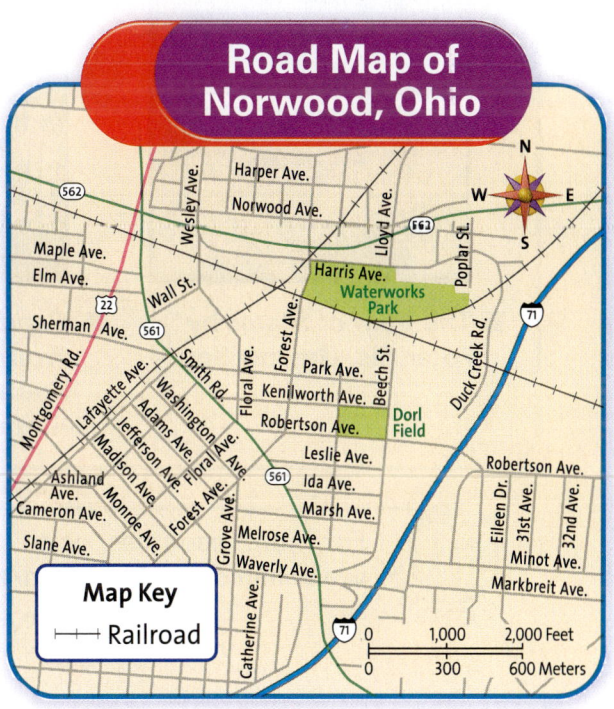

Road Map of Norwood, Ohio

Unit 4 • 311

Unit 4 Activities

Show What You Know

 Unit Writing Activity

Write a Summary Describe the relationship between citizens and the government.

- List some rights and responsibilities of citizens.
- Explain how the government serves and protects citizens.

 Unit Project

Government Handbook Make a handbook that tells about the government.

- Find out about the people and jobs in local, state, and national governments.
- Describe how each level works.

Read More

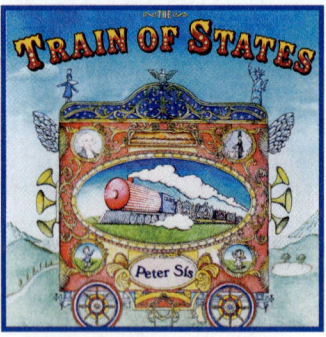

- *The Train of States* by Peter Sis. Greenwillow.

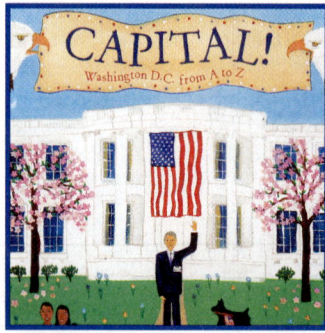

- *Capital! Washington D.C. From A to Z* by Laura Krauss Melmed. HarperCollins.

- *The Flag Maker* by Susan Campbell Bartoletti. Houghton Mifflin.

 For more resources, go to www.harcourtschool.com/ss1

People in Communities

Emma Lazarus
1849–1887
American poet whose poem "The New Colossus" was placed on the Statue of Liberty

Maya Lin
1959–Present
Artist who designed the Vietnam Veterans Memorial in Washington, D.C.

Unit 5 Preview
Vocabulary

diverse The variety of differences in a group, such as language or beliefs. (page 332)

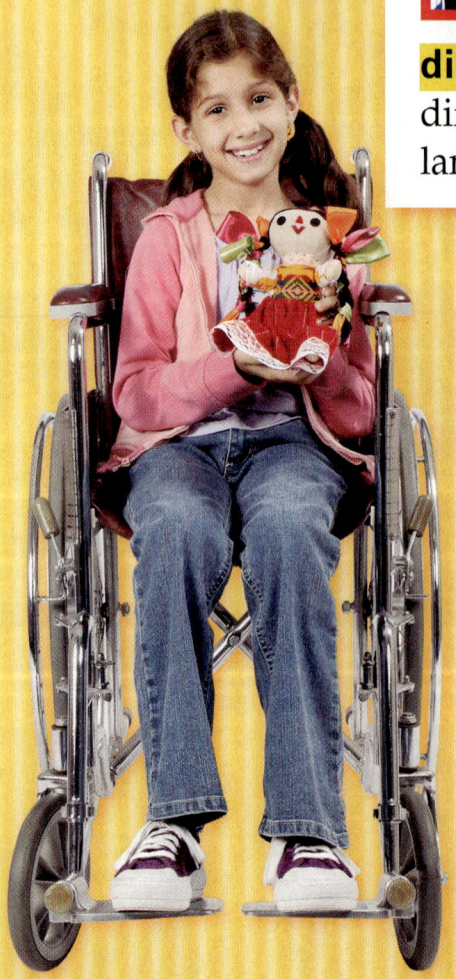

tradition A custom, or way of doing something, that is passed on to others. (page 335)

custom A people's way of doing something. (page 332)

landmark An important human or natural feature that marks a location. (page 338)

festival A joyful gathering for celebration. (page 359)

For more resources, go to www.harcourtschool.com/ss1

Unit 5 • 315

Unit 5

Reading Social Studies

Cause and Effect

Why It Matters Understanding cause and effect can help you see why events happen.

▶ Learn

A **cause** is something that makes something else happen. An **effect** is the thing that happens as a result of a cause.

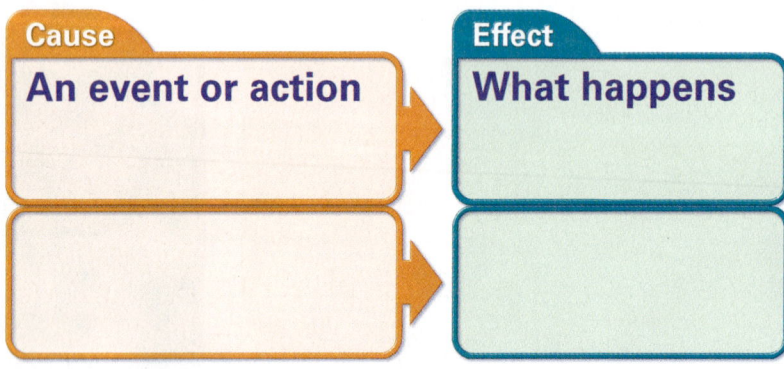

- Words and phrases, such as *because, as a result, since,* and *so,* can help you identify why something happens.
- An effect can also become a cause for another event.

▶ Practice

Read the paragraph. Find a cause and an effect.

In the past, people in the Appalachian Mountains did not travel far from home. **[Cause]** The steep mountains made it difficult to visit other communities, where they could have learned other ways of life. **[Effect]** As a result, the Appalachian region had a different culture from those in the rest of the country.

316 ▪ Unit 5

> Apply

Read the paragraphs, and answer the questions.

The Sound of Appalachian Music

The Appalachian region is known for its folk music, or popular music that people learn from each other. The first Europeans in the area came from many cultures. They included English, Scottish, Irish, German, and French settlers. African Americans and Native Americans also settled in the region. As a result, Appalachian folk music blends styles from around the world. Over time, this blend became its own unique, or special, mountain sound.

English settlers brought their love of ballads, or songs that tell stories. German settlers played the dulcimer, a stringed instrument held on the player's lap. A Scottish fiddler started playing the fiddle in a new way, using a short bow. The guitar, banjo, and mandolin were also popular in the region. Each style and instrument helped create the Appalachian sound.

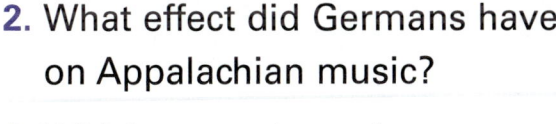 Cause and Effect

1. Why is Appalachian folk music made up of many styles?

2. What effect did Germans have on Appalachian music?

3. Which group brought ballads to Appalachian music?

Start with a Story

Dreaming of America
An Ellis Island Story

by Eve Bunting — illustrated by Ben F. Stahl

Annie Moore and her two brothers, Anthony and Philip, left Ireland to come to the United States. Annie's parents had come to this country earlier to work and save money. On January 1, 1892, Annie arrived at Ellis Island, a place where immigrants went before they were allowed to enter the country. This story shows what might have happened when Annie stepped off the ship.

With a squeak and a squeal, the gangplank was lowered.

Mr. Viktor gave Annie a little push. "Be first, Annie. First will be good."

The *Nevada* brought immigrants from Europe to America from 1869–1894.

The original Ellis Island immigration building was completed in 1891.

Annie stepped out, Anthony and Phillip at her heels.

The cheers were like thunder. Small American flags waved. Hats and caps flew in the air. The salty air smelled good. The smell of America.

Two important-looking gentlemen in suits took her hands. "Welcome. You are the first immigrant to enter our country through Ellis Island," one of the gentlemen said.

"First will be good," Mr. Viktor had said. This was what he'd meant. This was why there was a big celebration!

"I am Colonel Weber," the other gentleman said. "What is your name?"

Annie tried not to stammer. "I am Annie Moore of Cork, Ireland. These are my brothers, Anthony and Phillip." She stood, unsure and embarrassed, knowing everyone was watching them. All those hundreds of people pressed behind the barricades. She looked from side to side. Oh, if she could only see her parents!

"We want you to accept this ten-dollar gold piece to commemorate this important day in history," Colonel Weber said.

"And it's Annie's birthday, too," little Phillip piped up.

An important day in history, and she was a part of it! Annie stared down at the gold coin. It seemed to float in her hand, bright as sunshine. Ten dollars? That must be a fortune!

"I'll never part with it. Never," she whispered.

"Now, if you and your brothers will come with us, we will get you registered. . . ."

It was then Annie heard the shouts, so excited they rose above the noise around them.

"It's Annie and little Anthony and little Phillip!"

"Daddy!" Annie called. "Daddy!" She'd know that voice anywhere.

And there was her mother, pushing through to the front of the crowd, her face red with excitement, her hat and hair every which way. "Here we are, darlin's, here we are!" she called.

"How does it feel to be in America?" a man with a notepad asked.

"Grand altogether," Annie said. She looked down at her ring with the red stones that were more precious than rubies. The two hearts. Ireland and America. Was that what her auntie had known when she gave it?

I am Annie Moore of Cork, Ireland, she thought. And I am Annie Moore of America.

This is the real Annie Moore with her first-born child, Mary Catherine.

Response Corner

1. **Cause and Effect** Why did Colonel Weber give Annie a ten-dollar gold piece?

2. **Make It Relevant** Why do you think people might move to your community from another community?

STUDY SKILLS

USE AN ANTICIPATION GUIDE

An anticipation guide helps you anticipate, or predict, what you will read.

- Look at the lesson and section titles for clues about what you will read.
- Preview the Reading Check questions. Use what you know about the subject to predict the answers.
- Read to find out whether your predictions were correct.

Immigration and Migration

Reading Check	Prediction	Correct?
Why have immigrants come to the United States?	People move to find new opportunities.	✓

PREVIEW VOCABULARY

opportunity p. 324

multicultural p. 333

holiday p. 340

CHAPTER 9
Our American Culture

> A Native American celebration in Los Angeles, California

Lesson 1

Moving to New Places

What to Know
Why do people move to new places?

Vocabulary
opportunity p. 324
prejudice p. 325
migrate p. 328

Cause and Effect

People do not always live in the same place all their lives. Sometimes they move to another community or even another country.

A Nation of Immigrants

Immigrants have been coming to the United States for hundreds of years. Many have come to find new opportunities. An **opportunity** is a chance to have a better way of life. Some came here hoping to find more freedoms. Some came for a better education or job. Others wanted to escape dangers in their own countries.

› Immigrant children arriving in the 1930s wave at the Statue of Liberty.

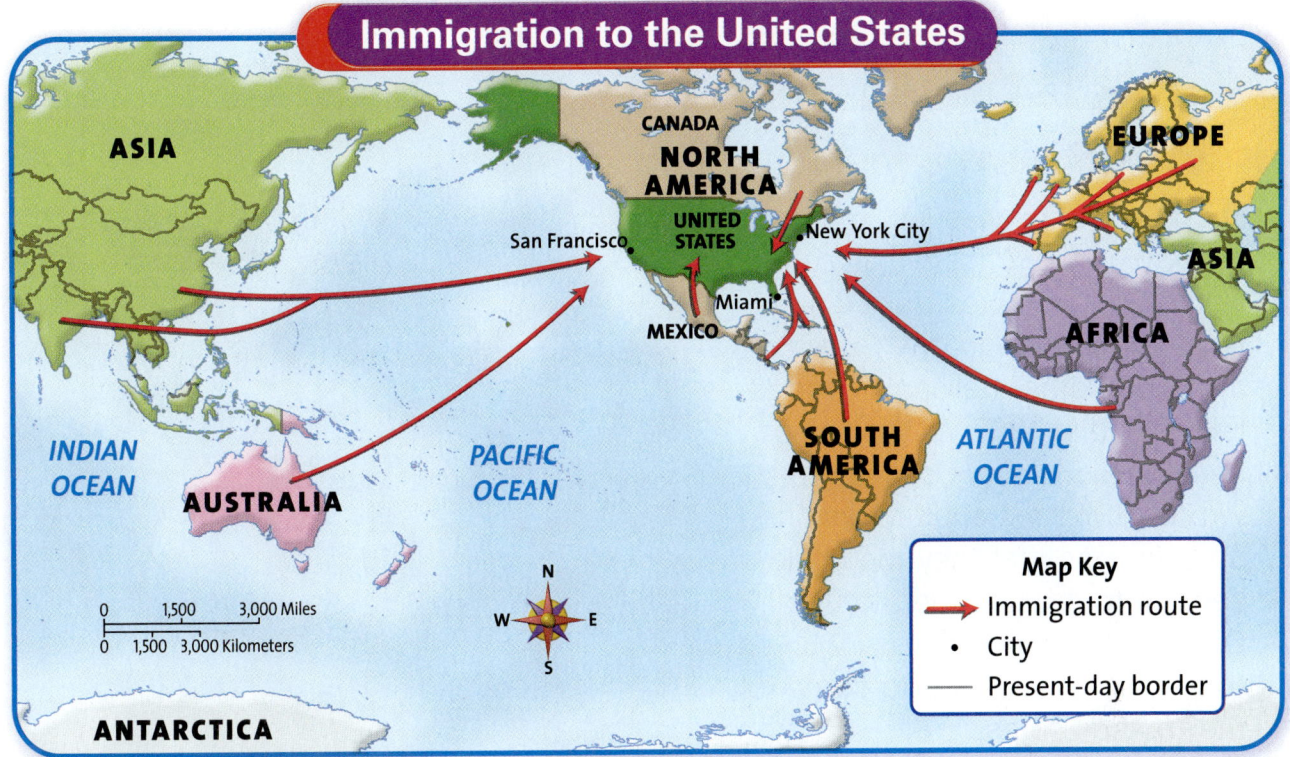

 Movement What part of the United States did most immigrants from Europe reach first?

Immigrants Face New Problems

In the past, immigrants to the United States faced many problems. They often had to live in crowded apartments in the older parts of big cities. They had little money for food.

Some immigrants also faced prejudice (PREH•juh•duhs). **Prejudice** is the unfair feeling of hate or dislike for people of a certain group, race, or religion. Immigrants were often paid less money than other workers for the same job. They also had fewer opportunities for good jobs.

▶ A passport of a Russian immigrant

Reading Check ŏ**Cause and Effect**
Why have immigrants come to the United States?

Chapter 9 ■ 325

Children in History

Edward Corsi

Edward Corsi was just ten years old when he and his family came to the United States from Italy. After a long voyage, the Corsis and 1,600 other Italians arrived at Ellis Island in 1907. As their ship neared Ellis Island, Corsi later wrote, "Mothers and fathers lifted up babies so that they too could see, off to the left, the Statue of Liberty." As an adult, Corsi worked to help other immigrants come to the United States.

› These children, like Corsi, were immigrants from Europe.

Beginning New Lives

Between 1880 and 1920, millions of new immigrants arrived in the United States. Most traveled on crowded ships. They wanted the chance to become United States citizens.

After they arrived, immigrants often had to wait in long lines. They had to answer many questions from immigration officers. Then they had to see doctors. They could enter the United States only if they passed all the tests.

Most immigrants from Europe arrived at Ellis Island, in New York Harbor. It was the nation's largest immigration center.

Most immigrants from Asia arrived on the west coast, at Angel Island. Angel Island is located in California's San Francisco Bay.

› More than 20 million immigrants passed through Ellis Island.

Building Communities

Many immigrants settled in cities close to Ellis Island or Angel Island. They found jobs and met people from their home countries.

Other immigrants moved to different areas of the country. Some started new communities. They often named these communities for their homelands. Germantown, in Tennessee, was named by the town's early German settlers.

Immigration Today

Today, immigrants arrive from countries all over the world. Most come from countries in Asia and Latin America. The United States government limits the number of immigrants that can enter the country each year.

Reading Check Generalize
Why did immigrants settle in cities near Ellis Island or Angel Island?

Immigrants and Their Countries

Country	Number of Immigrants
Mexico	173,664
India	65,472
Philippines	54,632
China	45,942
Vietnam	30,064
Dominican Republic	30,049

Table Many of the immigrants who came to the United States in 2004 were from these countries. How many people came from Vietnam?

▶ Immigrants being sworn in as United States citizens

▶ This African American family migrated from the rural South to Chicago.

Migration in the United States

People also **migrate**, or move, within their own country. Like immigrants, many of them are looking for better opportunities.

The Great Migration

Even after slavery ended, laws limited African Americans' freedoms. During the 1900s, many African Americans left rural areas in the South. They migrated to urban areas in the North and the West. They hoped to find jobs, homes, and equal rights. This movement became known as the Great Migration. African American populations grew in cities such as Detroit, Cleveland, Chicago, and New York City.

▶ A painting from *The Migration* series by Jacob Lawrence

Migration Continues

People still migrate to urban areas to find jobs and other opportunities. Other people migrate out of urban areas to suburban or rural towns. Often they are looking for less crowded or less expensive places to live.

Since the 1970s, many people from northern parts of the United States have moved to the Sun Belt. This wide region in the southern parts of the country has a mild climate.

Reading Check ○ **Cause and Effect**
What was one effect of the Great Migration?

> A family unpacks after moving to a new community.

Summary Immigrants come to the United States looking for opportunities. People already living here sometimes migrate to other areas.

Review

1. **What to Know** Why do people move to new places?
2. **Vocabulary** Use the term **opportunity** in a sentence about immigration.
3. **Geography** To what regions did African Americans move during the Great Migration?
4. **Critical Thinking** Why did immigrants who started new communities often name them for their homelands?
5. **Write a Diary Entry** Write a diary entry as if you are an early immigrant to the United States. Include details about the challenges you face.
6. **Cause and Effect** Copy and complete the graphic organizer below.

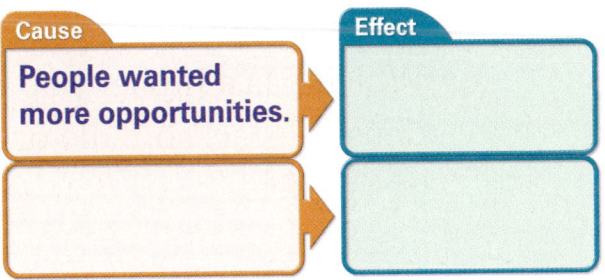

Map and Globe Skills

Use a Population Map

Why It Matters As communities change, so do their populations. Population maps can show you where most people live.

❯ Learn

People are not spread out evenly on Earth. Different areas have different population densities (DEN•suh•teez). **Population density** is the number of people living in an area of a certain size, such as 1 square mile. A square mile is a square of land that is 1 mile wide and 1 mile long. Places with higher population densities are more crowded. Cities usually have the highest population densities.

❯ Practice

Use the map of Illinois's population density on page 331 to answer these questions.

1. The map key shows four population densities. Which color is used for the highest population density?
2. What is the population density of Princeton?
3. Which has a higher population density—Jacksonville or Springfield?

330 ▪ Unit 5

 **For online activities, go to www.harcourtschool.com/ss1**

Population Map of Illinois

▸ Apply

Make It Relevant Look in an encyclopedia or on the Internet to find a population map for your state. Where is the population density the highest? Where is it the lowest?

Chapter 9 ▪ 331

Lesson 2
Sharing Cultures

What to Know
How do different groups in the United States share their cultures?

Vocabulary
custom p. 332
diverse p. 332
ethnic group p. 333
multicultural p. 333
tradition p. 335

Cause and Effect

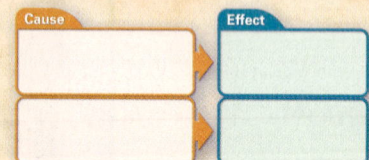

All people bring their own cultures and customs to communities. A **custom** is a way of doing something. For example, it is a custom in the United States for people to greet each other by shaking hands. In Japan, some people greet others by bowing.

Different customs make communities in the United States **diverse**, or different. These differences give people the opportunity to learn more about other cultures.

▶ In the Adams Morgan neighborhood of Washington, D.C., people share many cultures.

332 ■ Unit 5

▶ The Friendship Archway in Washington, D.C., shows the city's Chinese culture.

Washington, D.C.

Like most large cities, Washington, D.C., has many ethnic groups. An **ethnic group** is a group of people who have the same language, culture, and way of life. Each ethnic group brings some of its culture to the community.

Some neighborhoods are made up mainly of the same ethnic group. The Chinatown area of Washington, D.C., began when Chinese immigrants moved there in the 1800s. It has many Chinese restaurants and shops.

Other people live in more multicultural neighborhoods. **Multicultural** neighborhoods have many different cultures. Adams Morgan is a Washington, D.C., neighborhood where many Latin American, Caribbean, African, and Asian immigrants live.

Reading Check ✏ **Cause and Effect**
How do ethnic groups affect communities?

Chapter 9 ▪ 333

> The opening of the Hebrew Garden at the Cleveland Cultural Gardens

> The Hebrew Garden at the Cleveland Cultural Gardens

Cleveland, Ohio

Cleveland is another community with many cultures. Cleveland is located in northern Ohio on Lake Erie. African Americans make up one of its largest ethnic groups. Many African American families came to Cleveland during the Great Migration. The city also has large Italian, Czech (CHEK), Irish, and Polish groups, as well as many other groups.

The city's multiculturalism can be seen in the Cleveland Cultural Gardens. These gardens honor more than 20 different ethnic groups. Together, the gardens show Cleveland's ethnic diversity.

▶ African Americans are among the many groups who celebrate their culture in Cleveland's Parade the Circle Celebration.

A City of Traditions

Every ethnic group has its own beliefs and traditions. A **tradition** is a custom that is passed on to others. Visitors to Cleveland's Little Italy neighborhood enjoy traditional Italian foods. They can watch Italian musicians and traditional dancers at neighborhood events.

Visitors to Cleveland's Hough (HUFF) neighborhood enjoy African American traditions. They can visit the African American Museum to learn about their traditional art, culture, and history.

▶ These cooks prepare traditional foods in Cleveland's Little Italy.

Reading Check **Summarize**
What are some kinds of cultural traditions?

Chapter 9 ■ 335

Chamblee, Georgia

Chamblee (SHAM•blee) is a small city in Georgia. About 10,000 people live there. Like Cleveland, Chamblee has different ethnic neighborhoods. Its largest ethnic groups include Hispanic and Southeast Asian immigrants.

An International City

Visitors to Chamblee have many opportunities to enjoy the city's cultural diversity. It has about 100 different businesses owned by immigrants. Many of these are restaurants that offer traditional foods from other countries. There are Mexican, Vietnamese, Greek, Thai, and other restaurants. There are also Chinese bookstores and a Mexican music store.

▶ This market in Chamblee sells goods from many different countries.

Immigrant groups have brought many changes to Chamblee. They help the community grow. They bring money into the community with their businesses. They also continue to help build a diverse community by sharing their customs and traditions.

Reading Check ⊙ **Cause and Effect**
What effects have immigrants had on the city of Chamblee?

Summary Communities in the United States are made up of people from many different ethnic groups. People share their cultural traditions where they live.

▶ This sign shows some of the ethnically diverse businesses in Chamblee

Review

1. **What to Know** How do different groups in the United States share their cultures?

2. **Vocabulary** Use the term **tradition** in a sentence that explains its meaning.

3. **Your Community** What examples of different cultures are found in your community?

4. **Critical Thinking Make It Relevant** What cultural traditions are shared in your community?

5. **Make a Bulletin Board** Make a bulletin board about the different cultures in your community or state.

6. **Cause and Effect** On a separate sheet of paper, copy and complete the graphic organizer below.

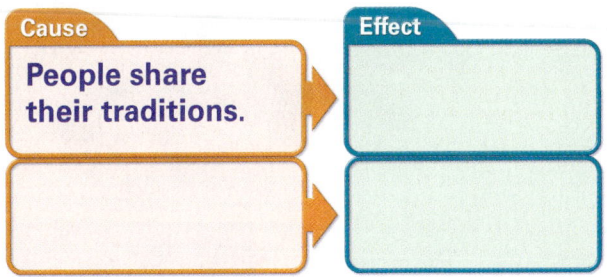

Chapter 9 ▪ 337

Lesson 3 Our American Heritage

 What to Know
What makes up our American heritage?

Vocabulary
landmark p. 338
statue p. 338
holiday p. 340

 Cause and Effect

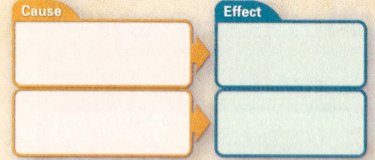

Belonging to the same community unites people of different cultures. In the United States, people share a common heritage, or set of beliefs and customs.

American Landmarks

American landmarks are a part of our national heritage. A **landmark** is an important natural or human feature that marks a location. The Statue of Liberty is one well-known landmark. A **statue** is a monument built to honor or remember a person, an idea, or an event.

The Statue of Liberty

1876

1878

338 ▪ Unit 5

The Statue of Liberty stands on an island in New York Harbor. France gave the statue to the United States in 1885. It was a sign of friendship.

The Statue of Liberty quickly became a symbol of freedom. A poem by Emma Lazarus on the statue reads, "Give me your tired, your poor, Your huddled masses yearning to breathe free."

Mount Rushmore

Another important national landmark in the United States is Mount Rushmore. This is a sculpture of four United States Presidents—George Washington, Thomas Jefferson, Theodore Roosevelt, and Abraham Lincoln. Images of their faces are carved into a cliff in South Dakota.

Reading Check **Cause and Effect**
What caused France to give the Statue of Liberty to the United States?

Fast Fact

It took more than 400 workers from 1927 to 1941 to complete Mount Rushmore's 60-foot sculptures of the Presidents.

1884   Today

Time Line It took eight years to build the Statue of Liberty. Why do you think it took this long to build the Statue of Liberty?

339

National Holidays

People in the United States often celebrate their American heritage on national holidays. A **holiday** is a day set aside for remembering a person, an idea, or an event.

Celebrating People

In January, people celebrate the birthday of Dr. Martin Luther King, Jr. This holiday honors his peaceful actions for civil rights.

In February, we celebrate Presidents' Day. This holiday once marked the birthday of George Washington. Today, we honor all United States Presidents on this day.

In November, we celebrate Veterans Day. On this day, we honor citizens who served in the military in all of our country's wars.

❯ A World War II veteran takes part in the Veterans Day parade in New York City.

❯ Marchers in St. Paul, Minnesota, celebrate Dr. Martin Luther King, Jr., Day.

Celebrating History

National holidays celebrate important events in history, too. Our country's Declaration of Independence was signed on July 4, 1776. Every year on the Fourth of July, we celebrate Independence Day. Many people across the country gather to watch fireworks and fly the American flag. They also show pride in the United States by wearing its colors—red, white, and blue.

Reading Check **Generalize**
Why do we celebrate national holidays?

> Students celebrate Independence Day.

Summary American landmarks remind us of our common national heritage. Holidays remind us of the people and events that make up our American heritage.

Review

1. **What to Know** What makes up our American heritage?
2. **Vocabulary** What clues can you use to remember the meaning of the term **landmark**?
3. **Your Community** How does your community celebrate national holidays?
4. **Critical Thinking** **Make It Relevant** How can national holidays help you and other people think about our heritage?
5. **Draw a Landmark** Draw a picture of a landmark in your community or state.
6. **Cause and Effect** On a separate sheet of paper, copy and complete the graphic organizer below.

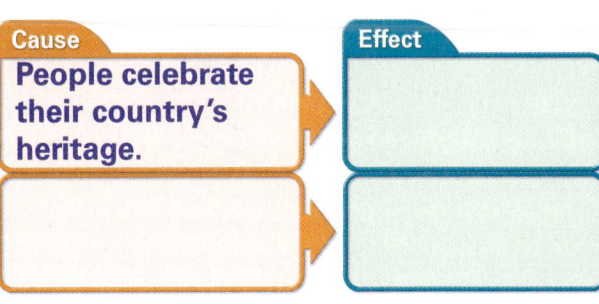

Chapter 9 ■ 341

Biography

- Trustworthiness
- **Respect**
- Responsibility
- Fairness
- Caring
- Patriotism

Maya Lin

"[The Wall] is like a thread of life."
— Maya Lin, 2002

When Maya Lin was just 21 years old, she won a contest to design the Vietnam Veterans Memorial. At the time, Lin was studying architecture at Yale University. Architecture is the art of designing buildings and other structures.

Lin was born in Athens, Ohio. Her parents had immigrated to the United States from China. Her father was also an artist. Lin sculpted art from clay with her dad.

Lin's Vietnam Veterans Memorial in Washington, D.C., is made up of two black granite walls. The names of soldiers who died in the Vietnam War are engraved on the stone. Millions of visitors come to see the memorial each year.

Maya Lin

Why Character Counts

How does Maya Lin's work show respect for her American heritage?

At the Vietnam Veterans Memorial, many visitors go to the names of the people they knew.

In 1989, Maya Lin designed the Civil Rights Memorial, in Montgomery, Alabama. This memorial shows respect for people, who were part of the Civil Rights movement.

Lin created an outdoor sculpture garden in 1998 for the Cleveland Public Library in Ohio. Called *Reading a Garden*, it includes poetry written by her brother Tan Lin. The garden is described as a "landscape of words."

Today, Lin lives in New York. She works as both an architect and an artist.

Water flows over the names of 40 people at the base of the Civil Rights Memorial.

 For more resources, go to www.harcourtschool.com/ss1

Time

1959 Born — **Present**

- **1982** Vietnam Veterans Memorial opens to the public in Washington, D.C.
- **1989** Designs the Civil Rights Memorial in Montgomery, Alabama
- **1998** Creates an outdoor sculpture garden for the Cleveland Public Library in Ohio

Chapter 9 • 343

Chapter 9 Review

Visual Summary

People move for new opportunities.

Summarize the Chapter

Cause and Effect Complete the graphic organizer to show that you understand the causes and effects of movement in the United States.

Cause	Effect
	People in other countries immigrated to the United States.
	African Americans moved from rural areas to urban areas.

Vocabulary

Write a short story. Use each of these vocabulary terms in your story. Show that you understand the meaning of each term.

1. **opportunity**, p. 324
2. **migrate**, p. 328
3. **ethnic group**, p. 333
4. **multicultural**, p. 333
5. **tradition**, p. 335
6. **landmark**, p. 338
7. **holiday**, p. 340

344 ■ Unit 5

 People share customs and make communities diverse.

 People in the United States share a common heritage.

Facts and Main Ideas

Answer these questions.

8. What problems did some immigrants to the United States face because of prejudice?

9. How is Adams Morgan in Washington, D.C., a multicultural community?

10. Why do we celebrate Presidents' Day?

Write the letter of the best choice.

11. Where did African Americans move during the Great Migration?
    A to rural areas
    B to urban areas
    C to the South
    D to suburban areas

12. What honors different ethnic groups in Cleveland, Ohio?
    A Friendship Archway
    B Chamblee
    C Cultural Gardens
    D African American Museum

Critical Thinking

13. **Make It Relevant** What symbols of American heritage are in your community?

14. Why do you think immigrants move to the United States today?

Skills

Use a Population Map
Use the population map on page 331 to answer the question.

15. Which color is used for the lowest population density in the map key?

writing

Write an Interview Suppose you are going to interview an immigrant. Write questions you want to ask this person.

Write a Poem Imagine that you are Emma Lazarus. Write another poem for the Statue of Liberty.

Chapter 9 ■ 345

STUDY SKILLS

WRITE TO LEARN

Write about what you read to better understand and remember information.

- Keep a learning log to write responses to what you read.
- Responses can be personal and creative to make the text more meaningful to you.

Cultures Around the World

What I Learned	My Response
People express their culture through storytelling and art.	I can tell a story or make artwork to express my culture.

PREVIEW VOCABULARY

folktale p. 349

folk song p. 350

worship p. 352

346 • Unit 5

Cultures Around the World

CHAPTER 10

> People celebrate the Fiesta of San Francisco in Teotihuacán, Mexico

Lesson 1

Expressions of Culture

What to Know
How do people express their culture?

Vocabulary
literature p. 348
myth p. 348
fable p. 348
folktale p. 349
legend p. 349
folk song p. 350
worship p. 352

Cause and Effect

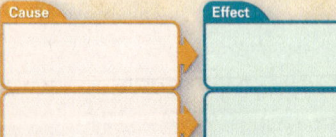

The world has many different cultures. Sometimes different groups express, or share, their cultures in some of the same ways.

Written and Oral Traditions

People can share their culture through literature. **Literature** includes the stories and poems that people use to share their ideas. A **myth** is a story made up to explain the world around us. Children in West Africa hear myths about how Anansi the Spider created the sun, moon, and stars.

A **fable** is a story in which animals speak and act like humans. People enjoy fables that were told by Aesop, a Greek storyteller.

▶ A storyteller tells folktales at a New York public library.

▶ People perform in a play. A play is a story acted out in front of an audience.

▶ Third graders listen to stories at their school in Hawaii.

Folktales and Legends

Folktales help keep the traditions of a culture alive. A **folktale** is a story passed from one generation to the next. A favorite Japanese folktale is about a man named Urashima Taro. While fishing, Taro rescues a turtle. He is rewarded with a visit to the Dragon Palace.

Many people share legends from their culture. A **legend** is a made-up story about a real person or event. One legend is based on John Chapman. He planted apple trees in the United States. He was given the nickname Johnny Appleseed.

Reading Check ⭐ **Cause and Effect**
Why was John Chapman called Johnny Appleseed?

Chapter 10 ■ 349

▶ *Detroit Industry*, a mural by Diego Rivera

The Arts

Storytelling is just one way people express their culture. Artists, musicians, dancers, and builders also use their talents to express their cultures.

Art and Music

Artists draw, paint, and sculpt artworks. Diego Rivera (ree•VAY•rah) expressed his Mexican culture with colorful murals. A mural is a large painting on a wall.

Musicians use sound to create music, another part of culture. In many African cultures, drums provide the beat for music. The *kalungu,* or "talking drum," comes from Nigeria. Its sounds can be high or low, like a human voice.

Folk songs express the culture of a group of people. In Eastern Europe, people play folk songs with accordions and other instruments.

▶ People dance to folk songs.

Dance

Dancers express culture through traditional clothes, music, and movement. In West Africa, people perform a welcome dance called the Yabara. This dance is named after the beaded rattles that the dancers carry. The rattles are thrown in the air and caught in rhythm.

Architecture

Architecture is the art of designing buildings. The ancient city of Tikal, in Guatemala, was a center of culture for the Maya. The large step pyramids they built there still stand today. The pyramids show the power and skill of the ancient Maya.

Reading Check **Summarize**
How can people express their culture through the arts?

> Women perform an African dance.

Fast Fact

Tikal includes the ruins of several step pyramids and a royal palace. There are also courts where the ancient Maya played a ball game.

► Church

► Mosque

► Buddhist Temple

► Synagogue

Religions

Religious traditions are also an important part of culture. In the United States, people have the right to choose which religion, if any, they will follow. Some choose to follow the teachings of Christianity or Judaism (JOO•duh•ih•zuhm). Others follow the teachings of Islam (is•LAHM), Hinduism (HIN•doo•ih•zuhm), or Buddhism (BOO•dih•zuhm).

Places of Worship

Communities have special places where people can **worship**, or pray, together. Christians worship in churches. Followers of Islam pray in a mosque (MAHSK), or masjid (MUS•jid). Jewish worshipers meet in a synagogue (SIN•uh•gahg), or temple. Buddhists and Hindus visit temples to meditate.

People gather at places of worship to share religious traditions. There, they meet with other people who share the same beliefs. Some offer programs that help the community. Some places of worship also have schools. These schools teach students about the religion and its beliefs and values. They may also teach regular school subjects.

Reading Check **Summarize**
What are the names of some kinds of places of worship?

Followers of Five Religions in the United States

Religion	Number of Followers
Buddhism	1,082,000
Christianity	159,030,000
Hinduism	766,000
Islam	1,104,000
Judaism	2,831,000

Table This table shows how many people follow the five largest religions in the United States. Which religion has the most followers?

Summary People around the world express their culture. They tell stories and create art. Some people express their culture through religious traditions.

Review

1. **What to Know** How do people express their culture?
2. **Vocabulary** Explain the difference between a **myth** and a **legend**.
3. **Culture** What are some of the different types of literature people use to share their culture?
4. **Critical Thinking** Why do you think people go to places of worship?
5. **Write a Folktale** Write a folktale that takes place in your community.
6. **Cause and Effect** On a separate sheet of paper, copy and complete the graphic organizer below.

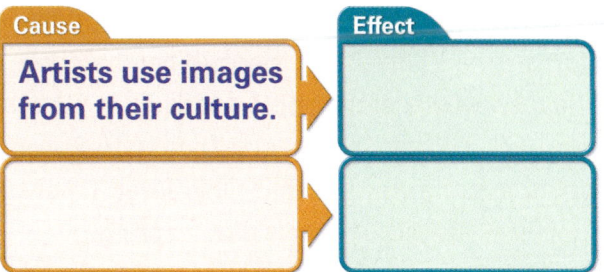

Chapter 10 ■ 353

Critical Thinking Skills

Tell Fact from Fiction

Why It Matters When you read something, it is important to know whether it is fact or fiction.

▶ Learn

Facts are statements that can be proved. They give names, places, and dates that you can check. You can look up these facts in reference works, such as encyclopedias.

Fiction is a story that is made up. The people and events in it may seem real, but they are imaginary. Some works of fiction, such as legends and historical fiction, tell about real people and events. However, many of the details are made up to add interest.

Johnny Appleseed

A long time ago, a man named Johnny decided he would plant apple seeds for settlers in the Ohio River valley. He left his home with only a bag and a cooking pot in which to make his meals. In the bag were so many apple seeds that there was no room for the cooking pot, so he wore it on his head like a hat!

As Johnny traveled, he would sleep outside at night. Once, during a snowstorm, he slept inside a log snuggled up with a bear. When he came to farms, he would plant apple seeds. The pioneers called him Johnny Appleseed. Thanks to Johnny Appleseed, the trees of the Ohio River valley bloom with apple blossoms every spring.

▶ Practice

Read the two selections about Johnny Appleseed. Then answer these questions.

1. Which selection is mainly fiction? Which selection contains the most facts? How do you know?
2. What sources could you use to check the facts?

▶ Apply

Make It Relevant Write a legend about someone you know or have read about. Include both facts and fiction.

John Chapman
(1774–1845)

John Chapman was an American pioneer born in Massachusetts. For more than 40 years, he traveled around Ohio, Indiana, and Illinois. He sold or gave away apple seeds to people he met. He helped hundreds of settlers set up apple orchards. The settlers began to tell stories about him. They gave him the nickname Johnny Appleseed. Chapman became an American legend during his life. He became a symbol of the pioneer spirit in the United States.

FIELD TRIP

http://www.harcourtschool.com/ss1

READ ABOUT

National Storytelling Festival

Good storytellers make you feel like you are a part of the story. Jimmy Neil Smith has heard many great storytellers spin their tales. These stories led him to create the first National Storytelling Festival in 1973. This festival is held every October in Jonesborough, Tennessee.

Each year, thousands of visitors make their way to Jonesborough. They come to hear stories told about the past. Storytellers take the stage over the festival weekend. Often, their stories share messages about the hopes and dreams of people around the world.

FIND

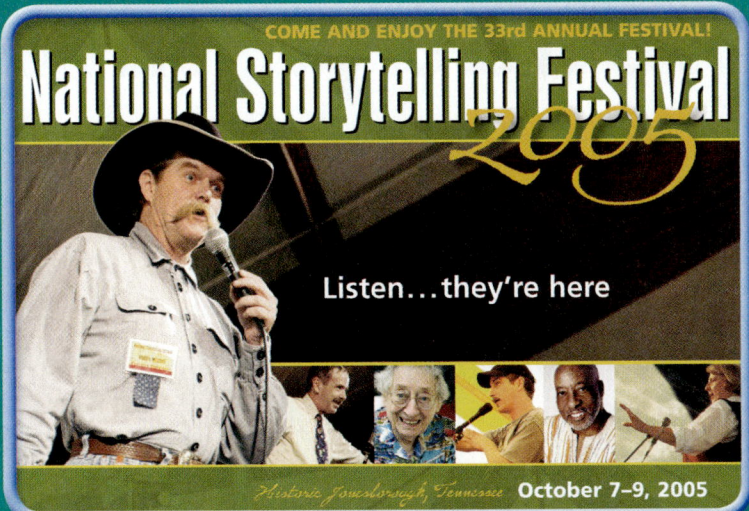

A poster for the National Stoytelling Festival

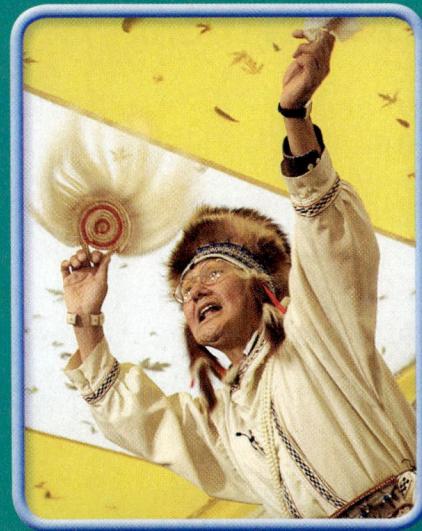

This Native American shares a story.

A festival performance

Listeners laugh at a story.

A VIRTUAL TOUR

GO ONLINE For more resources, go to www.harcourtschool.com/ss1

Lesson 2

Holidays and Traditions

What to Know
What are some holidays and traditions that people celebrate?

Vocabulary
festival p. 359

Cause and Effect

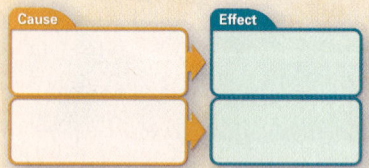

People around the world express their culture with holidays and celebrations. Many of these holidays are also celebrated in the United States.

Cultural Holidays

Some holidays come from different cultures. They are celebrated by many Americans, too.

Saint Patrick's Day

On March 17, the Irish celebrate Saint Patrick's Day. Saint Patrick's Day began as a religious holiday. It has grown to celebrate Irish culture.

> Saint Patrick's Day parades are held in many cities in the United States.

Cinco de Mayo and Mexican Independence

Cinco de Mayo is celebrated in Mexico. It is also celebrated in many communities in the United States. The name is Spanish for "the Fifth of May." On this day in 1862, a small Mexican army won an important battle against France.

Every September 16, people in Mexico also celebrate their independence from Spain. Many Mexican Americans living in the United States celebrate, too. They decorate their homes with lights. People enjoy food, music, and fireworks.

Kwanzaa

Kwanzaa is a week-long holiday in late December. It celebrates the importance of family and community in African American cultures. Many cities have a Kwanzaa **festival**, or a joyful gathering for celebration.

Reading Check ⚡ **Cause and Effect**
Why do people celebrate Kwanzaa?

▶ Cinco de Mayo is celebrated today with traditional Mexican dances and music.

▶ Each day of Kwanzaa honors a different value, or principle, in the community.

New Year's Day

New Year's Day is the beginning of a new calendar year. Countries around the world celebrate the new year in different ways. On New Year's Eve, people in New York City gather in Times Square. They watch as a giant crystal ball is lowered just before the new year begins. Children in Belgium write messages on decorated paper for their parents to read on New Year's Day.

Chinese New Year

The Chinese New Year falls on a different date each year. This date is between January 21 and February 20. Chinese New Year is celebrated in China and around the world. Chinese families gather for a special meal on New Year's Eve. Children receive red packets with money inside for good luck.

▶ New Year's Eve in Times Square

▶ On New Year's Day in China, people gather to watch traditional dragon dances.

Thai New Year

The Thai New Year is called Songkran. *Songkran* is a Thai word that means "to move" or "to change place." It is celebrated in April. April is a hot month in Thailand. People celebrate the new year by throwing cool water on one another. People walk on the streets with bowls of water or even garden hoses. Anyone who passes by is likely to get wet!

Reading Check **Main Idea and Details**
How do people in Thailand celebrate a new year?

Summary People express their culture by celebrating holidays. People of different cultures celebrate their new year with different traditions.

▶ Thai children at a Songkran festival

Review

1. **What to Know** What are some holidays and traditions that people celebrate?

2. **Vocabulary** What does the term **festival** mean?

3. **Geography** Where are some different places that the new year is celebrated?

4. **Critical Thinking Make It Relevant** How does your community celebrate New Year's Day?

5. **Write a Description** Write about a holiday that your community celebrates. Describe the traditions for this holiday.

6. **Cause and Effect** On a separate sheet of paper, copy and complete the graphic organizer below.

Cause		Effect
	→	People express their culture.
	→	

Lesson 3 Cultures of the World

What to Know
How are cultures around the world alike and different?

Vocabulary
cultural identity p. 364

Cause and Effect

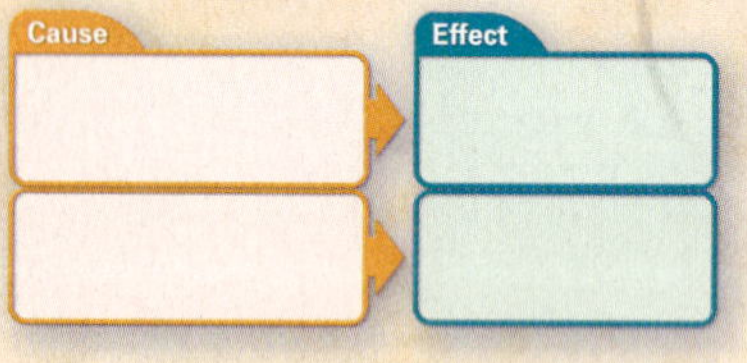

Culture groups around the world have similar and different ways of life. These customs affect family, school, language, food, and other parts of life.

Ways of Life

There are many different cultures throughout the world. Africa and Europe are two continents. Each continent has about 700 million people. The people of each continent make up hundreds of culture groups. The people in these groups speak different languages and eat different foods.

▶ Drummers and singers at the Timkat festival in Ethiopia

> A market in Spain

Life in Ethiopia

Africa has more than 50 countries. Hundreds of languages, such as Arabic and Somali are spoken. Students in Ethiopia learn different languages in school. At home, families eat vegetables and meat served on *injera* (in•JAIR•uh), a flat, spongy bread.

Life in Spain

Europe is made up of more than 40 countries. More than 40 languages are spoken. In Spain, the official language is Spanish. Other languages, such as Basque (BASK) and Catalan, are also spoken. Families in Spain eat their main meal of the day in the afternoon.

Reading Check **Cause and Effect**
Why are several languages spoken on each continent?

> An Ethiopian woman makes *injera*.

People of the World

People everywhere are proud of their own cultures. One way people show their cultural identities is through what they wear. A **cultural identity** is a collection of traits that are seen in a group.

This map shows children from some of the world's cultures. Some are wearing traditional clothing that is worn on special days. Others are in everyday clothes.

Reading Check **Main Idea and Details**
What is one way people show their cultural identity?

Expressions of Culture Around the World

People around the world express their culture in different ways. Architecture, music, and dance also help create a group's cultural identity.

Japanese Architecture

Many historic buildings in Japan share traditional features. They were designed to be close to the natural environment. Most older buildings are made of wood. Some buildings have many openings, so air can move easily through the rooms. In Japan, living close to nature is an important value.

▶ A room in a Japanese house

▶ The island of Itsukushima (it•soo•koo•SHEE•mah) in Japan is home to a shrine, or holy place.

Brazilian Music and Dance

Music and dance are important ways to express culture in Brazil. Samba music has a lively rhythm. The samba dance comes from Portuguese, African, and native traditions. Dancers and musicians practice all year for contests held during a festival called Carnaval.

Reading Check **Cause and Effect**
Why were buildings in Japan built with nature in mind?

Summary People around the world have similar and different customs and ways of life. They express their cultures in many different ways.

▶ Samba dancers in Rio de Janeiro, Brazil

Review

1. **What to Know** How are cultures around the world alike and different?
2. **Vocabulary** Explain the meaning of **cultural identity**.
3. **Culture** What cultures are celebrated when Brazilians dance the samba?
4. **Critical Thinking Make It Relevant** What cultures from around the world are expressed in your community?
5. **Make a List** List different cultural expressions you learned about in this lesson. Name the countries they came from and find these places on a world map.
6. **Cause and Effect** On a separate sheet of paper, copy and complete the graphic organizer below.

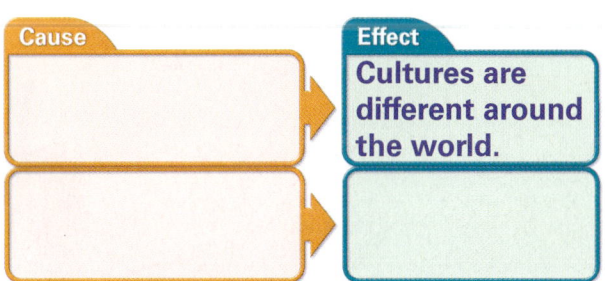

Chapter 10 ■ 367

Explore Your Community's Culture

In this unit, you learned about different cultures and the ways people share their culture with others. You can also explore the cultures in your own community.

- What ethnic groups live in your community?
- What are some ways that people in your community express their culture?
- Which cultural holidays or festivals are celebrated in your community?

Use Your Community's Resources

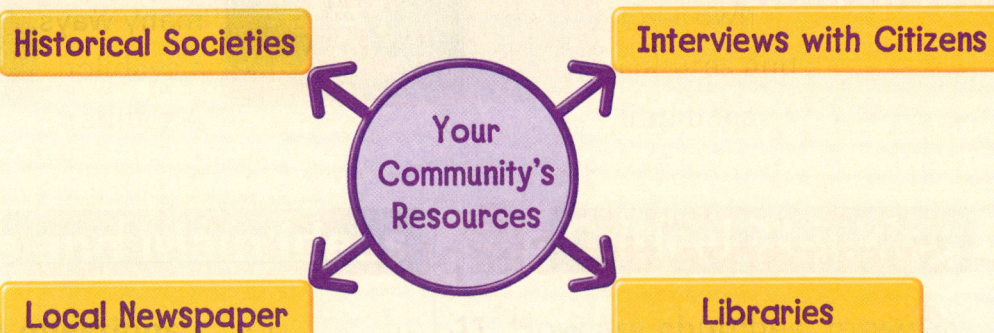

- Historical Societies
- Interviews with Citizens
- Local Newspaper
- Libraries

Your Community's Resources

Design a Culture Guide

Design a guide to the festivals and other cultural events in your community. List the events in order of when they happen in the year. Include a photo or drawing for each event. Describe the customs, food, music, dance, and artwork for each.

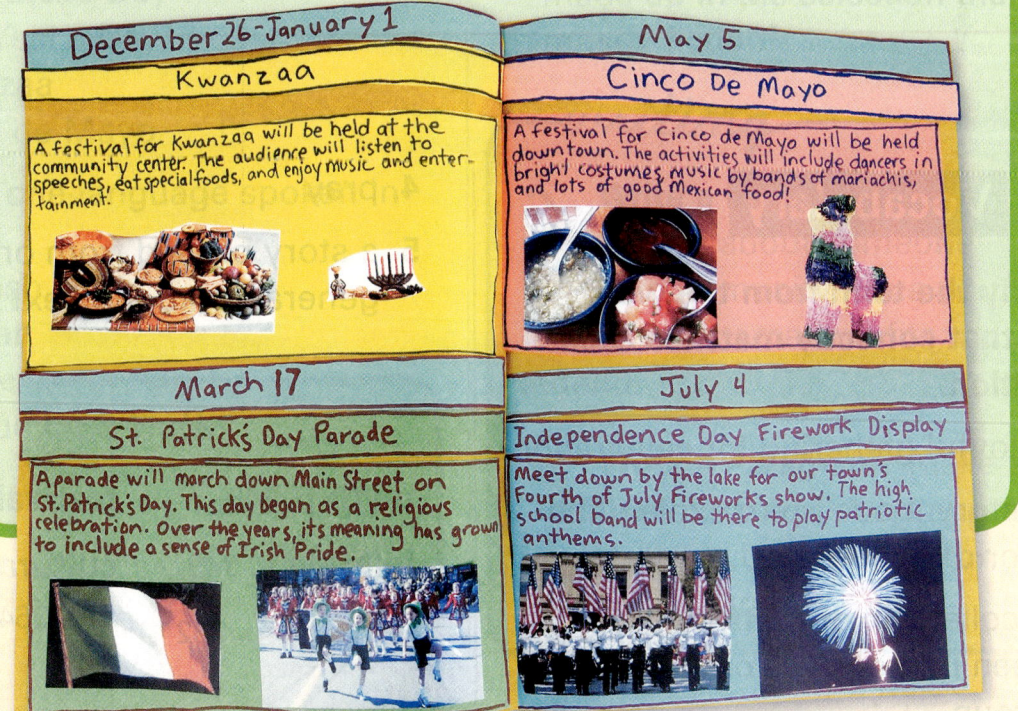

Fun with Social Studies

Button Craze

Calvin collects buttons. Where did he get each one?

1 mountain
4 Presidents

From France to U.S.
One Tall Lady

Taste the world in our town

Diversity grows in our Cultural Gardens

We open our door. Millions come in.

Pyramids—
The Maya made 'em

Alphabet Riddle

Put these words into the grid in alphabetical order. Read down the letters in the green squares to answer the riddle.

tradition
folktale
fable
festival
legend
folk song

Riddle:
How can you hear a pin drop?

Online Adventures

The cultural fair is in town today! Join Eco to play the online game and visit the fair. You'll get to see games, rides, and prizes. But be ready. To win, you'll need to remember what you learned about culture. Play now at www.harcourtschool.com/ss1

Unit 5 Review and Test Prep

The Big Idea

Culture Cultural differences enrich communities and make them diverse.

Reading Comprehension and Vocabulary

People in Communities

Immigrants move to the United States to find more opportunities. By sharing their cultures and customs, these different ethnic groups help make our communities diverse.

People share their cultures through written and oral traditions, such as myths, fables, folktales, and legends. They also express their cultures through art, music, dance, architecture, and religion. In the United States, people of all cultures are united in a common American heritage.

Read the summary above. Then answer the questions that follow.

1. Why do people move to the United States?
   A to find more opportunities
   B to celebrate holidays
   C to honor people
   D to share their art

2. What does diverse mean?
   A better
   B larger
   C different
   D traditional

3. What are some traditions that people share?
   A ethnic groups
   B opportunities
   C landmarks
   D folktales

4. How are all community members in our country united?
   A religious traditions
   B ethnic groups
   C common American heritage
   D art and music

Facts and Main Ideas

Answer these questions.

5. Where did most immigrants arrive in the United States in the past?

6. How is Cleveland, Ohio, multicultural?

7. What are some religions that people follow?

Write the letter of the best choice.

8. Where do most immigrants to the United States come from today?
   A Australia
   B Canada and Mexico
   C Europe
   D Asia and Latin America

9. Which holiday celebrates our common American heritage?
   A Cinco de Mayo
   B Saint Patrick's Day
   C Fourth of July
   D Kwanzaa

10. How do people celebrate the Thai New Year?
    A They gather in Times Square.
    B They write messages on decorated paper.
    C They throw cool water on one another.
    D They watch traditional dragon dances.

 Critical Thinking

11. **Make It Relevant** What values and beliefs are taught in your favorite stories?

12. What do you think Emma Lazarus's poem at the base of the Statue of Liberty means?

 **Skills**

Read a Population Map

Use the map below to answer the following questions.

13. Which color is used for the highest population density?

14. What is the population density of Columbia?

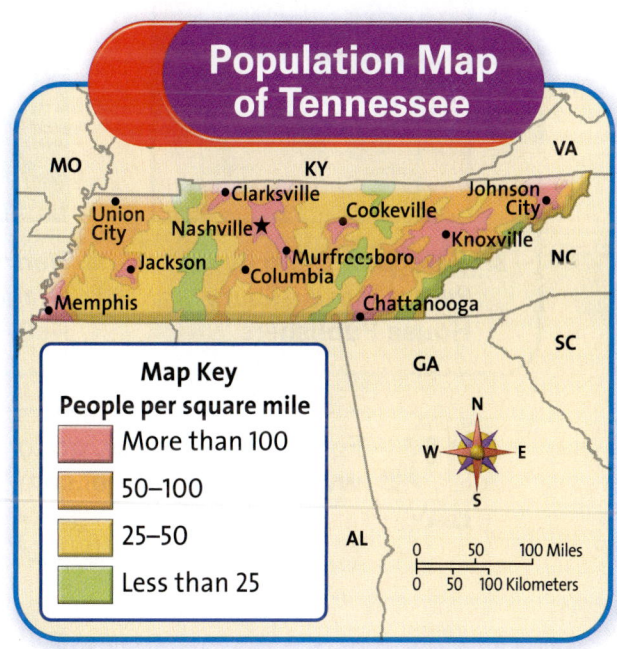

Unit 5 • 375

Unit 5 Activities

Show What You Know

 Unit Writing Activity

Write a Poem Write a poem about your community's cultures.

- Include details about cultural traditions, such as food, clothing, and art.
- Tell how the cultures make the community a better place to live.

 Unit Project

Culture Fair Create a fair exhibit about a culture.

- Research a culture in the United States.
- Make a poster that illustrates the customs of the culture.

Read More

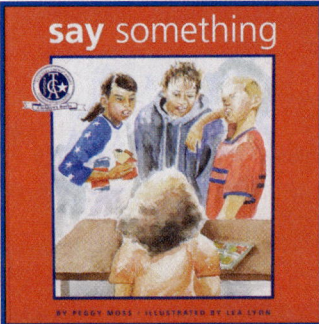

- *Say Something* by Peggy Moss. Tilbury House Publishers.

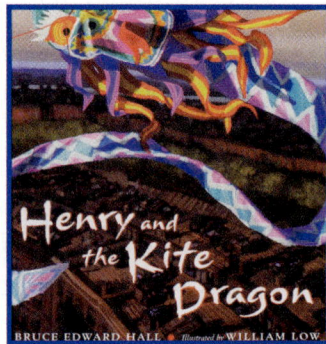

- *Henry and the Kite Dragon* by Bruce Edward Hall. Philomel.

- *Going North* by Janice N. Harrington. Farrar, Straus and Giroux.

 For more resources, go to www.harcourtschool.com/ss1

Working in Communities

Unit 6

Start with the Standards

OHIO SOCIAL STUDIES CONTENT STANDARDS

History 3.3A, 3.3D, 3.3G

Geography 3.1, 3.3, 3.6, 3.8

Economics 3.1, 3.2, 3.3, 3.4, 3.5, 3.6, 3.7

Citizenship 3.1B, 3.1C, 3.1D, 3.1E, 3.1F, 3.2C, 3.2F

Social Studies Skills 3.1A, 3.1B

The Big Idea

Economics

People depend on one another to produce, buy, and sell goods and services. Good decision-making helps the economy of a family or a community.

What to Know

✓ How do people in a community depend on one another?

✓ Why do people and countries trade with each other?

✓ How do families earn, spend, and save money?

✓ How do businesses around the world make money?

Unit 6

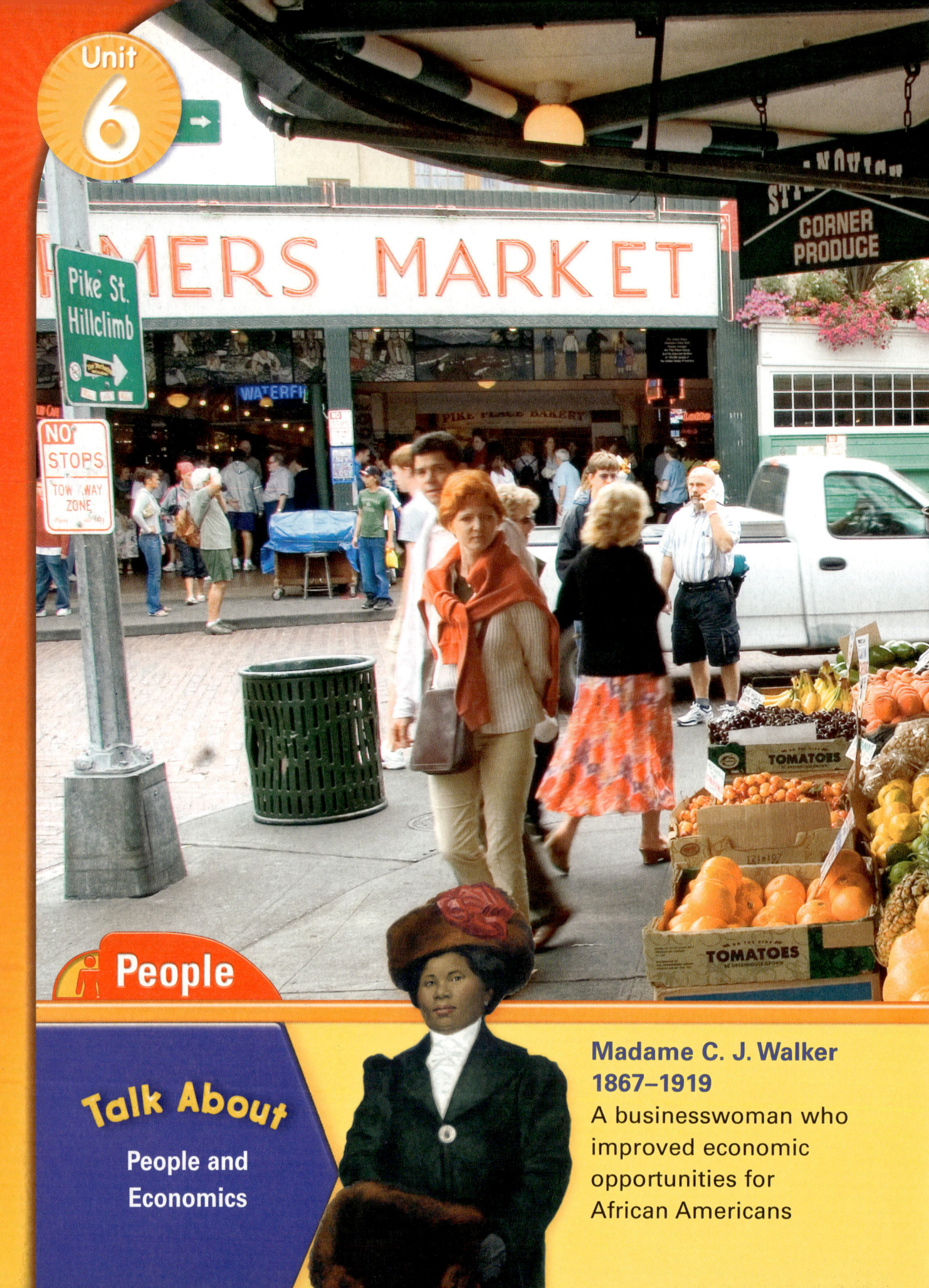

People

Talk About
People and Economics

Madame C. J. Walker
1867–1919
A businesswoman who improved economic opportunities for African Americans

Working in Communities

Katherine Ortega
1934–Present
Former United States treasurer

Ray Tomlinson
1941–Present
Massachusetts engineer who invented e-mail

Unit 6 Preview
Vocabulary

producer Someone who makes a product or provides a service. (page 389)

consumer A person who buys a product or service. (page 390)

barter To trade without using money. (page 418)

supply The goods or services that businesses provide. (page 424)

demand The willingness to buy a good or service. (page 424)

For more resources, go to www.harcourtschool.com/ss1

Unit 6 379

Reading Social Studies
Generalize
Focus Skill

Why It Matters Knowing how to generalize can help you understand and remember what you read.

▶ Learn

To **generalize** is to make a broad statement based on what you know about a group of ideas.

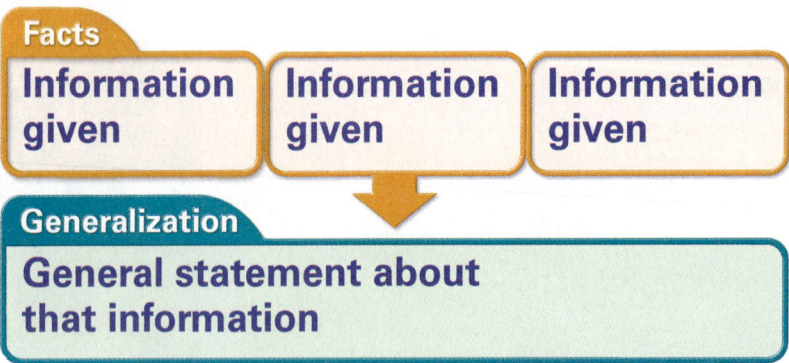

- A generalization should be based on facts.
- To generalize, think about what the facts have in common.

▶ Practice

Read the paragraph. Then make a generalization.

Fact — Ten years ago, the rural town of Alliance, Nebraska, was in trouble. Its agriculture industry was failing, and the railroad company was getting smaller. Community members feared **Fact** — that their town would become poor. They took action by starting new tourism businesses. Tourism businesses provide goods and services for visitors.

> Apply

Read the paragraphs, and answer the questions.

Tourism in Alliance, Nebraska

The people of Alliance, Nebraska, made tourism a major part of the economy. Visitors, or tourists, come to see things such as the huge sculpture Carhenge. The artist, Jim Reinders, modeled it after Stonehenge, an ancient monument in England. His whole family sculpted 38 cars to match the stones in Stonehenge.

Reinders gave the site to the city, and a community group now runs Carhenge. More than 80,000 tourists come each year to see the sculpture. Other tourist sites in town include several museums and a fine arts center.

Tourists bring money to Alliance. They pay to stay in hotels. They buy meals at restaurants and goods in the town's stores. Tourism also helps create jobs in the town. Some townspeople work in the hotels and restaurants. Others help keep the tourist sites clean and safe for visitors.

Focus Skill Generalize

1. What generalization can you make about the selection?
2. How did Jim Reinders help the economy of Alliance?
3. How do tourists help the economy of Alliance?

Unit 6 • 381

Start with a Story

Alex and the Amazing Lemonade Stand

by Liz and Jay Scott
illustrated by Pam Howard

Alexandra "Alex" Scott was only a baby when her family found out she had cancer. When Alex was eight years old, she decided that she wanted to do something to raise money to fight cancer. She decided to start her own lemonade business. Alex gave the money she made to doctors. She wanted to help find a cure for children's cancers.

Alex was smart. She developed a plan. She would sell lemonade from a lemonade stand. Keeping the money was not in her mind. She would give it to her hospital for the cure they might find.

When summer came, Alex told her mother that she would have her stand with the help of her brothers. They worked very hard getting everything ready, but this work was fun, and their progress was steady.

The day for the sale came around at last.
There were people outside;
they were lining up fast!
    Many people had heard about Alex's stand,
    about little Alex and her lemonade plan.

They waited in line, the young & the old,
for a cup of her lemonade,
    extra sweet and icy cold.

At the end of the day Alex was happy and amazed
to learn how much money her lemonade had raised.
    She also learned
    something else that was true.
    Other people cared about sick kids too.

Many people learned of Alex's determination.
They found her story an inspiration.
    They sent her cards and wrote her letters.
    They liked that she helped
    sick kids get better.
When next year came along,
    Alex stuck with her plan.

On another warm Saturday she set up her stand,
people arrived from near and far.
They had heard about Alex,
the Lemonade Star.

They waited in line, the young & the old,
for a cup of her lemonade,
extra sweet and icy cold.

This year was even better and as her line
grew longer...

...Alex's determination for a cure
grew stronger.
Again she gave the hospital her money
and a letter.

It said,

Please use my money to help ALL kids get better
♥ -alex

More and more people heard about the good things that were done By the girl named Alex and her Lemonade Fund.

The following year, Alex had a new plan —

"Now I'll sell lemonade
across this great land!
If more kids would help, wouldn't it be great,
we could have lemonade
stands in every state.
Think of the money we could raise to
help kids who are sick.
A cure might be found,
perhaps even quick!"

Other kids listened and held
their own stands,
to help support Alex with her lemonade plans.

Response Corner

1. **Focus Skill** **Generalize** Why did so many people line up to buy lemonade?

2. **Make It Relevant** Do you think you could start a business to make money and help others? What would the business be? Where would you donate the money?

STUDY SKILLS

CONNECT IDEAS

Web organizers can help you connect ideas.

- Write the chapter title in the top oval.
- Add ovals showing main ideas that support the theme.
- Add bubbles showing facts and details.

PREVIEW VOCABULARY

wage p. 392

human resource p. 395

capital resource p. 395

CHAPTER 11
Working in Our Community

This market in Cleveland, Ohio, has many booths that sell foods from different countries.

Lesson 1

Workers and Consumers

What to Know
How do people in a community depend on one another?

Vocabulary
product p. 388
producer p. 389
entrepreneur p. 389
consumer p. 390
interdependence p. 391
wage p. 392
income p. 392

Generalize

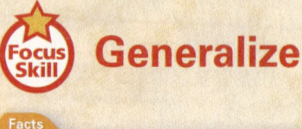

In a community, some people grow or make products to sell. A **product** is a good. Other workers provide services, such as haircuts and car washes.

People Work Together

Think about how busy you would be if you had to make all the things you use every day. You would have to grow your own vegetables. If you wanted meat, eggs, and milk, you would have to raise animals.

Early settlers had to make much of what they used. But as towns grew, people were able to share the work with others in their community.

› People in a community long ago work together to build a barn.

> Oscar Weissenborn's pencil-making business, long ago and today

People Depend on Producers

People in a community depend on producers for goods and services. A **producer** is someone who makes a product or provides a service.

Oscar Weissenborn learned how to use graphite and clay to make pencils. In 1889, he began making pencils in his home in New Jersey. At that time, most pencils were made in other countries.

People began buying Weissenborn's pencils. Weissenborn hired more people. He moved his business into a larger building.

Oscar Weissenborn was an entrepreneur (ahn•truh•pruh•NER). An **entrepreneur** is a person who starts and runs a business. Entrepreneurs provide goods or services and create jobs for workers.

Reading Check ⭐ **Generalize**
Why are producers important to a community?

Chapter 11 ■ 389

◗ Consumers have many choices in kinds of pencils to buy.

People Buy Things

A person who buys a product or a service is a **consumer**. Consumers buy pencils in all sizes, shapes, and colors. Students buy pencils for school. Some artists buy colored pencils to use for drawing. Other consumers buy pencils to write with at home or at work.

Producers are always trying to make new and better cars, computers, televisions, toys, cereals, and other products. As a result, consumers have more products to choose from all the time.

Reading Check ✪ **Generalize**
What is a consumer?

People Help Each Other

Producers and consumers in a community depend on one another. Producers depend on consumers to buy the goods they make. Consumers depend on producers to provide goods and services for them to buy. Depending on one another is called **interdependence**.

Consumers trade, or exchange, things for what they want. They usually trade money for goods or services.

Reading Check ⓞ **Generalize**
How do producers and consumers depend on one another?

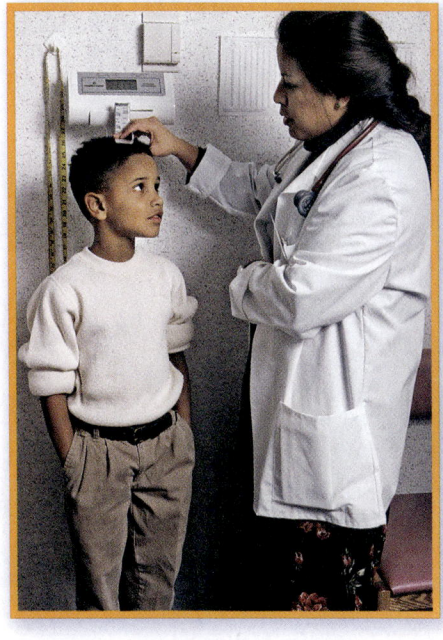

▶ People depend on the services doctors provide to help them stay healthy.

▶ Consumers buy goods at this farmers' market.

Chapter 11 • 391

People Start Businesses

▶ Leticia Herrera

Leticia Herrera (eh•REH•rah) runs a business that provides cleaning services to other businesses in Chicago. Her workers also fix up old buildings for businesses. Like people everywhere, Herrera's workers depend on their jobs for money.

The money people earn at work is called a **wage**. It is also called **income**. In the United States, people can choose the jobs they will do to make money.

Reading Check ⚡ **Generalize**
Why do people depend on their jobs?

Summary People depend on one another to provide and buy goods and services. They earn income for the jobs they do. Some start their own businesses.

Review

1. **What to Know** How do people in a community depend on one another?

2. **Vocabulary** Write a description of an **entrepreneur**.

3. **Economics** How do people pay for the goods they need?

4. **Critical Thinking Make It Relevant** What are some goods and services that you buy as a consumer?

5. **Write a Help Wanted Ad** Imagine that you are a business owner. Write an ad that describes a job for which you want to hire someone.

6. **Generalize** On a separate sheet of paper, copy and complete the graphic organizer below.

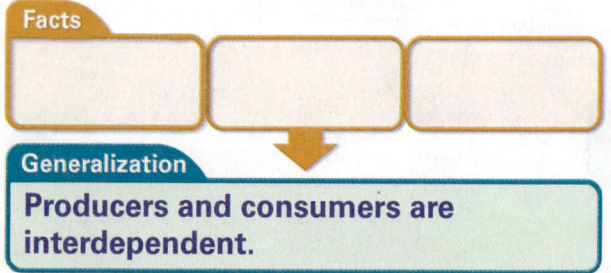

392 ■ Unit 6

Madame C. J. Walker

Biography

Trustworthiness
Respect
Responsibility
Fairness
Caring
Patriotism

"I have built my own factory on my own ground."
— Madame C. J. Walker, 1912

Madame C. J. Walker became one of the first women in the United States to make millions of dollars on her own. She turned her small hair product business, based in Indianapolis, Indiana, into a giant success.

Walker hired and trained many African American women to sell her products. She also donated money to create better opportunities for African Americans. By 1917, she had the largest business owned by an African American in the country. Her generosity and business skills made her a trusted community leader.

Why Character Counts

Why was Madame C. J. Walker trustworthy?

Madame C. J. Walker

GO ONLINE
For more resources, go to www.harcourtschool.com/ss1

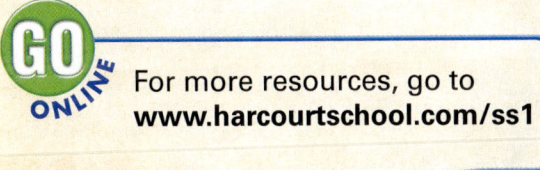

Time

- **1867** Born
- **1905** Moves to Denver to sell her hair products
- **1910** Has more than 1,000 employees
- **1919** Died

Chapter 11 ■ 393

Lesson 2: How Business Works

What to Know
What kinds of resources do businesses use?

Vocabulary
capital p. 394
raw material p. 394
human resource p. 395
capital resource p. 395
factory p. 396
manufacture p. 397

Focus Skill: Generalize

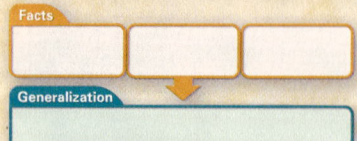

It takes more than just a good idea to start a business. All businesses use **capital**, or money. They also use different resources.

Businesses Start with Resources

Businesses use different resources to make products and provide services. Some businesses begin with a raw material. A **raw material** is a natural resource that can be used to make a product. Some raw materials that businesses use are metals, rock, wood, and water.

Resources Keep a Business Running

One business in Wilmore, Kentucky, uses the natural spring water that bubbles up in parts of central Kentucky. The company bottles the water for people to drink. Then it sells the bottled drinking water to the public.

In addition to natural resources, the business also depends on human resources. **Human resources** are the workers who produce goods and services. Workers at the business collect the water. They clean and bottle it. They also sell and deliver the bottles.

The business uses capital resources, too. **Capital resources** are the tools and buildings a business uses. These include the machines used to make and deliver products.

Reading Check ⚙ **Generalize**
What three kinds of resources do businesses need?

Natural Resources

Human Resources

Capital Resources

❯ Spring water is found in natural springs all over the United States.

❯ Products, such as bottled water, depend on these three types of resources.

Working with Resources

Many businesses need a factory to make their products. A **factory** is a building in which products are prepared and packaged. A yogurt factory in Minster, Ohio, is the largest yogurt producer in the world.

The yogurt factory depends on many resources to stay in business. It uses milk as a raw material to make the yogurt. It uses human resources to run the factory's machines and other capital resources.

A Yogurt Factory

Illustration The following steps show yogurt making.
1. Fresh milk arrives from farms.
2. The milk is heated.
3. Yogurt cultures are added to the warm milk.
4. Machines put the yogurt into containers.
5. The yogurt is ready to be delivered to grocery stores.

What do the workers do after the milk is delivered?

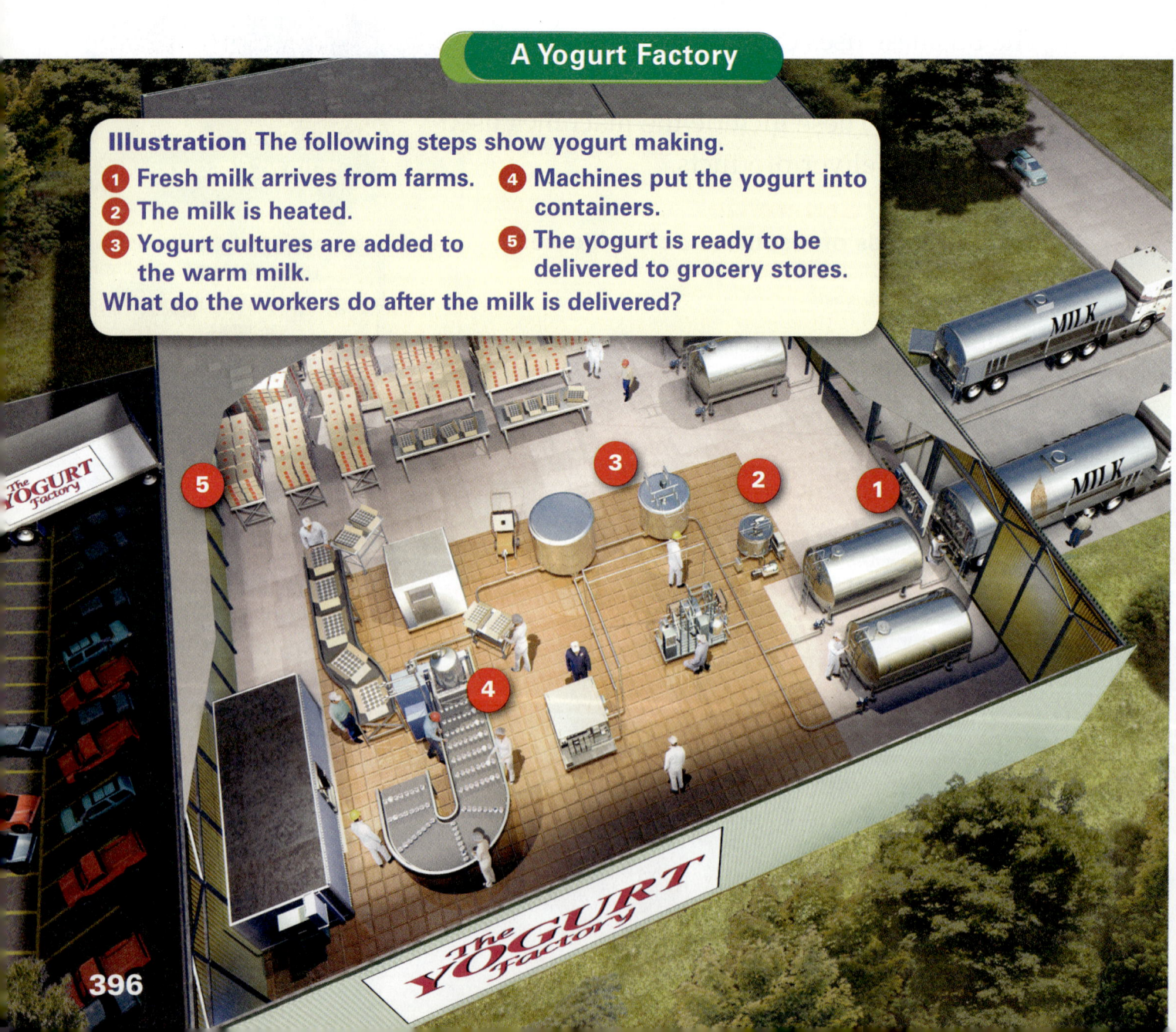

Factory Machines

The yogurt factory uses its resources to manufacture yogurt. To **manufacture** is to use machines to make something. Machines heat the milk and add the yogurt cultures. They also fill the yogurt containers and pack them for delivery to stores. Capital pays for these machines. Capital also helps buy the milk from farmers and pays the factory workers.

Reading Check ◎ Generalize
How do factories use resources?

> A factory worker uses machines to make yogurt.

Summary Businesses and factories use resources to make and sell products. They use natural, human, and capital resources.

Review

1. **What to Know** What kinds of resources do businesses use?
2. **Vocabulary** Explain the difference between **human resources** and **capital resources**.
3. **Your Community** What are some businesses found in your community?
4. **Critical Thinking Make It Relevant** What are some raw materials you might use to start a business? How would you use them?
5. **Make a Chart** Choose a business described in the lesson. Make a chart to show how it uses the three types of resources.
6. **Generalize** On a separate sheet of paper, copy and complete the graphic organizer below.

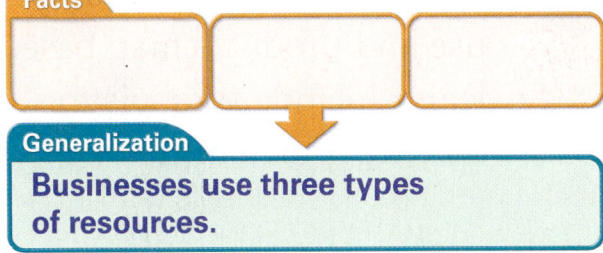

Chapter 11 ■ 397

Map and Globe Skills

Read a Land Use and Products Map

Why It Matters A land use and products map can help you learn about the economy of a region.

▶ Learn

The map on page 399 is a land use and products map. It uses color to show land use. **Land use** is the way most land in a place is used. The map key shows which color stands for each kind of land use.

The map uses symbols to show where products are grown or made. The map key explains what product each symbol stands for.

▶ Practice

Use the map on page 399 to answer these questions.

1. What color shows Minnesota's farmlands?
2. What symbol stands for Minnesota's dairy products?
3. In what type of land can you find trees?

▶ Apply

Make It Relevant Find out how land is used in your community. Draw a land use and products map based on what you learn. Include symbols to show the products that are grown or made in your area.

 For online activities, go to www.harcourtschool.com/ss1

Land Use and Products of Minnesota

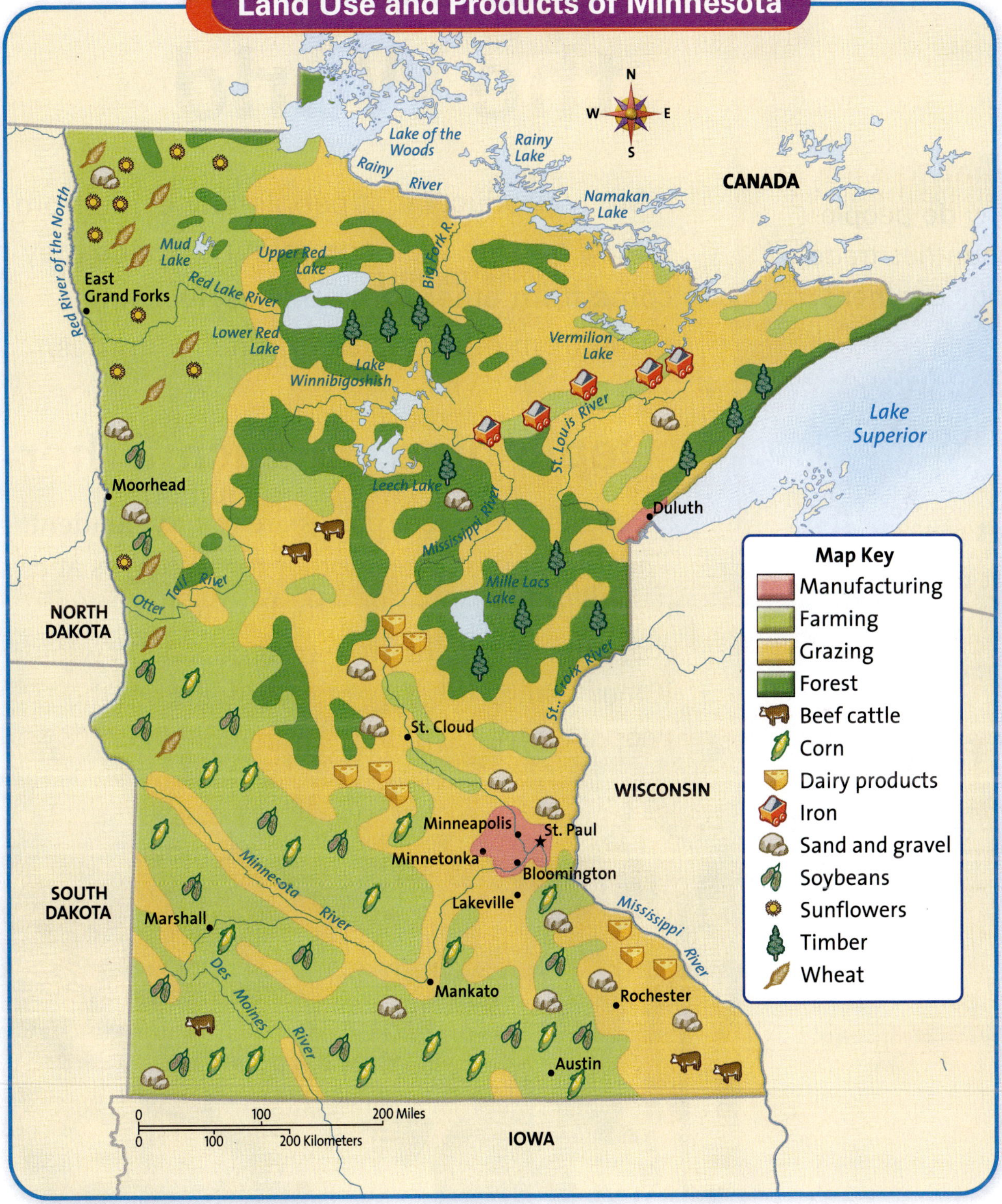

Map Key
- Manufacturing
- Farming
- Grazing
- Forest
- Beef cattle
- Corn
- Dairy products
- Iron
- Sand and gravel
- Soybeans
- Sunflowers
- Timber
- Wheat

Map and Globe Skills

Chapter 11 ■ 399

Lesson 3

Trading with the World

What to Know
Why do people and countries trade with one another?

Vocabulary
international trade p. 401
import p. 402
export p. 402

Generalize

Many products that people buy come from places outside their community. Goods may come from other communities. They may come from other states or other countries.

Depending on Each Other

People in different places are interdependent. They depend on one another for resources and products. For example, people who live in a cold climate cannot grow fruit outside in winter. If they want fruit, they often buy it from the people who grow it in a warmer climate.

400 • Unit 6

Moving Goods

Trucks, ships, trains, and airplanes move goods from place to place. On rivers, barges often move goods. A barge is a large, flat boat.

Improvements in transportation have made more trade possible. Today, fruits can be shipped so quickly that they are still fresh when they arrive. Keeping goods refrigerated, or cool, also allows goods to be moved over long distances.

Better transportation has also made more international trade possible. **International trade** is the buying and selling of goods between countries.

Reading Check **Generalize**
How do people buy goods that they cannot make or grow in their community?

▶ Workers load goods onto a plane.

▶ Shipping port in Seattle, Washington

Fast Fact

Container ships are loaded with shipping containers. Shipping containers can be 40 feet long, which is about the same length as one school bus!

Some Important Worldwide Exports

Map Key
- Beef
- Cars
- Citrus fruit
- Clothing
- Coal
- Coffee
- Corn
- Diamonds
- Electronics
- Oil
- Rice
- Ships
- Steel
- Tea
- Timber
- Toys
- Wheat

MAP SKILL **Movement** This map shows some of the goods exported around the world. What are two countries that export clothing?

Where Do Goods Come From?

▶ This toy is imported from China.

Each day, imports from all over the world arrive in the United States. An **import** is a good brought into one country from another country. Like the United States, most countries buy at least some goods from other countries.

The United States also sends exports to other countries. An **export** is a good shipped from one country to another. Many businesses make money selling exports to other countries.

402 ■ Unit 6

Countries import and export many products. The United States exports computers to countries around the world. It imports newsprint paper from Canada to make newspapers. Japan and other countries export automobiles. The United States imports many of these cars and trucks.

Some countries are known for large exports of one product. China is one of the world's main exporters of tea.

Reading Check **Main Idea and Details**
What is one good the United States exports?

Summary Countries trade goods with one another. People use transportation to ship goods from place to place.

▶ **These food items are imported from Sweden, Ireland, and Scotland.**

Review

1. **What to Know** Why do people and countries trade with one another?
2. **Vocabulary** Explain the difference between an **import** and an **export**.
3. **Economics** How does better transportation help trade?
4. **Critical Thinking Make It Relevant** What foods imported from other countries do you eat?
5. **Make a Bulletin Board Display** Find and draw an object that was made in another country. Label your drawing to tell where the object was made.
6. **Generalize** On a separate sheet of paper, copy and complete the graphic organizer below.

Chapter 11 ■ 403

Citizenship

Volunteering

"When you see families torn apart by this tragedy [disaster] . . . you realize that . . . we all have an obligation [duty] to help the victims of the tsunami have the blessings of a normal life."

—Former President Bill Clinton calling on volunteers to help the victims of the 2004 tsunami

People around the world take action to help one another. Volunteers donate their time, money, or skills to help other people in need. When a tsunami struck Asia in December 2004, many thousands of people were killed, injured, or made homeless. All around the world, people volunteered to help.

◗ Red Cross volunteers help people after Hurricane Katrina.

Focus On: Civic Participation

Volunteers with the Red Cross gave out blankets, water, food, and medical supplies. The Red Cross is a world wide organization that helps victims of natural disasters.

In August 2005, Hurricane Katrina destroyed many communities in Louisiana, Mississippi, and Alabama. People sent money, food, and other supplies to the Gulf Coast. Thailand donated 15 tons of rice, as well as other food and blankets. "In the tsunami, the United States helped [us] promptly [quickly]. . . . We feel obliged [a duty] to help the United States as well," said Songsak Saicheua (Sawng•sag Sygh•choo•ah), Thailand's minister-counselor.

Make It Relevant What volunteer opportunities are in your community?

❯ Volunteers prepare food for victims of the 2004 tsunami.

❯ A volunteer for the Salvation Army packs supplies to send to hurricane survivors.

Lesson 4

New Inventions

What to Know
How has new technology changed businesses?

Vocabulary
communication link p. 408
e-commerce p. 408
advertisement p. 409

Generalize

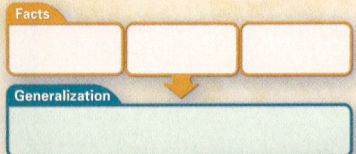

New inventions change the way people do business. Some inventions provide new ways to communicate. Other inventions give us new ways to buy and sell goods.

Moving Information

When telephones were first invented, people used them only to talk. Now people can also use phone lines to send written and visual information. Fax machines deliver the information on paper. People use cell phones to talk and to send pictures, music, and written and video messages.

> People can use cell phones to communicate from most places on Earth.

406 • Unit 6

▶ An Internet cafe provides temporary Internet service for a fee.

The Internet

In the late 1960s, computers at several California universities were connected by wires. This allowed them to "talk" to one another. One of the university students who worked on this project was Vinton Cerf. Along with many others, Cerf helped create what is now known as the Internet.

Ray Tomlinson, a Massachusetts engineer, found a way to use the Internet to send electronic messages. It was his idea to use the *at* symbol (@) in e-mail addresses. He said, "I thought about other symbols, but at [@] didn't appear in any names, so it worked."

E-mail and the Internet have changed the way people work. Both have made it faster and easier to send and receive information.

▶ An early computer

Reading Check ❂ **Generalize**
How has technology improved communication?

Chapter 11 ■ 407

Electronic Buying and Selling

The Internet is a **communication link**—a kind of technology that lets people share information instantly. Communication links have changed the way people buy and sell products. In the past, people had to meet face to face to buy and sell goods. Now, many businesses sell goods and services online, or on the Internet. Buying and selling in this way is often called **e-commerce**. *Commerce* means "business."

Another communication link that businesses use is the telephone. People place orders over the phone from catalogs. Catalogs are magazines with information about goods and services that can be ordered.

Diagram The flowchart shows how a consumer uses a computer to order a book. Which steps in the process use computers?

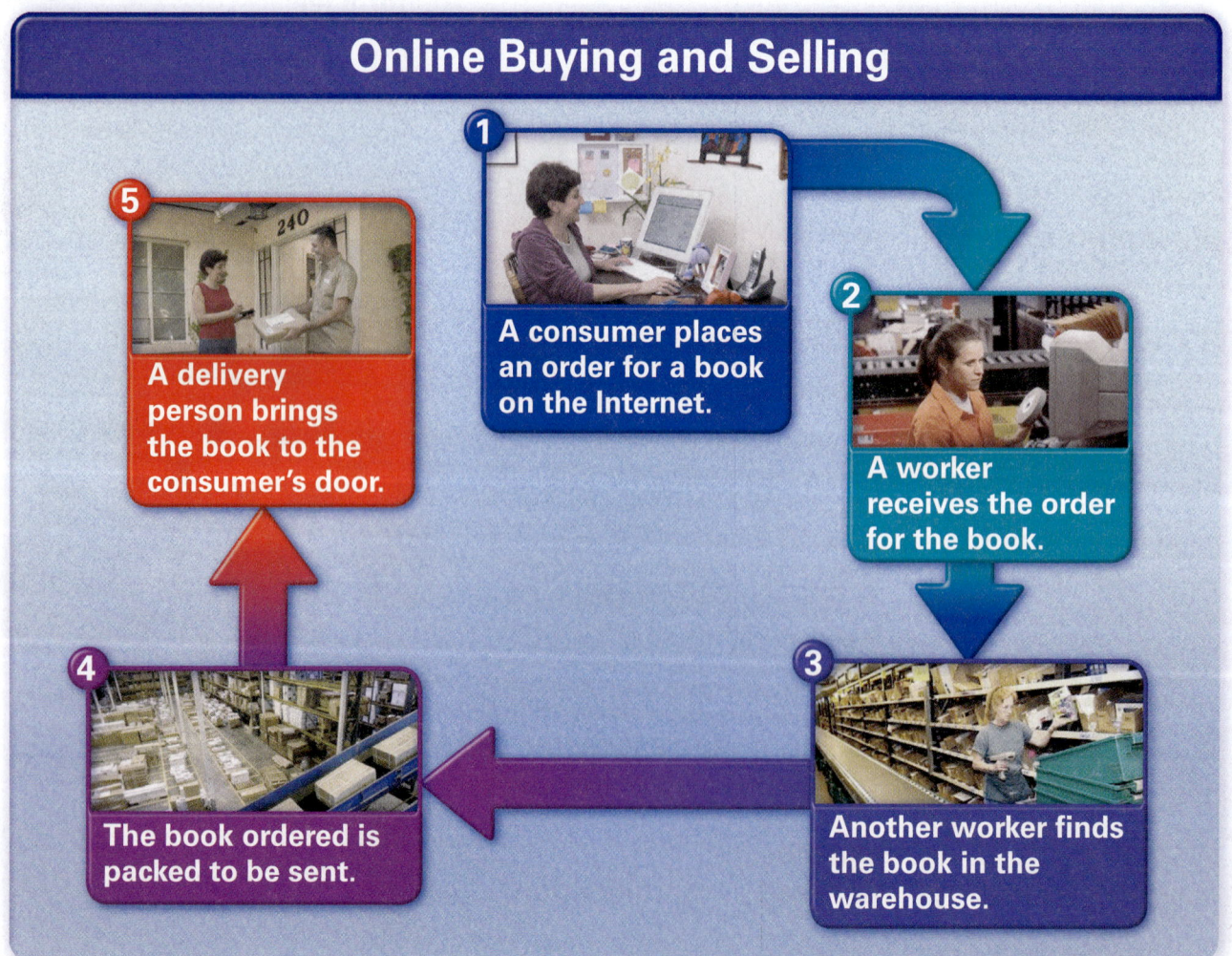

Online Buying and Selling

1. A consumer places an order for a book on the Internet.
2. A worker receives the order for the book.
3. Another worker finds the book in the warehouse.
4. The book ordered is packed to be sent.
5. A delivery person brings the book to the consumer's door.

Internet Advertising

Many businesses create Internet websites with advertisements about their goods and services. **Advertisements** are notices made to get people to buy something. Consumers around the world see these ads. They can order what they want from any computer that is connected to the Internet.

Reading Check ⭕ **Generalize**
How have communication links changed businesses?

Summary Technology has changed the way people do business. New inventions provide new ways to communicate. They also give us new ways to buy and sell products.

◗ A consumer orders products over the Internet.

Review

1. **What to Know** How has new technology changed businesses?
2. **Vocabulary** Use the term **communication link** in a sentence.
3. **Economics** Why might a business decide to sell goods on the Internet?
4. **Critical Thinking Make It Relevant** What technology do you use to communicate?
5. ✏️ **Write an E-mail** Write an e-mail to a local business owner. Ask how changes in technology have affected his or her business.
6. **Generalize** On a separate sheet of paper, copy and complete the graphic organizer below.

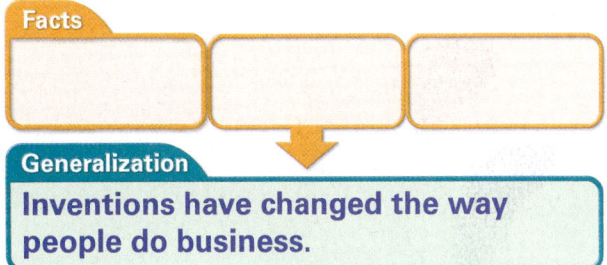

Chapter 11 ◾ 409

Critical Thinking Skills

Tell Fact from Opinion

Why It Matters To make good decisions, you need to know when a message tells you the facts.

❯ Learn

Many advertisements include both facts and opinions. A fact is a true statement. It can be proved. An **opinion** is a person's belief. Opinions may be supported by facts, but they cannot be proved.

❯ Practice

Study the advertisement on the next page. Read each message, and ask yourself *Can this statement be proved?* Then answer these questions.

1. Which statements are facts?
2. Which statements are opinions?
3. Why might people buy this product?

❯ Apply

Make It Relevant Create an advertisement for a product you enjoy. Share your ad with the class. Invite classmates to point out the facts and opinions.

Primary Sources

Computers, Past and Present

Background In 1974, the first personal computer was invented in California. Computers are machines that store information. People also use computers to solve problems, communicate, and play games. Computer technology has been improved many times.

 **Document-Based Questions** Study these primary sources, and answer the questions.

The First Personal Computer

This computer was the first personal computer made for the public.

DBQ ❶ How was this computer unlike computers used today?

People used a panel of switches to enter commands.

1980s Computer

This computer was a popular home computer in the 1980s. Games helped make this computer a hit.

DBQ ❷ Why do you think more of this computer were sold than the first personal computer?

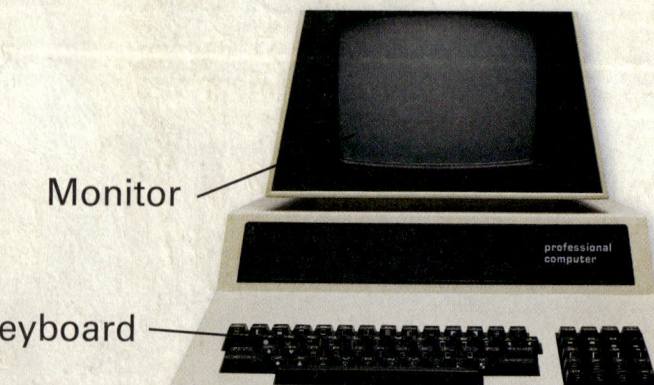

Monitor

Keyboard

Present-Day Computer

Speakers

Mouse

Computer with Modem

This computer was one of the first personal computers to include a modem, or a part that reads information shared through the Internet.

Icons

This computer used icons, or pictures, that could be clicked with a mouse.

Today's computers can store more information and work faster than computers in the past.

DBQ ❹ What features does this computer have that the computers on page 412 do not have?

DBQ ❸ Why do you think the use of a computer mouse became so popular?

WRITE ABOUT IT

Write a paragraph about how computers have changed.

GO ONLINE For more resources, go to www.harcourtschool.com/ss1

Chapter 11 ■ 413

Chapter 11 Review

Visual Summary

Producers and consumers depend on one another.

Summarize the Chapter

Generalize Complete the graphic organizer to make a generalization about what businesses need.

Facts
- People depend on one another.
- Businesses use different resources.
- People and countries trade with one another.

Generalization

Vocabulary

Identify the term from the word bank that correctly completes each sentence.

1. You are a _____ when you buy a product or a service.

2. The United States _____ products to other countries.

3. An _____ gets people to buy something.

4. A person who starts and runs a business is an _____.

5. All businesses need _____, or money.

Word Bank

entrepreneur p. 389
exports p. 402
consumer p. 390
advertisement p. 409
capital p. 394

414 ■ Unit 6

 People trade goods and services with people in other places.

 New technology helps businesses find new customers.

Facts and Main Ideas

Answer these questions.

6. Why do people need an income?
7. How do people transport goods from one place to another?
8. How have e-mail and the Internet changed the way people work?

Write the letter of the best choice.

9. Which is an example of a raw material?
   - A capital
   - B workers
   - C equipment
   - D water

10. What was made possible by improvements in transportation?
    - A international trade
    - B entrepreneurs
    - C manufacturing
    - D advertisements

Critical Thinking

11. **Make It Relevant** What are some communication links in your house?
12. Why is it better for some businesses to provide only one kind of product or service?

Skills

Read a Land Use and Products Map
Use the land use and products map on page 399 to answer the question.

13. What are some crops grown in Minnesota?

- **Write a Business Plan** Suppose you are an entrepreneur. Describe what you need to start and run your own business.

- **Write an E-mail** Write an e-mail to a business. Give its owners your opinion about how they can improve their product or service.

Chapter 11 ■ 415

STUDY SKILLS

ORGANIZE INFORMATION

A graphic organizer can help you make sense of the facts you read.

- Webs, charts, and tables can show main ideas and details.
- Use graphic organizers to classify and categorize information.

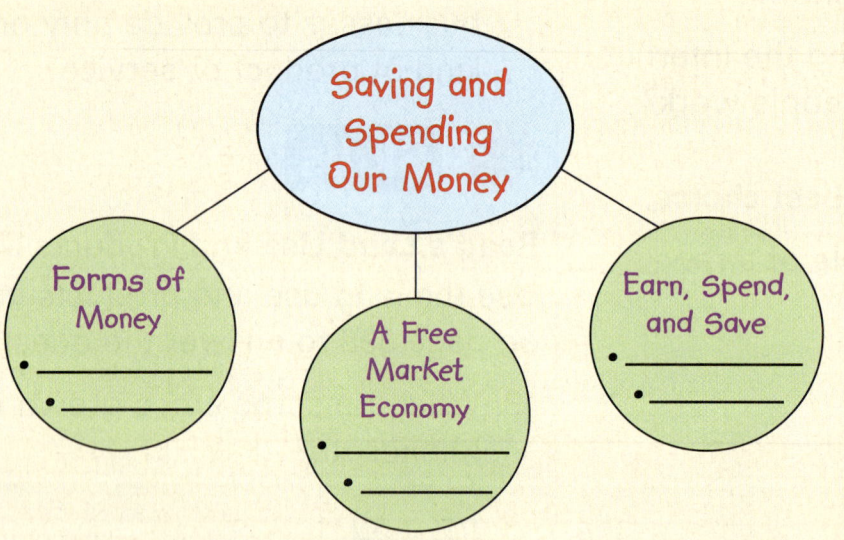

PREVIEW VOCABULARY

savings p. 429

deposit p. 429

budget p. 430

416 ■ Unit 6

CHAPTER 12
Saving and Spending Our Money

> New $100 bills are made at the Bureau of Engraving and Printing in Washington, D.C.

Lesson 1

Forms of Money

What to Know
Why do people use money?

Vocabulary
barter p. 418
mint p. 421

Focus Skill **Generalize**

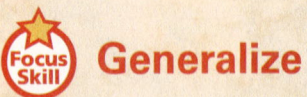

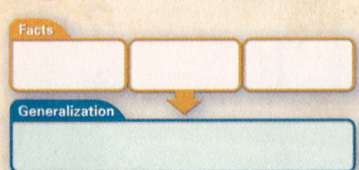

People use money to buy what they want. Different kinds of money are traded for goods and services.

Trading and Bartering

To get goods or services, people need to trade. In the past, people often traded by bartering. To **barter** is to trade without using money. A farmer might have bartered eggs for cloth. Bartering is not always possible. No one may want to trade for your product or service.

Some things are still bartered for, such as trading cards.

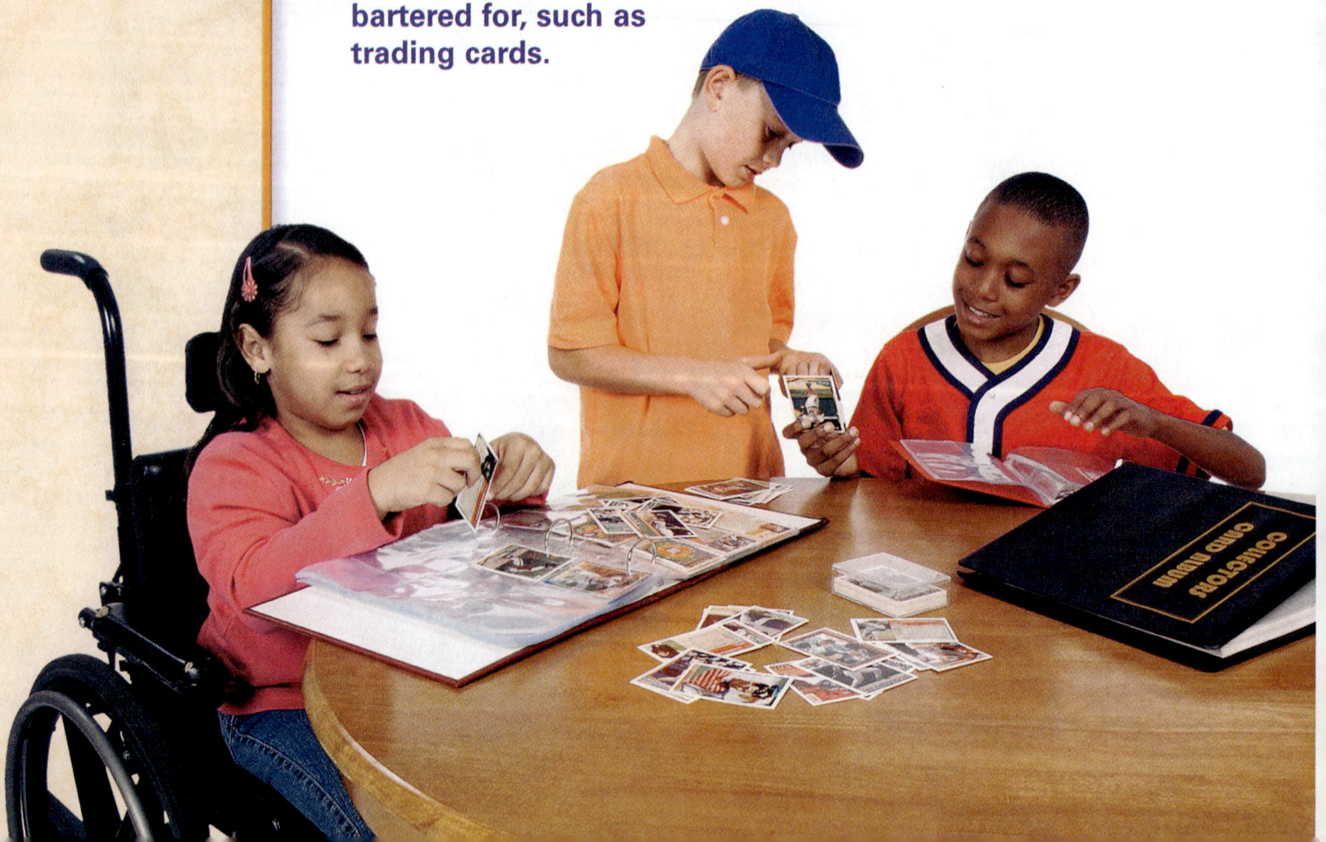

Using Money to Trade

Today, people often trade money for goods and services. Money makes trade easier. Coins and bills are small and light. They can be carried easily.

Checks can also be traded for goods and services. The buyer writes on a check the amount to be paid. The bank takes the money from the person's account and gives it to the seller.

Many consumers also use credit cards. Credit cards let people buy goods and services now and pay for them later. Information from their credit card is sent by computers to banks.

Reading Check **Generalize**
How does money make trade easier?

❯ Most goods can be paid for with money.

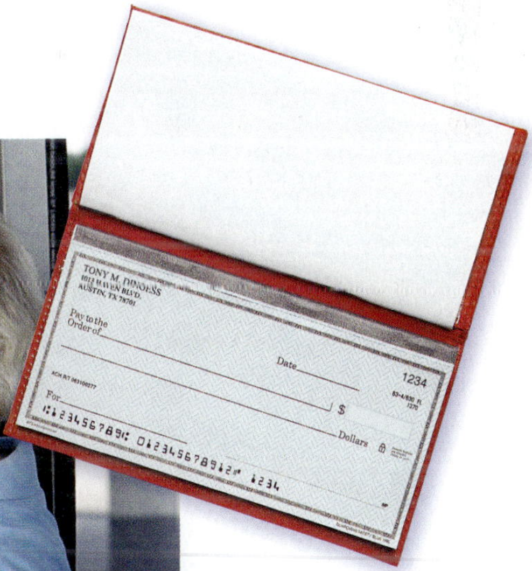

❯ People usually write checks to make large payments.

❯ This man is buying gas with his credit card.

Primary Sources

Money Through Time

Background People have been using money for thousands of years. But money was not always like the coins and paper bills that most people use today.

Cowrie shells were once used as money in India, Thailand, and countries in Africa.

Wampum belts were used as money by Native Americans.

Today, the euro is the money of countries in the European Union.

Turkish coins were the first coins ever to be used.

DBQ Document-Based Question
How is the euro different from cowrie shells?

United States Money

The United States Mint began making coins in Philadelphia in 1792. A **mint** is a place where coins are made. Metal strips are put into machines that punch out coin shapes. Designs are stamped on both sides of the new coins. The United States Bureau of Engraving and Printing in Washington, D.C., and Fort Worth, Texas, makes our paper money.

Reading Check **Main Idea and Details**
Where are United States coins made?

▸ Katherine Ortega was once United States treasurer. Each dollar has the signature of the treasurer.

Summary People trade money for goods and services. Money has many different forms and has changed over time.

Review

1. **What to Know** Why do people use money?
2. **Vocabulary** Use the term **barter** in a sentence.
3. **History** When were the first coins made in the United States?
4. **Critical Thinking** **Make It Relevant** What goods and services could you use to barter?
5. **Make a Coin Display** Draw a picture of several coins. Label each with its value.
6. **Generalize** On a separate sheet of paper, copy and complete the graphic organizer below.

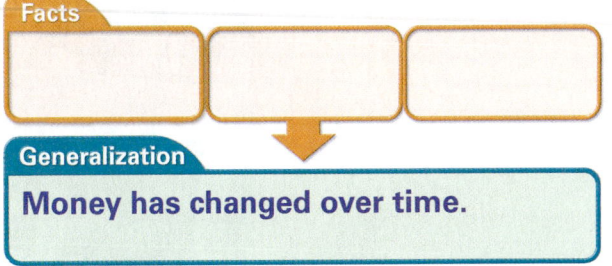

Chapter 12 ■ 421

Lesson 2

Free Market Economy

What to Know
How does a free market economy work?

Vocabulary
profit p. 422
free market p. 422
competition p. 423
demand p. 424
supply p. 424
scarcity p. 425

Generalize

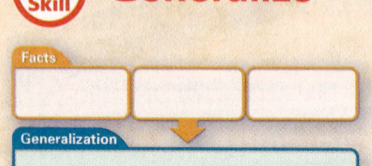

People in the United States have the freedom to start a business. When people start businesses, they hope to make a profit. A **profit** is the money left over after all the costs of running a business have been paid.

A Free Market Economy

The United States has a free market economy. In a **free market** economy, people can make and sell any product or service allowed by law. The government does not tell businesses what goods to make or services to provide.

› The Mall of America in Minneapolis, Minnesota

422 • Unit 6

Children in History

Kid Blink, A Famous Newsie

In the 1800s, New York City had many different newspapers. Young people sold the newspapers for a living. These "newsies" bought the papers at a low cost and sold them for more to make a profit.

When the newspaper companies raised their prices, the newsies could not make enough money. One boy, Kid Blink, tried to do something about the problem. He and other newsies refused to sell any newspapers. After two weeks, the newspaper companies agreed to lower their price. The newsies had won!

Make It Relevant What things do you do to earn money?

Competition in a Free Market

To make a profit, business owners must offer goods and services that people want to buy. Businesses are often in competition with one another. **Competition** is the contest among businesses to sell the most goods or services. For example, bookstore owners compete with each other. Each one tries to sell the most books.

Competition affects the prices of goods and services. Prices must be low enough to draw consumers from other businesses that sell the same good or service. However, prices must be high enough for the business to make a profit.

Reading Check ⭐ **Generalize**
How does competition affect prices?

❯ Bookstores and other businesses compete with one another to sell the most goods or services.

Supply and Demand

What consumers want helps business owners decide what to make or sell. Consumers' wants create a **demand** for, or willingness to buy, goods and services. The products and services that businesses provide are the **supply**.

Sometimes there is a high demand for a product or service. Businesses offer a greater supply of it to meet the demand. For example, if a community has many pets, there will be a demand for pet care products and services. The demand for these goods and services will affect their price.

Fast Fact

The hula hoop came onto store shelves in 1958. Demand for the new toy was so high, the business that made it sold more than 100 million hoops in two years.

Table This table shows how supply, demand, and price can change. How does high supply affect prices?

Supply and Demand Affects Prices		
Consumers and Producers	Supply and Demand	Usual Prices
Consumers want more	High demand	Higher prices
Consumers want less	Low demand	Lower prices
Businesses produce more	High supply	Lower prices
Businesses produce less	Low supply	Higher prices

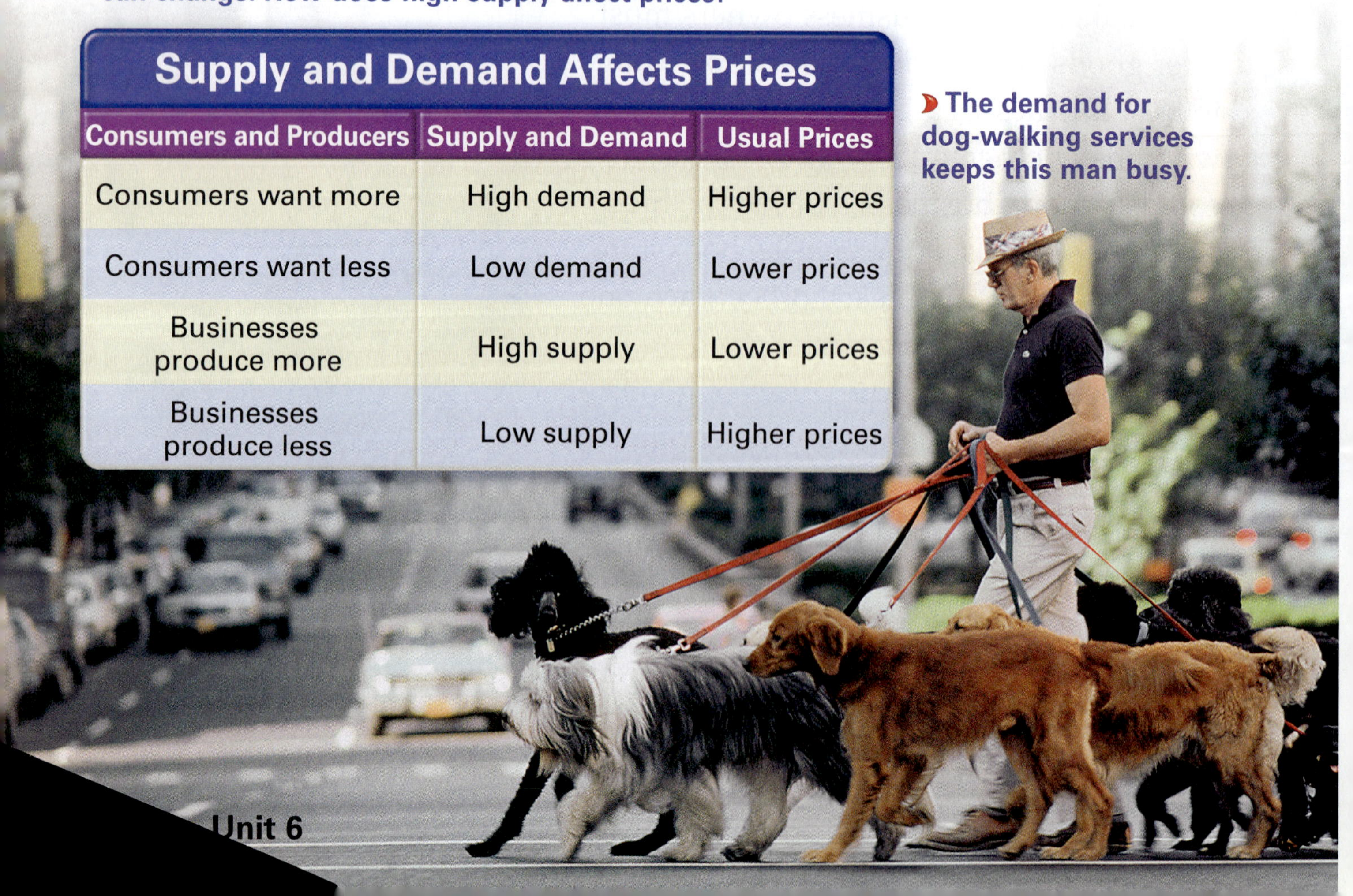

▶ The demand for dog-walking services keeps this man busy.

Scarcity of Products

Prices are also affected by the scarcity (SKAIR•suh•tee) of a product. **Scarcity** means that the supply of a product is not enough to meet the demand for it. Suppose that a drought, or a time of dryness, destroys all of the wheat crops. Wheat then becomes scarce, and its price rises.

Reading Check ⊙**Generalize**
How do consumers affect the prices of goods and services?

Summary The United States has a free market economy. Competition among businesses often helps keep their prices low. Supply and demand affect the prices of goods. Scarcity also affects prices.

▶ Cotton plants during a drought in North Carolina

Review

1. **What to Know** How does a free market economy work?
2. **Vocabulary** Explain how **scarcity** affects price.
3. **Your Community** How do businesses in your community compete to meet the needs of community members?
4. **Critical Thinking Make It Relevant** What is a product you would like to have that is scarce?
5. **Write a Paragraph** Choose a local business. Write a paragraph that explains how consumers affect what it sells.
6. **Generalize** On a separate sheet of paper, copy and complete the graphic organizer below.

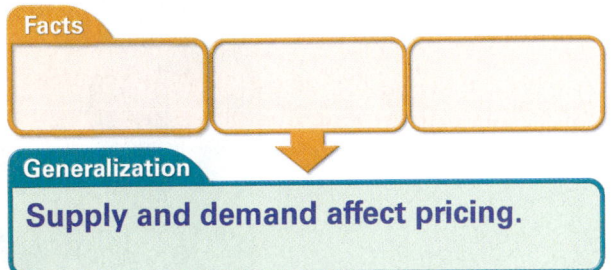

Chapter 12 ■ 425

Lesson 3

Earn, Spend, and Save

People must make choices about how they earn, spend, and save money. The choices they make can have big effects. Families make economic decisions every day.

A Family Earns Income

Each member of the Wright family earns an income. The youngest member, James, does yard work. He enjoys earning his own money. He is also glad to help people in his community.

> Watering flowers is one of the ways James can earn money.

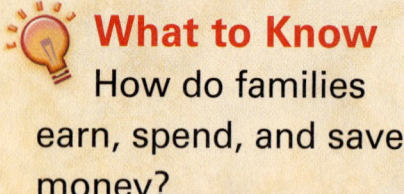

What to Know
How do families earn, spend, and save money?

Vocabulary
savings p. 429
deposit p. 429
interest p. 429
invest p. 429
budget p. 430

Generalize

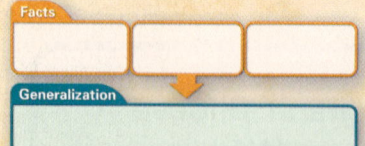

426 ■ Unit 6

▶ **Bonnie takes photos of children for her photography business.**

James's mother, Bonnie, owns a photography business. She takes pictures of people at special events, such as weddings. People pay money for her service. That money is her income.

James's father, Ed, worked at a car parts factory for more than 10 years. He made sure each part was made correctly. When the factory closed, he decided to learn a new skill. He took classes at a local college. He studied how to manage a factory. When he finished, he got a job as a manager in a steel factory. He now earns a higher income.

▶ **Ed studies for a test.**

Reading Check 🔥 **Generalize**
How do the members of the Wright family earn income?

> The Wrights use part of their income to buy food for their family.

A Family Spends and Saves

The Wrights make decisions about money as a family. They make choices about how to spend and save their income.

Spending Money

Like many families, the Wrights use their income to pay for things they use every day. Much of their income is spent to buy food and to pay for their house. They also buy clothing.

The Wrights buy other things with the money they have left. They spend money on karate lessons for James. James often uses his own money to buy movie tickets and music CDs.

The Wrights do not spend all their money on themselves. They share some with other people. The Wrights give some money to groups that help people in their community and around the world. They also choose to save some of their money.

> The Wright family spends money on karate lessons for James.

Saving Money

The money the Wrights save is called their **savings**. They **deposit**, or put, their savings into a bank.

A savings account in a bank earns interest. **Interest** is the money a bank pays people for keeping their money there. It is also the money a person pays to borrow money.

Banks loan to other people some of the money deposited in savings accounts. Those people often borrow that money to start businesses or to buy houses. They pay interest to the bank until all the money is paid back.

The Wrights also invest some of their money. To **invest** is to buy something that will grow in value. One kind of investment involves buying a small part of another person's business. The Wrights hope to make more money when the businesses grow.

Reading Check ⭐ **Generalize**
How do the Wrights save money?

▶ A bank keeps its customers' money in a vault, a room-sized safe with thick, steel walls.

▶ Bonnie Wright deposits at the bank some of the money she earns.

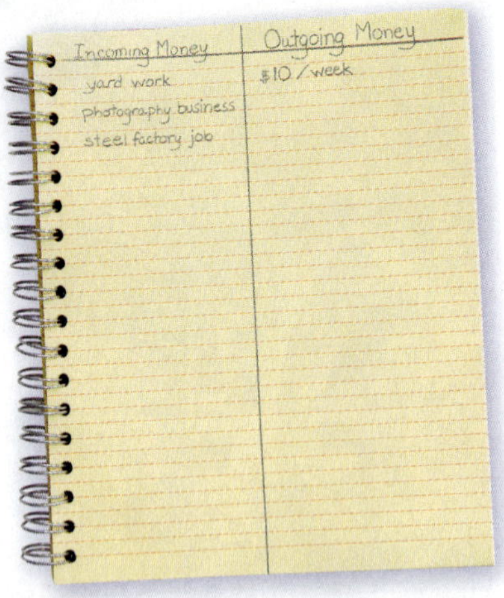

A Family Makes a Budget

The Wright family keeps a budget. A **budget** is a plan for spending and saving money.

To make a budget, the Wrights first list the ways they earn money. They write down each family member's job. Next to each job, they write the income from it. This part of the budget tells them how much money they have to spend or save.

The Wrights then list the ways they spend money. They organize their list into five groups—shelter, food and clothing, fun, giving, and savings. They add up the amounts of money they spend for different things. Then they write the total for each group.

The Wrights' family budget helps them see how they spend their money. It also helps them make plans to reach economic goals.

▶ In a note book, the Wright family keeps a budget.

▶ The Wright family works on their budget.

Reaching Economic Goals

The Wrights want to take a camping trip. They will need to buy a tent and other supplies before they go. Their budget shows them how much money they can save each week. This lets them see when they will have enough for the camping supplies. If the Wrights follow their budget, they will reach their goal.

Reading Check **Main Idea and Details**
How can a budget help people save money?

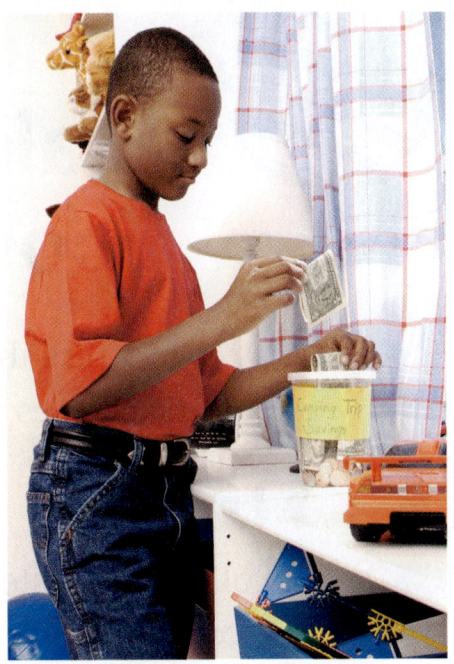

> James saves money to buy souvenirs on the family's camping trip.

Summary Families earn, spend, and save money. They use their income to pay for goods and services. Making a budget helps them spend and save wisely.

Review

1. **What to Know** How do families earn, spend, and save money?
2. **Vocabulary** Use the terms **savings** and **interest** in a sentence.
3. **Economics** Why might someone choose to put money in a bank?
4. **Critical Thinking** **Make It Relevant** What is something you want to save money to buy?
5. **Make a Budget** Make a budget that will help you reach an economic goal. Note how long you will need to save to reach your goal.
6. **Generalize** On a separate sheet of paper, copy and complete the graphic organizer below.

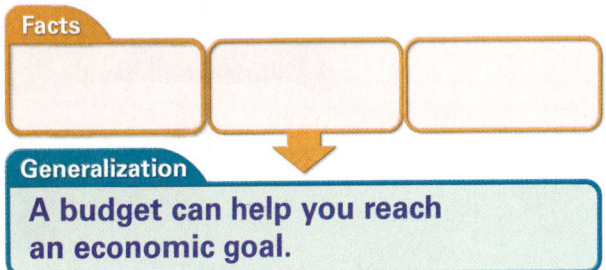

Chapter 12 ■ 431

Citizenship Skills

Make an Economic Choice

Why It Matters Knowing how to make good economic choices can help you spend money wisely.

▶ Learn

Follow these steps the next time you need to make an economic choice.

Step 1 Consider the **trade-off**. When you choose to buy one product or service, you give up the chance to buy a different one.

Step 2 Consider the **opportunity cost**. This is what you give up to get what you want.

Tent A

Tent B

› Practice

The Wrights have $120 in their budget to buy camping supplies. Tent A is $100. It is roomy and has two windows. Tent B is $80. It has less space and only one window.

1. What is the trade-off if the Wrights buy Tent A?
2. What is the trade-off if the Wrights buy Tent B?
3. What is the opportunity cost for each tent?
4. Which tent do you think they should buy? Why?

› Apply

Make It Relevant Think about a product or service you bought recently. What was the trade-off? What was the opportunity cost? Do you think you made a good economic decision? Explain.

Points of View

What Should You Do with Your Money?

Most people agree that it is important to make good decisions about money. Some people think it is best to save money. Others believe it is also important to share money with people who have less.

1 Lynnette Khalfani

Author Lynnette Khalfani has written several books about budgeting and saving money. She coaches people on how to manage their money.

"...Feel free to spend money on the things you need....Just live within your means."

2 Richard H. Moore

Richard H. Moore is the state treasurer of North Carolina. He believes North Carolina should save money for the future.

"The state should invest in projects that will make our communities stronger like schools and roads."

Benjamin S. Carson

Benjamin S. Carson is one of the country's leading brain doctors. Even though his family was poor, Carson was encouraged by his mother to be successful by studying hard. Dr. Carson often takes the time to talk to young people about giving.

❝Happiness doesn't result from what we get, but from what we give.❞

Andrew Carnegie

Andrew Carnegie believed people with riches, like himself, should share their money. He gave more than $300 million to help make the world a better place.

❝I resolved to stop accumulating [gathering] and begin the infinitely [endlessly] more serious and difficult task of wise distribution [giving].❞

It's Your Turn

Compare Points of View Summarize each point of view. Then answer these questions.

1. Who talks about spending money on needs?
2. How does Richard H. Moore feel about saving and investing money?
3. How is Benjamin S. Carson's view like that held by Andrew Carnegie?

Make It Relevant Which ideas about spending, saving, or sharing do you agree with most? Give your reasons.

Lesson 4

World Businesses

 What to Know
How do businesses around the world make money?

Vocabulary
cooperative p. 438

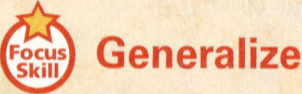 Generalize

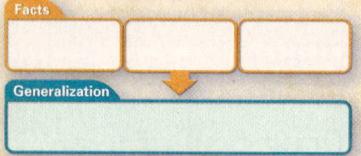

Families around the world depend on businesses. As in the United States, businesses in other countries provide goods, services, and jobs. Some sell goods to other countries. Others sell goods mainly to local markets.

A Business District

In Japan, the city of Tokyo is the main business center. Many Japanese businesses have their main office, or headquarters, in Tokyo. Companies with headquarters in other countries also keep offices in Tokyo.

Businesses Depend on One Another

As in most cities, Tokyo's businesses work together. Workers use technology to communicate with one another by telephone, fax, and e-mail.

Many businesses in Tokyo make goods that they export to other countries. Some high-tech businesses make computers, flat-panel television screens, and cell phones. They depend on other businesses for some of the parts they use. They also depend on transportation companies to ship the finished goods. They depend on stores to sell their products, too.

❯ These business people in Tokyo use cell phones to communicate.

Reading Check ❖ **Generalize**
How do Tokyo's businesses depend on other businesses?

❯ Tokyo has more than 800,000 businesses and 8 million workers.

A Community Cooperative

Manica (mah•NEE•kah) is a rural community in eastern Mozambique (moh•zahm•BEEK). The climate there is warm. It is just right for farming and raising animals. Some people in Manica raise chickens.

Some families in Manica are part of a farming cooperative. A **cooperative** is a group of workers who own a business together. Each worker has a vote when the group makes decisions about the business.

A farming cooperative depends on natural resources to survive. The farmers grow sunflowers, which are made into chicken feed. When the chickens are big enough, they are sold.

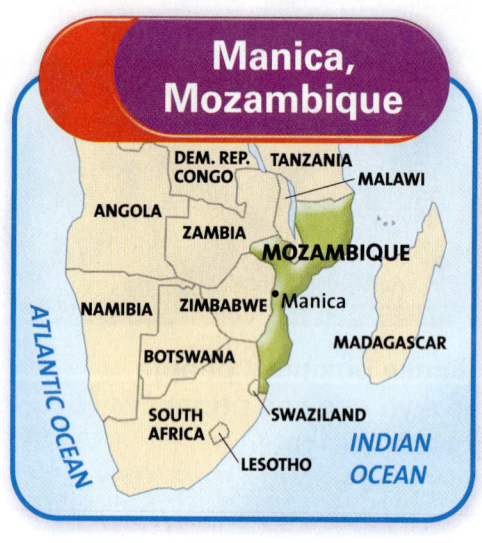

› Farmers raise chickens in Manica.

Cooperatives Help the Community

The money earned from selling the chickens helps the cooperative's economy. Some of the money pays for the cost of the business. The rest of the money pays for things that help the community.

Reading Check **Main Idea and Details**
How do cooperatives help their communities?

Summary Businesses around the world make money in different ways. Many companies in Tokyo sell their goods around the world. A cooperative in Mozambique sells its product to local markets.

▶ These farmers grow sunflowers, corn, and rice and raise chickens.

Review

1. **What to Know** How do businesses around the world make money?

2. **Vocabulary** What clues can you use to remember the meaning of **cooperative**?

3. **Your Community** Are there any businesses in your community like the ones from this lesson? If so, tell how they are the same.

4. **Critical Thinking** In what ways do businesses in Tokyo use technology?

5. **Make a Diagram** Make a Venn diagram to compare and contrast the ways the businesses in this lesson make their money.

6. **Generalize** On a separate sheet of paper, copy and complete the graphic organizer below.

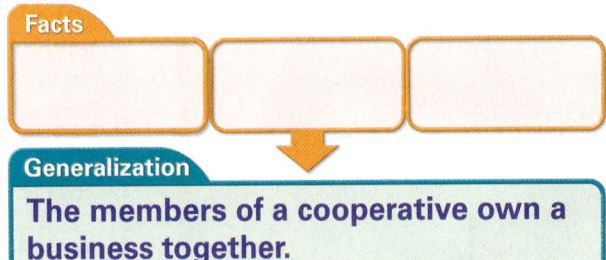

Chapter 12 ■ 439

Explore Your Community's Economy

In this unit, you studied the economies of communities around the world. You can also explore your own community's economy. These steps explain how to answer the following question.

What businesses make up my community's economy?

STEP 1 Use your community's resources, such as the newspaper and the Internet, to find what kinds of businesses are in your town.

STEP 2 Make a list of businesses in your community.

STEP 3 Categorize the types of businesses by whether they produce goods or provide services.

STEP 4 Then find out more about a business that interests you. Share it with the class.

Use Your Community's Resources

Make an Advertisement

Make an advertisement about a good or service provided in your community. Your advertisement should name the good or service and include its cost. Illustrate your advertisement, and display it together with your classmates' advertisements.

Fun with Social Studies

Woof Wash

abc VOCABULARY

Be an entrepreneur, and start a dog-washing business! Play this game with a partner. Be the first to go from START to FINISH!

- **START**
- Make a budget. Take an extra turn.
- Borrow $20 from Dad for shampoo and brushes. Lose a turn.
- There's a demand for your service. Go ahead 2 spaces.
- You need more human resources. Hire your little brother to help. Go back 2 spaces.
- Your monthly profit is $150! Take an extra turn.
- Deposit your profit in a savings account. Go to FINISH.
- **FINISH**

444 ■ Unit 6

You repay Dad his $20. Go back 1 space.

Barter for your older sister's nail polish. Take an extra turn.

It's slow work to polish a poodle's nails. Lose a turn.

You need an advertisement for your business. Create a website. Go ahead 1 space.

Demand for your service is up. Go ahead 2 spaces.

Take a 2-day vacation. Lose a turn.

E-commerce pays off! You get 5 new customers. Take 2 extra turns.

Let customers make reservations on your website. Go ahead 2 spaces.

Online Adventures

GO ONLINE

Do you think you have learned enough to run a business? In this online game, you and Eco will need to start two successful businesses. In one, you will grow your own vegetable garden on a farm. In the other, you will make and sell fresh-squeezed juice in the city. Play now at **www.harcourtschool.com/ss1**

Unit 6 ■ 445

Unit 6: Review and Test Prep

The Big Idea

Economics People depend on one another to produce, buy, and sell goods and services. Good decision-making helps the economy of a family or a community.

Reading Comprehension and Vocabulary

Working in Communities

Businesses and consumers are <u>interdependent</u>. People earn wages from their work. Then they spend their money on goods and services. Businesses could not make a profit without consumers. Producers also depend on resources. Competition, supply and demand, and scarcity affect prices set by businesses.

People use their <u>income</u> in many ways. They trade money for goods and services. People also put money into savings. Some invest their money in businesses or give money to help others.

Read the summary above. Then answer the questions that follow.

1. Why are businesses and consumers <u>interdependent</u>?
   A They like to make profits.
   B Both are human resources.
   C They depend on one another.
   D They import products.

2. What do businesses need to make a profit?
   A scarcity of products
   B savings
   C competition
   D consumers

3. Which of the following affects prices in a free market economy?
   A how money is earned
   B amount of profits
   C income
   D competition

4. What does <u>income</u> mean?
   A something bartered
   B money earned
   C plan for spending
   D goods or services

Facts and Main Ideas

Answer these questions.

5. How do businesses depend on natural, human, and capital resources?

6. When is bartering not possible?

7. What can people make and sell in a free market economy?

Write the letter of the best choice.

8. What are producers always trying to do?
   A start their own business
   B make better products
   C buy products
   D help each other

9. For which export is China well known?
   A computers
   B automobiles
   C clothing
   D tea

10. What was used for money in ancient times?
    A trading cards
    B bills
    C beads and shells
    D checks

Critical Thinking

11. **Make It Relevant** Which businesses in your community compete with one another?

12. How might our economy be different if there were no banks?

 **Skills**

Read a Land Use and Products Map

Use the map below to answer the following questions.

13. What color shows forest areas in New Jersey?

14. What symbol stands for New Jersey's dairy products?

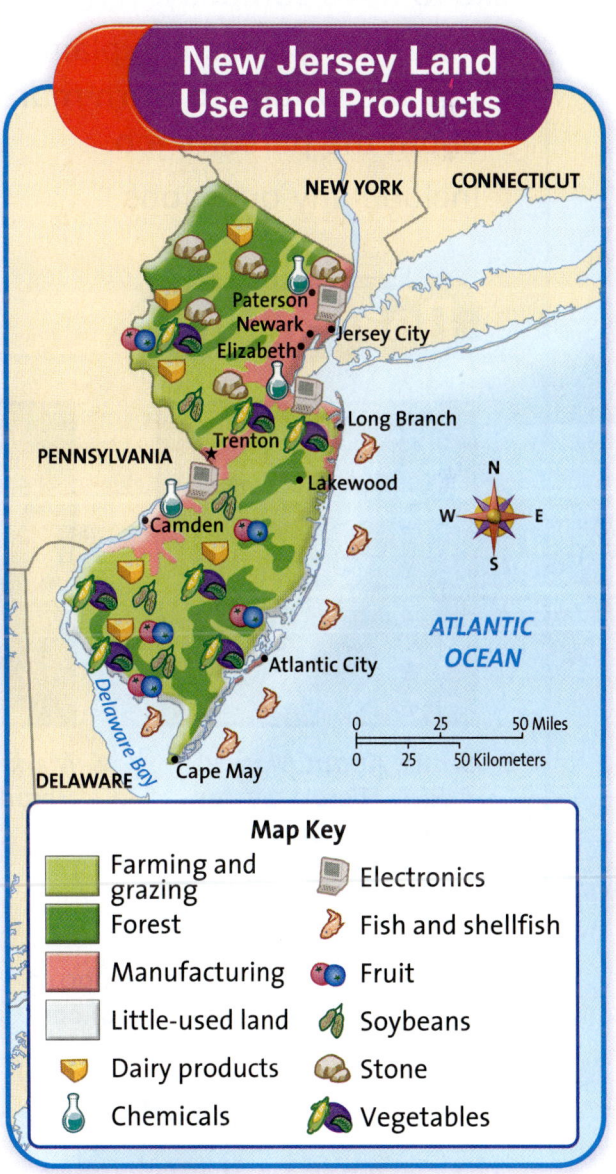

Unit 6 ■ 447

Unit 6 Activities

Show What You Know

 Unit Writing Activity

Write a Letter Write a letter to someone who has a job you might like to have someday.
- Introduce yourself. Explain that you are writing to learn more about the person's job.
- Include any questions.

 Unit Project

Community Newspaper Make a newspaper for your community.
- Research facts about the local economy to gather topic ideas.
- Write and illustrate the articles.
- Use articles and illustrations to complete the newspaper.

Read More

- *Smart About Money: A Rich History* by Jon Anderson. Grosset & Dunlap.

- *Market!* by Ted Lewin. HarperCollins.

- *Hard Hat Area* by Susan L. Roth. Bloomsbury USA Children's Books.

GO ONLINE For more resources, go to www.harcourtschool.com/ss1

For Your Reference

- ATLAS
- RESEARCH HANDBOOK
- BIOGRAPHICAL DICTIONARY
- GAZETTEER
- GLOSSARY
- INDEX

- ATLAS
- RESEARCH HANDBOOK
- BIOGRAPHICAL DICTIONARY
- GAZETTEER
- GLOSSARY
- INDEX

For Your Reference

ATLAS
- **R2** The World: Political
- **R4** The World: Physical
- **R6** Western Hemisphere: Political
- **R7** Western Hemisphere: Physical
- **R8** United States: Political
- **R10** United States: Physical

RESEARCH HANDBOOK
R12

BIOGRAPHICAL DICTIONARY
R22

GAZETTEER
R27

GLOSSARY
R33

INDEX
R40

Research Handbook

To write a report or complete a project, you must gather information about your topic. You can find information in different sources, such as maps, photos, illustrations, and artifacts. You can also find information in your textbook. Other sources of information are technology resources, print resources, and community resources.

Technology Resources
- Internet
- Computer disk
- Television or radio

Print Resources
- Almanac
- Atlas
- Dictionary
- Encyclopedia
- Nonfiction book
- Periodical
- Thesaurus

Community Resources
- Teacher
- Museum curator
- Community leader
- Older citizen

Technology Resources

The main technology resources you can use to find information are the Internet and computer disks. Your school or local library may have CD-ROMs or DVDs that contain information about your topic. Television or radio can also be good sources of information.

Using the Internet

The Internet contains large amounts of information. By using a computer to go online, you can read letters and documents. You can see pictures and artwork. You can listen to music or take a virtual tour.

Keep in mind that some websites have mistakes or incorrect information. To get accurate information, be sure to visit only trusted websites. These include museum and government sites.

▶ Plan Your Search

- Identify the topic.
- Make a list of questions that you want to answer.
- List key words or groups of words that you might want to use to write or talk about your topic.
- Look for good online resources to find answers to your questions.
- Decide if the information is relevant.

Use a Search Engine

A search engine is an online collection of websites. It can be sorted by entering a key word or group of words. Ask a librarian, a teacher, or a parent for suggestions about which search engine to use.

Search by Subject To search by subject, or topic, use a search engine. Choose from the list of key words that you made while planning your search. Enter a key word or group of words in the search engine field on your screen. Then click SEARCH or GO. You will see a list of websites that relate to your topic. Click on the site or sites you think will be most helpful.

Search by Address Each website has its own address, called a Uniform Resource Locator, or URL for short. To get to a website by using a URL, simply type the URL in the LOCATION/GO TO box on your screen, and hit ENTER or click GO.

Use Bookmarks The bookmark feature is an Internet tool for keeping and organizing URLs. If you find a website that seems helpful, you can save the URL. This way you can quickly return to it later. Click BOOKMARKS or FAVORITES at the top of your screen, and choose ADD. Your computer makes a copy of the URL and keeps a record of it.

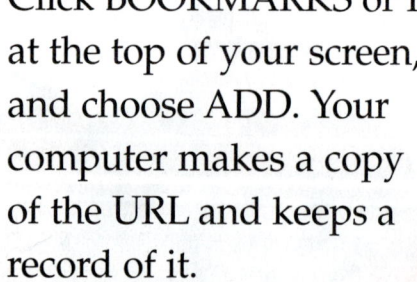

Print Resources

Books in libraries are organized through a system of numbers. Every book has its own title and call number. The call number tells where in the library the book can be found. You can then find information in the book by using its table of contents, title page, and index. You may also need to look at illustrations to learn more about the topic you are researching.

Some reference books, such as encyclopedias, are usually kept in a separate section of a library. Each book there has R or RE—for *reference*—on its spine.

❯ Almanac

An almanac is a book or an electronic resource that has facts about different subjects. The subjects are listed in alphabetical order in an index.

❯ Atlas

An atlas is a book of maps. It gives information about places. Different kinds of atlases show various places at different times. Your teacher or librarian can help you find the kind of atlas you need for your research.

❯ Dictionary

A dictionary gives the correct spelling of words and their definitions, or meanings. It also gives the words' pronunciations, or how to say the words aloud.

Research Handbook ■ R15

❱ Encyclopedia

An encyclopedia is a book or set of books that gives information about many different topics. The topics are arranged alphabetically. An encyclopedia is a good source to use when beginning your research.

❱ Nonfiction Books

A nonfiction book gives facts about real people, places, and things. All nonfiction books in a library are arranged in order and by category according to their call numbers. To find a book's call number, you use a library's card file or computer catalog. You can search for a book in the catalog by subject, by author, or by title.

❱ Periodicals

A periodical is a publication that appears each day, each week, or each month. Periodicals are good resources for current information on topics not yet recorded in books.

❱ Thesaurus

A thesaurus (thih•SAWR•uhs) lists words that mean the same or nearly the same as another word. A thesaurus also lists words that have the opposite meaning. Using a thesaurus can help you find words that better describe your topic and make your writing more interesting.

Community Resources

People in your community can share oral histories or information about your research topic. Before you talk to any of them, always ask a teacher or a parent for permission.

Listening to Find Information

It is important to plan ahead whenever you talk with people as part of your research.

◗ Before

- Find out more about the topic you want to discuss.
- List the people you want to talk to.
- Make a list of questions you want to ask.

◗ During

- Speak clearly and loudly when asking questions.
- Listen carefully. Make sure you are getting the information you need.
- Be polite. Do not talk when the other person is speaking.
- Take notes to help you remember important ideas.
- Write down the person's exact words if you think you will want to use them in your report. If possible, use a tape recorder. Be sure to ask the speaker for permission in advance.

◗ After

- Thank the person you spoke with.
- Later, write a thank-you note.

Research Handbook ■ R17

Writing to Get Information

You can also write to people in your community to get information. You can send them an e-mail or a letter. Keep these ideas in mind as you write:

- Write neatly or use a computer.
- Say who you are and why you are writing. Check your spelling and punctuation.
- If you are writing a letter, always provide a self-addressed, stamped envelope. The person can use it to send you a response.
- Thank the person.

Reporting

❱ Written Reports

Your teacher may ask you to write a report about the information you find. Knowing how to write a report will help you make good use of the information. These tips will help you write your report.

❱ Before Writing

- Choose a main idea or topic.
- Think of questions about your topic.
- Gather information from more than one source.
- Take notes on the information you find.
- Review your notes to be sure you have the information you need. Write down ideas to put in your report.
- Use your notes to make an outline of the information you found.

❱ Citing Sources

An important part of research and writing is citing, or listing, sources. When you cite a source, you write down where you got your information. The list of sources will make up a bibliography. A bibliography is a list of the books and other sources that you used to find the information in your report.

Bibliography Card

Wyatt, Adam. *The History of Arkansas*. Philadelphia, Pennsylvania: Scenic River Publishing, 2003, page 25.

In 1820, Little Rock became capital of the Arkansas Territory.

Write a First Draft

- Use your notes and your outline to write a draft of your report. Keep in mind that your purpose is to share information.
- Write in paragraph form. Develop your topic with facts, details, and explanations. Each paragraph should focus on one idea.
- Get all your ideas down on paper.

Revise

- Read over your draft. Does it have a beginning, a middle, and an end?
- Rewrite sentences that are unclear or poorly worded. Move sentences that seem out of place.
- Add details to support your ideas.
- If too many sentences are alike, make some sentences shorter or longer.
- Check any quotations to be sure you have shown someone's exact words and that you have noted the source correctly.

Proofread and Edit

- Proofread your report, checking for errors.
- Correct any errors in spelling, capitalization, or punctuation.

Publish

- Make a neat, clean copy of your report.
- Include pictographs, bar graphs, maps, or other illustrations to help explain your topic.

Proofreading Marks and Their Meanings	
Word	Meaning
∧	Insert word.
∧,	Insert comma.
¶	Start a new paragraph.
≡ cap	Use a capital letter.
⌒	Delete.
lc	Use a lowercase letter.

Marta Berzina
Social Studies

A History of Little Rock, Arkansas

Little Rock is the capital of the state of Arkansas. the city has a rich history. In 1722, the site where Little Rock is located was explored by a French trapper. He named the area Little Rock after a rock formation that he saw there. About 100 years later, in 1820, Little Rock became the capital of the Arkansas Territory.

During the Civil War, Arkansas was one of the states in the Confederacy. In 1881, Confederate troops took over a Union arsenal in Little Rock. the Union captured Little Rock in 1883.

After the Civil War, Little Rock's economy grew. In the 1880s railroads began to connect the industries in Little Rock with the natural resources around Arkansas. Timber and coal, especially, were important natural resources for Little Rock. Also, farmers from around the state of Arkansas sold their produce in markets in Little Rock. In 1969 a network of canals and dams linked Little Rock to the Mississippi River, bringing more trade to the city.

Little Rock is also famous for what happened there during the Civil Rights movement. After the Civil War, Arkansas, like most other states in the South, became segregated. Segregation meant that African Americans and whites were separated. They ate in different restaurants, used different restrooms, and attended different schools. In 1954, the Supreme Court decided that segregation was unconstitutional. The Little Rock Nine were nine African American students from Little Rock who, in 1957, were the first to be sent to a school that before had only allowed white students to attend. Central High School, the school where this took place, is now a national historic site.

◗ Oral Presentations

Sometimes you may be asked to give an oral presentation. The purpose of an oral presentation is to share information. These tips will help you prepare an oral presentation.

- Follow the steps described in Before Writing to gather and organize information.
- Use your notes to plan and organize your presentation. Include an introduction and a conclusion in your report.
- Prepare note cards that you can refer to as you speak.
- Prepare visuals such as illustrations, diagrams, graphs, or maps to help listeners understand your topic.
- Give your audience the main idea about your topic. Support your main idea with details.
- Practice your presentation.
- Be sure to speak clearly and loudly enough. Keep your listeners interested in your report by using facial expressions and hand movements.

Biographical Dictionary

The Biographical Dictionary provides information about many of the people introduced in this book. Names are listed alphabetically by last name. Pronunciation guides are provided for hard-to-pronounce names. After each name are the birth and death dates of that person. If the person is still alive, only the year of birth appears. A brief description of the person's main achievement is then given. The page number that follows tells where the main discussion of that person appears in this book. (You can check the Index for other page references.) Guide names at the top of the pages help you quickly locate the name you need to find.

A

Adams, John *(1735–1826)* The second President of the United States (1797–1801) and a signer of the Declaration of Independence. p. 206

Aesop (EE•sahp) *(620 B.C.?–560 B.C.?)* A Greek storyteller who was famous for telling fables. p. 348

Aldrin, Edwin "Buzz" *(1930–)* An American astronaut who was the second human to walk on the moon. p. 219

Alito, Samuel Anthony, Jr. *(1950–)* An American appointed as a justice of the United States Supreme Court. p. 284

Angelou, Maya (AN•juh•loo) *(1928–)* An African American poet and author. p. 60

Anthony, Susan B. *(1820–1906)* A leader in the women's rights movement who worked alongside Elizabeth Cady Stanton to earn women the right to vote. p. 165

Armstrong, Neil *(1930–)* An American astronaut who was the first human to walk on the moon. p. 219

B

Bell, Alexander Graham *(1847–1922)* An American, born in Scotland, who built a telephone in 1876. The next year he started the first telephone company. p. 171

Breyer, Stephen Gerald *(1938–)* An American appointed as a justice of the United States Supreme Court. p. 284

Buffalo Tiger *(1920–)* A leader of the Miccosukee tribe. p. 195

Burnham, Daniel *(1846–1912)* An American architect and urban planner who helped plan the city of Chicago. p. 50

Burr, Richard *(1955–)* A United States senator from North Carolina. p. 283

Bush, George W. *(1947–)* The forty-third President of the United States (2001–). p. 282

C

Camarena, Guillermo González *(1917–1965)* A Latin American scientist who invented color television and the remote control. p. 175

Carnegie, Andrew *(1835–1919)* A wealthy businessman who was known for his generous gifts to make the world a better place. p. 435

Carson, Benjamin S. *(1951–)* A leading brain doctor in the United States who grew up very poor. p. 435

Carter, James "Jimmy" *(1924–)* The thirty-ninth President of the United States (1977–1981). p. 254

Carter, Rosalynn *(1927–)* The wife of former President Jimmy Carter. p. 254

Cerf, Vinton *(1943–)* A scientist who helped create the Internet. p. 407

Chapman, John *(1775?–1845)* An American pioneer nicknamed "Johnny Appleseed" because he planted apple trees in large parts of Ohio, Indiana, and Illinois. pp. 349, 355

Chavez, Cesar *(1927–1993)* A farmworker and American leader who worked for fair treatment of all farmworkers. p. 258

Clark, George Rogers *(1752–1818)* An American military leader during the Revolutionary War. p. 23

Clark, William *(1770–1838)* An explorer who, with the help of Meriwether Lewis, led the Corps of Discovery in the exploration of the Louisiana Purchase. p. 213

Clinton, William Jefferson "Bill" *(1946–)* The forty-second President of the United States (1993–2001). p. 404

Cochran, Josephine *(1839–1913)* An American who invented the first dishwasher. p. 175

Coleman, Michael B. *(1954–)* A mayor of Columbus, Ohio, elected in 1999. p. 273

Columbus, Christopher *(1451–1506)* An Italian explorer, working for Spain, who sailed to the Americas while trying to reach Asia from Europe. p. 196

Corsi, Edward *(1896–1965)* An Italian immigrant who came to the United States in 1907. p. 326

de Soto, Hernando *(1496?–1542)* A Spanish explorer who explored southwestern Tennessee. p. 149

Dole, Elizabeth A United States senator from North Carolina. p. 283

Douglass, Frederick *(1817–1895)* A leader and writer who was born enslaved in Maryland. He escaped in 1838 and helped in the fight against slavery. p. 216

Earle, Sylvia *(1935–)* An American oceanographer who has written many stories and books about the ocean. p. 119

Edison, Thomas *(1847–1931)* An inventor who, along with Lewis Latimer, created the electric lightbulb. He also invented the phonograph, the movie camera, and the microphone. p. 174

Emerson, Jo Ann *(1950–)* A United States representative from Missouri. p. 63

F

Ford, Henry *(1863–1947)* The founder of the Ford Motor Company. He produced the Model T, the first affordable and widely available automobile. p. 172

Franklin, Benjamin *(1706–1790)* An American leader, writer, and scientist. He helped work on the Declaration of Independence. p. 210

G

Gandhi, Mohandas (moh•HAHN•dahs GAHN•dee) *(1869–1948)* An Indian leader who used peaceful tactics to change India into a free country. p. 166

Ginsburg, Ruth Bader *(1933–)* An American appointed as a justice of the United States Supreme Court in 1993. p. 284

Gomez, Joel *(1981–)* A United States soldier from Wheaton, Illinois, who was injured in the war in Iraq. p. 250

Granholm, Jennifer *(1959–)* The first female governor of Michigan, elected in 2003. p. 280

Grant, Ulysses S. *(1822–1885)* The eighteenth President of the United States. He was the leader of the Union army during the Civil War. p. 100

Hancock, John *(1737–1793)* The first signer of the Declaration of Independence. p. 206

Hatshepsut (hat•SHEP•soot) *(1503 B.C.–1482 B.C.)* A female Egyption pharaoh. p. 180

Herrera, Leticia An entrepreneur who runs a cleaning service company in Chicago. p. 392

Hreljac, Ryan (1992–) At the age of six, he started the Ryan's Well Foundation to help people gain access to clean water. p. 257

Huerta, Dolores (1930–) A teacher who worked alongside Cesar Chavez to help farmworkers become citizens, vote, and earn more money. p. 256

James I of England (1560–1625) King of England (1603–1625). Jamestown, the first lasting English settlement in North America, was named after him. p. 200

Jefferson, Thomas (1743–1826) The third President of the United States (1801–1809). He wrote the first draft of the Declaration of Independence. p. 210

Jenney, William (1832–1907) An American architect and engineer who designed the first steel-frame skyscraper. p. 164

Joseph (1840–1904) Known as Chief Joseph, a leader of the Nez Perce tribe. p. 194

Kennedy, Anthony M. (1936–) An American appointed as a justice of the United States Supreme Court in 1988. p. 284

Kennedy, John F. (1917–1963) The thirty-fifth President of the United States (1961–1963). p. 291

Key, Francis Scott (1779–1843) A lawyer and poet who wrote the words of "The Star-Spangled Banner." Congress adopted the song as the national anthem in 1931. p. 294

Khalfani, Lynnette (1967–) An African American author who has written several books about budgeting and saving money. p. 434

Khufu (2500s B.C.) A pharaoh in ancient Egypt. p. 180

Kid Blink A newsboy who led a strike against New York City newspapers in 1899. p. 423

King, B. B. (1925–) An African American guitarist and blues musician. p. 149

King, Dr. Martin Luther, Jr. (1929–1968) An American minister and civil rights leader who worked to change unfair laws. He received the Nobel Peace Prize in 1964. p. 167

Laclède, Pierre (lah•KLED) (1729–1778) A French explorer who founded St. Louis, Missouri. p. 198

Langdon, Phillip An American author who writes about communities and design. p. 63

Latimer, Lewis (1848–1928) An African American inventor who, along with Thomas Edison, created the electric lightbulb. p. 174

Lawrence, Jacob (1917–2000) An American artist who was famous for his paintings of historic events. p. 328

Lazarus, Emma (1849–1887) An American writer who wrote the poem printed at the base of the Statue of Liberty. p. 339

Leigh, Louise (1914–) A senior citizen from California who invented the idea for Constitution Day. p. 270

Lewis, Meriwether (1774–1809) An explorer who, along with William Clark, led the Corps of Discovery in the exploration of the Louisiana Purchase. p. 213

Lin, Maya (1959–) A Chinese American artist and architect who designed the Vietnam War Memorial in Washington, D.C. p. 342

Lincoln, Abraham (1809–1865) The sixteenth President of the United States (1861–1865). He was President during the Civil War. p. 217

Louis XV of France *(1710–1774)* King of France (1715–1774). St. Louis, Missouri, was named after him. p. 198

M

Maathai, Wangari *(1940–)* The first African woman to win the Nobel Peace Prize and the first woman in eastern or central Africa to earn a doctoral degree. She founded the Green Belt Movement in Kenya. p. 135

Madison, James *(1751–1836)* The fourth President of the United States (1809–1817) and a writer of the Bill of Rights, the first ten amendments to the Constitution. p. 270

Mansa Musa *(?–1332)* A ruler of ancient Mali. p. 184

Mead, Margaret *(1901–1978)* An American scientist who studied people and places. p. 62

Menéndez de Avilés, Pedro (may•NAYN•days day ah•vee•LAYS) *(1519–1574)* A Spanish explorer who founded St. Augustine, the oldest European settlement in the United States. p. 197

Moore, Richard H. The state treasurer of North Carolina. p. 434

Morganfield, McKinley. *(1915–1983)* An African American blues musician known as Muddy Waters. p. 149

Morse, Samuel *(1791–1872)* An American artist and inventor known for his work on the telegraph and Morse code. p. 171

Muir, John *(1838–1914)* An American naturalist, born in Scotland, who was largely responsible for the creation of many of the conservation programs in the United States. p. 106

N

Nelson, Gaylord *(1916–2005)* A Wisconsin senator who founded Earth Day in 1970. p. 134

O

Olmsted, Frederick Law *(1822–1903)* An American landscaper who designed many important parks. p. 50

Ortega, Katherine *(1934–)* The thirty-eighth treasurer of the United States (1983–1989). p. 421

Otis, Elisha *(1811–1861)* An engineer who designed the first elevator that could safely carry people. p. 164

P

Parks, Rosa *(1913–2005)* An African American civil rights leader. She refused to give up her seat on a bus to a white man. p. 255

Pocahontas (poh•kuh•HAHN•tuhs) *(1595–1617)* Indian chief Powhatan's daughter. p. 201

Ponce de Leon, Juan *(1460?–1521)* A Spanish explorer who claimed the land that is now Florida for Spain. p. 197

Powhatan (pow•uh•TAN) *(1550?–1618)* The chief of the Indian tribes who lived in the area where English settlers started Jamestown. p. 201

R

Ralston, Alexander *(1771–1827)* A city planner who planned Indianapolis. p. 237

Reinders, Jim *(1927–)* An American artist who created Carhenge in Nebraska. p. 381

Rivera, Diego *(1886–1957)* A Mexican painter known for his colorful murals. p. 350

Roberts, John *(1955–)* Chief Justice of the United States. He was appointed in 2005. p. 284

Rolfe, John *(1585?–1622?)* A citizen of Jamestown who began growing the first tobacco in North America. p. 201

Sacagawea (sa•kuh•juh•WEE•uh) *(1787?–1812)* A young Shoshone woman who helped the Corps of Discovery talk to Native Americans and led the explorers through paths in the Rocky Mountains. p. 213

Saicheua, Songsak (SAWNG•sag SY•choo•ah) The minister-counselor of Thailand. p. 405

Satanta *(1820–1878)* A Kiowa chief. p. 194

Scalia, Antonin *(1936–)* An American appointed as a justice of the United States Supreme Court. p. 284

Silko, Leslie Marmon *(1948–)* An author from the Laguna Pueblo tribe. p. 195

Smith, Jimmy Neil *(1947–)* An American who created the National Storytelling Festival. p. 356

Smith, John *(1579?–1631)* An early leader of Jamestown who helped maintain peace by trading for food with early Native Americans. p. 200

Souter, David Hackett *(1939–)* An American appointed as a justice of the United States Supreme Court in 1990. p. 284

Stanton, Elizabeth Cady *(1815–1902)* A leader in the women's rights movement who worked alongside Susan B. Anthony to earn women the right to vote. p. 165

Stephens, John Paul *(1920–)* An American appointed as a justice of the United States Supreme Court in 1975. p. 284

Stephenson, George *(1781–1848)* A British engineer and inventor who made the first modern locomotive. p. 163

T

Thomas, Clarence *(1948–)* An American appointed as a justice of the United States Supreme Court in 1991. p. 284

Tomlinson, Ray *(1886–1957)* An engineer who invented e-mail. p. 407

Tubman, Harriet *(1820–1913)* A person who escaped slavery and who used the Underground Railroad to lead more than 300 slaves to freedom. p. 216

W

Walker, Madame C. J. *(1867–1919)* An African American businesswoman who became the first female in the United States to make millions of dollars on her own. p. 393

Wangchuck, King Jigme Singye (JEE•mee SING•ee WANG•choo) *(1955–)* The King of Bhutan (1973–). p. 302

Washington, George *(1732–1799)* The first President of the United States (1789–1797). He is known as "the father of our country." p. 207

Weissenborn, Oscar An American entrepreneur who sold many pencils in the United States. p. 389

Wright, Orville *(1871–1948)* An American who, with his brother, Wilbur, built the first working airplane. p. 173

Wright, Wilbur *(1867–1912)* An American who, with his brother, Orville, built the first working airplane. p. 173

York *(1770?–1831?)* Enslaved African American who was a part of the Corps of Discovery. p. 213

Gazetteer

The Gazetteer is a geographical dictionary that can help you locate places discussed in this book. Place-names are listed alphabetically. Hard-to-pronounce names are followed by pronunciation guides. A description of the place is then given. The page number that follows tells where each place is shown on a map. Guide words at the top of the pages help you locate the place-name you need to find.

A

Afghanistan A country in south central Asia. p. 365
Africa The second-largest continent. p. 85
Akron A city in northeastern Ohio. p. 89
Alabama A state in the Southeast region of the United States. p. 103
Alaska A state of the United States, in the northwestern corner of North America. p. 103
Albany The capital of New York. p. 281
Ancient China An ancient civilization in Asia that developed into present-day China. p. 181
Ancient Egypt An ancient civilization in Africa. p. 180
Ancient Greece An ancient civilization where the world's first democracy was developed. p. 182
Ancient Mali An ancient civilization in Africa. p. 184
Ancient Mesopotamia An ancient civilization in southwestern Asia. p. 179
Ancient Rome An ancient civilization that ruled most of what is now Europe. p. 183
Annapolis The capital of Maryland. p. 266
Antarctica Continent located at the South Pole, covered by an ice cap. p. 85
Appalachian Mountains A low and rounded mountain range in the eastern United States. p. 99
Arctic Ocean The body of water surrounding the North Pole. p. 85
Arizona A state in the Southwest region of the United States. p. 103
Arkansas A state in the Southeast region of the United States. p. 103
Arkansas River A river that runs through Colorado, Kansas, Oklahoma, and Arkansas. p. 59
Asia The largest continent. p. 85
Atlanta The capital of Georgia. p. 281
Atlantic Ocean The body of water that separates North and South America from Europe and Africa. p. 85
Augusta The capital of Maine. p. 281
Austin The capital of Texas. p. 281
Australia The smallest continent. p. 85

B

Baltimore A city in Maryland. p. 49
Baton Rouge The capital of Louisiana. p. 281
Bhutan (boo•TAHN) A kingdom in Asia, located between India and China. p. 302
Bismarck The capital of North Dakota. p. 281
Bogor (BOH•gawr) A city in Indonesia. p. 28
Boise The capital of Idaho. p. 281
Boston The capital of Massachusetts. p. 281
Brazil A country in South America. p. 402
Buffalo National River A river in northern Arkansas. p. 59

Gazetteer ■ R27

California A state in the West region of the United States. p. 103

Canada A country in North America. p. 86

Carson City The capital of Nevada. p. 281

Chamblee A city in northern Georgia. p. 336

Charleston The capital of West Virginia. p. 281

Cheyenne The capital of Wyoming. p. 281

Chicago The third-largest city in the United States, located in northeastern Illinois. p. 331

Cincinnati A city in southwestern Ohio. p. 89

Cleveland A city in northeastern Ohio. p. 334

Coastal Plain A large area of plains in the United States that stretches along the Atlantic Ocean and the Gulf of Mexico. p. 99

Colorado A state in the West region of the United States. p. 103

Columbia The capital of South Carolina. p. 281

Columbus The capital of Ohio. p. 89

Concord The capital of New Hampshire. p. 281

Connecticut A state in the Northeast region of the United States. p. 103

Crater of Diamonds State Park A state park in southwest Arkansas. p. 59

Cuba A country in the Caribbean, south of Florida. p. 103

D

Delaware A state in the Northeast region of the United States. p. 103

Denver The capital of Colorado. p. 281

Des Moines The capital of Iowa. p. 281

Dover The capital of Delaware. p. 281

E

Eastern Hemisphere The eastern half of Earth. p. 83

Europe The second-smallest continent. p. 85

F

Fayetteville A town in northwest Arkansas, home to the University of Arkansas. p. 279

Florida A state in the Southeast region of the United States. p. 103

Frankfort The capital of Kentucky. p. 281

G

Georgia A state in the Southeast region of the United States. p. 103

Germany A country in Europe. p. 402

Great Lakes Large lakes located along the border of the United States and Canada; the largest body of freshwater lakes in the world. p. 99

Great Plains A large area of plains that stretches across the middle of the United States. p. 99

Greenland An island north of Canada, ruled by Denmark, part of North America. p. 86

Gulf of Mexico A body of water on the southeastern coast of North America. p. 103

Harrisburg The capital of Pennsylvania. p. 281
Hartford The capital of Connecticut. p. 281
Hawaii A state of the United States, made up of a string of volcanic islands in the north-central Pacific Ocean. p. 103
Helena The capital of Montana. p. 281
Helena Bridge A bridge in Helena, Arkansas. p. 59
Holla Bend National Wildlife Refuge A wildlife refuge in north central Arkansas. p. 59
Honolulu The capital of Hawaii. p. 281
Hot Springs National Park A national park in south Arkansas. p. 59
Hudson A county in New Jersey. p. 274

Idaho A state in the West region of the United States. p. 103
Illinois A state in the Midwest region of the United States. p. 103
Indian Ocean The smallest of the world's three major oceans, stretching between the southern tips of Africa and Australia. p. 85
Indiana A state in the Midwest region of the United States. p. 103
Indianapolis The capital of Indiana. p. 281
Iowa A state in the Midwest region of the United States. p. 103
Italy A country in Europe. p. 183

Jackson The capital of Mississippi. p. 281
Jamaica A country in the Caribbean, south of Florida. p. 364
Japan A country in northeast Asia. p. 365
Jefferson City The capital of Missouri. p. 281
Jersey City A city in New Jersey. p. 274
Jonesborough A city in eastern Tennessee. p. 356
Juneau The capital of Alaska. p. 281

Kansas A state in the Midwest region of the United States. p. 103
Kansas City The largest city in Missouri. p. 31
Kentucky A state in the Southeast region of the United States. p. 104
Knoxville A city in eastern Tennessee. p. 99

L

Lake Erie One of the Great Lakes. p. 89
Lake Huron One of the Great Lakes. p. 99
Lake Michigan One of the Great Lakes. p. 99
Lake Ontario One of the Great Lakes. p. 99
Lake Superior One of the Great Lakes. p. 99
Lansing The capital of Michigan. p. 281
Lexington A city in central Kentucky. p. 104
Lima (LY•muh) A city in northwest Ohio. p. 89
Lincoln The capital of Nebraska. p. 281
Little Rock The capital of Arkansas. p. 59
Los Angeles The second-largest city in the United States, located in southern California. p. 98
Louisiana A state in the Southeast region of the United States. p. 103

M

Madison The capital of Wisconsin. p. 281
Maine A state in the Northeast region of the United States. p. 103
Mali A country in western Africa. p. 365
Manica (mah•NEE•kah) A small farming region in Mozambique. p. 438
Maryland A state in the Southeast region of the United States. p. 103
Massachusetts A state in the Northeast region of the United States. p. 103
Mercer A county in New Jersey. p. 274
Mexico A country in southern North America that borders on the Pacific Ocean and the Gulf of Mexico. Mexico is on the United States' southern border. p. 85
Michigan A state in the Midwest region of the United States. p. 103
Millwood Lake A lake in southwest Arkansas. p. 59
Minnesota A state in the Midwest region of the United States. p. 103
Mississippi A state in the Southeast region of the United States. p. 103
Mississippi River The second-longest river in the United States. It runs from Minnesota to the Gulf of Mexico. p. 99
Missouri A state in the Midwest region of the United States. p. 31
Montana A state in the West region of the United States. p. 103
Montgomery The capital of Alabama. p. 281
Montpelier The capital of Vermont. p. 281
Mount Vernon A neighborhood in Baltimore, Maryland. p. 49
Mozambique (moh•zahm•BEEK) A country in southeastern Africa. p. 438

N

Nashville The capital of Tennessee. p. 281
Nebraska A state in the Midwest region of the United States. p. 103
Nevada A state in the West region of the United States. p. 103
New Hampshire A state in the Northeast region of the United States. p. 103
New Jersey A state in the Northeast region of the United States. p. 274
New Mexico A state in the Southwest region of the United States. p. 103
New York A state in the Northeast region of the United States. p. 103
Newark A city in New Jersey. p. 274
North America The continent that includes the United States, Canada, Mexico, and Central America. p. 86
North Carolina A state in the Southeast region of the United States. p. 103
North Dakota A state in the Midwest region of the United States. p. 103
North Pole The northernmost tip of Earth. p. 83
Northern Hemisphere The northern half of Earth. p. 83

O

Ohio A state in the Midwest region of the United States. p. 89
Ohio River A branch of the Mississippi River; runs from Pennsylvania to Illinois. p. 99
Oklahoma A state in the Southwest region of the United States. p. 103
Oklahoma City The capital of Oklahoma. p. 281
Olympia The capital of Washington. p. 281
Oregon A state in the West region of the United States. p. 103
Ouachita Mountains (WAHSH•uh•tah) A mountain range in Arkansas and Oklahoma. p. 59

Pacific Ocean The body of water that separates North America and South America from Australia and Asia. p. 85

Pennsylvania A state in the Northeast region of the United States. p. 103

Phoenix The capital of Arizona. p. 281

Pierre (PIR) The capital of South Dakota. p. 281

Poison Spring State Park A state park in south Arkansas. p. 59

Providence The capital of Rhode Island. p. 281

Raleigh The capital of North Carolina. p. 281

Rhode Island A state in the Northeast region of the United States. p. 103

Richmond The capital of Virginia. p. 281

Rocky Mountains A tall and sharply pointed mountain range in the western United States. p. 99

Russia A country in northern Europe and Asia. p. 365

Sacramento The capital of California. p. 281

Salem The capital of Oregon. p. 281

Salt Lake City The capital of Utah. p. 84

Santa Fe The capital of New Mexico. p. 281

Searcy (SER•see) A rural community in central Arkansas. p. 59

Sherwood A suburb of Little Rock, Arkansas. p. 59

South Africa A country in southern Africa. p. 365

South America The fourth-largest continent. p. 85

South Carolina A state in the Southeast region of the United States. p. 103

South Dakota A state in the Midwest region of the United States. p. 103

South Pole The southernmost tip of Earth. p. 83

Southern Hemisphere The southern half of Earth. p. 83

Springfield The capital of Illinois. p. 281

St. Louis A city in western Missouri. p. 28

St. Paul The capital of Minnesota. p. 281

Stillwater A town in north central Oklahoma. p. 71

Tallahassee The capital of Florida. p. 281

Tennessee A state in the Southeast region of the United States. p. 103

Texas A state in the Southwest region of the United States. p. 103

Tokyo A city in Japan that is also Japan's main business center. p. 437

Toledo A city in northwestern Ohio. p. 89

Topeka The capital of Kansas. p. 281

Trenton The capital of New Jersey. p. 274

United Kingdom A country in western Europe that includes England, Wales, Scotland, and Northern Ireland. p. 365

United States A country on the continent of North America. p. 86

Utah A state in the West region of the United States. p. 103

Venezuela A country in South America. p. 364

Vermont A state in the Northeast region of the United States. p. 103

Virginia A state in the Southeast region of the United States. p. 103

Washington A state in the West region of the United States. p. 103

Washington, D.C. The capital of the United States. p. 281

West Virginia A state in the Southeast region of the United States. p. 103

Western Hemisphere The western half of Earth. p. 83

Wisconsin A state in the Midwest region of the United States. p. 103

Wyoming A state in the West region of the United States. p. 103

Yellowstone National Park The world's first national park, located in the northwestern United States. It covers parts of Idaho, Montana, and Wyoming. p. 100

Glossary

The Glossary contains important history and social science words and their definitions, listed in alphabetical order. Each word is respelled as it would be in a dictionary. When you see this mark ´ after a syllable, pronounce that syllable with more force. The page number at the end of the definition tells where the word is first used in this book. Guide words at the top of the pages help you quickly locate the word you need to find.

add, āce, câre, pälm; end, ēqual; it, īce; odd, ōpen, ôrder; to͝ok, po͞ol; up, bûrn; yo͞o as *u* in *fuse*; oil; pout; ə as *a* in *above*, *e* in *sicken*, *i* in *possible*, *o* in *melon*, *u* in *circus*; **ch**eck; **r**ing; **th**in; **th**is; **zh** as in *vi***s***ion*

A

absolute location (ab´sə•lo͞ot lō•kā´shən) The exact location of a place. p. 88

adapt (ə•dapt´) To change. p. 116

advertisement (ad´vər•tīz•mənt) A notice made to get people to buy something. p. 409

agriculture (a´gri•kul•chər) The growing of crops and the raising of farm animals for sale. p. 60

amendment (ə•mend´mənt) A change to something that is already written. p. 217

ancestor (an´ses•tər) Someone in a person's family who lived long ago. p. 34

ancient (ān´shənt) Happening or existing very long ago. p. 178

anthem (an´thəm) A patriotic song. p. 294

appointed (ə•point´əd) Chosen. p. 284

artifact (är´tə•fakt) An object that was used by people in the past. p. I2

assembly line (ə•sem´blē līn) A process to make a product in which each person adds one part as the product passes on a moving belt. p. 176

authority (ə•thôr´i•tē) The right given to leaders to give orders, make decisions, and take action for a community. p. 266

B

ballot (ba´lət) A list of the choices in an election. p. 246

bank (bangk) A business that keeps money safe. p. 25

bar graph (bär graf) A graph that uses bars to show amounts. p. 120

barter (bär´tər) To trade without using money. p. 418

biography (bī•ä´grə•fē) The story of a person's life. p. I2

border (bôr´dər) On a map, a line that shows where a state or a nation ends. p. 86

boycott (boi´kät) A decision by a group of people not to buy or use something. p. 255

budget (bu´jət) A plan for spending and saving money. p. 430

business (biz´nəs) An activity in which workers make or sell goods or do work for others. p. 16

C

canal (kə•nal´) A human-made waterway dug across land. p. 123

capital (kap´ə•təl) Money to start a new business. p. 394

capital resource (kap´ə•təl rē´sôrs) A tool or building that a business needs to make and deliver a product. p. 395

capitol (ka´pə•təl) The government building in a capital city where lawmakers meet. p. 281

cardinal directions (kär´də•nəl di•rek´shənz) The main directions *north*, *south*, *east*, and *west*. p. I13

century (sen´shə•rē) 100 years. p. 156

character trait (kar´ik•tər trāt) A quality that a person has. p. 253

citizen (sit´ə•zən) A person who lives in and belongs to a community. p. 14

civil rights (si´vəl rīts) Rights that give everyone equal treatment under the law. p. 167

civil war (si´vəl wôr) A war in which the citizens of a country fight each other. p. 216

civilization (si•və•lə•zā´shən) A large group of people living in a very organized way. p. 178

claim (klām) To say that something belongs to you. p. 197

climate (klī´mət) Weather that a place has over a long period of time. p. 20

colony (käl´ə•nē) A place that is ruled by another country. p. 204

common good (kä´mən good) The good of everyone in a community. p. 250

communication (kə•myoo´nə•kāshən) The sharing of information. p. 27

communication link (kə•myoo´nə•kā•shən lingk) A kind of technology that lets people who are far apart share information instantly. p. 408

community (kə•myoo´nə•tē) A group of people who live and work in the same place. p. 14

compass rose (kum´pəs rōz) A drawing on a map that shows directions to help people use the map. p. I13

competition (käm•pə•ti´shən) The contest among businesses to sell the most goods or services. p. 423

compromise (käm´prə•mīz) When each person gives up some of what he or she wants in order to agree. p. 288

conflict (kän´flikt) A disagreement. p. 200

Congress (kän´grəs) The legislative branch of the national government. p. 283

consequence (kän´sə•kwens) Something that happens because of what a person does. p. 249

conservation (kon•sər•vā´shən) Working to save resources to make them last longer. p. 130

constitution (kän•stə•too´shən) A written set of laws that describe how a government will work. p. 208

constitutional monarchy (kän•stə•too´shən•əl män´är•kē) A kind of government that has both a monarch and a government elected by the people. p. 302

consumer (kən•soo´mər) Someone who buys a product or service. p. 390

continent (kon´tən•ənt) One of the seven large land areas on Earth. pp. I10, 82

continuity (kon•tə•noo´i•tē) Continuing without changing. p. 157

cooperate (kō•ä´pə•rāt) To work together. p. 252

cooperative (kō•ä´pə•rə•tiv) A group of workers who own a business together. p. 438

council (koun´səl) A group of people chosen to make laws. p. 273

county (koun´tē) A section of a state, including cities and towns in an area. p. 272

county seat (koun´tē sēt) The city or town in which the main government offices of the county are located. p. 274

court (kôrt) A place where a judge or a jury decides if someone has broken the law. p. 275

cultural identity (kul´chər•əl ī•den´ti•tē) A collection of traits that are seen in the members of a group. p. 364

culture (kul´chər) A way of life shared by members of a group. p. 15

custom (kus´təm) A way of doing something. p. 332

dam (dam) An earthen or concrete structure that holds back water. p. 126

decade (de´kād) Ten years. p. 156

decision (di•si´zhən) A choice. p. 260

demand (di•mand´) A willingness of consumers to buy goods and services. p. 424

democracy (di•mä´krə•sē) The form of government in which citizens have the right to vote. p. 182

deposit (di•pä´zət) To put money into a bank account. p. 429

desert (de´zərt) An area with a hot, dry climate. p. 21

diverse (dī•vûrs´) Different. p. 332

e-commerce (ē•kä´mərs) Buying and selling goods and services on the Internet. p. 408

economy (i•kä´nə•mē) The ways a country or community makes and uses goods and services. p. 60

ecosystem (ē´kō•sis•təm) The plants, animals, land, water, and climate that make up an area. p. 97

elect (i•lekt´) To choose by voting. p. 246

election (i•lek´shən) A time set aside for voting. p. 246

empire (em´pīr) All of the land and people under the control of a powerful nation. p. 184

engineer (en•jə•nir´) A person who designs ways to build and make things. p. 164

entrepreneur (än•trə•prə•nûr´) Someone who starts and runs a business. p. 389

environment (in•vī´rən•mənt) The physical and human features that make up a place. p. 114

equality (i•kwä´lə•tē) Equal treatment. p. 166

equator (i•kwā´tər) On a map or globe, a line that appears halfway between the North Pole and the South Pole. pp. I11, 83

erosion (i•rō´zhən) The wearing away of Earth's surface over a period of time. p. 96

ethnic group (eth´nik groop) A group of people who share the same language, culture, and way of life. p. 333

executive (ig•ze´kyə•tiv) Having to do with the branch of government that sees that laws are obeyed. p. 268

explorer (ik•splōr´ər) A person who goes to find out about a place. p. 196

export (eks´pôrt) To send products and resources to other countries to sell. p. 402

fable (fā´bəl) A story in which animals speak and act like humans. p. 348

fact (fakt) A statement that can be proved. p. 354

factory (fak´tə•rē) A building where products are prepared and packaged. p. 396

festival (fes´tə•vəl) A joyful gathering for celebration. p. 359

fiction (fik´shən) A story that is made up. p. 354

flowchart (flō´chärt) A drawing that shows how to do something or how something works. p. 176

folk song (fōk sông) A song that expresses the culture of a group of people. p. 350

folktale (fōk´tāl) A story passed from one generation to the next. p. 349

free market (frē mär´kət) The freedom to make and sell any product or service that is allowed by law. p. 422

freedom (frē´dəm) The right to make your own choices. p. 204

fuel (fyool) A natural resource that is burned to make heat or energy. p. 108

geographic tool (jē•ə•graf´ik tool) A tool that tells where a place is and what it looks like. p. 82

geography (jē•ä´grə•fē) The study of Earth's surface and the ways people use it. p. 18

globe (glōb) A model of Earth. p. I10

good (good) Something that can be bought or sold. p. 24

government (guv´ərn•mənt) A group of people who make laws for a community. p. 19

government service (guv´ərn•mənt sûr´vəs) The work that the government does for everyone in its area. p. 267

governor (guv´ər•nər) The elected leader of a state's government. p. 280

grid system (grid sis´təm) A set of lines the same distance apart that cross each other to form boxes. p. 48

growing season (grō´ing sē´zən) The time in which plants can grow. p. 94

H

harbor (här´bər) A protected place with deep water that allows ships to come close to the shore. p. 45

hemisphere (hem´ə•sfir) Half of the globe when it is divided into either northern and southern halves or eastern and western halves. pp. I11, 83

heritage (her´ə•tij) A set of values and traditions handed down from those who lived earlier. p. 34

hero (hir´ō) A person who does something important and sets an example for others. p. 257

historic site (hi•stôr´ik sīt) A place that is important in history. p. 36

historical society (hi•stôr´i•kəl sə•sī´ə•tē) An organization of people who are interested in the history of their community. p. 36

history (his´tə•rē) The story of what has happened in the past. p. I2

Glossary ■ R35

history map (his′tə•rē map) A map that shows what a place looked like at an earlier time. p. 220

holiday (hä′lə•dā) A day set aside for remembering a person, an idea, or an event. p. 340

human feature (hyōō′mən fē′chər) Something that people add to a landscape. p. 114

human resource (hyōō′mən rē′sôrs) The workers who produce goods and services. p. 395

immigrant (im′ə•grənt) A person who comes to live in a country from somewhere else in the world. p. 218

import (im′pōrt) To bring in products and resources from other countries to sell them. p. 402

income (in′kəm) Money paid to a worker for the work he or she does. p. 392

independence (in•də•pen′dəns) Freedom from another country's control. p. 206

inset map (in′set map) A small map within a larger map. p. I12

interdependence (in•tər•də•pen′dəns) The reliance of producers and consumers on each other for products and resources they need. p. 391

interest (in′trist) The money a bank pays people for keeping their money there. p. 429

intermediate directions (in•tər•mē′dē•ət də•rek′shənz) The in-between directions that give more exact information about location, such as northeast, southeast, northwest, and southwest. pp. I13, 30

international trade (in•tər•nash′ə•nəl trād) The buying and selling between countries. p. 401

Internet (in′tər•net) A system that links computers around the world. p. 27

invention (in•ven′shən) Something that is made for the first time. p. 162

invest (in•vest′) To buy something that will grow in value. p. 429

irrigation (ir•ə•gā′shən) The moving of water to dry areas. p. 124

judicial (jōō•di′shəl) Having to do with the branch of government that decides whether laws are fair or are based on the Constitution. p. 268

jury (joor′ē) A group of citizens that meets to decide whether a person has broken the law. p. 248

justice (jus′təs) Fairness. p. 253

land use (land yōōs) The way most land in a place is used. p. 398

landform (land′fôrm) A physical feature, such as a mountain, valley, plain, or hill. p. 21

landform map (land′fôrm map) A map that shows a place's physical features. p. 98

landmark (land′märk) An important natural or human feature that marks a location. p. 338

language (lang′gwij) A set of words a group of people use to communicate. p. 190

latitude (la′tə•tōōd) Lines that run east and west around a globe. p. 88

law (lô) A rule that a community makes. p. 18

legend (le′jənd) A made-up story about a real person or event. p. 349

legislative (le′jəs•lā•tiv) Having to do with the branch of government that makes laws. p. 268

line graph (līn graf) A graph that uses a line to show patterns in information formed over time. p. 296

literature (li′tə•rə•chər) Stories and poems that people use to share their ideas. p. 348

locator (lō′kā•tər) A small map or picture of a globe that shows where an area on the main map is found in a state, on a continent, or in the world. p. I12

longitude (län′jə•tōōd) Lines that run north to south on a globe, from pole to pole. p. 88

majority rule (mə•jôr′ə•tē rōōl) Accepting the choice that more than half the people vote for. p. 247

R36 ■ Reference

manufacture (man•yə•fak´chər) To make something with machines. p. 397

map (map) A picture that shows the location of things. p. I3

map key (map kē) A box on a map in which map symbols are explained; also called a map legend. p. I12

map scale (map skāl) A part of a map that compares a distance on the map to a distance in the real world. p. I12

map title (map tī´təl) A title that tells what a map is about. p. I12

mayor (mā´ər) A leader of a community government. p. 273

mediator (mē´dē•ā•tər) A person who helps other people settle a conflict. p. 288

memorial (mə•môr´ē•əl) Something that helps keep a memory of a person or event alive. p. 292

migrate (mī´grāt) To move within one's country. p. 328

millennium (mə•len´ē•əm) 1,000 years. p. 160

mineral (min´ər•əl) A kind of natural resource found in the ground, such as iron or gold. p. 107

minority rights (mə•nôr´ə•tē rīts) The rights kept by a smaller group that did not vote for the same thing or person most people voted for. p. 247

mint (mint) A place where coins are made. p. 421

modern (mäd´ərn) Having to do with the time we live in today. p. 178

modify (möd´ə•fī) To change. p. 122

monument (män´yə•mənt) Something that is built to honor or remember a person or an event in history. p. 292

mountain range (moun´tən rānj) A large chain of mountains. p. 91

multicultural (mul•tē•kul´chər•əl) Having to do with many different cultures. p. 333

museum (myoō•zē´əm) A place that keeps and displays objects from other places and times. p. 17

myth (mith) A story made up to explain the world around us. p. 348

N

nation (nā´shən) An area of land with its own people and laws. Another name for a country. p. 26

natural disaster (nach´ər•əl di•zas´tər) An event in nature that causes great harm or damage to people and their property. p. 117

natural resource (na´chə•rəl rē´sôrs) Something from nature that people can use, such as trees, water, or soil. p. 106

nonrenewable (nän•ri•noō´ə•bəl) Not able to be made again quickly by nature or people. p. 108

O

opinion (ə•pin´yən) A person's belief that can be supported by facts but cannot be proved. p. 410

opportunity (ä•pər•toō´nə•tē) A chance to have a better way of life. p. 324

opportunity cost (ä•pər•toō´nə•tē kôst) What someone gives up to get what he or she wants. p. 432

oral history (ôr´əl his´tə•rē) Spoken history. p. 190

P

Parliament (pär´lə•mənt) The legislative branch of Canada's government. p. 301

patriotic symbol (pā•trē•ä´tik sim´bəl) A symbol, such as a flag, that stands for the ideas in which people believe. p. 290

patriotism (pā´trē•ə•ti•zəm) A feeling of pride in one's country. p. 208

physical feature (fi´zi•kəl fē´chər) A feature of a place's land, water, climate, or plant life. p. 90

pictograph (pik´tə•graf) A graph that uses pictures or symbols to show the numbers of things. p. 120

pioneer (pī•ə•nir´) A person who settles a new land. p. 214

plateau (pla•tō´) A landform with steep sides and a flat top. p. 91

pollution (pə•lōō´shən) Anything that makes a natural resource dirty or unsafe to use. p. 128

population (pä•pyə•lā´shən) The total number of people in a place. p. 42

population density (pop•yə•lā´shən den´sə•tē) The number of people living in an area of a certain size. p. 330

port (pōrt) A place where ships dock to pick up goods or passengers. p. 185

prejudice (prej´ə•dis) The unfair treatment of a person because of his or her background, race, or religion. p. 325

preserve (pri•zərv´) To save. p. 104

President (pre´zə•dənt) The title given to the leader of the United States of America. p. 209

primary source (prī´mer•ē sôrs) A record of an event made by someone who saw or took part in the event. p. 168

prime meridian (prīm mə•rid´ē•ən) The meridian of 0 degrees longitude. p. 88

prime minister (prīm min´i•stər) The head of an executive branch of some countries' governments, such as Canada's. p. 301

problem (prob´ləm) Something that is difficult or hard to understand. p. 132

producer (prə•dōō´sər) Someone who makes and sells a product or service. p. 389

product (prod´əkt) A good. p. 388

profit (prä´fət) The amount of money that is left over after all the costs of running a business have been paid. p. 422

public works (pu´blik wərks) A department of a community government that provides services to meet the daily needs of citizens, such as repairing streets, collecting trash, or making sure that there is clean water. p. 277

R

raw material (rô mə•tir´ē•əl) A natural resource that can be used to make a product. p. 394

recreation (re•krē•ā´shən) Any activity done just for enjoyment. p. 276

recycle (rē•sī´kəl) To reuse resources. p. 130

reference work (re´frəns wûrk) A source of facts. p. 33

region (rē´jən) A large area with at least one feature that makes it different from other areas. p. 42

relative location (re´lə•tiv lō•kā´shən) The location of a place in relation to another place. p. 86

religion (ri•li´jən) A person's belief system. p. 197

renewable (ri•nōō´ə•bəl) Able to be made or grown again by nature or people. p. 108

representative (re•pri•zen´tə•tiv) A person chosen by a group of people to act or speak for them. p. 283

republic (ri•pub´lik) A type of government where citizens vote for leaders to make decisions for them. p. 183

reservoir (re´zə•vwär) A human-made lake used for collecting and storing water. p. 126

responsibility (ri•spon•sə•bil´ə•tē) Something a person should do because it is necessary and important. p. 248

revolution (re•və•lōō´shən) A fight for a change in government. p. 205

right (rīt) A freedom. p. 165

road map (rōd map) A map that shows the roads and other local features of a community. p. 278

rural (rōōr´əl) Having to do with the countryside, farms, and small towns. p. 56

S

savings (sā´vingz) The money that people save. p. 429

scarcity (skâr´sə•tē) What happens when the supply of a product is not enough to meet the demand for it. p. 425

secondary source (se´kən•der•ē sôrs) A record of an event made by a person who was not present at the event. p. 168

service (sûr´vəs) Work that someone does for someone else. p. 24

settlement (se´təl•mənt) A new community. p. 197

settler (set´lər) One of the first people to live in a new community. p. 199

shelter (shel´tər) A home or building that protects people from the weather. p. 191

R38 ■ Reference

slavery (slā´və•rē) A system under which people have no choices. p. 201

slogan (slō´gən) A short phrase used to deliver a message. p. 165

solution (sə•lōō´shən) An answer to a problem. p. 132

statue (stach´ōō) A monument built to honor or remember a person, an idea, or an event in history. p. 338

suburb (sub´ûrb) A smaller community built near a larger city. p. 52

suburban (sə•bûr´bən) Having to do with smaller communities around cities. p. 52

suffrage (suf´rij) The right to vote. p. 165

supply (sə•plī´) The products and services that businesses provide consumers. p. 424

supreme court (sə•prēm´ kôrt) The highest court in any state. The United States Supreme Court is the most important court in the nation. p. 281

tax (taks) The money that citizens pay to the government for goods and services. p. 205

technology (tek•nä´lə•jē) All of the tools people can use every day. p. 170

terrace (ter´əs) Giant steps cut into hillsides for farming. p. 124

territory (ter´ə•tôr•ē) Land that belongs to a government but is not a state or a colony. p. 217

time line (tīm līn) A drawing that shows when and in what order events took place. p. 160

trade (trād) To exchange one good or service for another. p. 184

trade-off (trād´ôf) The giving up of one thing in return for something else. p. 432

tradition (trə•di´shən) A custom that is passed on to others. p. 335

transportation (trans•pər•tā´shən) The movement of people, goods, and ideas. p. 46

tunnel (tun´əl) A path that runs through or under something. p. 123

urban (ûr´bən) Having to do with a city. p. 43

valley (va´lē) A lowland that lies between hills or mountains. p. 91

vegetation (ve•jə•tā´shən) The plants that grow in a place. p. 94

volunteer (vä•lən•tir´) A person who chooses to work without getting paid. p. 251

vote (vōt) A choice that gets counted. p. 165

wage (wāj) Money paid to a worker for the work he or she does. p. 392

worship (wûr´shəp) To pray together. p. 352

Index

The Index lets you know where information about important people, places, and events appear in the book. All key words, or entries, are listed in alphabetical order. For each entry, the page reference indicates where information about that entry can be found in the text. Page references for illustrations are set in italic type. An italic *m* indicates a map. Page references set in boldface type indicate the pages on which vocabulary terms are defined. Related entries are cross-referenced with *See* or *See also*. Guide words at the top of the pages help you identify which words appear on which page.

A

Absolute location, **88**
Acropolis, *182*
Activities
   brochure, 159
   budget, 431
   bulletin board, 337, 403
   coin display, 421
   diagram, 277
   flyer, 55
   landmark, 341
   map, 87, 193
   picture, 109, 127
   postcard, 47
   radio interview, 185
   time line, 209
   web page, 37
   word web, 19
Adams, John, 206, *206*
Adams, Morgan, Washington D.C., *332–333*
Adapt, **116**
Adopt-a-Highway program, 253
Advertisements, 409–411
Aerial, **84**
Aesop, 348
Afghanistan, *m365*
Africa, 180, 184, 201, 362–363, *362–363*
African American Museum, 335
African Americans
   African American Museum, 335
   civil rights and, **167**, 255, 340, *340*
   as entrepreneur, 393
   Great Migration and, 328, *328*, **334**
   Kwanzaa and, 359, *359*
Agriculture, **60**
Air pollution, 129
Ajmera, Maya, 6–11
Alaska, 218
Albuquerque, New Mexico, *20*
Aldrin, Edwin, 219
"Alex and the Amazing Lemonade Stand" (Scott), 382–385
Alliance, Nebraska, 381–382
Amendment, **217**
American Red Cross, *404*, 405
American Revolution. *see* Revolutionary War
Anansi the Spider, 348
Ancestor, **34**
Ancient, **178**
Angel Island, 326–327
Angelou, Maya, *1*, 60
Anthem, **294**
Anthony, Susan B., 165, *165*
Appalachia, 104, 317
Appalachian Mountains, *90–91*, 91, 104, 212, 316–317
Appleseed, Johnny, 349, 354–355, *354–355*
Appointed, **284**
Arabic, 363
Architecture, 342, 351, 366, *366*
Armstrong, Neil, 219
Art, 350
Art activities. *see* Activities
Artifacts, **I2**, *207*, *213*, *214*, *215*, *220*, *222–223*, *325*, *412–413*
Asia, 179, 196, 326–327
Asian immigrants, 326–327, 333
Assembly, **245**
Assembly line, *176–177*, **176–177**
Atlantic Ocean, 21, 46, 91, 123, 196, 202
Atlas, R2–R11
Australia, 27, *m365*
Authority, **266**
Automobile, 172, 403

B

Bagnell, Dam, 126, *126*
Bald Eagle, 291, 296, *297*
Ballot, **246**, *247*
Baltimore, Maryland, 44–46, *44–45*, 294
Bank, 25, 419, 429, *429*
Bank vault, *429*
Bar graph, 120–121
Barges, 401
Barter, **418**
Basque, 363
Bay, **93**
"Becoming a Citizen —Just Like Me" (Hoyt-Goldsmith), 238–241
Belgium, 360
Bell, Alexander Graham, 171, *171*
Bhutan, 302–303

R40 ▪ Reference

Bill of Rights

Bill of Rights, 244–245, *245*
Biographical dictionary, R22–R26
Biography, I2
   Chavez, Cesar, (civil rights worker) 233, 258–259, *258–259*
   Earle, Sylvia (oceanographer), *73*, 119, *119*
   Franklin, Benjamin (patriot), *210*, 210–211
   Jefferson, Thomas (patriot), *210*, 210–211
   Lin, Maya (artist), *313*, *342*, 342–343
   Olmsted, Frederick Law (landscape artist), *1*, *50*, 50–51
   Walker, Madame C.J. (entrepreneur), *393*, *393*
Bogor, Indonesia, *m*28, 28–29
Border, 86, *m*301
Boston Tea Party, *204*, 205
Boycott, 255
Branches of government
   executive, **268**, 280, 282, 300–301, 303
   judicial, **268**, 275, 280–281, 284, 300
   legislative, **268**, 273, 280–281, 283, 300, 303
Brazil, 367, *367*
Britain, 123, 166, 204–207, 209. *see also* England
Buddhism, *352*, 352–353
Budget, 430–431
Buffalo, 192
Buffalo Tiger, 195, *195*
Bunting, Eve, 318–321
Bush, George W., 268, 282
Business, 16, *16*, 55, 392–393, 394–397, 406–409, 422–424, 427, 429, 436–440
Business district, 45

Buying online, *see* Online buying and selling

C

Cabinet of Ministers, 301
Camarena, Guillermo, *175*
Canada, 93, 198, 301, *m*364
Canal, 123, 163, 172
Capital, 394, 397
Capital city, 281
Capital of the United States. *see* Washington, D.C.
Capital resources, 395, 397
Capitol, 281, 286–287
Caravan, 184, *184*
Caring, 50–51
Carnaval, 367
Carnegie, Andrew, 435, *435*
Cars, hybrid, 129, *129*
Carson, Benjamin S., 435, *435*
Carter, Jimmy, 254, *254*
Catalan, 363
Catalog, 408
Cell phones, 406
Central Park, 51, *51*
Century, 156
Cerf, Vinton, 407
Chamblee, Georgia, 336–337, *336–337*
Channel, 92
Chapman, John, 349, 354–355, *354–355*
Character trait, 253
   caring, 50–51, 253
   fairness, 258–259
   patriotism, 210–211, 253
   respect, 253, 342–343
   responsibility, 119, 253
   trustworthiness, 253, 393
Charlotte, North Carolina, 25
Chart and Graph Skills
   bar graph, **120–121**

Citizenship Feature

   flowchart, **176–177**
   line graph, **296–297**
   pictograph, **120–121**
   time line, **160–161**
Chavez, Cesar, *233*, 258–259, *258–259*
Chicago, Illinois, *42–43*, 46, *156–158*, 156–158, *160–161*, 160–161, 164, 328
Chickasaw tribe, 149
Chief Joseph, 194, *194*
Children in History
   Angelou, Maya, 60, *60*
   Corsi, Ed, 326
   first Earth Day, 130
   Kid Blink, 423, *423*
   living American flag, 294, *294*
   pioneer children, 215, *215*
China, 342
China, ancient, 181, *m*181
Chinatown, 333, *333*
Chinese New Year, 360, *360*
Christianity, *352*, 352–353
Chocolate, 25, *25*
Chunnel (Channel Tunnel), 123
Cinco de Mayo, 359, *359*
Citizens, 14, 19
   becoming, 256, *327*
   being a good, 252–257
   duties of, 248–251
   responsibilities of, 248–251
   rights of, 244–247
Citizenship
   cooperation, 252
   voting, 246–247
Citizenship Feature
   Citizen Participation
      Volunteering, 404–405
   Constitutional Principles
      Consitution Day, 270–271
   Democratic Values
      Working for the Environment, 134–135

Citizenship Skills

Citizenship Skills
  make an economic choice, 432–433
  resolve conflicts, 288–289
City, 43, 46–47
City council, 273
City manager, 273
Civil rights, 167
Civil Rights Memorial, 343
Civil War, 216–217
Civilization, 178
Claim, 197
Clark, George Rogers, 23
Clark, William, *212,* 213–214, *m*213
Clarksville, Indiana, 22–23, *23*
Cleveland Cultural Gardens, 334, *334*
Cleveland, Ohio, 334–335, *334–335*
Cleveland Public Library, 343, *343*
Climate, 20–21, 42, 94, 114, 438
Coastal Plain, 91
Cochran, Josephine, *175*
Coleman, Michael, *273*
College, 60
Colonists, 205, 207
Colony, 204, *m*205
Columbus, Christopher, 196, *196*
Commerce, 408
Common good, 250
Communication, 27–28, 170–171, 406–409
Communication link, 408–409
Community, 14
  ancient, 178–185
  building, 196–203
  changes in, 156–159, 162–167, 170–175
  Chinatown, 333, *333*
  climate of, 20–21
  continuity in, 157
  culture, 15, 332–337
  differences among, 20–25, 332
  of different nations, 26–29
  early, 190–193
  economy of your, 440–441
  environment and, 114–118
  farming, 192–193
  government, 19, 267, 272–273
  growth, 162–164
  heritage, 338–341
  history, I2–I3, 22–23, 178–185, 190–193
  heroes, 257
  inventions in, 170–175
  jobs in, 24–25
  laws, 18–19
  location, 82–87
  Native American, 190–195
  places, 17
  researching, 32–37, 440–441
  rural, 56–61
  services in, 276
  sister cities, *m*28, 28–29
  suburban, 52–56, 58
  urban, *42–43,* 43–47, 54, 58
  your own, 32–37, 64–65, 87, 136–137, 224–225, 304–305, 368–369, 440–441
Compass rose, I13, *30,* 30–31, *86*
Competition, 423
Compromise, 288–299
Computers, 27, 157, 412–413
Confederacy, *m*216, 217
Conflict, 200, 215, 288
Conflict resolution, 288–289
Congress, United States, 283, *283*
Consequence, 248–249, *249,* 261, 275
Conservation, 130
Constitution, 208

Culture

Constitution, United States, *208,* 208–209, *244, 244,* 266–268, 284
  Bill of Rights, 244–245, *245*
  Thirteenth Amendment, 217
Constitutional monarchy, 302
Consumers, 390–391, 409, 419, 423, 424
Continental Congress, *208*
Continents, I10, 82, 92
Continuity, 157
Cooperate, 252
Cooperative, 438–439
Copper, 159
Corps of Discovery, 213–214
Corsi, Edward, 326
Council, 273
Council of Ministers, 303
Council-manager government, 273
County, 272
County board, 274, *274*
County seat, 274
Court, 275
Credit card, 419
Critical Thinking practice, 39, 67, 71, 139, 143, 187, 227, 231, 263, 307, 311, 345, 371, 375, 415, 443, 447
Critical Thinking Skills
  compare primary and secondary sources, 168–169
  make a thoughtful decision, 260–261
  solve a problem, 132–133
  tell fact from fiction, 354–355
  tell fact from opinion, 410–411
Cultural identity, 364
Culture, 15,
  communities and, 34, 332–337, 368–369

Custom

communities, urban and, 44, 47
community, your, and, 368–369
expressions of, 348–353
holidays and, 358–361
preservation of, 104
world, 362–367
Custom, 332

Dam, *126*, **126**–127
Dance, 351, 367
De Soto, Hernando, 149
Decade, 156
Decision, 260
Declaration of Independence, *206*, 206–207, 210, *211*, 291, 341
Delta, 93
Demand, 424–425
Democracy, 182, 230, 300
Deposit, 429
Desert, I14, 21, 94
Details, 76. *see also* Main Idea
Detective, 32–33
Directions,
  cardinal, I3, 30–31
  intermediate, I3, 30–31
Disaster, 117–118
Distance, 30–31
Diverse, 332
Documents
  Bill of Rights, 244–245, *245*
  Constitution, United States, 208–209, *208*, 244, *244*, 266–268, 284
  Declaration of Independence, *206*, 206–207, 210, *211*, 291, 341
Douglass, Frederick, *216*
Dr. Martin Luther King, Jr. Day, 340, *340*
"Dreaming of America: An Ellis Island Story" (Bunting), 318–321
Drought, 425, *425*

Earle, Sylvia, *73*, 119, *119*
Earth, 122
Earth Day, 134
Earthquake, 96, 117
Eastern hemisphere, *m*83
E-commerce, 408
Economic choice, 432–433
Economics
  choices and, 428–431, 432–433, 434–435
  consumers, 388–392
  free market, 422–425
  money, 418–421
  technology and, 406–409, 437
  trade, international, 400–403
  transportation and, 401, 437
  workers, 388–392
  world business, 436–439
Economy, 60, 422–425, 439
Ecosystem, 97
Edison, Thomas, 174, *174*
Education, 276
Egypt, ancient, 180, *m*180
Elect, 246, 280
Election, 246, *246*
Electricity, 126–127, 174
Elevator, 164
Ellis Island, 318–321, *326*, 326–327
E-mail, 407, 437
Emancipation Proclamation, 217
Emerson, Jo Ann, 63
Empire, 184
Energy, 116
  hydroelectric, **127**
  wind power, 127
Engineers, 164
England, 200–203. *see also* Britain
English explorers, 200–203
Entrepreneur, 389
Environment, 114–118
  adapting to, 116
  caring for, 128–131
  modifying, 122–127
Equal rights, *see* Rights of citizens
Equality, 166
Equator, I11, 83, 94
Erosion, 96
Ethiopia, 363
Ethnic group, 333–337
Europe, 182, 326, 362–363
European immigrants, 326
Executive branch, 268, 280, 282, 300–301, 303
Explore Your Community, 64–65, 136–137, 224–225, 304–305, 368–369, 440–441
Explorers, 196–198, 230
  Aldrin, Edwin, 219
  Armstrong, Neil, 219
  Clark, William, *212*, 213–214, *m*213
  Columbus, Christopher, 196, *196*
  English, 200–203
  French, 198–199
  Lacléde, Pierre, 198, *198*, 202
  Lewis, Meriwether, *212*, 213–214, *m*213
  Menédez, Pedro de Avilés, 197, *202*
  Ponce de Leon, Juan, 197, *197*
  Spanish, 197
Export, 402–403, 437

Index ■ R43

F

Fable, 348
Fact, 354, 410
Factory, 396–397, 427
Farm, 124
Farm workers, 256
Fax machines, 406, 437
Federal government. *see* Government
Festival, 359
Fiction, 354
Field Trip
    National Storytelling Festival, 356–357, *356–357*
    The United States Capitol, 286–287, *286–287*
    Yellowstone National Park, 100–101, *100–101*
Fire department, 276
Flag, American, 290, *290*, 294
Flatiron Building, *164*
Flooding, 126
Florida Wetlands Park, Christmas, FL, 277
Flowchart, 176–177
Focus Skills
    cause and effect, 317, 329, 337, 341, 353, 361, 367
    compare and contrast, 19, 25, 29, 37, 47, 55, 61
    generalize, 381, 392, 397, 403, 409, 421, 425, 431, 439
    main idea and details, 87, 97, 105, 109, 118, 127, 131
    sequence, 149, 159, 167, 175, 185, 193, 203, 209, 219
    summarize, 247, 251, 257, 269, 277, 285, 295, 303
Folk songs, 350
Folktale, 349
Ford, Henry, 172, *172*
Forest, I14, 24, 107
Forest fire, 117

Fort, 199
Fort Mackinac, 61
Forum, Roman, *183*
France, 123, 198, 339
Franklin, Benjamin, 206, *206*, 210, 210–211
Franklin Delano Roosevelt Memorial, *293*
Free market economy, 422–426
Freedom, 204. *see also* Rights of citizens
Fuel, 108, 116
Fun with Social Studies, 68–69, 140–141, 228–229, 308–309, 372–373, 444–445

G

Gazetteer, R27–R32
General Pencil Company, 389, *389*
Geographers, 82, 102, 104
Geographic tools, 82
Geography, 20, 90
    themes of, I8–I9
    terms, I14
Geography features. *see* Physical features
Germantown, Tennessee, 327
Germany, *m*402
Gettysburg Address, *217*
Ghandi, Mohandas, 166, *166*
Ghost town, 159, *159*
Globe, I10, 82–85, 87
Glossary, R33–R39
Goal, 431
Gomez, Joel, 250–251, *251*
Goods, 24–25, 184, 205, 301, 388–389, 391–392, 395, 400–403, 408, 418–419, 421, 423–424, 436–437
Government, 19
    Bhutan, 302–303

branches of, 268–269, 280–284
Canadian, 301
Constitution, United States, *208*, 208–209, *244*, *244*, 266–268
democracy, *182*
local, 266–267, 269, 272–277
Mayflower Compact, *203*
Mexican, 300–301
national, 266–268, 282–285
services of, 267, 276, 285
state, 266–267, 269, 280–281, 285
structure of, 266–269
world, 300–303
Governor, 280
Grand Canyon, The, *96*
Granholn, Jennifer, 280, *280*
Graphic organizers
    cause and effect, 316, 322
    compare and contrast, 38, 66
    main idea, 40, 76, 110, 138, 188
    sequence, 148, 186, 226
    web, 64, 137, 225, 369, 386, 416, 441
Graphs, *see* Chart and Graph Skills
Gravel, 125
Great Chicago Fire, The, 158
Great Lakes, 76–77, *77*, 93
Great Migration, The, 328, *328*, 334
Great Mosque, The, *185*
Great Plains, 91, 192
Great Pyramid, 180, *180*
Greece, ancient, 182, *m*182, 348
Greenbelt, Maryland, 22, *22*
Grid system, 48–49
Growing season, 94
Guatemala, 351

Guggenheim Museum

Guggenheim Museum, 17, *17*
Gulf, I14, 92
Gulf of Mexico, 91, 119

H

Habitat for Humanity, 254
Harbor, 45–46, 202
Hatshepsut, *180*
Hawaii, 218
Headquarters, 436
Hemispheres, I11, *mI11*, 83, *m83*
Heritage, 34, 197, 338–341
Hero, 257
Herrera, Leticia, 392, *392*
Hershey, Pennsylvania, 25, *25*
Highway sign, *330*
Highways, 172
Hill, I14
Hinduism, 352–353
Hispanic immigrants, 336
Historians, I2–I3
Historic site, 36–37
Historical society, *36*, 36–37
History, I2, 420
Holiday(s), 340–341, 358–361
Holidays, national, 340
Horses, 105
House of Representatives, 283
Hoyt-Goldsmith, Diane, 238–241
Huerta, Dolores, 256, *256*
Hula Hoop, *424*
Human features, 114, 122
Human resources, 395–396
Human-environment interactions, I9
Hurricane, 117
Hurricane Katrina, 117, *117*, 405, *405*
Hybrid, 129, *129*

Hydroelectric power, 127

I

"I Have a Dream" speech by Martin Luther King, Jr., 168, *168*
Immigrants, 218, 324–327, 336–337
  Asian, 333, 336, 342
  European, 326
  Hispanic, 336
  Irish, 358
  Latin American, 327
Imports, 402–403
Inca culture, 124
Income, 392, 426–428, 430
Independence, 206–207
Independence Day, 341
India, 166
Indian Ocean, 29
Indianapolis, Indiana, 236–237, *237*
Indians. *see* Native Americans
Indies, 196
Information, 406–408
Injera, 363
Inner Harbor, 45, *45*
Innovations, 406–410
Interdependence, 391, 400
Interest, 429
International Space Station, *219*
International trade, 401–403
Internet, 27, 407–409
Interview plan, 34–35
Inventions, 162–163, 170–175, 230, 406–410
  fireworks, 181
  lightbulb, 174
  Model A Flyer, 173, *173*
  Model T Ford, 172, *172–173*
  paper, 181
  printing, 181
  telegraph, 171

Johnson, Lyndon B.

  telephone, 171, *171*
  television, *174*, 175
  vacuum, *174*
  wheeled cart, 179, *179*
  writing, 179
Inventors
  Bell, Alexander Graham, 171, *171*
  Camarena, Guillermo Gonzalez, 175
  Cochran, Josephine, 175
  Edison, Thomas, 174, *174*
  Ford, Henry, 172, *172*
  Latimer, Lewis, 174, *174*
  Morse, Samuel, 171, *171*
  Stephenson, George, 163, *163*
  Tomlinson, Ray, 407
  Wright, Orville, 173
  Wright, Wilbur, 173
Invest, 429
Iraq, 250
Irish immigrants, 358
Iroquois tribe, 193
Irrigation, 124, *124*
Islam, *352*, 352–353
Island, I14, 92, 93
Italy, 183
Ivanko, John D., 6–11

J

Jamaica, 364
James I (King of England), 200
Jamestown, Virginia, *200–201*, 200–201
Japan, 332, 365, 366, *m402*, 403
Japanese shrine, *366*
Jefferson, Thomas, 206, *206*, *210*, 210–211, 212–213, 339
Jenney, William, 164
Jerome, Arizona, 159, *159*
Jobs, 389, 392, 436
Johnson, Lyndon B., I1

Jonesboro, Tennessee

Jonesboro, Tennessee, *m*356, 356–357
Judaism, *352*, 352–353
Judges, 275, 284
Judicial branch, 268, 275, 280–281, 284, 300
Jury, *249*, 249–250
Justice, 253
Justices, 284

Kalungu, 350
Kennedy, John F., 291
Kenya, Africa, *135*
Key, Frances Scott, 294, *294*
Khalfani, Lynnette, 434, *434*
Khufu, 180
Kid Blink, 423, *423*
Kiowa tribe, 194
King, Martin Luther, Jr., *145*, 166–167, *167*, 168, *168–169*, 340
Korean War Veterans Memorial, *293*
Kwanzaa, 359, *359*

Laclède, Pierre, 198, *198*, *202*
Lagos, Nigeria, 4–5, *5*
Lake, I14, 21, 92–93
Lake Erie, *77*, 334
Lake Huron, 77
Lake Michigan, 46, 61, 77
Lake Ontario, 77
Lake of the Ozarks, 126
Lake Superior, 77
Land features, 90–91
Land use, 398
Landfill, 130
Landforms, 21, 42, 91, 114
  climate and, 42, 94, 438
Landforms, types of
  desert, I14, 21
  hill, I14
  lake, I14, 21, 92–93
  mountain, I14, 21, 91
  ocean, I14, 92–93
  peninsula, I14
  plain, I14, 21, 91
  plateau, 91
  pond, 92
Landform map, 98–99, *m*98–99
Landmark, 338–339
Landscaping, 51–52
Langdon, Philip, 63, *63*
Language, 190
Latimer, Lewis, 174, *174*
Latin American immigrants, 327
Latitude, *m*88, 88–89
Laws, 18–19, 249, 252, 255
Lazarus, Emma, *313*, 339
Leaders, 266, 280, 282
Legend, 349
Legislative branch, 268, 273, 280–283, 300, 303
Levee, 126
Lewis Meriwether, *212*, 213–214, *m*213
Lexington, Kentucky, *104*, 104–105
Liberty, 206
Liberty Bell, 291, *291*
Library, 17, 33, *33*
Light rail, 45
Lightbulb, 174
Limestone, 125
Lin, Maya (artist), *313*, *342*, 342–343
Lincoln, Abraham, *145*, 217, *217*, 292, 339
Lincoln Memorial, 292
Line graph, 296–297
Literature
  "Alex and the Amazing Lemonade Stand" (Scott, Howard), 382–385
  "Be My Neighbor" (Ajmera, Ivanko), 6–11
  "Becoming a Citizen—Just Like Me" (Hoyt-Goldsmith, Suarez, Migdale), 238–241
  "Dreaming of America: An Ellis Island Story" (Bunting, Stahl), 318–321
  "A Place Called Freedom" (Sanders, Allen), 150–153
  "Walk Lightly" (Lewis), 78–79
Literature (author)
  Ajmera, Maya, 6–11
  Bunting, Eve, 318–321
  Hoyt-Goldsmith, Diane, 238–241
  Ivanko, John D., 6–11
  Lewis, Patrick, 78–79
  Sanders, Scott Russell, 150–153
  Scott, Jay, 382–385
  Scott, Liz, 382–385
Little Italy, Cleveland, Ohio, 335, *335*
Little Rock, Arkansas, 58–59, *59*
Loan, 429
Location, I8, 82–87, 94
  absolute, 88
  relative, 86, 102
Locator, I12
Log cabins, 215
Longhouse, 193, *193*
Longitude, *m*88, 88–89
Los Angeles, California, 47
Louis XV (King of France), 198
Louisiana Purchase, 212–213, *m*213, 220, *m*221

M

Maathai, Wangari, *73*, 135, *135*
Mackinac Island, 61, *61*
Main Idea, 76–77

Majority rule, 247
Mali, *m*184, 184–185, *m*365
Mall of America, Minnesota, 422
Manica, Mozambique, *438,* 438–439
Mansa Musa, 184
Manufacture, 397
Map and Globe Skills
   directions and distances, 30–31
   grid system, 48–49
   history maps, compare, 220–221
   land use and product map, 398–399
   landform map, 98–99, *m*98–99
   latitude and longitude, *m*88, 88–89
   map grid, 48–49
   population map, 330–331
   road map, 278–279
Maplewood, New Jersey, *52–53,* 52–54
Map, I3, 84–85
   Annapolis, Maryland, *m*266
   Arkansas, *m*59
   Baltimore, Maryland, *m*49
   Bhutan, *m*302
   Chamblee, Georgia, *m*336
   China, *m*181
   Cleveland, Ohio, *m*334
   Earth's hemispheres, *m*83
   Egypt, *m*180
   Fayetteville, Arkansas, *m*279
   Greece, *m*182
   historical, 220, *m*221
   Illinois, *m*331
   immigration routes, *m*325
   Jonesboro, Tennessee, *m*356
   land use and product, 398–399, *m*399
   landform, *m*98–99
   latitude, *m*88, *m*89
   Lewis and Clark, *m*213, *m*221
   Lexington, Kentucky, *m*104
   longitude, *m*88, *m*90
   Mali, *m*184
   Mesopotamia, *m*179
   Minnesota, *m*399
   Missouri, *m*31
   Mount Vernon, *m*49
   Native American groups, *m*191
   New Jersey, *m*274
   North America, *m*86, *m*301
   Ohio, *m*89
   population, *m*331
   regions of the United States, *m*103
   road, *m*279
   Rome, Italy, *m*183
   immigration routes, *m*325
   Salt Lake City, Utah, *m*84
   sister cities, *m*28
   southeast, *m*104
   Stillwater, Oklahoma, *m*71
   thirteen colonies, *m*205
   United States, *m*86, *m*98–99, *m*103, *m*191, *m*213, *m*221, *m*267, *m*281
   using, 84–85, 87
   Washington, D.C., 333
   world, I10, *m*85, *m*325, *m*364–365, *m*402, *m*437
   Yellowstone National Park, *m*100
Maps, parts of
   borders, *m*301
   cardinal directions, I13
   compass rose, I13, 30
   inset, **I12–I13**
   key, I12, 398
   legend, I12
   locator, I12
   map grid, 48–49
   scale, I12, 30–31
   symbols, 398
   title, I12
Markets, 9, *9*
Masjid, 352
Maxton Historical Society, The, *36–37*
Maya, 351
Mayflower, 202
Mayflower II, *202*
Mayflower Compact, 203
Mayor, 273
Mayor-council government, 273
Mead, Margaret, 62, *62*
Media, 245
Mediator, 288–289
Memorials, 292
   Civil Rights Memorial, 343, *343*
   Franklin Delano Roosevelt Memorial, *293*
   Korean War Veterans Memorial, *293*
   Lincoln Memorial, 292
   Mount Rushmore, 339
   National World War II Memorial, *292, 293*
   Vietnam Veterans Memorial, 293, 313, 342–343, *343*
   Washington Memorial, *293*
Memphis, Tennessee, 149
Menéndez, Pedro de Avilés, 197, *202*
Mesopotamia, 179, *m*179
Mexican Americans, 359
Mexico, 197, 238–241, 256, 300–301, 359
Miccosukee tribe, 195
Michigan, 61, *281*

Midwest region, 102, *m*103, 328
Migrate, 328
Millennium, 160
Mine, 124–125, *125*, 159
Minerals, 107–108, 125
Minister, Ohio, 396
Minnesota, 93
Minority rights, 247
Mint, 421
Mississippi River, 93, *93*, 198, 212
Missouri, 126
Model T Ford, 172, *172–173*
Modern, 178
Modify, 122, 124, 126
Money, 418–422
   bills, 419, 421
   checks, 419
   coins, 419–420
   credit cards, 419
Montgomery, Alabama, 255, 343
Monuments, 292, *see also* Memorials
   in Washington D.C., *292*, 292–293
   Washington Monument, 292, *292*
Moore, Annie, *321*
Moore, Richard, 434, *434*
Morse, Samuel, 171, *171*
Mosque, 352, *352*
Mount Rushmore, *339*, 339
Mountain, I14, 21, 91
Mountain range, 91
Movement, I9
Muir, John, 106
Multicultural, 333–334
Munster, Ohio, 396
Mural, *350*
Museum, 17, 36–37, 45, 55
   African American Museum, 335
   Guggenheim Museum, *17*

Music, 350, 367
Myth, 348

Nashville, Tennessee, *34–35*
Nation, 26–28
Nation, symbols of, 290–299
   Bald Eagle, 291, *291*
   Liberty Bell, 291, *291*
National anthem, 294
National Assembly, 303
National Farm Workers Association, 256, 259
National government. *see* Government
National Mall, *293*
National Park Ranger, *285*
National World War II Memorial, *292*, 293
Native Americans
   change and, 194–195
   Chickasaw, 149
   conflicts and, 200, 215
   farming, 193
   groups, *m*191
   hunting, 192
   Iroquois, 193
   Kiowa, 194
   language, 190
   longhouse, 193, *193*
   Miccosukee, 195
   natural resources and, 191–193
   Nez Perce, 194
   Peace Medals, 223
   Pocahontas, *201*
   Powhatan, *201*
   Sacagawea, 145, 212, 213
   shelters of, 191–193
   Shoshone, 213
   teepees, 192, *192*
   transportation, 191
   Wampanoag, 202

Natural disaster, 117–118
Natural resources, 106–109. *see also* Resources
   business use of, 394–396, 438
   fuel, 108
   land, 107
   living, 109
   minerals, 107
   Native Americans and, 191–193
   non-living, 109
   non-renewable, 108
   protection of, 128–131
   renewable, 108
   trees, 107
   use of, 127
   water, 107, 395, *395*
Need, 9, 16
Neighborhood, 6–11
Nelson, Senator Gaylord, 134, *134*
New Jersey, 389
New Year's Day, 360
New York City, New York, 46, 51, 52–54, 130, 328, 360
New York Harbor, 326, 339
Nez Pierce tribe, 194
Nigeria, 350
Nobel Peace Prize, 135, *168*, 254, *254*
North America, 86, 123, 196, 197, 200
North Carolina Senators, 283
Northeast region, 102, *m*103, 328

Ocean, I14, 92–93
Oceanographer, 119
Ohio, 334
Ohio River, 93
Oil well, *109*

Oklahoma

Oklahoma, 60, 118
Oklahoma State University, 60, *60*
Olmsted, Frederick Law, *1*, *50*, 50–51
Online buying and selling, 408
Open pit mines, 125, *125*
Opinion, 410
Opportunity, 324
Opportunity cost, 432
Oral history, 190
Ortega, Katherine, 377, *421*
Otis, Elisha, 164

Pacific Ocean, 21, 123, 191, 213
Panama Canal, 123, *123*
Paper making, 181, *181*
Parks, Rosa, *233*, 255, *255*
Parliament, 301
Patapsco River, 44
Patriotic symbol, 290
Patriotism, 208, 210–211, 290, 294–295
People, I1
Peninsula, I14
Peru, 124
Philadelphia, Pennsylvania, 208, 291
Physical features, 90–95
    climate, 90, 94–95
    land, 90–91
    landforms. *see* landforms
    vegetation, 94
    water, 90, 92–93
    weather, 94–95
Physical processes, 96–97
    erosion, 96
Pictograph, 120–121
Pilgrims, 202–203
Pioneers, *214*, 214–215
Place, I1, I9
"Place Called Freedom, A" (Sanders), 150–153
Plain, I14, 21, 91
Plantations, 216
Plateau, 91
Pledge of Allegiance, The, 295
Plymouth, Massachusetts, 202–203
Pocahontas, *201*
Points of View Feature
    How Did Change Affect Native Americans?, 194–195
    What Is Best About Your Community?, 62–63
    What Should You Do With Your Money?, 434–435
Police department, 276
Pollution, 128–129, 131
Ponce de Leon, Juan, *197*
Ponds, 92
Population, 42–43, 283, 330
Population density, 330–331, *m*331
Port, 185, 199
Prejudice, 325
Preserve, 104
President, 209, 282–284, 300
Presidential Medal of Freedom, 134
Presidents
    Bush, George W., *268*, *282*, *300*
    Carter, Jimmy, 254, *254*
    Clinton, Bill, 404
    Jefferson, Thomas, 206, *206*, *210*, 210–211, 212–213, 339
    jobs of, 282–284, 300
    Johnson, Lyndon B., I1
    Kennedy, John F., 291

Reading Social Studies

    Lincoln, Abraham, 145, *145*, 217, *217*, 292, 339
    Washington, George, 209, *209*, 339–340
Presidents' Day, 340
Primary sources, 168–169
    Computers, Past and Present, 412–413
    The Corps of Discovery, 222–223
    State Symbols, 298–299
Prime Meridian, 88
Prime Minister, 301
Printing, 181
Problems, solving, 132–133
Producer, 389–391
Product, 388–390, 394–396, 398, *m*399, 400, 402–403, 409, 437
Profit, 422–423
Public works, 277
Pyramid, 180, *180*, 351

Railroads, 163, 172
Raw materials, 394, 396
"Reading a Garden," Cleveland Public Library, 343, *343*
Reading Social Studies
    cause and effect, 164, 316–317, 325, 329, 333, 337, 339, 349, 359, 363, 367
    compare and contrast, 4–5, 15, 21, 23, 25, 27, 33, 37, 43, 47, 53, 57, 61, 85
    generalize, 16, 327, 341, 380–381, 389, 391, 392, 395, 397, 401, 407, 409, 423, 425, 427, 429, 437
    main idea and details, 17, 19, 29, 45, 55, 76–77, 83,

Index ■ R49

Recreation
87, 91, 93, 94, 97, 102, 105, 107, 109, 115, 116, 118, 123, 125, 127, 129, 165, 182, 183, 193, 201, 361, 364, 403, 431, 439
  sequence, 35, 148–149, 157, 159, 163, 171, 173, 179, 191, 197, 199, 203, 205, 207, 209, 213, 215
  summarize, 58, 131, 180, 181, 219, 236–237, 245, 247, 249, 251, 253, 254, 255, 256, 257, 267, 269, 273, 275, 277, 281, 284, 285, 291, 295, 301, 303, 335, 351, 353
Recreation, 276
Recycle, 130
Reference works, 33
Refrigeration, 401
Region, I9, 42, 102–105, *m103*
  Midwest, 102, *m103*
  Northeast, 102, *m103*
  rural, 56
  Southeast, 102, *m103*
  Southwest, 102, *m103*
  suburban, 52, 55
Relative location, 86, 102
Religion, 197, 202, 352–353
Representative, 283
Republic, 183, 208
Research Handbook, R12–R21
Reservation
  Laguna Pueblo, 195
Reservoir, 126
Resources. *see also* Natural resources
  capital, 395, 397
  human, 395–396
Respect, 252–253, 342–343
Responsibility, 10, 248–249
Revolution, 205
Revolutionary War, 205, 207, 212
Rights of citizens, 165, 230

  assembly, freedom of, 245
  civil, 167
  equal, 166, 328
  limits to, 249
  press, freedom of, 245
  religion, freedoms of, 245, 352
  speech, freedom of, 245
  voting, 165, 246
River, I14, 21, 92
Rivera, Diego (artist), 350, *350*
Riverboats, *116*
Road map, 278
Roads, 163, 183, 278
Rocky Mountains, 91
Rolfe, John, 201
Rome, ancient, 183, *m183*
Routes, 218
Rules, 18
Rural communities, 56–61, 328–329
Russia, *m365*

Sacajawea, 145, *212*, 213
Saicheua, Songsak, 405
St. Augustine, Florida, 197, *197*, 202
St. Louis, Missouri, *m28*, 28–29, 198–199, *199*, 202
St. Patrick's Day, 358, *358*
Salt Lake City, Utah, *84*, *m84*
Samba, 367, *367*
Sami people, 116
San Francisco Bay, 326
Satanta, 194, *194*
Savings, 429–431
Scarcity, 425
"School of the air," 27
School board, 276
Searcy, Arkansas, 56–60, *59*
Seasons, 95, *95*

Seattle, Washington, *20*
Secondary sources, 168–169
Senate, 283
Service, 24–25, 184, 388–392, 395, 408, 418–419, 423–424, 436
Services, government, 267, *276*, 276–277, *277*
Settlement, 197–203, 204
Settler, 199–200, 230
Shells and beads, 420, *420*
Shelter, 191
Sherwood, Arkansas, 58–59, *59*
Shipping Port, *400*
Silko, Leslie Marmon, 195, *195*
Skyscraper, 45, 164, *164*
Slavery, 201, 216–217
Slogans, 165
Smith, John, 200
Smog, *128–129*, 129
Society, 36
Soil, 107
Solution, 132–133
Sources
  primary, 168
  secondary, 168
South Africa, *m365*
South America, 123, 196, 197, *m402*
South Dakota, 339
Southeast region, 102–104, *m103*
Southwest region, 102–103, *m103*
Space exploration, 219, *219*
Spain, 196–197, 363
Spanish, 197
Spanish market, *363*
Spending, 426, 428, 430–431
Square mile, 330
SS *Nevada*, *318*
Stanton, Elizabeth Cady, 165
"Star-Spangled Banner, The" (song), 294
State constitution, 281

R50 ■ Reference

State government

State government, 266–267, 269, 280–281
Statue, 338
Statue of Liberty, 338–339, *338–339*
Steamboat Springs, Colorado, *114–115*
Stephenson, George, 163, *163*
Stillwater, Oklahoma, 60, *60*
Storyteller, 348, *348*
Stream, 92, 93
Study Skills
    anticipation guide, using, 322
    connecting ideas, 386
    K-W-L chart, 242
    note taking, 188
    organizing information, 416
    outlining, 154
    preview and question, 40
    questions, 112
    skim and scan, 264
    visuals, 80
    vocabulary, 12
    write to learn, 346
Suburban communities, 52–56, 58, 329
Suburbs, 52–55, 172
Subway, 46, *46*
Suffrage, 165
Sumer, 179
Summarize the Chapter, 38, 66, 110, 138, 186, 226, 262, 306, 344, 370, 414, 442
Sun Belt, 329
Supply, 424–425
Supreme Court, United States, 284, *284*
Supreme Court Seal, *284*
Supreme courts, state, 281
Symbols
    national, 290–295, 339
    state, 298–299
Synagogue, 352, *352*

Taro, Urashima, 349
Tax, 205, 252, 267, 283
Technology, 170, 437, *437*
    communication, 27, 170–171
    computers, 157, 412–413
    home, 174–175
    Internet, 27, 407–409
    transportation, 172–173
Telegraph, 171
Telephone, 27, 171, *171*, 406
Temple, 352, *352*
Terraces, 124, *124*
Territory, 217
Textbook, reading, I4–I7
Thai New Year, 361, *361*
Thanksgiving, *203*
Thirteenth Amendment, 217
Tiber River, 183
Tikal, Guatemala, 351, *351*
Time, I1
Time line, 160–161
Time period, 160
Times Square, New York City, New York, 360, *360*
Tokyo, Japan, *436*, 436–437
Tokyo business district, *436*
Tomlinson, Ray, *377*, 407
Tornado, 117–118, 120–121
Tourism, 381–382
Town government, 272–273
Town meeting, *19*, 272
Trade, 184, 391, 400–404, 418–419
Trade-off, 432
Tradition, 335, 337, 349, 352–353, 358–361
Traditions, religious, 352–353
Transportation, 46
    changes in, 172–173
    environment and, 122–123
    Native Americans and, 191
    suburban communities, and, 54, 172

United States of America

    trade, and, 401
    urban communities and, 45–46
Tree farm, *108*
Trees, 215
Tribe, 190
Trustworthiness, 393
Tsunami, 29, 404
Tubman, Harriet, *216*
Tunnel, 123

Unit project
    Community Catalogue, 72
    Community History Scrapbook, 232
    Community Nature Center, 144
    Community Newspaper, 448
    Culture Fair, 376
    Government Handbook, 312
United Kingdom, *m*365
United States of America, 206, 211
    bodies of water in, 93
    citizens' rights in, 244–247
    communities of, 26
    flag of, 290
    free market economy of, 422–426
    geography of, 90–97
    government of, 266–268, 282–285
    heritage of, 338–341
    history of, 190–195, 196–203, 204–209, 212–218
    immigration to, 324–327
    landmarks of, 338–339
    migration in, 328–329
    money in, 420–421
    regions of, 102–104
    resources of, 106–109

symbols of, 290–295
trade in, 400–403
United States Bureau of Engraving and Printing, 421
United States Constitution. *see* Constitution, United States
United States Mint, 421
United States Postal Service, 285
Urban communities, 43–52, 54–55, 58, 328–329

Valley, I14, 91
Vegetation, 94
Venezuala, *m*364
Veterans Day, 340, *340*
Vietnam Veterans Memorial, 293, 313, 342–343, *343*
Vietnam War, 343
Virginia, 210
Volcano, 96
Volunteers, 251, 254, 404–405
Voting, 246–247, 248, 252, 266

Wage, 392
"Walk Lightly" (Lewis), 78–79
Walker, Madame C. J., 393, *393*
Wamponoag, 202–203
Wangchuck, King Singye, *302*, 302–303
Want, 16
War of 1812, 294

Washington, D.C., 4–5, *5*, 22, 130, 282, 292, 292–293, 333, *332–333*
Washington, George, 207, *207*, 209, *209*, 339–340
Washington Monument, 292, *292*
Water
bodies of, 21, 24, *92*, 92–93
business use, 395, *395*
communities and, 21, 24
electricity and, 126–127
pollution of, 128–129
as resource, 107
Waterfall, 92, *92*
Weather, 20, 94
Weissenborn, Oscar, 389
Well, 215
Western region, 102, *m*103, 328
Wetlands, 92
Wheaton, Illinois, 250–251
White House, 282, *282*
Wilmore, Kentucky, 395
Wind power, 127
Wind turbines, 127, *127*
Women, voting rights of, 165
Workers, 388, 395–397, *397*
Worship, 352–353
Wright, Orville, 173
Wright, Wilbur, 173
Write for information, 36
Writing Activity
Write an Article, 72
Write a Journal Entry, 232

Write a Letter, 448
Write a Poem, 376
Write a Story, 144
Write a Summary, 312
Writing Skills
article, 39, 263
brochure, 159, 263
description, 25, 97, 361
diary entry, 61, 187, 329
e-mail, 29, 409
fable, 353
help wanted ad, 392
interview, 345
invitation, 67
legend, 371
letter, 139, 285
log entry, 227
journal entry, 219
narrative, 139
paragraph, 111, 167, 307, 371, 425
persuasive letter, 131
poem, 39, 345
post card, 111
report, 251
song, 307
speech, 227, 247
story, 67, 118
thank-you note, 187
travel brochure, 105

Yabara, 351
Yellowstone National Park, 100–101, *100–101*
Yogurt, 396–397

For permission to reprint copyrighted material, grateful acknowledgment is made to the following sources:

Atheneum Books for Young Readers, Simon & Schuster Children's Publishing Division: From *A Place Called Freedom* by Scott Russell Sanders, illustrated by Thomas B. Allen. Text copyright © 1997 by Scott Russell Sanders; illustrations copyright © 1997 by Thomas B. Allen.

Bloomsbury Children's Books, a division of Walker and Company: Cover illustration from *Hard Hat Area* by Susan L. Roth. Copyright © 2004 by Susan L. Roth.

Charlesbridge Publishing, Inc.: From *Be My Neighbor* by Maya Ajmera and John D. Ivanko. Text copyright © 2004 by SHAKTI for Children.

Children's Press, a Scholastic Library Publishing Company, Inc., a division of Scholastic Incorporated: Cover illustration from *mi barrio/my neighborhood* by George Ancona. Children's drawings © 2004 by Marc Anthony and Christina Ortiz; photograph © 2004 by George Ancona.

Dial Books for Young Readers, a Division of Penguin Young Readers Group, a Member of Penguin Group (USA) Inc., 345 Hudson Street, New York, NY 10014: "Walk Lightly" from *A World of Wonders: Geographic Travels in Verse and Rhyme* by J. Patrick Lewis, illustrated by Alison Jay. Text copyright © 2002 by J. Patrick Lewis; illustrations copyright © 2002 by Alison Jay.

Farrar, Straus and Giroux, LLC: Cover illustration by Jerome Lagarrigue from *Going North* by Janice N. Harrington. Illustration copyright © 2004 by Jerome Lagarrigue.

Grosset & Dunlap, a Division of Penguin Young Readers Group, a Member of Penguin Group (USA) Inc., 345 Hudson St., New York, NY 10014: Cover illustration by Thor Wickstrom from *Money: A Rich History* by Jon Anderson. Illustration copyright © 2003 by Thor Wickstrom.

Harcourt, Inc.: Cover illustration by Wendell Minor from *Rachel: The Story of Rachel Carson* by Amy Ehrlich. Illustration copyright © 2003 by Wendell Minor. Cover illustration © 2003 by Emily Arnold McCully from *Old Home Day* by Donald Hall. Illustration copyright © 1996 by Emily Arnold McCully.

HarperCollins Publishers: Cover illustration from *Market!* by Ted Lewin. Copyright © 1996 by Ted Lewin. Cover illustration by Frané Lessac from *Capital! Washington D. C. from A to Z* by Laura Krauss Melmed. Illustration copyright © 2003 by Frané Lessac. Cover illustration from *The Train of States* by Peter Sís. Copyright © 2004 by Peter Sís.

Henry Holt and Company, LLC: Cover illustration from *Mapping Penny's World* by Loreen Leedy. Copyright © 2000 by Loreen Leedy.

Houghton Mifflin Company: Cover illustration by Claire A. Nivola from *The Flag Maker* by Susan Campbell Bartoletti. Illustration copyright © 2004 by Claire A. Nivola.

Kids Can Press Ltd., Toronto: Cover illustration by Shelagh Armstrong from *If the World Were a Village: A Book about the World's People* by David J. Smith. Illustration © 2002 by Shelagh Armstrong.

Philomel Books, a Division of Penguin Young Readers Group, a Member of Penguin Group (USA) Inc., 345 Hudson St., New York, NY 10014: Cover illustration by Ted Lewin from *High as a Hawk* by T. A. Barron. Illustration copyright © 2004 by Ted Lewin. Cover illustration by William Low from *Henry and the Kite Dragon* by Bruce Edward Hall. Illustration copyright © 2004 by William Low.

Scholastic Inc.: From *Dreaming of America: An Ellis Island Story* by Eve Bunting, illustrated by Ben F. Stahl. Text copyright © 2000 by Edward D. Bunting and Anne E. Bunting, Trustees of the Edward D. Bunting and Anne E. Bunting Family Trust; illustrations copyright © 2000 by Ben F. Stahl. Cover photograph by Russ Kendall from *Sarah Morton's Day: A Day in the Life of a Pilgrim Girl* by Kate Waters. Photograph copyright © 1989 by Russell Kendall.

Jay Scott: From *Alex and the Amazing Lemonade Stand* by Liz and Jay Scott with help from Alex Scott, illustrated by Pam Howard. Text copyright © 2004 by Liz and Jay Scott; illustrations copyright © 2004 by Pam Howard.

Tilbury House, Publishers: Cover illustration by Lea Lyon from *Say Something* by Peggy Moss. Illustration copyright © 2004 by Lea Lyon.

PHOTO CREDITS FOR GRADE 3 SOCIAL STUDIES

Placement Key: (t) top; (b) bottom; (l) left; (r) right; (c) center; (tl) top left; (tc) top center; (tr) top right; (cl) center left; (cr) center right; (bl) bottom left; (bc) bottom center; (br) bottom right; (bg) background; (fg) foreground; (i) inset

COVER

ENDSHEET

FRONTMATTER

Blind (b) David Lawrence/Panoramic Images; iv (bg) Joe Sohm/PictureQuest; vi (bg) Photodisc Red/Getty Images; (b) Kwame Zikomo/SuperStock; vii (t) Royalty-Free/Corbis; (fg) David Young-Wolff/PhotoEdit; viii (fg) David W Hamilton/Getty Images; (bg) Steve Vidler/SuperStock; (b) Richard T. Nowitz/Corbis; xii (bg) Index Stock Imagery; (fg) John Wang/Getty Images; xiii (fg) Kevork Djansezian/AP Images; x (b) PhotoDisc/Media Bakery; (bg) Maryland Historical Society; (fg) Michael Ventura/PhotoEdit; xi (fg) Comstock/PictureQuest; xiv (bg) Minnesota Historical Society/Corbis; (b) Jamie & Judy Wild/Danita Delimont Stock Photography; (t) Joe Tree/Alamy; I2 (bc) Brand X/SuperStock; (bl) Corbis; (br) Library of Congress; I3 (bl) Alan King/Alamy; (br) Jeremy Woodhouse/Getty Images; I8 (c) Danny Lehman/Corbis; (b) age fotostock/SuperStock; I9 (t) Gail Mooney/Masterfile; (c) Peter Christopher/Masterfile; (b) age fotostock/SuperStock.

UNIT 1

1 (bl) Used with permission from The Biltmore Company, Asheville, North Carolina (t), (b) Panoramic Images; 2 (t) Robert Harding World Imagery/Getty Images; 3 (tl) Gary Conner/PhotoEdit; (c) Lenny Ignelzi/AP Images; (tr) Masterfile Royalty-Free; (b) Artiga Photo/Corbis; 5 (t) Greg Pease/Photographer'sChoice/Getty Images; (b) Bruno Barbey/Magnum Photos; 6 (c) Josef Polleross/The Image Works; (b) Ken Cavanagh/Photo Researchers, Inc.; 7 (b) Nik Wheeler Photography; (t) Momatiuk-Eastcott/Woodfin Camp; 8 (t) Robert Frerck/Woodfin Camp; (b) Adam Tanner/The Image Works; 9 (t) Ray Roberts/Topham/The Image Works; (b) Robert Fried/Alamy; 10 (b) Richard Hutchings/Photo Researchers, Inc.; (t) Sean Sprague/Sprague Photo Stock; 11 (b) Jim Mahoney/The Image Works; (t) David Austin/Woodfin Camp; 12 (b) James Lemass/Index Stock Imagery; (br) HIRB/Index Stock Imagery; (bl) Diaphor Agency/Index Stock Imagery; (bg) J Sohm/Voa LLC/Panoramic Images; 14 (b) Jon Arnold/Danita Delimont; 15 (t) Rudi Von Briel/PhotoEdit; 16 (b) Jacqueline Larma/AP Images; (c) Terry Gilliam/AP Images; 17 (b) Scott Barrow,Inc./SuperStock; (t) Monika Graff/The Image Works; 19 (t) Toby Talbot/AP Images; 20 (bl) Charles Crust Photographer; (b) Claver Carroll/Panoramic Images; 21 (bc) age fotostock/SuperStock; (bl) Jim Wark/AirPhoto; (br) Rafael Macia/Photo Researchers, Inc.; 22 (t) Beverly Palau/City of Greenbelt; (b) Tom Carter/PhotoEdit; 23 (b) Clarksville Historical Society; (t) Indiana Historical Society; 24 (bl) Jack Kurtz/The Image Works; (br) Masterfile Royalty-Free; 25 (t) Pickerell/Folio; 26 (b) Peter Adams/Panoramic Images; 27 (t) Evan Collis/Australian Picture Library; 28 (tr) Medio Images/Getty Images; (tl) Bjorn Grotting/Indonesia Photo; (b) St.Louis Center for International Relations; 29 (t) Jordan R. Beesley/US Navy/NewsCom 33 (t) Mark Richards/PhotoEdit; 34 (bg) Gerald L. French/Panoramic Images;36 (bg), (inset) North Carolina ECHO; 37 (t) Michael Jaenicke/The Robesonian/AP Images; 38 (t) Jacqueline Larma/AP Images; 39 (tl) age fotostock/SuperStock; 40 (bg) SpotWorks, Inc.; (bl) Henry T. Kaiser/Stock Connection/Workbook; (bc) Michael Melford/Getty Images; (br) Grandmaison Photography; 42 (b) SpotWorks, Inc.; 43 (c) Joe Sohm/PictureQuest; 44 (bg) age fotostock/SuperStock; 45 (t) Photodisc Green/Getty Images; (c) Gail Mooney/Masterfile; 46 (b) Julie Jacobson/AP Images; (c) SpotWorks, Inc.; 47 (t) Michael Newman/PhotoEdit; 50 (b) AP Images; 51 (t) Walter Bibikow/Getty Images; (c) U.S. Postal Service/AP Images; 52 (b) BerylGoldberg; 53 (t) Emily Shur/Getty Images; 54 (b) Peter Byron/PhotoEdit; 56 (bg) Gary McMichael/Grant Heilman Photography; 57 (t) Philip Holsinger/The Daily Citizen; 58 (b) Randall Hyman/AGPix; 59 (br) R. Krubner/Robertstock.com; (t) Paul Rezendes Photography; 60 (t) John Elk III; 61 (t) Steve Warble/Mountain Magic Photography; 62 (c) Bettmann/Corbis; 63 (tl) Knight Programing Community Building/University of Miami School of Architecture; (tr) U.S. Representative JoAnn Emerson; 64 (cl) Paul Barton/Corbis; (cr) Susan Van Etten/PhotoEdit; 66 (t) Joe Sohm/PictureQuest; 67 (tl) Beryl Goldberg; (tr) Gary McMichael/Grant Heilman Photography; 70 (t) age fotostock/SuperStock; (b) Tom Carter/PhotoEdit.

UNIT 2

73 (b) The Granger Collection, New York; (bg), (t) Chad Ehlers/Stock Connection/Workbook; 74 (t) Royalty-Free/Corbis; (br) Ariel Skelley/Masterfile; 75 (tl) Jupiter Images/PictureQuest; (tr) Stockbyte/Media Bakery RF; (c) Sal Maimone/SuperStock; (b) Douglas Peebles/Corbis; 77 (b) Jeremy Frechette/The Image Bank/Getty Images; 80 (bg) Adam Jones/Danita Delimont Stock Photography; (bc) Paul Rezendes; (br) Macduff Everton/Iconica/Getty Images; 84 (t) Tim Thompson/Corbis; 90 (b) Photodisc Red/Getty Images; 91 (t) Kwame Zikomo/SuperStock; 92 (t) Darrell Gulin/Getty Images; 93 (t) Tom Bean/Corbis; 94 (c) Art Wolfe/Getty Images; (bl) Gary Conner/Index Stock Imagery; (br) Frank Krahmer/zefa/Corbis; 95 (bl), (br), (tl)Todd Pearson/Getty Images; 96 (t) David Muench/Getty Images; 97 (t) Norbert Wu/Minden Pictures; 100 (bg) Willard Clay/Getty Images; (b) Bob and Suzanne Clemenz/AGPix; 101 (tr) Gunter Marx/Corbis; (cr) Byron Jorjorian/Alamy; (tl), (c) Paul Uhl; (cl) Dewitt Jones/Corbis; 102 (bl) Tim Fitzharris/Minden Pictures; (br) Yva Momatiuk/John Eastcott/Minden Pictures; 103 (bl) Glen Allison/Getty Images; (b) Masterfile Royalty-Free; (br) Digital Vision/Getty Images; 104 (t) Jeff Rogers Photography; 105 (c) Kevin R. Morris/Corbis; (t) Jeff Spradling/University of Kentucky Appalachian Center; 106 (bg) Ike Geib/Grant Heilman Photography; (c) Denny Eilers/Grant Heilman Photography; 107 (fg) Peter Dean/Grant Heilman Photography; 108 (t) Jason Turner/The Journal/AP Images; (b) Grant Heilman/Grant Heilman Photography; 109 (t) Photodisc Collection/Getty Images; 110 (t) Photodisc Red/Getty Images; 111 (tl) Digital Vision/Getty Images; (tr) Jason Turner/The Journal/AP Images; 112 (bg) James M Phelps, Jr/ShutterStock; (bc) Denny Eilers/Grant Heilman Photography; (bl) Yann Arthus-Bertrand/Corbis; (br) Karl Weatherly/Corbis; 114 (b) James Schwabel/Panoramic Images; 116 (t) W. Robert Moore/Getty Images; (c) Bryan & Cherry Alexander Photography; 117 (b) Mario Tama/Getty Images; 119 (b) Macduff Everton/Corbis; 120 (t) Weatherstock/Peter Arnold, Inc.; (b) Stephen Holman/Stillwater News Press/AP Images; 122 (b) Sergio Pitamitz/Getty Images; 123 (b) Hulton Archive/Getty Images; 124 (t) Tom Brownold/AGPix; (b) Johan Elzenga/Foto Natura/Minden Pictures; 125 (t) Kevin R. Morris/Corbis; (b) Bernhard Lang/The Image Bank/Getty Images; 126 (b) Photos courtesy of Lake of the Ozarks CVB/800-FUNLAKE/funlake.com; (t) Royalty-Free/Corbis; 127 (t) Glen Allison/Getty Images; 128 (b) Photodisc Collection/Getty Images; 129 (c) Hand Out/AP Images; 130 (b) JP Laffont/Sygma/Corbis; (t) David Young-Wolff/PhotoEdit; 131 (t) Shipley's Choice Elementary/Maryland Department of the Environment; 134 (b) Tom Lynn/Journal Sentinel Inc.; (c) Gregory Berger/Pomegranate Design/Sacramento Area Earth Day Network; 135 (t) Ron Wurzer/Nature Consortium/AP Images; (t) Karen Prinsloo/AP Images; 138 (t) Mario Tama/Getty Images; 139 (tl) Photos courtesy of Lake of the Ozarks CVB/800-FUNLAKE/funlake.com; (tr) David Young-Wolff/PhotoEdit; 142 (b) Hand Out/AP Images.

UNIT 3

145 (bl) Jean Leon Jerome Ferris/Private Collection/Bridgeman Art Library; (bg) Prisma/SuperStock; 146 (t) Bettmann/Corbis; (br) Mark Richards/PhotoEdit; 147 (tl) Masterfile Royalty-Free; (c) Larry Ulrich; (tr) Art Resource, NY; (b) Paul Johnson/Index Stock Imagery; 149 (b) Sylvia Pitcher Photolibrary/Alamy; 154 (bg) K. Yamashita/PanStock/Panoramic Images/Workbook; (bc) Brad Wrobleski/Masterfile; (bl) Noel Hendrickson/MasteFile; (br) Scala/Art Resource, NY; 156 (b) Adam Jones/Getty Images; 157 (cl) New York Public Library Picture Collection; (cr) Hisham F Ibrahim/Photodisc Green/Getty Images; 158 (tl) Corbis; (tr) Scala/Art Resource; 159 (t) Bob Landry/Time Life Pictures/Getty Images; (c) Herb Levart/SuperStock; 160 (t) Lawrence Carmichael Earle/Chicago Historical Society/Bridgeman Art Library; (br) Chicago Historical Society; 161 (bl) Library of Congress; (b) Bettmann/Corbis; (br) Images.com/Corbis; 163 (t) John Seymour Lucas/Institute of Mechanical Engineers/Bridgeman Art Library; 164 (t) Raymond Patrick/Getty Images; 165 (br) California Historical Society; (b), (bl) National Museum of Women's History; 166 (c) Robin Nelson/PhotoEdit; (t) Douglas Miller/Getty Images; 167 (t) Bob Fitch/Stock Photo; 168 (br) Stephen Chernin/Getty Images; (bl) Flip Schulke/Corbis; (c) Ted Spiegel/Corbis; 169 (inset) Getty Images; 170 (b) Gilcrease Museum; 171 (tl) Corbis; (tr) Bettmann/Corbis; (bl) Ryan McVay/Getty Images; (c) Scott Milless/ShutterStock; (br) Getty Images; (b) The Granger Collection, New York 172 (t) Bettmann/Corbis; 173 (t) Underwood & Underwood/Corbis; 174 (c) J. Walter Thompson/AP Images; (b) Queens Borough Public Library; (tl), (tr) The Granger Collection, NY; 175 (t) Judy Rosella Edwards/Ecolitgy Communications; 178 (b) Nik Wheeler Photography; 179 (tr) Réunion des Musées Nationaux/Art Resource; (tl) Werner Forman/TopFoto/The Image Works; 180 (b) Travel Ink Photo Library/Index Stock Imagery; (t) Deir el-Bahri, Temple of Hatshepsut/Metropolitan Museum of Art Excavations; 182 (b) Johnny Stockshooter/Robertstock.com; 184 (b) Ali Murat Atay/Coral Planet/AGPix; (t) Bibliotheque Nationale de France, Paris; 185 (t) Bruno Morandi/Corbis; 186 (t) Bob Fitch/Stock Photo; 187 (tl) Bettmann/Corbis; (tr) Réunion des Musées Nationaux/Art Resource; 188 (bg) John Neubauer/PhotoEdit; (bl) Scott Olson/Getty Images; (bc) Michael Pasdzior/The Image Bank/Getty Images; (br) John Elk III/Lonely Planet Images/Getty Images; 190 (b) David W Hamilton/Getty Images; 191 (b) Private Collection/Peter Newark Western Americana/Bridgeman Art Library; 193 (t) Nathan Benn/Corbis; 194 (cl) Picture History, LLC; (cr) W.S. Soule/Picture History, LLC; 195 (tl) http://www.mrp.txstate.edu/mrp/publications/hillviews/2001/winter/page4.html; (tr) Marilyn "Angel" Wynn/nativestock.com; 196 (br) Private Collection, Index/Bridgeman Art Library; (bl) Sebastiano del Piombo/Metropolitan Museum of Art/Bridgeman Art Library; 197 (c) Bettmann/Corbis; (t) Steve Vidler/SuperStock; 198 (t) MPI/Getty Images; (b) David Schultz/Missouri Historical Society;

199 (b) The Granger Collection; (t) Airphoto; 200 (b) Richard T. Nowitz/Corbis; 201 (t) David Muench/Corbis; 202 (bl) Snark/Art Resource, NY; (cl) Jeff Greenberg/PhotoEdit; (cr) Bettmann/Corbis; (br) Tom Horlacher; (t) Brand X/SuperStock; 203 (t) Burstein Collection/Corbis; 204 (b) Bettmann/Corbis; 206 (t) Bettmann/Corbis; 207 (t) Morristown National Historic Park/National Park Service Museum Collection; (b), (c) Military and Historical Image Bank; 208 (b) The Granger Collection, New York; 209 (t) Arsene Hippolyte Rivey/New-York Historical Society/Bridgeman Art Library; 210 (bl), (br) The Granger Collection, New York; 211 (t) Courtesy of the Historical Society of Pennsylvania; (c) The Granger Collection, New York; 212 (b) "Lewis and Clark at Three Forks" by E.S. Paxson, Oil on Canvas 1912, Courtesy of the Montana Historical Society, Don Beatty photographer; 213 (b) National Museum of American History, Smithsonian Institution; 214 (b) Comstock Images/Alamy; 215 (b) Montana Historical Society, Helena.; 216 (c) National Archives; (t) Library of Congress; 217 (t) National Portrait Gallery, Smithsonian Institution/Art Resource, NY; (b) Library of Congress; 218 (b) Royalty-Free/Corbis; 219 (fg) NASA Kennedy Space Center; (bg) Worldspec/NASA/Alamy; 220 (c) David Schultz/Missouri Historical Society Collections; 222 (bl) Geography and Map Division/The Library of Congress; (br) Oregon Historical Society; 223 (bl), (br) Oregon Historical Society; (t) Erich Lessing/Art Resource, NY; (c) The Granger Collection, New York; 226 (t) Bettmann/Corbis; 227 (tr) National Portrait Gallery, Smithsonian Institution/Art Resource, NY; 229 (tc) U.S. Postal Service, HO/AP Images; (c) NASA Kennedy Space Center; (cl) Picture History LLC; (cr) Kean Collection/Getty Images; (bl) AP Images; (bc) Bettmann/Corbis; 230 (t) Scott Milless/ShutterStock; (b) National Museum of Women's History.

UNIT 4

233 (bg), (t) San Rostro/AGE Fotostock; 234 (t) David Butow/Corbis Saba; (br) Getty Images; 235 (tl) Jeffrey Greenberg/Photo Researchers, Inc.; (c) Gary Conner/PhotoEdit; (tr) C Squared Studios/Getty Images; (b) Park Street/PhotoEdit; 237 (b) George & Monserrate Schwartz/Alamy; 238 (b) Lawrence Migdale; 239 (tl), (tr) Lawrence Migdale; 240 (bl), (br) Lawrence Migdale; 241 (t) Lawrence Migdale; 242 (bg) Nanine Hartzenbusch/Getty Images; (bl) St. Cloud Times, Kimm Anderson/AP Images; (bc) John Neubauer/PhotoEdit; (br) Paul Conklin/PhotoEdit; 244 (b) Alex Wong/Getty Images; 245 (t) The Granger Collection, New York; (br), (cl) David Young-Wolff/PhotoEdit; (cr) Richard Hutchings/PhotoEdit; (bl) Lisa Law/The Image Works; 246 (t) Spencer Platt/Getty Images; (b) Jeff Greenberg/The Image Works; 247 (t) Jonathan Nourok/PhotoEdit; 249 (t) John Neubauer/PhotoEdit; (b) Bob Stern/The Image Works; 250 (b) Jesse Chehak; (t) Tanit Jarusan/The Daily Herald Photo Archives; 251 (t) Jesse Chehak; 252 (b) David Schmidt/Masterfile; 253 (t) Beach/Kentucky Transportation Cabinet; (c) Vincent/Kentucky Transportation Cabinet; 254 (t) Pat Roque/AP Images; (b) Bjoern

Sigurdsoen/Pool/AP Images; 255 (t) Take Stock; (b) Paul Warner/AP Images; 256 (t) Bob Fitch/Take Stock; (c) Library of Congress; 257 (t) Ryan's Well Foundation; 258 (b) Najlah Feanny/Corbis; 259 (t) Sakuma/AP Images; (c), (b) Spotworks; 263 (tl) John Neubauer/PhotoEdit; (tr) Pat Roque/AP Images 264 (bg) Mark Gibson Photography; (bc) Ted Soqui/Corbis; (bl) Rebecca Cook/Reuters/Corbis; (br) Ron Chapple/Taxi/Getty Images; 266 (b) Office of the City Clerk/Annapolis, Maryland; 267 (c) Douglas Kirkland/Corbis; (b) Marland State Archives; 268 (tl) PhotoDisc/Media Bakery; (tr) Larry Fisher/Masterfile; (b) Ron Edmonds/AP Images; 269 (t) Ed Reinke/AP Images; 270 (br) Jim Rider/South Bend Tribune/AP Images; (bl) Musee Franco-Americaine, Blerancourt, Chauny, France, Giraudon/Bridgeman Art Library; 271 (b) Bob Child/AP Images; (t) National Archives; 272 (b) Lee Snider/Photo Images/Corbis; 273 (t) Columbus City Council; (b) Terry Gilliam/AP Images; 274 (b) Warren County Public Information & Tourism Department; 275 (b) Brian Rose; 276 (t) Kayte M. Deioma/PhotoEdit; (b) Comstock Images/PictureQuest RF; 277 (t), (c) Stephen Wirt; 280 (b) Jim LeMays/Michigan Department of Transportation/Gov. Jennifer M. Granholm; 281 (b) SuperStock; 282 (b) Getty Images; 283 (b) 2005 Getty Images; (t) U.S. Senator Richard Burr; 284 (t) Jason Reed/Reuters/Corbis; (c) Bettmann/Corbis; 285 (t) Jeffrey Greenberg/Photo Researchers, Inc.; (c) Byron Jorjorian Photography; 286 (bg) Lester Lefkowitz; (b) Royalty-Free/Corbis; 287 (c) Peter Gridley/Getty Images; (br) Mark Wilson/Getty Images; (tl) Brand X Pictures/Alamy; (tr) Kelly-Mooney Photography/Corbis; (bl) Craig Aurness/Corbis; 288 (inset) Catherine Karnow/Folio, Inc.; 290 (b) PhotoEdit; 291 (c) Bob Daemmrich/The Image Works; (b) Comstock/PictureQuest; 292 (t) National Geographic/Getty Images; 293 (c) Pablo Martinez Monsivais/AP Images; (t) Photo Disc/Media Bakery; (c) Richard T. Nowitz/Corbis; 294 (t) Library of Congress Prints and Photographs Division Washington, D.C. 20540 USA; 295 (b) Maryland Historical Society; (t) Michael Ventura/PhotoEdit; 296 (b) age fotostock/SuperStock; 298 (c), (b) Flags: The Americas/PictureQuest; 299 (tl), (b) Vector-Images.com; (tr) Stockbyte/PictureQuest; 300 (b) J. Scott Applewhite/AP Images; 301 (t) Business Wire/Getty Images; 302 (t) Robert Nickelsberg/Time Life Pictures/Getty Images; (b) National Geographic/Getty Images; 303 (t) Anupam Nath/AP Images; (cl) Peter Arnold, Inc./Alamy; (b) Robert Harding Picture Library Ltd/Alamy; (cr) Colin Young-Wolff/PhotoEdit; 306 (t) Lee Snider/Photo Images/Corbis; 307 (tl) 2005 Getty Images; (tr) Comstock/PictureQuest; 309 (l) Library of Congress Prints & Photographs Division; 310 (t) The Granger Collection, New York; (b) Douglas Kirkland/Corbis.

UNIT 5

313 (t) Panoramic Images/Getty Images; 314 (t) James J. Bissell/SuperStock; (br) Bill Aron/PhotoEdit; 315 (tr) Creatas/SuperStock; (c) North Wind Picture Archives/Alamy; (b) Jack Kurtz/The Image Works; (tl) Ryan McVay/Getty Images; 317 (t) Tom Stewart/Corbis; 318 (b) The Mariners' Museum; 319 (c) AP Images; 321 (c) Ellis Island Immigration Museum; 322 (bg) Gary Conner/PhotoEdit; (bl) Photodisc Red/Getty Images; (br) Howie McCormick/AP Images; (bc) Michael Goldman/The Image Bank/Getty Images; 324 (b) Bettmann/Corbis; 325 (b) Royalty-Free/Corbis; 326 (t) National Archives Washington DC/The Art Archive; (b) Underwood & Underwood/Corbis; 327 (b) Kathy Willens/AP Images; 328 (b) Digital Image © The Museum of Modern Art/Licensed by Scala/Art Resource, NY; 329 (t) Pluriel Phototheque/SuperStock; 330 (c) Jim Hartman/Division of Streets/ Department of Public Properties/City of Aurora; 332 (b) Elliot Teel Photography; 333 (t) Index Stock Imagery; 334 (tl), (tr) Cleveland Public Library Photograph Collection; 335 (b) John Kuntz/The Plain Dealer; (t) Jeff Greenberg/Courtesy of Convention & Visitors Bureau of Greater Cleveland; 336 (b) SpotWorks, Inc.; 337 (t) SpotWorks, Inc.; 338 (bl), (br) Corbis; 339 (br) John Wang/Getty Images; (t) age fotostock/SuperStock; (bl) Bettmann/Corbis; 340 (b) Janet Hostetter/AP Images; (t) Spencer Platt/Getty Images; 341 (c) Comstock/Media Bakery RF; (t) Ariel Skelley/Corbis; 342 (b) Ohio University; 343 (t) Dennis Brack Photography; (c) Andre Jenny/Alamy; 344 (t) Bettmann/Corbis; 345 (tl) Index Stock Imagery; (tr) Ariel Skelley/Corbis; 346 (bg) Russell Gordon/Danita Delimont Stock Photography; (br) Catherine Karnow/Corbis; (bc) Pat & Chuck Blackley; (br) Myrleen Ferguson Cate/PhotoEdit; 348 (b) Syracuse Newspapers/John Berry/The Image Works; 349 (t) Bonnie Kamin/PhotoEdit; (c) Carol Cunningham/AP Images; 350 (b) Erin Patrice O'Brien/Getty Images; (t) Gift of Edsel B. Ford(33.10.N)/Detroit Institute of Arts; 351 (t) Gibson Stock Photography; (b) Robert Frerck and Odyssey Productions, Inc; 352 (cr) age fotostock/SuperStock; (cl) John Elk III; (tr) Martin Puddy/Getty Images; (tl) Spotworks, Inc; 356 (bg) Fresh Air Photo; 357 (tl) Hillhouse Graphic Design; (cl), (tr), (cr) Fresh Air Photo; 358 (b) Thomas Cain/Getty Images; 359 (b) Dave Scherbenco/Citizens Voice/AP Images; (t) Kevork Djansezian/AP Images; 360 (t) Julie Jacobson/AP Images; (b) Liu Liqun/Corbis; 361 (t) AFP Photo/Pornchai Kittiwongsakul/Getty Images; 362 (b) Dave Bartruff/Corbis; 363 (b) Brian Seed/Alamy; (t) Jon Hicks/Corbis; 364 (t) Galen Rowell/Corbis; (cl) Ned Frisk Photography/Brand X Pictures/Adobe Stock Photos; (b) Mark Eveleigh/Alamy; (cr) Gen Nishino/Taxi/Getty Images; 365 (t) Richard Kolker/Getty Images; (c) Adam Buchanan/Danita Delimont Stock Photography; (br) Darroch Donald/Alamy; (cl) Ariadne Van Zandbergen/Lonely Planet Images/Getty Images; (tr) Oleg Nikishin/Getty Images; (cr) J Kim/Stone/Getty Images; (bl) Peter Turnley/Corbis; (tl) Tony Latham/Getty Images; 366 (t) Akira Kaede/Getty Images; (b) Sylvain Grandadam/Stone/Getty Images; 367 (t) travelstock44/Alamy; 370 (t) Erin Patrice O'Brien/Getty Images; 371 (tl) Thomas Cain/Getty Images; (tr) Adam Buchanan/Danita Delimont Stock Photography; 374 (t) Comstock/Media Bakery RF; (b) Royalty-Free/Corbis.

UNIT 6

377 (t) David R. Frazier/PhotoLibrary Inc/Alamy Images; 378 (t) Getty Images; (br) Laura Rauch/AP Images; 379 (tl) Gift; State Historical Society of Colorado; 1949/Library of Congress; (br) Royalty-Free/Corbis; (bl) Francisco Cruz/SuperStock; 381 (b) Glen Allison/Stone/Getty Images; 385 (t) Alex's Lemonade Stand; 386 (bg) Jeff Greenberg/Courtesy of Convention & Visitors Bureau of Greater Cleveland; (br) J. Silver/SuperStock; (b) Richard Shock/Stone/Getty Images; (bl) Michael Newman/PhotoEdit; 388 (b) Minnesota Historical Society/Corbis; 389 (tl), (tr) The General Pencil Co.; 391 (t) Barbara Stitzer/PhotoEdit; (b) Lawrence Migdale; 392 (t) ECI; 393 (b) A'Lelia Bundles/Walker Family Collection/Wash, DC; 394 (b) Andre Jenny/The Image Works; 395 (t) Hans Strand/Corbis; (c) Mark E. Gibson/Corbis; (b) Roy Ooms/Masterfile; 397 (t) Bob Krist/Corbis; 398 (b) Christine Osborne/Worldwide Picture Library/Alamy; 400 (b) Jamie & Judy Wild/Danita Delimont Stock Photography; 401 (t) Bob Krist/Corbis; 402 (b) Joe Tree/Alamy; 403 (t) SpotWorks, Inc.; 404 (b) Ethan Miller/Getty Images; 405 (t) Gautam Singh/AP Images; (b) Rogelio Solis/AP Images; 406 (fg) Royalty-Free/Corbis; (bg) Franz Marc Frei/Corbis; 407 (t) Photodisc Blue/Getty Images; (b) Index Stock/Alamy; 408 (cr) Ed Wheeler/Corbis; (br) Scott Sady/AP Images; (bl) Chuck Savage/Corbis; 409 (t) Gary Conner/Index Stock Imagery; 412 (bl) National Museum of American History, Smithsonian; (br) Index Stock RF; 413 (c) Smithsonian Institute, Computers and Communications; (t) Wikimedia Foundation Inc.; 414 (t) Lawrence Migdale; 415 (tl) Bob Krist/Corbis; (tr) Gary Conner/Index Stock Imagery; 416 (bg) Doug Mills/AP Images; (bc) Ariel Skelley/Corbis; (bl) Royalty-Free/Corbis; 419 (t), (inset) Royalty-Free/Corbis; (b) Bill Bachmann/Index Stock Imagery; 420 (tl) Helene Rogers/Alamy; (bl) The British Museum; (tr) Werner Forman/Art Resource, NY; (cr) Gary Conner/PhotoEdit; (b) The British Museum; 421 (t) Scott Stewart/AP Images; (bg) SpotWorks, Inc.; 422 (b) Owaki - Kulla/Corbis; 423 (b) Frances Roberts/Alamy; 424 (b) John Dominis/Index Stock Imagery; (t) Hulton Archive/Getty Images; 425 (t) Don Smetzer/PhotoEdit; 429 (t) Royalty-Free/Corbis; 434 (cl) The Money Coach; (cr) North Carolina Department of State Treasurer; 435 (tr) Bettmann/Corbis; (tl) Carson Scholars Fund; 436 (b) José Fuste Raga/zefa/Corbis; 437 (t) David Guttenfelder/AP Images; 438 (b), (c) John Robinson; 439 (t) John Robinson; 442 (t) Royalty-Free/Corbis; 443 (tl) Hulton Archive/Getty Images.

All other photos from Harcourt School Photo Library and Photographers: Ken Kinzie, Weronica Anakaron, Eric Camden, Doug Dukane.

All Maps created by MAPQUEST.COM.